Medical Liability and Artificial Intelligence

Rafaella Nogaroli

Medical Liability and Artificial Intelligence

Brazilian and European Legal Approaches

Springer

Rafaella Nogaroli
President's Office – Scientific Direction and Events Coordination
Miguel Kfouri Neto – Medical and Health Law Institute
Curitiba, Brazil

ISBN 978-3-031-94305-8 ISBN 978-3-031-94306-5 (eBook)
https://doi.org/10.1007/978-3-031-94306-5

English translation of the original Portuguese language edition published by Thomson Reuters, 2023

Translation from the Portuguese language edition: "Responsabilidade Civil Médica e Inteligência Artificial " by Rafaella Nogaroli, © Author 2023. Published by Thomson Reuters Revista dos Tribunais.

This Springer imprint is published by the registered company Springer Nature Switzerland AG
The registered company address is: Gewerbestrasse 11, 6330 Cham, Switzerland

In a world linked with unceasing advance, the physician strides, a figure of balance, transcending boundaries of medicine's traditional sphere, a Master of Art, of science, and technologies' reign. Through the cadence of progress, they adapt and refine, perpetual learners, embracing the design of AI, robotics, and telemedicine's rise, guided by innovation beneath ever-changing skies.
AI, the pioneer, with insights profound, shapes tailored visions where solutions abound, illuminating histories, preferences, and more, empowering decisions as never before.
Steering from generalities, their path is clear: each patient, a sun, their orbit held near. Human-centred care, with precision imbued, a symphony of healing, where the humanity is renewed.
Yet caution remains, for technology must serve, guided by ethics, a resolute curve, the physician's touch, its warmth to retain, human connection, medicine's enduring refrain.
The new specialist embodies a vision complete, where science and compassion harmoniously meet, delivering care, both tailored and wide, a pulse of accessibility, humanity as guide.
Let AI's implementation be gentle, humane, enhancing the bond, not letting it wane, for in Medicine's theatre, its purpose must hold, enriching the meaning of stories untold.
Thus, the sacred bond shall flourish and thrive, if technology bridges, ensuring it's alive. Across the vast realms of this noble domain, humanity and heart will forever remain.
(Authored by Rafaella Nogaroli and 'ChatGPT')[1]

[1] The poem transcribed here illustrates the symbiosis between human and machine. Based on a few inputs—three paragraphs written by this book's author discussing ethical principles and the duties guiding physicians in their interaction with AI systems—ChatGPT was requested to transform the text into a poem. Regarding the interaction with ChatGPT and its designation as a co-author, it is worth noting the existence of an intense international debate on the (im)possibility of an AI being recognised as the author of an intellectual work. The debate remains ongoing, sparking new reflections and insights.

I dedicate this work to my dearest parents, Ana Flávia Evangelista Nogaroli and José Renato Nogaroli, whose constant support and unconditional love have been the foundation of my journey. Their boundless generosity and selfless sacrifices have been a source of profound inspiration, encouraging me to pursue excellence and imbuing me with the resilience and determination to achieve my academic and professional aspirations. This book is also devoted to my esteemed academic mentor, Professor Judge Miguel Kfouri Neto, a revered master, trusted guide, and pre-eminent authority on medical law in Brazil. His profound wisdom, steadfast encouragement, and enduring friendship have been invaluable in shaping my path. As his disciple, I hold the hope that this work may serve as a meaningful contribution to the advancement of medical law doctrine, reflecting the depth of his teachings and the honour of his legacy.

Foreword by Professor André Gonçalo Dias Pereira[1]

I first met the author, Rafaella Nogaroli, before the pandemic, in Coimbra, during the 2019 edition of the *International Civil Law Congress*. In the presentation's competition, the quality of her research, the strength and elegance of her discourse, and her confidence during the debate phase stood out. Rightfully, she was awarded first place in that competition, in which I had the honour of serving as a jury member, invited by the Vice-Rector for International Relations and Alumni of the University of Coimbra, Prof. Dr João Nuno Calvão da Silva. The commendable and intensive activity of this Curitiba-born jurist within IBERC (the Brazilian Institute for Civil Liability Studies) and IMKN (the Miguel Kfouri Neto Medical Law Institute) is widely acknowledged by all its members. Furthermore, the volume and quality of her scientific publications are already recognised by the international legal community.

Everything pointed to this work being of exceptional quality. Combining her personal skills as a researcher with the expert guidance of Professor Dr Paulo Nalin, a renowned academic at the Federal University of Paraná, and drawing from her activities within a Medical Law research group and the Paraná Court of Justice, under the mentorship of remarkable jurists and exceptional individuals such as Appellate Judges Prof. Dr Miguel Kfouri Neto and Prof. Dr Clayton Maranhão, the intellectual and human conditions were in place for this work to emerge with brilliance. And it most certainly did!

It was with great honour that I served on the panel for the evaluation of this thesis in Brazil, in March 2023, awarding it the highest grade! It is a privilege now to share some reflections that may provide insights for engaging with this book, which addresses topics of such importance to Civil Law—and, therefore, to society at large—such as medical liability and artificial intelligence.

[1] Professor at the Faculty of Law, University of Coimbra, Director of the Centre for Biomedical Law—University of Coimbra, Vice-President of the National Council for Ethics in Life Sciences—Portugal, Fellow of ECTIL—European Centre of Tort and Insurance Law, Chair of the Education Committee—World Association for Medical Law.

Scientific and technological advancements in the biomedical sciences and their application to healthcare are a daily subject in the news, transforming individuals' relationships with the healthcare system and reshaping healthcare professions themselves. Telemedicine, robotics, artificial intelligence, nanotechnology, genetic editing, and the so-called *P4 Medicine are no longer distant promises, but concrete realities influencing diagnosis, treatment, and overall healthcare delivery.* Additionally, the concept of One Health–*shared health*–requires a new perspective on health, integrating human, animal, and environmental health. These techno-scientific transformations also prompt epistemological reconfigurations, particularly in Civil Law itself. As the foundational and primary branch of legal science, Civil Law adapts to the present day, tackling the challenges posed by emerging controversies.

This is precisely what we find in this book: contemporaneity, scientific dialectics, rigorous research, and proposed solutions to problems that once seemed distant but have now become central to courtroom debates.

The advantages of these technologies are vast. In the case of telemedicine, it facilitates access to medical specialists, reduces the need for geographical travel, improves equity in accessing specialised healthcare, and lowers the risk of nosocomial infections. In robotics, it enhances precision and accuracy in surgical procedures, reduces pharmaceutical costs, and addresses labour shortages in specific healthcare areas. Artificial intelligence reduces the costs of complex diagnostic procedures, increases decision-making accuracy, adapts robotics to individual patient needs, and facilitates more secure and effective pandemic management.

Nanotechnology enables the targeted delivery of active substances to specific cells and allows medical devices to be embedded in clothing, enabling patient monitoring. The properties of certain nanomaterials are also ideal for improving early diagnosis and treatment of neurodegenerative diseases or cancer, selectively targeting cancer cells without harming healthy ones. Genetic editing is revolutionising pharmacy and medicine, from prevention to diagnosis and treatment, and will be analysed in this work.

As we can see from these brief examples, we are witnessing a proliferation of new technologies with the potential to alter the very nature of the doctor–patient relationship. These innovations are not merely tools but catalysts for reshaping how care is delivered and experienced. They have played a pivotal role in advancing what is known as *P4 Medicine*, which stands for Prevention, Prediction, Participation, and Personalisation—a paradigm that prioritises patient-centred, data-driven, and proactive healthcare.

Artificial intelligence plays a pivotal role in all these technologies, accelerating the technological and scientific progress of the others, with a profound impact on healthcare. Through a dialectical process, the development of these technologies has led to a transformation in the structure of healthcare relationships. From a vertical relationship where the doctor held authority, we now move to a networked relationship in which the doctor becomes a manager of information, much of which is provided by other disciplines and professionals: biologists, geneticists, pharmacists, engineers, physicists, computer scientists, mathematicians, statisticians, and

AI-powered robots. Medicine is losing its centrality, and doctors are losing exclusivity—and, undoubtedly, the monopoly on knowledge.

Simultaneously, the medical industry has become coveted by other market players—powerful, organised, transnational entities with access to funding—who benefit from the ingenuity and innovation of Information and Communication Technology (ICT) experts. Medicine is under siege. Representing 10–20% of the GDP in developed countries, it is a stable and predictable sector, attractive for capital seeking long-term, secure investments. Penetrating this territory requires only a law that removes doctors' monopoly on medical acts or regulations favouring the free provision of health services without human contact. Soon, an AI-powered robot will offer free diagnoses and propose low-cost therapies, hosted on some social network already controlling much of our private lives.

This is why the Portuguese Medical Association has proposed that the Medical Act be recognised as Intangible Cultural Heritage of Humanity. It is therefore essential to safeguard the dignity and specificity of the medical act. Equally important, today's and tomorrow's doctors must cultivate humanistic skills that nurture compassion and enable moments of emotional connection (António Damásio) in clinical relationships—moments that have proven to yield significant therapeutic effects.

This backdrop calls for calm and informed reflection on these topics. Ethical challenges can be framed within the three values of the Enlightenment—Liberty, Equality, and Fraternity—which we still consider the most suitable for promoting the ideals of Order and Progress, so well expressed in Brazil's flag.

The Enlightenment values that brought us science must now be reinterpreted in light of the radical challenges that AI poses to human life itself. Liberty calls for an urgent warning against the totalitarianism of the global healthcare project. Major ICT and AI companies aim to dominate the healthcare market, equating health with well-being and disease with nonconformity, creating an Orwellian dystopia that undermines diversity, autonomy, and freedom. Equality requires defending equal access to modern healthcare and fighting against discrimination.

The *homo sanitas dystopia* risks leading to health insurance discrimination and unequal access to healthcare. Fraternity here means equity in healthcare access and the bioethical principle of justice, requiring a financially sustainable system, democratic access to approved and subsidised medicines, and the promotion of treatments for rare diseases. This is even more urgent in an era of ageing populations and increasing healthcare demands, calling for intergenerational solidarity, solidarity with future generations, and solidarity among classes, regions, countries, and continents.

The advancements and ethical challenges outlined above provide the crucial backdrop for understanding the issues of medical liability and AI's impact on healthcare, which form the foundation of Rafaella Nogaroli's work. Starting from these specific concerns, her book takes us further, inviting reflection on the meaning and scope of the patient-citizen, inherently vulnerable, in the face of a profoundly transforming medical industry. It calls for addressing the challenges of regulating the advances of AI-driven medicine while preserving the human being as the subject of action and human dignity as the ultimate goal of techno-scientific progress—in short, maintaining a medicine with a human face.

As the French philosopher Gilles Lipovetsky states, *conformism is the opposite of the ethics of authenticity*. In a society pursuing the maxim *be yourself*, the domination of AI risks reifying—or worse, commodifying—the patient and the doctor, turning these actors from subjects of action into mere extras or, worse, objects. Against this backdrop, Rafaella Nogaroli's work emerges as a counterpoint, an act of authenticity that reaffirms a Civil Law framework centred on the individual. It stands as an ethical endeavour, making it essential reading and reference material for anyone wishing to study Biomedical Law today.

It is worth mentioning that, in October 2023, this work was first published in Portuguese by Thomson Reuters Brazil, with launch events held in both Brazil and Portugal. The Portuguese launch, organised in collaboration with the Centre for Biomedical Law, which I have the honour of directing, at the University of Coimbra, took place in January 2024. The publication was met with remarkable acclaim from both medical and legal communities across the two countries, achieving the milestone of approximately 700 copies sold within its first year.

With the publication of this English edition, I extend my sincere congratulations to Springer Nature for recognising the significance of this work and to the author for achieving the distinction of having her book published by one of the world's leading publishers of legal scholarship.

This edition has been thoughtfully adapted to address topics relevant to Medical Law in European jurisdictions, enhancing its multijurisdictional applicability. The discussions on medical liability and the ethical and legal duties involved in the integration of artificial intelligence into healthcare systems transcend the Brazilian context, offering valuable insights for various European nations and beyond.

This book's contributions to the fields of Medical Law and artificial intelligence regulation are both timely and indispensable. It provides a robust analytical framework for understanding how emerging technologies reshape the practice of medicine and the legal principles that govern it. As healthcare systems globally grapple with the challenges of AI integration, this work serves as a vital resource for scholars, practitioners, and policymakers alike.

By addressing issues of such universal significance, this book affirms its place not only as a cornerstone in the study of Medical Law in Europe but also as a guide for navigating the ethical and legal dimensions of healthcare innovation on a global scale.

Coimbra, Portugal
January 2025

André Gonçalo Dias Pereira

Preface

This work represents the complete development of my thesis research, successfully defended in March 2023 at the Federal University of Paraná in Curitiba, Brazil, under the supervision of Professor Paulo Nalin. On that occasion, the examining board – comprising Professors Paulo Nalin, Clayton de Albuquerque Maranhão, Miguel Kfouri Neto, and André Dias Pereira – awarded my dissertation work the highest distinction, with a recommendation for conversion to a doctoral thesis. Professors Kfouri and Pereira are widely recognised as leading authorities in Medical Law in Brazil and Portugal, respectively.

In October 2023, the work was published in Portuguese by Thomson Reuters Brazil, with launch events in both Brazil and Portugal, the latter in collaboration with the Centre for Biomedical Law at the University of Coimbra, in January 2024. The publication received an exceptional reception from both medical and legal audiences in both countries, with approximately 700 copies sold within a year.

Now, with the publication of this English edition, I wish to extend my deepest gratitude to Springer Nature, and in particular to Karolina Araújo and Peter Pushpanathan, professionals responsible for the project coordination of this book. It is a true honour to publish with the world's foremost publisher of legal books, with nearly two centuries of history, whose reputation for disseminating high-calibre legal scholarship is unparalleled.

The work has been subtly adapted for its English edition, incorporating specific topics on Medical Law in European countries, with the objective of highlighting the book's multijurisdictional relevance. The concepts discussed concerning the assessment of medical liability and duties of conduct in artificial intelligence systems are applicable not only in Brazil but also in various European nations.

It is worth emphasising that this work does not solely address the civil liability of medical professionals within the specific context of artificial intelligence systems. The first half of the book provides an overview of the evolution of Medical Law in Brazil and Europe, alongside a detailed examination of the fundamental concepts underpinning this field. Only in the second half does the book engage more specifically with issues of medical fault and duties of conduct in the context of AI. This broad survey of the current state of the art is the culmination of my research from 2017 to 2023 within a research group that I co-directed with Professor Miguel Kfouri Neto. In October 2023, this group evolved into one of Brazil's foremost institutes of Medical Law—of which I am honoured to serve as president for the inaugural term of 2024–2027.

I would further emphasise that the practical insights presented in this work are largely drawn from my experience, between 2017 and 2023, as an legal advisor to Appellate Judges Clayton Maranhão and Miguel Kfouri Neto at the Court of Justice of the State of Paraná. Professor Kfouri, an eminent jurist and the foremost authority on Medical Law in Brazil, has been my esteemed mentor and friend since 2017. I am profoundly honoured to have had the privilege of learning from his lectures, presentations, and discussions.

Building on these preliminary considerations, I shall now present an overview of the key themes discussed in this book.

The book explores the pivotal intersection of medical practice and artificial intelligence, addressing the benefits, risks, and challenges that AI introduces within the physician–patient relationship. It provides in-depth insights into the redefinition of medical duties, highlighting both their ethical aspects and binding legal force. Focusing on issues of medical malpractice and medico-legal duties, the book explores the ethical principles of AI in medicine and their relationship with legal obligations.

Additionally, the book offers a general overview of AI regulation within the European Union, providing valuable perspectives for comparison with existing legal concepts in the Brazilian system. This analysis seeks to identify suitable solutions to emerging conflicts, thereby contributing to the development of medical civil liability jurisprudence on a global scale.

An in-depth analysis of medical liability is presented, featuring hypothetical cases of adverse events involving automated decision-making systems in healthcare. The purpose is to provide practical guidance for lawyers and judges in addressing future legal claims related to AI in medicine. The reflections presented here begin with an analysis of the Brazilian legal framework, respecting its unity and complexity while diverging from doctrinal perspectives that suggest substantial gaps in civil liability laws concerning AI-related issues.

It is important to emphasise that this book adopts a multijurisdictional perspective, highlighting the adaptability of core concepts in medical law and artificial intelligence across various legal systems. The approach to investigating medical liability or ethical principles in the use of AI systems is applicable on a global scale, making this book relevant to a wide range of countries and increasing its potential to reach consumer markets across multiple jurisdictions. By transcending specific legal frameworks, the insights and guidance offered possess universal applicability, thereby enhancing the book's appeal and relevance in overseas markets.

This multijurisdictional approach is further developed in the section on legal frameworks for medical law and liability across Europe, which examines key aspects of European medical law and includes a discussion on AI regulation within the European Union. Particular attention is given to the ongoing influence of the AI Act in shaping current discussions on AI regulation in Brazil.

The topics explored include a comparative analysis of medical law and patient autonomy in Portugal and Spain, regulatory approaches to healthcare liability in France, Germany, and Italy, and the management of medical malpractice in the United Kingdom. This comparative analysis provides a solid foundation for understanding how different European jurisdictions address medical liability, patient autonomy, and regulatory frameworks, thereby enhancing the book's relevance and accessibility across diverse legal systems.

Detailed Description of the Scope, Aim, and Approach of the Book

This book aims to offer a comprehensive examination of the ethical, legal, and practical implications of artificial intelligence within the medical field, with a specific focus on medical liability and physician–patient relationships. By bridging core concepts in medical law, AI technology, and civil liability, the book provides valuable guidance for professionals in law, healthcare, and policy. The approach is both theoretical and practical, incorporating case law, hypothetical scenarios, and comparative legal analysis across multiple jurisdictions.

Chapter-by-Chapter Descriptions

- *Chapter 1* provides a foundational overview of the subject matter, presenting the latest technological advancements in AI and their relevance to medicine. This chapter includes a glossary of essential concepts, an overview of AI applications in 'P4 Medicine', and an outline of the ethical and legal considerations in clinical practice.
- *Chapter 2* examines the historical and legal evolution of the physician–patient relationship, focusing on medical duties and their legal impact. The chapter also explores Brazilian case law and compares legal obligations and patient autonomy frameworks across European jurisdictions, with emphasis on informed consent.
- *Chapter 3* delves into civil liability in healthcare, with a particular focus on medical negligence under Brazilian law. It discusses the allocation of liability among healthcare professionals, hospitals, and manufacturers, and further provides a comparative analysis of liability frameworks in Europe.
- *Chapter 4* analyses the ethical and legal aspects of AI in medical contracts, covering the benefits and risks of AI in clinical decision-making, ethical principles of AI in Europe, and the regulatory landscape in both the EU and Brazil. This chapter highlights the influence of the AI Act on emerging regulations.

- *Chapter 5* uses hypothetical cases to illustrate medical liability issues arising from AI-related adverse events. This chapter is designed to provide practical insights and guidance to legal and medical professionals when addressing future claims, with an emphasis on the duty of care, informed consent, and the evolving nature of medical responsibility.
- *Chapter 6* concludes the book by synthesising fifteen legal and ethical lessons regarding medical liability in the Age of AI. It reflects on AI's potential to enhance healthcare efficiency while reinforcing the indispensable role of physicians in patient care. The chapter underscores the need for a balanced approach that combines technological advancement with strong ethical and legal safeguards, advocating for continued adaptation by healthcare professionals to meet evolving responsibilities in patient-centred care.

This book represents a comprehensive resource for understanding the transformative impact of AI on medical practice and the ethical and legal responsibilities that arise within the physician–patient relationship. By combining theoretical insights with practical guidance, it offers an invaluable tool for legal and healthcare professionals navigating the rapidly evolving landscape of AI in medicine.

May this work inspire thoughtful reflection and offer meaningful insights for legal and medical professionals as they navigate the integration of AI into healthcare.

Curitiba, Brazil
January 2025

Rafaella Nogaroli

Acknowledgements

This work stands as a testament to an extraordinary journey, shaped by the wisdom, support, and inspiration of countless individuals. On that sublime, sunlit morning of 3 March 2023, my heart beat in harmony with the golden rays that danced through the celestial ether. In the majestic historic building of the Federal University of Paraná, Brazil, where wisdom permeates every stone walked upon by the most renowned Brazilian jurists, the defence panel for my thesis convened with brilliance and prestige. The illustrious presence of Professors Nalin, Kfouri, Maranhão, and Pereira elevated the occasion, akin to constellations guiding my path. There, amidst ancient books and the echoes of sagacious voices, I entrusted my work to the universe of knowledge, hopeful for it to be embraced by the symphony of approval.

The conclusion of this work marks a 6-year period of study (2017–2023) alongside the research group on Medical Law, coordinated by myself and the Appellate Judge Professor Dr *Miguel Kfouri Neto*, my academic master and mentor, to whom I owe eternal gratitude for his daily teachings and constant encouragement over the last decade. I had the unique opportunity to learn from and contribute to the updates of approximately three editions of his seminal works, *Civil Liability of the Physician* and *Civil Liability of Hospitals*. I can proudly say that I have the honour of being both a disciple and a friend of the leading authority on Medical Law in Brazil. Our partnership has strengthened over the years, and in 2024, we established the *Miguel Kfouri Neto Medical Law Institute*, of which I have the honour of serving as president, organising discussions and academic events with nearly 200 members from across the country, as well as engaging external audiences.

I am deeply grateful to my supervisor in the Postgraduate Programme in Law at the Federal University of Paraná, Professor Dr *Paulo Nalin*, an eminent Brazilian jurist for whom I hold profound admiration. His unparalleled cordiality and willingness to share his extensive knowledge were instrumental in refining the theoretical propositions contained in the thesis that underpins this book. I extend my sincere thanks for his invaluable guidance and oversight.

I also express my gratitude to Appellate Judge Professor Dr *Clayton Maranhão*, a distinguished jurist whose extensive knowledge of Medical Law and Civil Procedural Law helped refine many of the ideas presented in this book during our daily conversations. Moreover, several reflections contained herein about the redefined concept of Medical Law in the twenty-first century stem from my work as his legal adviser on cases cases adjudicated by the Paraná State Court of Justice.

Furthermore, I extend my heartfelt thanks to Portuguese Professor Dr *André Dias Pereira*, the foremost authority on Medical Law in Portugal, whose brilliant books and papers have always inspired my studies in this field. Since 2019, when I began my academic research on the ethical and legal aspects of emerging health technologies, his presence has marked significant milestones in my international academic journey. That year, I received an honourable mention at the International Congress of Civil Law at the University of Coimbra, where I had the privilege of having my paper on patient consent in robotic surgery evaluated by a panel that included Professor Pereira. More recently, since 2021, I have been deeply honoured to accept his invitation to lecture on Medical Law and artificial intelligence in the specialisation programme at the Centre for Biomedical Law at the same university.

Undoubtedly, strong academic ties connect me to these four distinguished jurists. Their wise counsel, unwavering support, and enriching knowledge have been crucial pillars for my intellectual and professional growth.

I also extend my thanks to Professor Dr *Nelson Rosenvald*, the leading Brazilian authority on civil liability and, indeed, the foremost living jurist in the country. Over recent years, he has been one of the most supportive figures in my pursuit of a doctor's degree, providing me with numerous learning opportunities, particularly through our work in the leadership of the Brazilian Institute for Civil Liability Studies (IBERC), which has become a highly fertile ground for academic exchange. Besides, he is the person who most strongly encouraged me to publish this book in English, firmly believing in its perspective and international significance.

Moreover, no expression of gratitude would be complete without acknowledging my beloved family, whose unwavering support has been the cornerstone of my academic journey over the years, especially during the completion of this book in both its Portuguese and English editions. I recognise the pivotal role played by my cherished parents Ana Flávia and Renato, my godfather Augusto César, my dear siblings José Renato, Lorena, Diogo, and Gustavo, and my grandparents Edezir, Ico, Maria do Socorro, and Augusto. At every challenging stage of my academic and professional journey, their words of encouragement and acts of affection fortified me, nurturing my determination and belief in my potential. Sharing my dreams and achievements with them is an indescribable privilege. The dedication, patience, and love they have always shown are precious balms that sustained me when my steps faltered. I know that every achievement I have reached is a shared victory, as they stood by my side, providing a foundation of constant support and love affection.

I am also deeply grateful to my friends *Juliano Ralo*, *Romualdo Baptista dos Santos*, *José Faleiros Júnior*, and *Igor Mascarenhas*, brilliant professors who generously dedicated their time and expertise to carefully reviewing my work, offering valuable insights that enriched the essence of the text. Their perceptive observations and guidance have served as beacons of wisdom, illuminating the paths of my research. I deeply appreciate their sensitivity to understanding the purposes and challenges of my work and for sharing their perspectives and expertise, making this academic journey all the more enriching.

Additionally, I record my admiration and affection for Professor *Rodrigo da Guia Silva*, my first academic collaborator and co-author of an article on Medical Law and artificial intelligence, which kindled my deeper interest in expanding my studies in this field. I also extend my gratitude to the brilliant Professors Dr *Romualdo Baptista dos Santos* and Dr *Fernanda Schaefer* for graciously agreeing to write in the Portuguese version of my book, respectively, the sections 'about the book' and 'afterword'. These scholars, with their inspiring academic trajectories and admirable methodological rigour, have made invaluable contributions, greatly enriching this work.

I also have to mention some friends who are distinguished Brazilian researchers in Medical Law and have played pivotal roles in my academic journey. Friendship, that divine bond that synchronises souls, reveals its magic when we share happiness in its fullness. It is in shared laughter and intertwined tears that we find life's true treasures. In the last years, I have been blessed with a precious group of invaluable friends—Caroline Cavet, Isadora Pagliari, Maitê Machado, Maria Teresa Oliveira, Mayara Medeiros, Natasha Gelinski, Patricia Bortolotto, and Yasmin Folha—who are cosmic sparks illuminating my path, providing essential support and encouragement throughout my academic and professional journey.

I express my immense joy and honour at having attended the Postgraduate Programme in Law at the Federal University of Paraná in Brazil, which, in the realm of Civil Law, brings together some of the most brilliant minds in the country. I hope that, through this work, I can, in some way, repay society for the investment and trust placed in me.

With the publication of this English edition, I would like to express my profound gratitude to *Springer Nature*, particularly to *Karolina Araújo* and *Peter Pushpanathan*, whose expertise and dedication were fundamental in coordinating this project. It is a privilege to collaborate with one of the most esteemed publishers of legal literature worldwide, boasting an unparalleled legacy of nearly two centuries in advancing high-quality legal scholarship.

Finally, I must extend my deepest gratitude to three distinguished professors who played a pivotal role in the publication of this English edition.

Professor Dr *Nelson Rosenvald*, as mentioned before, the most pre-eminent legal scholar and civil law authority in Brazil, deserves particular recognition. He was the driving force behind my decision to publish this work in English, recognising its multijurisdictional perspective and its potential to contribute to global legal discourse.

Professor Dr *André Dias Pereira*, previously mentioned as the leading authority on Medical Law in Portugal, has likewise honoured me profoundly by contributing the foreword to this edition. His unmatched expertise and unwavering support have enhanced this work in myriad ways, and I am deeply thankful for his invaluable contribution.

Finally, Professor Dr *Valterlei da Costa* has guided me into the profound realm of legal philosophy, broadening my intellectual perspective and inspiring a deeper contemplation of the philosophical foundations underpinning the redefinition of legal concepts and institutions. His invaluable insights have significantly influenced the English edition of this book, particularly through the integration of philosophical frameworks that reinterpret and transform fundamental juridical principles.

To all the remarkable individuals who have played a role in this endeavour, your contributions have been the foundation of this work. I am profoundly grateful for your guidance, inspiration, and unwavering belief in the potential of this project. This book stands as a reflection of collective effort, a synthesis of shared knowledge, and a testament to the enduring power of academic friendship and collaboration.

January 2025
Curitiba, Brazil

Rafaella Nogaroli

Competing Interests The author has no competing interests to declare that are relevant to the content of this manuscript.

Contents

1 Introduction: Artificial Intelligence (AI) and P4 Medicine in the Twenty-First Century 1
1.1 Glossary: Fundamental Concepts Used in This Work 1
1.2 Global Overview of AI Applications in P4 Medicine 11
1.3 Purpose of This Book: Navigating the Ethical and Legal Landscape of AI Integration in Clinical Practice 14
References 16

2 Ethical and Legal Aspects of the Physician-Patient Relationship . . . 19
2.1 The Historical Evolution of the Physician-Patient Relationship Worldwide 19
2.1.1 Medical Service Contracts Under Brazilian Law 31
2.1.2 A Proposed Classification of Physicians' Duties of Conduct in Brazil 34
2.2 A Detailed Analysis of Duties Related to Disclosure, Loyalty, and Protection in Brazil 39
2.2.1 The Duty of Disclosure and the Reinterpretation of Informed Consent 39
2.2.2 Duties Related to Loyalty and Protection 51
2.2.3 Professional Accountability and Legal Consequences of Breaching Duties, with Focus on Informed Consent 60
2.3 European Law on Patient Consent: Jurisprudential and Doctrinal Perspectives 63
References 77

3 Civil Liability in Healthcare 81
3.1 Spheres of Medical Liability: Civil, Criminal, and Ethical 81
3.1.1 Medical Malpractice Cases Under the Brazilian Legal System 85
3.1.2 Concurrence of Causes and Exclusions of Causality in the Healthcare Sector 88

3.2 Allocation of Civil Liability Among Physicians, Hospitals, and Manufacturers 94
3.2.1 Adverse Events Involving Medical Technologies 96
3.2.2 Accountability and Unknowable Risks in Medical Devices 100
3.3 Legal Frameworks on Liability for Medical Negligence in European Countries 105
References 120

4 Ethical and Legal Aspects of Artificial Intelligence (AI) in Medical Service Contracts 123
4.1 The Emergence of AI in Clinical Decision-Making Worldwide . . . 123
4.1.1 Applications of Artificial Intelligence in Brazilian and European Medical Practice 128
4.1.2 Key Risks and Challenges in the Implementation of Algorithms in Medicine 140
4.2 Ethics and Regulation of Artificial Intelligence in Europe 151
4.2.1 Ethical Principles of AI in Medicine and Their Impact on Physician's Duties of Conduct 153
4.2.2 The AI Act and the European Framework for Civil Liability for Damages Involving AI Systems in Healthcare 172
4.3 Frameworks and Perspectives for Regulation of Artificial Intelligence in Brazil 193
References 201

5 Artificial Intelligence and Medical Liability in Hypothetical Cases 207
5.1 Medical Malpractice in Errors Related to Diagnosis, Prognosis, and Treatment Through AI Systems 207
5.2 Data-Informed Duties (Duty of Vigilance) and the Multifunctionality of Medical Liability in the Twenty-First Century 224
5.3 Breach of Patient Trust as a Basis for Medical Liability in AI 233
5.4 Medical Liability and Patient Consent in AI-Assisted Clinical Decisions 237
References 244

6 A New Chapter for Medical Liability: Fifteen Legal and Ethical Lessons in the Age of AI 247

About the Author

Rafaella Nogaroli (nogaroli@gmail.com/https://www.linkedin.com/in/rafaellanogaroli/)

Researcher and Author in Medical Law, Civil Liability, and Healthcare Technologies

Served as an Appellate Judge's Advisor at the Court of Justice of the State of Paraná, Brazil (2017–2023).

Master of Laws from the Federal University of Paraná (Brazil), awarded the highest grade by the examination board and recommended for conversion of the degree to a doctorate.

President of the Miguel Kfouri Neto Institute—Medical and Health Law (2024–2027), a Brazilian institution that promotes academic activities in the field of Medical and Health Law, with nearly 200 members, including judges, prosecutors, lawyers, doctors, and nurses from different states across the country.

Coordinated the research group 'Healthcare Law and Medical Companies' at UNICURITIBA (2017–2023), overseeing a diverse membership of around 100 researchers.

Professor in short courses and in the specialisation course in Medical Law at the Centre for Biomedical Law, University of Coimbra, Portugal, and in various specialisation courses in Brazil.

Professor and Academic Supervisor of the specialisation course in Medical Law and Bioethics at EBRADI.

Director and Member of the Brazilian Institute for Civil Liability Studies (IBERC).

Author of more than 80 papers published in journals and books worldwide about Medical Law, Civil Law, artificial intelligence and emerging healthcare technologies. (curriculum: http://lattes.cnpq.br/2511396886621893/https://independent.academia.edu/rafaellanogaroli).

Coordinator of the column 'Migalhas on Medical Law and Bioethics'. (https://www.migalhas.com.br/coluna/migalhas-de-direito-medico-e-bioetica).

Chapter 1
Introduction: Artificial Intelligence (AI) and P4 Medicine in the Twenty-First Century

1.1 Glossary: Fundamental Concepts Used in This Work

At the dawn of the third millennium, human life has become closely intertwined with artificial intelligence (AI) algorithms, which play an essential role in supporting decision-making within the healthcare sector. Medical companies, laboratories, and healthcare institutions are intensely focused on developing and implementing increasingly sophisticated algorithms capable of performing predictive analyses to enhance diagnostic accuracy, improve patient outcomes, and streamline clinical workflows (Topol 2013, 2016, 2019a, b).

To better understand the intersections between artificial intelligence and medicine, as well as the legal implications of this phenomenon, it is essential to take a step back and revisit some fundamental concepts related to so-called 'intelligent' systems: (i) artificial intelligence; (ii) augmented intelligence; (iii) algorithms; (iv) robotics; (v) predictive analytics; (vi) machine learning; (vii) deep learning; (viii) natural language processing; (ix) Large Language Models (LLMs); (x) expert systems; and (xi) general purpose AI.

(i). *Artificial Intelligence* is a term that was first coined by John McCarthy in 1956, who was then an assistant professor of mathematics at Dartmouth College in Hanover, New Hampshire (USA). Together with three other researchers—Marvin Minsky of the Massachusetts Institute of Technology (MIT), Nathan Rochester of IBM, and Claude Shannon of Bell Telephone Laboratories—McCarthy proposed the "Dartmouth Summer Research Project on Artificial Intelligence Conference", which brought together a number of prominent scientists. This event created an opportunity for foundational contributions that served as a driving force in the scientific study of the field (Russell and Norvig 2022).

R. Nogaroli, *Medical Liability and Artificial Intelligence*,
https://doi.org/10.1007/978-3-031-94306-5_1

However, AI began to develop substantially from the early twenty-first century, particularly due to advancements in the Internet and microprocessors, as well as reductions in cloud data storage costs. This resurgence occurred during a period scientists refer to as the "AI Spring". According to Turner (2019), Artificial Intelligence "is the ability of a non-natural entity to make choices based on a process of evaluation"—with AI potentially classified according to its level of autonomy.

The origin of reflections that would lead to theoretical developments concerning the transcendence of human-machine distinctions—as well as the developmental challenges and evolution of this technology—can be traced to the seminal work of Alan Turing and his so-called *Turing Test*. This test was designed to examine whether a machine could process information to such a degree as to produce responses indistinguishable from those of a human. It was posited that, through data processing, a machine might ultimately achieve a level of autonomy, potentially emulating human behaviour (Russell and Norvig 2022).

To pass the Turing Test, a human interrogator would need to be unable to determine, after posing certain written questions, whether the responses were given by a person or by a computer. For this, the machine would need to exhibit the following capabilities: (i) natural language processing, (ii) knowledge representation, (iii) automated reasoning, and (iv) machine learning to adapt to new situations. Turing posited that if a computer could convince a third of its interlocutors that it was human, it could be said to be 'thinking' for itself and would have passed the test.

Today, a portion of legal doctrine—with which we concur—interprets the term 'Artificial Intelligence' (AI) as broad in scope, encompassing two distinct areas of research: 'General AI' (or Strong AI) and 'Specific AI' (or Weak AI).

"General AI" refers to a futuristic concept frequently depicted in films such as 'I, Robot' (2004), in which society creates a superintelligent entity with robots that act and behave similarly to human beings, including possessing feelings and emotions. However, at the current stage of technical and scientific development, such a technological threshold (artificial superintelligence) and the so-called "technological singularity"—a term coined by Vinge (1993) and later explored by Kurwzeil (2005)—have not yet been achieved.

In contrast, "Specific AI"—the primary focus of this book—encompasses a repertoire of techniques aimed at creating automated solutions for individual (specific) problems. Examples include document translation (e.g., Google Translate), content searching (e.g., Bing, Google), voice recognition (e.g., Siri, Alexa), autonomous vehicles, and data and image processing (such as health records or diagnostic imagery). Throughout this book, any reference to "Artificial Intelligence" pertains exclusively to Specific AI.

Autonomous systems may be purely software-based, functioning in the virtual realm (such as voice assistants, image analysis software, search engines, and systems for voice and facial expression recognition), or they may be integrated into hardware devices (such as advanced robots, autonomous vehicles, drones, and Internet of Things applications).

In the healthcare sector, according to the American Medical Association (2021), a machine's work is considered autonomous ("intelligent") when it involves the automatic interpretation of data to reach clinically relevant and independent conclusions, without reliance on the physician's input. This includes the capability to distinguish biomedical data (such as the likelihood of a particular pathophysiology) in order to establish a diagnosis or implement a therapeutic intervention.

According to the American Medical Association (2021), automated systems can be categorised into three levels based on the degree of physician involvement in the AI's decision-making: (1) Level I: AI generates predictions and clinical conclusions that are subject to review and require a physician's approval for implementation. These systems generally assist healthcare professionals in routine tasks, such as patient triage or organising medical data; (2) Level II: AI presents conclusions and proposes diagnostic and/or healthcare management options, along with alerts that may require medical intervention. These systems can assist in detecting diseases or medical conditions but rely on the physician to interpret and validate the automated decisions; (3) Level III: AI generates predictions and conclusions and autonomously initiates healthcare management, although the physician retains the authority to override the AI's decision.

It is noteworthy that recent documents, such as the United States' 2022 Algorithmic Accountability Act (an update to the 2019 version) and the European Artificial Intelligence Act (AI Act) of 2021, amended in 2024, avoid engaging in terminological debates over the semantic scope of the term "intelligence," opting instead to refer to "AI systems" or "automated decision-making systems."

In this regard, it is important to emphasise to readers of this book that, whenever the term "artificial intelligence" appears in the text, it should be understood as synonymous with "automated decision-making system".

The concept of an "AI system" in the AI Act is defined to align closely with the work of international organisations focused on AI, aiming to ensure legal certainty, facilitate international convergence and broad acceptance, while providing the flexibility needed to accommodate rapid technological advancements in this field. The definition is based on "key characteristics of AI systems that distinguish it from simpler traditional software systems or programming approaches and should not cover systems that are based on the rules defined solely by natural persons to automatically execute operations. A key characteristic of AI systems is their capability to infer. This capability to infer refers to the process of obtaining the outputs, such as predictions, content, recommendations, or decisions, which can influence physical and virtual environments, and to a capability of AI systems to derive models or algorithms, or both, from inputs or data. The techniques that enable inference while building an AI system include machine learning approaches that learn from data how to achieve certain objectives, and logic- and knowledge-based approaches that infer from encoded knowledge or symbolic representation of the task to be solved. The capacity of an AI system to infer transcends basic data processing by enabling learning, reasoning or modelling".

(ii). *Augmented intelligence* is the term adopted by the American Medical Association (American Medical Association 2021) and the World Medical Association (2019) as a substitute for "artificial intelligence", to emphasise

AI's assistive role—that is, technology enhances human intelligence rather than replaces it. In its Statement on augmented intelligence in Medical Care (2019), the WMA adopts the term "augmented intelligence" to describe systems intended to coexist with human decision-making, stressing that such systems are designed to support, rather than replace, the judgement of healthcare professionals. The AMA similarly promotes the term to underscore that artificial intelligence is designed to enhance human capabilities, not replace them. This emphasis is evident across several AMA documents, which highlight the value of augmented intelligence in supporting medical care and its complementary role in clinical practice.

(iii). *Algorithms* are structured sets of instructions or rules that a computer or machine follows to perform calculations, process data, or solve specific problems. They operate through a sequence of steps that convert input data into a desired output, enabling automated decision-making and problem-solving processes (Faleiros Júnior 2021).

The functioning of an artificial intelligence algorithm is based on the calculation of probabilities, which result from multiplying an input vector by millions of parameters, whose values were determined through training. Algorithms should not be conflated with robots, as the latter represent, at most, the physical framework within which all such processing occurs. Algorithms are, therefore, sets of instructions or sequences of rules that, when applied to datasets, enable the solution of similar classes of problems (Flasiński 2016).

Data train the algorithm to recognise patterns through examples, which is why, the larger the dataset processed by the algorithm, the greater the learning it will acquire, theoretically resulting in an algorithm with improved accuracy. In this regard, Donald Knuth (1973) states that "an algorithm is a set of rules or instructions for obtaining a specific output from given input". Put simply, data can be considered the *fuel* of AI.

For example, in the case of automated decision-making systems for diagnosing patients with Covid-19, thousands of data points from infected patients—or from those with suspected infection but negative results—were inputted into the algorithm, along with their respective chest CT scans (Topff et al. 2023). Using this dataset, the algorithm was then programmed to analyse a patient's CT scan and, within mere seconds, distinguish between patients infected with the novel coronavirus and those with other pulmonary conditions (output).

(iv). *Robotics* are machines (hardware) and, more specifically, electronic components that form a physical object which, on its own, is inoperative; however, it can produce actions in response to mechanical, electrical, or informational influences. Robots may take various physical forms: robotic arms, robotic platforms, exoskeleton robots, morphic robots, humanoid robots, as well as nano and microrobots.

The term "robot" was coined by the Czech playwright, novelist, and journalist Karel Čapek (1880–1938), who introduced it in his successful 1920 play Rossum's

Universal Robots. "Robot" originates from the old Slavic word *robota*, which means "servitude" or "forced/arduous labour".

According to the Cambridge Dictionary, a robot is "a machine controlled by a computer that is used to perform jobs automatically", such as "a robot-performed surgery". In other words, a robot is a machine programmed by a computer, designed to respond to input received either manually or from its environment, and capable of carrying out a series of actions autonomously.

At present, the most widely used surgical assistance robot globally is the da Vinci system, manufactured by Intuitive Surgical. This robotic platform enables surgeons to operate with greater precision and efficiency. Although this robot possesses advanced automation capabilities, it is not considered an artificial intelligence system, as understood in this work.

The da Vinci is a robot and, more precisely, classified as a medical device. It is worth noting that the robot is controlled by a computer system that uses an algorithm to interpret the surgeon's movements and translate them into precise actions of the robotic arms. Additionally, the software within this robotic platform includes an algorithm to minimise hand tremors and compensate for any unintended movement of the robotic arms.

The da Vinci robot utilises advanced data and image processing technology to assist surgeons in performing procedures with greater precision and safety. The system includes high-definition cameras and instruments with a far greater range of motion than the human hand, allowing the surgeon to conduct complex operations with enhanced ease. Furthermore, the system provides the surgeon with real-time information on the patient's anatomy, enabling a more precise visualisation of the surgical area (Iavazzo et al. 2014).

However, the da Vinci robot is fully controlled by the surgeon and has no autonomy to make decisions or perform tasks without human intervention. It accurately reproduces the surgeon's movements and can filter hand tremors but lacks the capability to make independent decisions or learn from experience.

Significant scientific research is currently underway to integrate surgical robots with autonomous functions, that is, artificial intelligence algorithms, as exemplified by the STAR (Smart Tissue Autonomous Robot), developed by researchers at Johns Hopkins University in the United States (Saeidi et al. 2022).

(v). *Predictive analytics* is the use of data, statistical algorithms, and machine learning techniques to identify the likelihood of future outcomes based on historical data. The aim is to move beyond understanding what has happened to provide a more accurate assessment of what may occur in the future.

In hospitals, predictive analytics is applied through AI algorithms to forecast hospital readmissions, risks of falls, and potential deterioration in a patient's clinical condition. Hundreds or thousands of biomedical data points are analysed to predict the likelihood of a particular health event occurring.

In clinical diagnostics, predictive analytics involves the use of AI algorithms to assess the likelihood of various health conditions before they fully manifest. By analysing vast datasets that include patient history, genetic information, and other biomedical indicators, predictive models can help clinicians identify individuals at higher risk of developing certain conditions. This proactive approach enables earlier interventions, more personalised treatment plans, and optimised resource allocation, ultimately improving patient outcomes and reducing healthcare costs.

(vi). *Machine learning* is a technique used in the field of Artificial Intelligence to train computational systems to identify patterns in data and make decisions based on those patterns. Machine learning models are fed large quantities of data and use algorithms to learn from these data and improve their ability to perform specific tasks.

It is a trial-and-error process that "gradually logs results, thereby preparing algorithms to solve problems more effectively, as the ongoing attempts 'train' them to deliver better outcomes" (Ashley 2017).

Machine learning encompasses various methods, including supervised, unsupervised, and reinforcement learning (Alloghani et al. 2020). Supervised learning involves training an algorithm on a labelled dataset, where each input is linked to a known output. The algorithm learns the mapping between inputs and outputs, allowing it to predict outcomes accurately when presented with new, unseen data.

Unsupervised learning operates without labelled data, meaning that the algorithm must uncover hidden patterns or groupings within the dataset without predefined outcomes. It is frequently used for clustering and dimensionality reduction, where the goal is to group data into meaningful segments or reduce the complexity of data for easier analysis. This type of learning is valuable for exploratory analysis, customer segmentation, anomaly detection, and recommendation systems. By revealing inherent structures in the data, unsupervised learning can provide insights that were previously unknown.

Reinforcement learning is a dynamic approach in which an algorithm, known as an "agent", learns by interacting with an environment. Through trial and error, the agent receives feedback in the form of rewards or penalties, allowing it to improve its decision-making over time. The objective is to maximise cumulative rewards by learning the best actions to take in various states within the environment. This method is particularly useful in applications requiring complex decision-making, such as robotics and autonomous driving, where the agent must adapt to changing conditions and continuously optimise its actions to achieve long-term goals.

These machine learning techniques enable systems to become increasingly autonomous, adaptable, and efficient, enhancing their ability to solve complex, real-world problems across fields such as healthcare, finance, and law. This evolving capacity to improve through continuous data intake and processing is fundamental to the broader applications of AI, where machine learning serves as a cornerstone for creating predictive models and automated decision-making tools.

(vii). *Deep learning* constitutes a subfield of machine learning that employs artificial neural network algorithms to perform complex tasks, such as image recognition and natural language processing. As Taulli (2019) explains, deep learning enables the processing of large quantities of data to identify specific patterns that humans would generally be unable to detect. The term "deep" refers to the number of hidden layers in the neural network, which contribute significantly to its learning capacity (Goodfellow et al. 2016).

In other words, deep learning is a subset of machine learning in which multiple layers of information-processing stages within hierarchical architectures are exploited for pattern classification and feature learning. It involves the development and testing of algorithms that enable a computer to extract (or learn) functions from a dataset shared with a neural network, emulating the synaptic structure of the human brain and employing a 'divide and conquer' strategy—whether supervised or unsupervised—to learn a function.

The primary distinction, therefore, between machine learning and deep learning is that the latter refers to a more advanced technique that leverages neural networks inspired by the structure and functions of the human brain and the interconnection of neurons. Deep learning is particularly valuable for tasks involving large quantities of data, such as speech recognition, automatic translation, object detection in images, and medical diagnostics.

(viii). *Natural language processing* (NLP) is a subfield of AI that enables computers to understand and process human languages in a meaningful and valuable way. It focuses on interactions between human (or "natural") languages, such as English or Portuguese, and computers, allowing systems to interpret, analyse, and even generate language that resembles human communication (Russell and Norvig 2022).

NLP employs a combination of machine learning techniques, linguistic processing methods, and computational linguistics to examine and understand the meaning of words, phrases, and sentences used in human communication. The ultimate goal is to enable machines to comprehend human language in a manner similar to human understanding, so that they can perform tasks such as automatic translation, text summarisation, information extraction, and question answering.

The technology involves several stages, including tokenisation (dividing text into smaller units like words or phrases), syntactic analysis (understanding grammatical structure), and semantic analysis (interpreting meaning in context). Furthermore, NLP allows for natural language generation, whereby machines create responses or generate text in human-like language.

The practical applications of NLP are extensive, from personal assistants like Siri, Alexa, and Google Assistant to healthcare chatbots, which are increasingly used for patient triage by gathering responses related to symptoms. Such applications demonstrate NLP's potential to transform not only daily interactions but also healthcare services by allowing more efficient, responsive, and accessible care. As technology advances, NLP continues to shape the ways people interact with machines, as well as the manner in which medical and other service-based industries deliver their services, contributing to a more dynamic and accessible interface between humans and digital systems.

(ix). *Large Language Models* (LLMs) refer to a category of artificial intelligence models designed to understand, generate, and interpret human language at an advanced level. These models are typically trained on vast datasets comprising text from diverse sources, such as books, articles, websites, and other written materials. Their training involves processing billions of words, enabling them to identify patterns in language, context, syntax, and semantics, which allows them to generate responses that closely mimic human writing and conversation (Chiarello et al. 2024).

LLMs operate based on deep learning techniques, often relying on a specific type of neural network architecture called transformers. Transformers enable these models to handle long-range dependencies in text, effectively understanding context over lengthy passages, which is critical for coherent and contextually appropriate responses. Examples of popular LLMs include OpenAI's GPT series, Google's BERT and T5, and Meta's LLaMA.

These models are first trained on general data (pre-training) and can then be fine-tuned on specific datasets or tasks, such as legal analysis, healthcare documentation, or customer service, making them versatile for domain-specific applications. LLMs are capable of performing a variety of language-based tasks, including: (a) text generation: creating coherent paragraphs of text on a given topic; (b) translation: translating between languages with a high degree of accuracy; (c) summarisation: condensing large bodies of text while preserving key information; (d) sentiment analysis: identifying and interpreting emotional tone within text; (e) question-answering: responding to factual or context-based questions accurately.

In summary, LLMs represent a breakthrough in natural language processing, providing refined tools for managing complex linguistic tasks across diverse industries. Nevertheless, these models are limited to language-specific functions and lack the broader, adaptable problem-solving capabilities characteristic of Artificial General Intelligence (AGI), with which they are often contrasted.

(x). *Expert systems* are specialised artificial intelligence (AI) frameworks crafted to address specific problems within defined fields of knowledge. In the medical domain, these systems are widely utilised to enhance clinical decision-making by aiding physicians in tasks such as diagnosis, prognosis, and treatment planning. Equipped with structured knowledge bases and sophisticated inference mechanisms, they analyse patient data and reach informed conclusions, thereby offering significant support in medical evaluations (Fieschi 1990).

The first medical expert system was developed in the 1970s by Edward Shortliffe at Stanford University. Named MYCIN, this programme recommended antibiotic treatments for patients with conditions such as bacteraemia and meningitis, utilising data pertaining to the infectious organism and patient-specific clinical details, including infection sites, symptoms, and other relevant medical conditions. Although not the initial computational tool for clinical support, MYCIN is widely regarded as the pioneering system for employing symbolic knowledge in a rule-based format (Shortliffe 1974, 1981).

In medical applications, an expert system's knowledge base may be organised in one of three primary configurations: (a) rule-based or frame-based structures, (b) cause-and-effect models, or (c) case-based systems. Each structure offers distinct functionalities and supports the system's inference mechanism, which employs an algorithm to draw conclusions based on data provided by the user in conjunction with its internal knowledge repository.

(a) Rule-Based or Frame-Based Systems: These systems operate on associative logic, linking clinical concepts without directly invoking causal relationships. For instance, rules may include associations such as "Osborn waves (ECG alterations) are associated with hypothermia". In these systems, the inference mechanism tests the validity of rules for a given case, often combining multiple rules to reach a probabilistic conclusion. An example might be: "If the patient presents with respiratory stridor and a history of congestive respiratory failure, the likely diagnoses are – pulmonary oedema (80% probability), asthma (50% probability), or pulmonary embolism (20% probability)" (Widman 1989).
(b) Cause-and-Effect Model-Based Systems: In this model, the knowledge base is organised around causal associations, such as, "a stroke may lead to symptoms like speech and comprehension difficulties, vision changes, and impaired balance and coordination." These systems are not designed to store specific clinical data but rather to represent causal pathways. The inference process navigates these causal chains; for example, "If the patient presents with jaundice, then hyperbilirubinaemia is likely. Should unconjugated bilirubin be elevated, liver dysfunction is implicated. The presence of fever suggests a viral or bacterial infection, potentially indicative of hepatitis." Another example might be, "If the patient has progressive difficulty with speech and comprehension, accompanied by weakness and partial paralysis, this symptomatic profile may indicate a potential stroke" (Widman 1989).
(c) Case-Based Systems: In these systems, the knowledge base is composed of historical clinical cases, which serve as a reference for decision-making and recommendations in comparable current cases. These systems analyse the present clinical scenario—including biomedical data, laboratory results, diagnoses, and previous treatments—and match it against similar cases in their database to propose the most suitable course of action. The inference mechanism utilises analogical reasoning; for instance, "If a patient with the same diagnosis and symptoms was previously treated successfully with a particular intervention, it is probable that the same treatment will be effective in this instance" (Widman 1989).

Numerous significant studies and authors have advanced the field of medical expert systems. Aris Persidis and Andreas Persidis, in their paper 'Medical Expert Systems: An Overview' (1991), published in the Journal of Management in Medicine, emphasise the significance of medical expert systems. They demonstrate how these systems emulate clinical reasoning to aid healthcare professionals by processing vast amounts of medical data, thereby supporting diagnostic and management decisions and optimising patient care.

These contributions underscore the essential role expert systems play in modern healthcare, enhancing the accuracy of clinical decisions, streamlining medical processes, and supporting educational needs in the medical profession (Levine et al. 1986). Through structured knowledge bases and inference mechanisms, medical expert systems provide a robust framework for clinical support, helping practitioners to deliver more informed and effective patient care.

(xi). *General purpose AI* (GPAI) refers to an advanced category of artificial intelligence models designed to perform a broad spectrum of tasks across diverse domains with considerable competence. Unlike more specialised AI systems, which are trained for specific functions such as image recognition or language translation, GPAI is characterised by its adaptability and versatility. Such models are trained on extensive datasets, often using large-scale self-supervision, allowing them to apply learned knowledge across various applications without the need for task-specific training. This adaptability makes GPAI distinct from other AI forms that are typically limited in scope and functionality.

A GPAI model is understood as an AI framework that, once developed, can operate effectively across multiple contexts and use cases, regardless of how it is marketed. This model's generality enables it to integrate seamlessly with a range of downstream systems, making it suitable for a variety of complex tasks without substantial modifications. GPAI models have a potential that underpins several applications, such as medical diagnostics, autonomous driving, or financial analysis, due to their ability to draw inferences and make decisions based on large and diverse datasets.

In contrast to models used exclusively in research or prototyping, GPAI systems are implemented for practical and commercial purposes, both as stand-alone applications and as foundational layers within other AI systems. By serving as a versatile platform, GPAI systems facilitate the development of more complex AI applications, streamlining integration across sectors while enabling innovation and efficiency. As such, GPAI serves as a critical foundation in the pursuit of Artificial General Intelligence (AGI), representing a significant leap towards AI models that exhibit a higher degree of adaptability and general intelligence.

The integration of artificial intelligence, particularly through the development of specific and general-purpose models, has ushered in a transformative era across various fields, notably within healthcare. From predictive analytics to expert systems and advanced language models, AI enhances clinical precision, optimises workflows, and offers unprecedented support for complex decision-making. As advancements continue, the distinctions between AI types—such as specific AI, augmented intelligence, and general-purpose AI—highlight both the opportunities and challenges in leveraging these technologies responsibly. This evolving landscape underscores the need for comprehensive legal frameworks to address ethical, operational, and regulatory concerns, ensuring AI remains a beneficial, trustworthy ally across sectors. These reflections will be further explored and developed throughout this book.

1.2 Global Overview of AI Applications in P4 Medicine

In light of the above discussion on the eleven fundamental concepts surrounding artificial intelligence, it is necessary to advance towards a broad analysis of certain applications of this technology in medicine, providing an overview of the benefits and risks, as well as the potential legal issues that may arise in this context. This approach aims to enable the reader to understand the main discussions that will permeate this book.

The entire new technological framework and the digitalisation of the healthcare sector form part of a broader global transformation phenomenon, defined by Klaus Schwab (2017) as the "Fourth Industrial Revolution". We are now in the "Era of Health 4.0," which introduces the concept of *smart health*, aligning with the shift from conventional medicine—primarily focused on treating diseases—to what is called "P4 Medicine". This term, coined by Leroy Hood (2006), describes the new paradigm of preventive, predictive, personalised and proactive medicine.

In this context, healthcare is increasingly focused on the implementation of preventative measures, aiming to reduce the risk of disease and maintain overall health (Preventive Medicine). Additionally, there is a growing emphasis on enhancing diagnostic accuracy with risk analysis and enabling early detection through advanced algorithms and AI-driven analytics, thereby allowing for more efficient and anticipatory care (Predictive Medicine).

Furthermore, patients receive more individualised care—moving away from the standardised approaches "one-size-fits-all"—based on their genomic and health data (Personalised or Precision Medicine), utilising genetic testing, biomarker identification, and the development of targeted therapies (Shaban-Nejad and Michalowski 2020). Finally, the physician-patient relationship has evolved from isolated interactions to continuous engagement, with patients actively and continuously participating in their healthcare, especially through new AI-enabled wearable technologies (Proactive or Participatory Medicine) (Bautista et al. 2021; Jeddi and Bohr 2020).

In recent decades, both medical practice and the physician-patient relationship have undergone significant transformations. These changes stem not only from an increased emphasis on humanism and personalised care but, more importantly, from the dynamic influence of AI integration (Balicer and Cohen-Stavi 2020). While technology will not replace physicians, it is fundamentally reshaping—and will continue to reshape—the functioning of healthcare systems. This evolution is particularly evident in the shift towards a more proactive, preventive, precise, and patient-centred model of care that respects and responds to each patient's unique needs (Hood 2013; Holzinger et al. 2015).

It is important to highlight that regulations such as the General Data Protection Regulation (GDPR) in Europe and the Brazilian General Data Protection Law (*Lei Geral de Proteção de Dados* –LGPD) in Brazil have emerged with, among their objectives, the creation of a secure framework for the expansion of digital health, establishing Medicine 4.0 as an integrated, personalised, and technologically advanced model. The digital era in medicine has been made possible by the convergence of advances in information technology, artificial intelligence, and digital health policies. Increased capacity for data processing and storage, coupled with the development of machine learning algorithms, has led to healthcare systems capable of managing vast volumes of data and facilitating predictive and personalised analyses essential for precision medicine. At the same time, advances in communication networks have enabled the development of telemedicine and remote patient monitoring.

With the emergence of the digital era in healthcare, patients' physical records have gradually transitioned from paper files to electronic health records (EHRs). Decades of digitalisation, combined with advances in cloud storage capacity and the growing power of computational analysis, have generated a vast and continuously expanding repository of health data. This data is increasingly collected from internet-connected medical devices (the Internet of Medical Things, or IoMT), as well as from clinical and pharmaceutical research (Degos 2020).

The most significant and valuable source of health data resides in electronic health records, which offer a comprehensive account of patient information. According to Wang (2023), 'EHRs are not only the base for storing clinical information for archival purposes, but they are also the bedrock on which clinical research and data science thrive'. These records capture every stage of medical intervention, from the initial anamnesis and diagnostic results to therapeutic medical-surgical procedures, as well as the patient's progress throughout treatment. In summary, the strategic use of EHRs not only enhances patient care but also drives innovation, enabling more precise healthcare delivery and fostering advancements in medical research and clinical decision-making.

In this context, AI holds the promise of enabling more precise and effective medical decisions based on data, processing vast amounts of information to transform health data into highly functional tools. Its capacity to identify patterns and correlations within complex datasets provides healthcare professionals enhanced diagnostic accuracy, optimising treatment plans and reducing the margin for human error. Moreover, AI facilitates continuous learning from new data inputs, ensuring that healthcare delivery advances in step with emerging medical knowledge and innovations.

Radiology, a field deeply reliant on imaging technologies, has quickly become a focal area for AI applications, given AI's capacity to swiftly and accurately process vast volumes of data. AI's pattern-recognition capabilities and its ability to detect abnormalities beyond human visibility present significant opportunities for early diagnosis, particularly in conditions like cancer, where subtle tissue variations can have substantial clinical implications (Toruner et al. 2024).

Medical devices with AI algorithms have been widely utilised globally as an essential support tool for the diagnostic analysis of Covid-19 during the pandemic, given their capacity to swiftly process and analyse large volumes of data—often more efficiently. AI was also used in patient triage to prevent hospital overcrowding, enabling prioritisation of care for those most in need. The pandemic period acted as a catalyst for numerous applications of artificial intelligence and emerging technologies in the treatment and monitoring of the disease, as well as in the prevention and control of virus transmission (Vaishya et al. 2020).

Another factor underpinning the development of AI in medicine is the evolving reality of healthcare systems worldwide, which have been facing increasing challenges over recent decades due to the rising demand from an ageing global population, particularly among those over the age of 65. Concurrently, morbidity from chronic diseases across all age groups has become increasingly prevalent. Moreover, the majority of individuals over the age of 50 present with comorbidities or multimorbidities (that is, two or more chronic conditions), which significantly impacts the nature of healthcare needs Balicer and Cohen-Stavi 2020).

In this context, the standard hospital room is highly susceptible to replacement, in certain situations, by the comfort and convenience of the patient's home, particularly for elderly individuals and those with chronic illnesses who require constant medical monitoring, thus creating opportunities for the emergence of so-called "virtual hospitals" (Topol 2019a). Medical care and monitoring are provided via telemedicine, supported by artificial intelligence algorithms, big data, and a range of emerging digital technologies.

Furthermore, Topol (2019a) envisions a near future in which technological innovations will permanently transform the hospital experience, with the spread of so-called "smart hospitals" and "virtual hospitals" around the world. Smart hospitals are connected facilities—with electronic medical records, interconnected smart devices, and cloud-based data storage—that enhance the quality of patient care through various technologies associated with Medicine 4.0. In hospital rooms, smartphones are employed for medical examinations, allowing access to previous test results, while biosensors continuously record vital signs and other relevant physiological metrics, transmitting the information to the medical team. For simple services, the patient can use a tablet or smartphone app to control the bed position, adjust the room temperature, close the curtains, or request meals (Holzinger et al. 2015).

The increase in demand for virtual care has driven the expansion of telehealth and the development of remote monitoring solutions through wearable devices. These "smart" devices can play a central role in disease management across various stages, including early screening, diagnosis, and post-discharge care (Jeddi and Bohr 2020). Studies indicate that implementing these tools for biomedical data monitoring in patients with chronic diseases reduces hospital admissions and treatment costs, while also improving efficiency and patient adherence to medical treatment (Kim and Lee 2017).

Broadly speaking, hospitals and healthcare systems around the world are increasingly investing in the development and implementation of AI for various valuable applications, both clinical and non-clinical, including:

1. *the analysis of medical tests and imaging* to enhance the accuracy of diagnoses, prognoses, and treatment recommendations in fields such as radiology, dermatology, and pathology;

2. *patient self-management* through wearable devices, such as smartwatches, particularly for the management of diabetes, hypertension, and other chronic conditions;
3. *AI-driven clinical research and drug discovery*, enabling the rapid prediction of drug efficacy and identification of promising compounds for further investigation;
4. *automation of administrative functions* within hospital operations, such as appointment scheduling, billing, and data entry, thus alleviating the administrative burden on healthcare professionals;
5. *medical risk management*, where predictive algorithms are employed to identify potential risks and adverse events, allowing healthcare providers to take preventive measures and improve patient safety;
6. *robotic assistance in hospitals, caregiving, and surgeries*, designed to support healthcare professionals in routine tasks, assist in surgical procedures, and provide physical support and monitoring for patients, thereby enhancing operational efficiency and patient care;
7. *digital twins in personalised and precision medicine,* where virtual models of patients' biological systems are created to simulate and predict individual responses to treatments, facilitating highly tailored therapeutic approaches.

Artificial intelligence is at the forefront of a transformative era in healthcare worldwide, reshaping medical practices and the physician-patient relationship. From its integration into *P4 Medicine* to its applications in various areas such as radiology, oncology, remote monitoring, and hospital management, AI has become an indispensable tool in addressing the complex challenges faced by modern healthcare systems.

1.3 Purpose of This Book: Navigating the Ethical and Legal Landscape of AI Integration in Clinical Practice

Given the overview of these technologies' applications in the healthcare sector, it is evident that integrating medical professionals with AI holds significant potential to improve clinical workflow, enhance individual performance, and reduce the risk of human error, making clinical decision-making considerably more accurate and efficient.

Nevertheless, despite the substantial advantages presented by this technological arsenal, there remains a potential for harm associated to automated decision-making systems and the inherent risks of these technologies. Such risks include the intrinsic fallibility of algorithms, unforeseen outcomes resulting from machine learning, and the training of algorithms on datasets that may be inaccurate, incomplete, or inadequate. These factors may expose patients to potential harm (Ross 2021).

In this context, the purpose of this book is to provide a comprehensive analysis of the following key questions:

1) If a harmful outcome occurs that could, in theory, have been avoided by following the AI-proposed diagnosis, can the physician be held liable?
2) How should the physician's conduct be evaluated if he or she modified the treatment based on an AI-generated diagnosis or recommendation, but a flaw in the algorithm's conclusion resulted in the patient's death due to inappropriate treatment?
3) To what extent should a physician critically evaluate and question algorithmic recommendations before integrating them into clinical decision-making?
4) Is it the physician's responsibility to evaluate whether he or she should use AI in each specific situation? If so, if the professional decides to follow or reject an algorithmic recommendation, can he or she be held liable for that decision, including the initial choice to utilise the technology?
5) When AI systems eventually become just one of many tools available in clinical practice, how should the physician use them to ensure that his or her conduct remains diligent?
6) What ethical principles should the physician follow when using AI in clinical practice, and what are the legal consequences of failing to comply with these principles?

The implementation of automated decision-making systems in medical practice gives rise to numerous ethical and legal implications, extending the discussion into contract law, medical law, and the doctrine of civil liability, particularly in cases where patients may suffer harm.

This book, adopting a hypothetical-deductive approach and aiming to provide a comprehensive overview of medical liability and professional duties within this context, seeks to address the six questions outlined above. To this end, it will examine the civil liability framework at the intersection of Medicine and AI. Additionally, it will offer reflections on causation, concurrent causes, and exclusions of liability, with a focus on identifying the efficient cause of harm—that is, whether the damage arises from a medical intervention, a hospital service, or even a product defect related to AI.

The ultimate objective of this book is to establish appropriate criteria for resolving future case law—particularly concerning the duty to compensate—in situations where there may (or may not) be a discrepancy between the diagnostic, prognostic, or treatment recommendations provided by AI and those determined independently by a physician without technological assistance. This book also aims to offer guidance for future cases in which patients may not be adequately informed about the use of such technology. Furthermore, it seeks to educate physicians on the importance of adhering to specific professional duties and ethical principles.

References

Alloghani M et al (2020) A systematic review on supervised and unsupervised machine learning algorithms for data science. In: Berry M, Mohamed A, Yap B (eds) Supervised and unsupervised learning for data science. Springer, Cham

American Medical Association (2021) Artificial intelligence taxonomy for medical services and procedures. https://www.ama-assn.org/system/files/cpt-appendix-s.pdf. Accessed 5 Nov 2024

Ashley KD (2017) Artificial intelligence and legal analytics: new tools for law practice in the digital age. Cambridge University Press, Cambridge

Balicer RD, Cohen-Stavi C (2020) Advancing healthcare through data-driven medicine and artificial intelligence. In: Nordlinger B, Villani C, Rus D (eds) Healthcare and artificial intelligence. Springer, Cham

Bautista M, Cifuentes CA, Munera M (2021) Conversational agents for healthcare delivery: potential solutions to the challenges of the pandemic. In: Cardona M, Solanki VK, Cena CG (eds) Internet of medical things: paradigm of wearable devices. CRC Press, Florida

Chiarello F et al (2024) Future applications of generative large language models: a data-driven case study on ChatGPT. Technovation 133

Degos L (2020) International vision of big data. In: NordlingerB VC, Rus D (eds) Healthcare and artificial intelligence. Springer, Cham

Faleiros Júnior JLM (2021) A evolução da Inteligência Artificial em breve retrospectiva. In: Barbosa MM (ed) Direito Digital e Inteligência Artificial: diálogos entre Brasil e Europa. Foco, Indaiatuba

Fieschi M (1990) Artificial intelligence in medicine: expert systems. Springer, New York

Flasiński M (2016) Introduction to artificial intelligence. Springer, Cham

Goodfellow I, Bengio Y, Courville A (2016) Deep learning (adaptive computation and machine learning series). The MIT Press, Cambridge

Holzinger A, Röcker C, Ziefle M (2015) From smart health to smart hospitals. In: Holzinger A, Röcker C, Ziefle M (eds) Smart health: open problems and future challenges. Springer, Cham

Hood L (2006) Health care of the 21st century: predictive, preventive, personalized and participatory (P4) medicine. J Oral Maxillofac Surg 64(9)

Hood L (2013) Systems biology and P4 medicine: past, present, and future. Rambam Maimonides Med J 4(2):e0012

Iavazzo C et al (2014) Evolution of robots throughout history from Hephaestus to da Vinci robot. Acta Med Hist Adriat 12(2):247–258

Jeddi Z, Bohr A (2020) Remote patient monitoring using artificial intelligence. In: Bohr A, Memarzadeh K (eds) Artificial intelligence in healthcare. Elsevier Inc., Amsterdam

Kim BY, Lee J (2017) Smart devices for older adults managing chronic disease: a scoping review. JMIR Mhealth Uhealth 5(5):e69

Knuth D (1973) The art of computer programming, 3rd edn. Addison-Wesley Professional, Massachusetts

Kurwzeil R (2005) The singularity is near: when humans transcend biology. Viking Penguin, Nova York

Levine RI, Drang DE, Edelson B (1986) Artificial intelligence and expert systems: a comprehensive guide. McGraw-Hill, New York

Persidis A, Persidis A (1991) Medical expert systems: an overview. J Manag Med 5(3):27–34

Ross C (2021) Machine learning is booming in medicine. It's also facing a credibility crisis. Available via Stat News. https://www.statnews.com/2021/06/02/machine-learning-ai-methodology-research-flaws/

Russell S, Norvig P (2022) Artificial intelligence: a modern approach, 4th edn. Pearson Education, Harlow

Saeidi H et al (2022) Autonomous robotic laparoscopic surgery for intestinal anastomosis. Science Robotics 7(62)

Schwab K (2017) The fourth industrial revolution. Crown Currency, New York

Shaban-Nejad A, Michalowski M (2020) From precision medicine to precision health: a full angle from diagnosis to treatment and prevention. In: Shaban-Nejad A, Michalowski M (eds) Precision health and medicine. A digital revolution in healthcare, studies in computational intelligence, vol v. Springer, Cham, p 843

Shortliffe EH (1974) MYCIN: A rule-based computer program for advising physicians regarding antimicrobial therapy selection. Dissertation, Standford University

Shortliffe EH (1981) Consultation systems for physicians: the role of artificial intelligence techniques. In: Webber BL, Nilsson NJ (eds) Readings in artificial intelligence. Tioga Publishing Company, Palo Alto

Taulli T (2019) Artificial intelligence basics: a non-technical introduction. Apress, New York

Topff L et al (2023) A deep learning-based application for Covid-19 diagnosis on CT: the imaging Covid-19 AI initiative. PLoS One 18(5):e0285121

Topol E (2013) The creative destruction of medicine: how the digital revolution will create better health care. Basic Books, New York

Topol E (2016) The patient will see you now: the future of medicine is in your hands. Basic Books, New York

Topol E (2019a) Deep medicine: how artificial intelligence can make healthcare human again. Basic Books, New York

Topol E (2019b) High-performance medicine: the convergence of human and artificial intelligence. Nat Med 25(1):44–56

Toruner MD et al (2024) Artificial intelligence in radiology: where are we going? EBioMedicine 109

Turner J (2019) Robot rules: regulating artificial intelligence. Palgrave Macmillan, Cham

Vaishya R et al (2020) Artificial intelligence (AI) applications for Covid-19 pandemic. Diabetes Metab Syndr 14(4):337–339

Vinge V (1993) The coming technological singularity: how to survive in the post-human era. Paper presented at Vision-21 Symposium: interdisciplinary science and engineering in the era of cyberspace, NASA Lewis Research Center, Cleveland, Ohio, March 30–31, 1993. https://edoras.sdsu.edu/~vinge/misc/singularity.html

Wang W et al (2023) Electronic health records as source of research data. In: Colliot O (ed) Machine learning for brain disorders. Springer, Humana Press, New York

Widman LE (1989) Expert system reasoning about dynamic systems by semi-quantitative simulation. Comput Methods Prog Biomed 29(2):95–113

World Medical Association (2019) WMA statement on augmented intelligence in medical care. Adopted by the 70th WMA General Assembly, Tbilisi, Georgia, 2019. https://www.wma.net/policies-post/wma-statement-on-augmented-intelligence-in-medical-care/

Chapter 2
Ethical and Legal Aspects of the Physician-Patient Relationship

2.1 The Historical Evolution of the Physician-Patient Relationship Worldwide

The field of medicine has advanced in remarkable ways over the last decades, simultaneously undergoing profound transformations in the traditional concepts in Medical Law. Before delving into a detailed examination of medical liability—particularly in the context of artificial intelligence (AI) systems—it is essential to adopt a retrospective view. This approach facilitates the examination and understanding of key fundamental concepts that form the foundation of the evolution of the physician-patient relationship throughout history, as well as the principles of Medical Law as they have developed in the early twenty-first century.

Wittgenstein (1953), one of the most influential philosophers of the twentieth century, advanced the concept of *language games* to illustrate that language does not possess a singular, fixed purpose or structure. His work profoundly reshaped the understanding of linguistic function and the construction of meaning. The concept of language games underscores the critical role of social and contextual usage in determining how words acquire their meaning. Rather than being statically tied to an external reality, the meaning of words is rooted in their usage within specific contexts, governed by the social rules and practices of the relevant environment.

Building upon this perspective, the reader may ask: In what way does this theory relate to patient consent or the physicians' duties of conduct? The connection is both significant and illustrative. For instance, the term *consent* can be understood as a *language game*, wherein the meaning of *to consent* adapts and evolves in alignment with prevailing social practices and the specific context in which it is expressed.

The doctrine of informed consent has received significant worldwide influence, with its formal incorporation being notably marked in the United States. Civil liability decisions concerning violations of informed consent can be traced back to the early twentieth century in both Europe and the United States. In 1914, in the

R. Nogaroli, *Medical Liability and Artificial Intelligence*,
https://doi.org/10.1007/978-3-031-94306-5_2

landmark case *Schloendorff v. Society of New York Hospital*, Justice Benjamin Nathan Cardozo famously affirmed the right of patients to self-determination with a statement that has since become iconic: *"Every human being of adult years and sound mind has a right to determine what shall be done with his own body*; and a surgeon who performs an operation without his patient's consent commits an assault, for which he is liable in damages". It was only in the past 50 years, however, that the legal duty of healthcare professionals to provide comprehensive information gained substantial recognition.

In 1957, the concept of informed consent was first articulated by a California court in *Salgo v. Leland Stanford Jr. University Board of Trustees*. This case established that physicians have a legal duty to disclose sufficient information about the risks, benefits, and alternatives of medical procedures, solidifying the foundation of modern informed consent. While the concept of consent had been recognized earlier in the 1914 *Schloendroff case*, its practical application and the extent of disclosure were clarified and formalized through the *Salgo decision*. Over time, subsequent American judicial decisions expanded and refined this obligation, emphasising the need for physicians to disclose sufficient information about medical treatments, including the associated risks, to enable patients to make informed choices.

This legal evolution quickly influenced other jurisdictions worldwide, not only in common law systems but also in continental Europe and American countries like Brazil, where the principle of informed consent has gradually become firmly grounded in the ethical and legal imperative of respecting human autonomy.

Each stage in the historical development of consent within the medical field reflects transformations in power dynamics and modes of communication between physicians and patients, shaped by historical, political, and cultural contexts. This evolution has also given rise to new legal duties for physicians, such as the duties of cooperation and loyalty, care and vigilance, accurate documentation, and confidentiality.

In this context, understanding patient consent and physician's duties of conduct as a dynamic, context-dependent process is crucial for addressing the ethical and legal complexities introduced by artificial intelligence in healthcare—a topic that will be explored in greater depth in a subsequent chapter of this book. Such an approach encourages a nuanced perspective on physicians' duties, recognising them as practices that evolve in response to shifting societal values, expectations, and technological advancements.

Throughout human history, various models of communication between patients and physicians have developed. These models, as outlined in the comparative Table 2.1, are further classified based on whether clinical practice adopts an *illness-centred approach* or a *patient-centred approach* (Veatch 1972).

The *Priestly Model* represents one of the earliest forms of medical practice, originating in the dawn of human civilisation, when medicine was administered by religious or shamanic figures. In this nascent phase, communication between physician and patient was strictly one-directional. The physician or healer possessed exclusive knowledge and authority, granting the patient no opportunity to question or comprehend the treatment. The physician-patient relationship was marked by profound

Table 2.1 Comparative table created by the author of this book, based on the studies of the following scholars: Veatch (1972), Stewart and Roter (1989), Balint (2000), Schermer (2002), Sandman and Munthe (2009), Mezzich (2011), Stewart (2013), Pereira (2015), Fitzharris (2017), Talukdar (2020), and Kfouri Neto (2024)

Typology/models of the physician-patient relationship	
Illness-centred medicine	Patient-centred medicine
Priestly Model ➔ The physician is portrayed as a figure of religious authority, comparable to shamans and deities, embodying a position of power. The physician-patient relationship is unidirectional and hierarchical. This model advocates for the near-total submission of the patient to the physician, who assumes responsibility for diagnosing, forming opinions on the patient's condition, and determining treatment, typically without regard for the patient's benefit. Consequently, the patient's role is reduced to mere compliance with the physician's decisions and instructions.	**Collegial Model ➔** This model underscores the principles of patient consent and autonomy, highlighting the importance of the patient's active participation in healthcare decisions. Trying to departing from paternalistic frameworks, the collegial model encourages a collaborative approach, where decision-making is shared between the patient and the physician. Its objective is to foster a balanced and equitable relationship. However, in practice, elements of persuasion may still arise, as physicians might feel a professional obligation to guide patients towards what they consider the optimal medical choice. Despite its aspiration for equality, the model occasionally reverts to subtle forms of paternalism, reflecting the inherent complexities of balancing professional expertise with patient autonomy.
Engineering Model ➔ This model reveals the physician as a technical expert who applies specialised knowledge to diagnose and treat medical conditions, comparable to a mechanic repairing a machine. The patient is seen as a passive recipient of technical expertise, with minimal participation in the decision-making process. This approach emerged within the context of the so-called *Spectacular Medicine*, characterised by public dissections and open surgeries conducted to both educate and captivate audiences. The interaction remains largely impersonal, with the physician maintaining emotional detachment and prioritising problem-solving and procedural tasks over the patient's individual needs, preferences, or emotional well-being.	**Contractual Model ➔** This model is widely regarded as the standard for physician-patient relationships and is arguably the most appropriate. Humanity is now in an era of growing knowledge and information sharing. The patient's rights and awareness are highly valued, ensuring patient autonomy, while the physician retains responsibility as a healthcare expert. Decision-making is collaborative, with information exchange and mutual agreements, placing the patient at the centre of the decision-making process, promoting not only better adherence to treatments but also greater satisfaction and trust in the physician. Moreover, other professional duties have begun to be redefined and emphasised, including the duty of cooperation and loyalty, the duty of care and vigilance, proper documentation, and confidentiality.

deference, as patients regarded the physician as a figure endowed with supernatural powers. The discourse here was both hierarchical and mystical, and no concept of consent existed, with the patient wholly subject to the spiritual authority of the *healer*.

With the advent of the Scientific Revolution in the sixteenth and seventeenth centuries, the advancement of the scientific method led to the development of the *Engineering Model*, which applied scientific methods to diagnose and treat disease, and conceptualised the human body as comparable to a machine. This period saw the emergence of the so-called *Spectacle Medicine*, characterised by the public display of medical procedures, diseases, and treatments, intended to educate or even entertain spectators and students driven by a desire to witness scientific progress. Public dissections and demonstrations of medical techniques were frequent, driven by a fascination with the human body and the advancements in medical science.

As modern medicine advanced, the focus increasingly centred on technical precision. However, the hierarchical structure of the physician-patient relationship remained largely unchanged, with the physician positioned as the technical expert and the patient relegated to the role of a passive observer. The rhetoric of modern scientific tradition further reinforced the view of the physician as a *pure scientist*, whose role was confined to executing procedures in strict adherence to established scientific knowledge. Consequently, the physician was likened to an engineer or even a plumber, tasked with performing repairs, connecting systems, and resolving blockages, often without deeper ethical engagement or consideration. Patient consent was largely absent from this framework, as the emphasis remained exclusively on technical treatment, with minimal or no active participation by the patient in the decision-making process.

It was only in the aftermath of the Nazi medical experiments on human beings during the Second World War (1939–1945) that the international community began to fully recognise the dangers of advancing and applying scientific knowledge in the absence of ethical principles and values (Thomasma and Bergsma 2000). The *Engineering Model* subsequently faced significant criticism for its reductive approach to medicine, which prioritised the diagnosis and treatment of disease (*illness-centred medicine*) to the exclusion of broader considerations of patient care and well-being).

The experiments conducted in concentration camps under Adolf Hitler's regime in Germany served multiple purposes, including medical research ostensibly aimed at benefiting German soldiers, the development of surgical techniques, and pseudo-scientific studies intended to validate Nazi racial theories. These experiments were frequently justified under the pretext of advancing medical science, conducted with a complete disregard for ethical principles or the intrinsic value of human life.

Prisoners were used as test subjects to evaluate the efficacy of various chemical agents and medical drugs, often resulting in painful deaths or permanent injury. Additionally, these experiments aimed to validate racial superiority theories, employing brutal procedures such as forced sterilisation and attempts to alter eye colour. These horrific acts led to the deaths and suffering of tens of thousands of individuals, and the full extent of the trauma and loss of life caused by these experiments is incalculable. After the war, during the Nuremberg Trials, many of the physicians involved were prosecuted and convicted for war crimes and crimes against humanity (Lifton 1986).

These trials led to the formulation of the Nuremberg Code (1947), which established fundamental principles for the ethical conduct of researches involving human beings, emphasising the necessity of voluntary, informed, and enlightened consent. This marked a historical milestone—a turning point in the history of medicine—as global society began to recognise the critical importance of requiring voluntary consent from individuals participating in medical experiments.

Subsequently, international human rights movements and foundational documents emerged, initiating the first formal discussions on medical ethics and the requirement for patient consent in medical treatments. On an international scale, patient autonomy gained recognition primarily in the twentieth century, particularly through foundational documents such as: the Nuremberg Code of 1948 (Article 1); the Oviedo Convention of 1997 (Convention for the Protection of Human Rights and Dignity of the Human Being with regard to the Application of Biology and Medicine—Articles 5 and 24); the Charter of Fundamental Rights of the European Union of 2000 (Article 3); and UNESCO's Universal Declaration on Bioethics and Human Rights of 2005 (Article 6, Section 1).

These documents underscore the humanisation of healthcare by establishing patient consent within the framework of the right to personal integrity, which significantly advanced the doctrine of informed consent. Furthermore, the emergence of bioethics in the 1970s and the establishment of the classic utilitarian bioethical principles—autonomy, beneficence, non-maleficence, and justice—are also noteworthy, as they are essential to understanding the current state of the physician-patient relationship (Durand 2005).

On this subject, the insights of Vasconcelos (2020) are particularly pertinent, highlighting that Bioethics arose worldwide from two decisive factors. The first is of a scientific and technological nature, reflecting the growing recognition of the need to impose external limits on scientific advancement, prompted by the far-reaching consequences of rapid progress. The second factor is socio-cultural, arising from a new perspective regarding individual and collective rights, which were both achieved and reaffirmed in the post-war period, culminating in a renewed commitment to ethical reform (Fürst 2023).

During the decade of the 1950 e 1980, the *Collegial Model* of the physician-patient relationship prevailed, introducing the concept of informed patient consent, which assumed a prominent role in theory. In practice, however, patients frequently failed to exercise their right to self-determination, as consent was often overly general and lacked the specificity necessary to ensure meaningful autonomy. The notion of patient consent began to take shape, although in a very preliminary form. Until the mid-twentieth century, medical practice largely adhered to a directive approach, with the physician perceived as the one who *knows best*, leaving the patient with limited real autonomy.

In the early development of patient consent doctrine, it was noted that, in practice, physicians often continued to make decisions based on what they believed to be in the patient's best interests. The physician assumed a paternalistic role, with the patient regarded as incapable of making fully informed decisions and therefore reliant on the physician's guidance and ultimate authority—founded upon the physician's mastery of the leges artis of the profession.

The reinforcement of patient autonomy and the introduction of the concept of informed consent were significantly shaped by constitutional advancements in various countries during the post-Second World War era. For example, Germany's 1949

Constitution enshrined the concept of human dignity as inviolable. Likewise, the Italian Constitution of 1948, in Article 32, stipulates that "no one may be compelled to undergo medical treatment except as provided by law". These post-war constitutions reflect a global shift towards the protection of human dignity and the promotion of fundamental rights, including the right to autonomy in medical decision-making. This shift helped establish and consolidate the concept of informed consent across jurisdictions. The focus on protecting human rights and affirming self-determination, in response to abuses committed in previous periods—such as during the Second World War—also extended to bioethics, influencing the physician-patient relationship on a global scale.

As Michael Balint observed, the 1970s reinforced the concept of *patient-centred medicine*. The physician continued to hold a position of authority; however, the discourse between physician and patient began to shift, placing more emphasis on the patient's well-being rather than solely on the illness.

In the 1970s and 1980s, social movements and civil rights reforms further impacted the physician-patient relationship, promoting individual autonomy and the right to self-determination. The physician has gradually moved away from the role of the one who *knows what is best* for the patient, becoming instead a *participant in shared decision-making* (Albuquerque and Bacelar 2021).

In Brazil, a major milestone for patient autonomy was reached with the *Constitutionalisation of Civil Law* through the enactment of the 1988 Constitution. This movement brought constitutional principles—such as human dignity, equality, solidarity, and fundamental rights—into private relations, leading to a reinterpretation of Civil Law concepts, including contracts, property, and family law, through the lens of constitutional values. The shift moves Brazilian Civil Law from an individualistic approach to one that recognises the social function of private relationships and promotes collective well-being. For instance, in contracts, the Constitution mandates that agreements must adhere to principles of good faith and fairness, aiming to prevent abuses and inequalities that might infringe on individual autonomy and dignity. In family law, constitutional principles uphold equality among spouses and children, ensuring fairness regardless of factors like marital status or parental lineage.

In Medical Law, this constitutionalised approach in Brazil reinforces patient rights by prioritising autonomy, informed consent, and dignity in healthcare. Physicians' duties are increasingly guided by these constitutional principles, emphasising patient-centred care, informed decision-making, and respect for individual values. This alignment of medical practice with fundamental rights reflects the broader goal of safeguarding individual autonomy and dignity within private relationships.

A key development is the recognition of human dignity (Article 1, III) as a foundational principle of the Brazilian Republic, reinforcing the rights to self-determination and individual choice across various domains, including healthcare decisions. The Brazilian Constitution also guarantees the rights to life and to physical and psychological integrity (Article 5), which are intrinsically linked to patient autonomy, as the ability to make decisions regarding one's own body is essential for the preservation of personal integrity. Moreover, the Brazilian Civil Code of 2002 directly addresses this issue in Article 15, stipulating that "no one may be compelled to undergo medical treatment or surgical intervention at the risk of life".

At this stage in the history of the physician-patient relationship, the *Collegial Model* represents an effort to transcend medical paternalism, yet it still falls short of fully recognising the patient's individuality. While attempts are made to balance power within the physician-patient dynamic, informed consent in this model remains more formalistic than genuinely dialogical. The use of standardised consent forms, although legally valid, tends to reduce the consent process to a procedural formality, limited to the provision of information about the treatment. As a result, the patient's role in decision-making regarding their treatment—based on personal beliefs, values, and preferences—is somewhat limited, as the interaction remains predominantly informative rather than genuinely participatory.

In the 1990s, a new historical milestone emerged, set to revolutionise the understanding of the physician-patient relationship: the advent and widespread dissemination of the internet, followed in subsequent years by the fast expansion of artificial intelligence systems in the medical field. This evolution led to the emergence of the *Contractual Model* of the physician-patient relationship, which is currently in effect. More precisely, the current phase can be characterised as *transitional*, marked by a shift from the *Collegial Model* to the *Contractual Model*, a framework that still requires further reinforcement and consolidation to achieve its full potential.

The internet has had a profound impact on the physician-patient relationship. The exponential growth in home computer usage, which began in the 1980s, and became firmly established during the 1990s and 2000s, was driven by increasing internet accessibility, declining costs, and technological advancements that made personal computers more affordable and user-friendly. Over the past decade, access to the internet and computational devices has grown at an accelerated pace, particularly through smartphones, tablets, and other mobile technologies. Herring (2020) explains, with the advent of the Internet, patients are encouraged to ask questions, leading doctors to assume that they possess some level of knowledge about their conditions.

The advent of the internet provided patients with access to an unprecedented volume of health information, resulting in several significant effects on the physician-patient dynamic:

(i) Patient empowerment: before the internet, patients relied exclusively on physicians for information about their health conditions. Today, patients often arrive at consultations already equipped with information (or misinformation) they have found online. This shift has made them more questioning and active participants in the decision-making process regarding their treatment.

(ii) Challenges for physicians: the availability of information from diverse, often unreliable sources has created new challenges for physicians, who must now manage patients with potentially unrealistic expectations or self-diagnoses based on internet sources. This trend has highlighted the need for more extensive dialogue, as physicians work to address questions, clarify doubts, and correct myths and misconceptions.

(iii) Changes in informed consent: with patients now better informed, the conversation surrounding informed consent has become more detailed. Physicians must not only inform the diagnosis and treatment options but also explain, clarify and demystify information the patient may have encountered online, ensuring that consent is truly based on clear and accurate information.

These developments underscore the evolving nature of the physician-patient relationship, which is now moving towards a more collaborative and contractual framework. This model seeks to balance both parties' roles more equitably, promoting an informed and participatory relationship while aiming to consolidate a new standard in patient autonomy and decision-making in healthcare. Thus, in the dynamic interplay of social practices and evolving contexts, patient consent emerges not as a fixed notion, but as a language game (Wittgenstein, 1953)—its meaning forever shaped by the rules and shared understandings of those who speak it.

In parallel with the spread of the internet, digital technologies and artificial intelligence (AI) systems began appearing in clinics and hospitals from the early 2000s, initially in developed countries and predominantly within major medical centres. However, the COVID-19 pandemic in 2020 accelerated the global adoption of AI, driving its rapid expansion across diverse regions and further integrating digital tools into healthcare practices. Nevertheless, despite the potential benefits offered by these technologies, substantial risks have surfaced—some inherent to AI itself and others, more alarmingly, stemming from its irresponsible application. These risks present challenges that must be carefully addressed to protect the quality of care, ensuring that technology serves to enhance, rather than compromise, the physician-patient relationship.

Moreover, numerous national legislations and Codes of Medical Ethics began to emphasise not only the content of information provided but also the quality of communication by healthcare professionals. As a result, mere formal consent has become insufficient; it must be accompanied by the patient's full exercise of autonomy. Over recent decades, there has also been an increased focus on teaching clinical communication skills at all levels of healthcare education, whether in undergraduate training, medical residency, or continuing education programmes.

However, with the expansion of AI in medical practice worldwide—especially from 2020 onwards—additional documents became necessary, going beyond traditional bioethical principles to specifically address the unique risks associated with this new technological arsenal.

AI systems in healthcare offer remarkable benefits, but it also introduce significant risks, both intrinsic to the technology and due to irresponsible usage. One major concern is the overreliance on AI-driven decisions, which can dehumanise care by reducing the clinical interactions between physicians and patients, potentially neglecting nuanced aspects of patient health. When improperly implemented, AI systems can result in diagnostic errors or incorrect treatment recommendations, posing a direct risk to patient safety.

In addition to dependency risks, AI brings intrinsic challenges to clinical practice, particularly when algorithms are inaccurate, discriminatory, or opaque in their decision-making processes. Biases within AI algorithms, often stemming from unrepresentative or flawed data, may lead to disparities in care. This is especially concerning as algorithmic fallibility and discriminatory patterns can emerge, disadvantaging specific patient groups and leading to unequal healthcare outcomes.

Regulatory oversight presents another critical risk, especially given the powerful influence of the medical technology industry. Insufficiently rigorous regulation, as explained in documentaries such as *The Bleeding Edge*, can prioritise profit over patient safety, resulting in devices and AI systems entering the market without adequate safeguards. Additionally, as highlighted in *Coded Bias*, algorithms may replicate social biases, with serious implications in healthcare; for example, underdiagnosis of Black women with breast cancer by systems like Watson for Oncology reveals how AI bias can worsen health disparities.

This new era in medicine calls for redefined ethical standards, focusing on enhanced consent models and responsible AI integration to protect patient autonomy and equity in healthcare.

The advent of new technologies, particularly AI, has expanded the concept of consent, necessitating consideration of specific risks and uncertainties associated with complex, innovative treatments. Medical practice, once solely reliant on human judgement, now incorporates algorithm-driven decision-making tools, reframing the duties surrounding patient autonomy, physician responsibility, and informed consent. The integration of AI systems and decision algorithms into patient diagnosis and treatment presents new ethical challenges.

In response to these changes, the WHO published its first global report on artificial intelligence in healthcare in 2021, setting out six guiding principles for its design and use. The WHO's guidelines are essential for ensuring that AI technologies in healthcare are employed ethically, safely, and effectively. Among these principles, a key directive emphasises transparency and informed consent, establishing that patients must be informed and fully briefed on the use of AI in their treatment and care.

In light of the recent integration of new technologies, medical practice and the physician-patient relationship have been significantly transformed. Within the *Contractual Model*, which characterises the modern era driven by technological advancements, there is now a heightened emphasis on patient autonomy.

The incorporation of technologies such as AI systems has fundamentally shifted the language and dynamics of medical practice. Additionally, with the widespread availability of information online, patients today are more proactive and informed participants. Consent now requires a higher standard, with detailed explanations of the risks and benefits of technological innovations. The physician-patient relationship has evolved into a partnership where transparent dialogue is encouraged, and patients actively engage in decision-making about their treatment. This approach fosters collaboration, as medical knowledge is shared, and patients are encouraged to take an active role in their care.

In this *gold standard* of the physician-patient relationship, shared decision-making underscores the professional's responsibility to place the patient's reality at the centre of the decision-making process. This approach aims to foster a truly inclusive relationship, highlighting a two-way exchange where the patient's individual circumstances, values, and preferences are integral to medical decisions.

The physician has an obligation to provide information regarding the risks and benefits of treatment options and to ensure that the patient truly understands the information conveyed. Furthermore, the physician must consider and incorporate the patient's values and preferences when recommending therapeutic options or preventive care. For instance, individuals may vary in their responses to the prospect of a few additional months of life when balanced against the significant side effects of certain medications or interventions, depending on their values and life goals. In this regard, as Fachin explains (2006), critical discussions have emerged concerning patient autonomy at the end of life, since determining what constitutes a *dignified life* is inherently subjective and should be assessed on a case-by-case basis. Ultimately, each individual holds the right to decide which life they find worth living.

Our society worldwide is increasingly trending towards placing the patient's reality and individual perspective at the heart of healthcare decision-making. This shift recognises the vital importance of aligning medical decisions with the patient's own values, preferences, and beliefs.

The concept of *patient-centred medicine* has finally gained ground, requiring a significant shift in the physician's mindset, whereby the illness is examined from the patient's own perspective on their health and experience of the disease (Stewart et al. 2013; Balint 2000). In this approach, patients actively participate in their healthcare planning, with emphasis on the context of care and the relationship between healthcare professional and patient. The aim is to ensure that medical treatment addresses the patient's social, emotional, and physical needs, taking into account their personal preferences and wishes. This model challenges the hierarchical notion of the healthcare professional as the authoritative figure and the patient as a passive recipient of care; it calls for relinquishing traditional control to share power within the relationship (Sandman and Munthe 2009, 2010).

Both patient and healthcare professional are expected to contribute preferences and information to the decision-making process, working together to reach a joint decision. In this context, an active role is demanded of the physician to ensure the information is understood and valued by the patient. The physician must assess and address any vulnerabilities, including the patient's understanding and knowledge of the information received. This recognition of patient autonomy and self-determination fosters the practice of *shared decision-making*, whereby a collaborative plan is formed with the patient for managing their illness, with the physician seeking to understand the patient's personal experience of the disease.

Person-Centred Medicine (PCM) has gained significant traction in recent years as a core ideology of modern medicine. It is often described as an approach in which the physician seeks to enter the patient's world, seeing the illness through the patient's eyes (Stewart and Roter 1989). In 2008, the first Conference on Person-Centred Medicine was held in Geneva, affirming the notion that the twenty-first century is indeed the century of PCM (Mezzich 2011).

A crucial observation here is the growing societal trend of prioritising the patient's perspective in healthcare decisions, including end-of-life decisions—a principle that has gained recognition in judicial rulings across the globe.

In the United States, a landmark 2017 case (*O'Donnell v. Harrison*) established judicial precedent when a hospital was found liable for *wrongful prolongation of life*. In this case, the court recognised that healthcare professionals had violated the patient's autonomy by disregarding a previously issued do-not-resuscitate (DNR) order. The ruling affirmed that the patient's explicit wishes should have been respected, and the hospital's failure to comply with the DNR order constituted an unjustifiable extension of the patient's life, thus setting a legal standard for respecting end-of-life directives.

This type of legal action recognises the autonomy of patients to make decisions about their own end-of-life care, including the right to refuse treatments such as ventilators, feeding tubes, or resuscitation efforts. When healthcare providers do not comply with these wishes—whether due to miscommunication, oversight, or deliberate actions—they may be accused of *wrongful prolongation of life*. In essence, the claim suggests that the physician or healthcare provider caused harm by unnecessarily extending life and disregarding the patient's right to die with dignity.

This decision underscores the growing recognition of the need to respect patient autonomy, emphasising that extending life against a patient's wishes can infringe upon their rights. Together, these developments reflect a societal shift toward aligning healthcare decisions with the patient's own values, preferences, and beliefs, reinforcing the importance of respecting individual choice in medical treatment.

In summary, in line with the growing emphasis on patient autonomy, courts worldwide are increasingly recognising patients' rights to control their own healthcare decisions, including decisions about life-sustaining treatments.

In September 2024, the Brazilian Supreme Federal Court (STF) ruled on two cases involving medical decisions affected by religious values, affirming the importance of respecting a patient's right to self-determination over existential choices. These cases, Themes 952 and 1069, established the right of Jehovah's Witnesses to refuse blood transfusions and ruled that the State must, where possible, offer alternative treatments available within the public health system. This decision underscores a broader societal shift towards a model of healthcare that prioritises the individual's values and preferences, reflecting the importance of placing the patient's perspective at the centre of medical decision-making and reinforcing the Contractual Model of partnership in physician-patient relationships.

In Europe, recent court rulings have similarly advanced the principle of patient autonomy, affirming individuals' rights to make personal healthcare decisions. For example, in 2016, the Federal Court of Justice in Germany (Case No. XII ZB 61/16) has reinforced the significance of advance healthcare directives, asserting that physician must honour these directives and respect patients' choices, even in critical care situations. This decision also highlights a consistent trend across Europe, placing individual autonomy at the heart of medical practice and strengthening the Contractual Model, where healthcare decisions are collaborative and centred on the patient's informed preferences.

Similarly, in the United Kingdom, the 2015 ruling in *Montgomery v. Lanarkshire Health Board* marked a pivotal shift towards prioritizing patient autonomy. The UK Supreme Court ruled that physicians must disclose all material risks associated with treatment and any reasonable alternatives, abandoning the paternalistic approach where physicians solely determined what information to share. This decision solidified the patient's right to make informed decisions about their care, underscoring that true consent requires transparency and respect for the patient's values and choices.

To conclude this Subchapter, it is important to note that, philosophically, the evolution of consent can be understood through Ludwig Wittgenstein's concept of *language games* (1953). Wittgenstein proposed that the meaning of language is derived from its use within specific social contexts and governed by rules that adapt to the circumstances in which communication occurs. Applying this concept to the physician-patient relationship, the rules and meanings of consent have evolved in tandem with historical, cultural, and technological developments. Initially, under the *Priestly Model*, consent was not a matter of patient autonomy but rather a passive acknowledgment of the physician's authority. Over time, as societal values shifted, the physician-patient relationship transformed into the *Contractual Model*, where informed consent and patient autonomy became central. Within this framework, the language of consent itself has taken on new meanings, reflecting a shift from hierarchical communication to a more participatory dialogue.

The advent of the internet and modern technologies has further altered this dynamic, introducing new challenges and opportunities in the language game of consent. Patients now arrive better informed—sometimes misinformed—armed with knowledge gleaned from sources like *Doctor Google* or *Doctor ChatGPT*. This change requires physicians to navigate and respond to these inputs effectively. They must not only address the validity of such information but also provide clear, contextualised explanations to ensure patients fully understand their medical conditions and treatment options.

Consequently, the linguistic interplay between physician and patient has undergone a profound transformation. It is no longer sufficient to simply convey information; physicians must actively engage in detailed, patient-tailored communication that fosters understanding, respect, and trust. This more dialogical and explanatory approach is critical to upholding the principles of informed consent and strengthening the foundation of patient trust within modern medical practice.

Additionally, drawing on Michel Foucault's insights, all this paradigm shift can be understood through his analysis of the *Microphysics of Power*, where power is relational, fluid, and embedded within social structures and practices. Foucault (1977, 1978) demonstrated that power is not a fixed or centralised entity but is instead distributed across networks of relationships, constantly evolving in response to societal transformations and discursive shifts. In the physician-patient relationship, this dynamic is particularly evident in the transition from the *Priestly and Engineering Models*—where the physician has a paternalistic view and exerted near-absolute authority over the patient's body—to a framework of the *Collegial and Contractual Models* that increasingly recognises the patients' autonomy and capacity to exercise control over their own body.

This transformation was significantly influenced by a global movement that emerged in the post-Second World War period, marked by the adoption of various national and international documents focused on safeguarding human rights and patient rights. As discussed above, these instruments elevated individual dignity and autonomy as central principles, profoundly impacting healthcare practices and medical ethics. From a Foucauldian perspective, this evolution exemplifies how changes in societal structures and discourses realign power, redefine professional authority, and reshape the ethical foundations of medicine.

This shift represents a decentralisation of medical authority, where the body is no longer solely subject to external decisions imposed by the physician. Instead, the patient gains greater power to make informed choices about their healthcare, challenging the traditional hierarchical structure of the relationship. Over time, the patient's role has evolved from passive compliance to active participation, reflecting broader societal movements that prioritise individual agency and self-determination.

By reconceptualising the body as a locus of personal autonomy, this transformation underscores a fundamental realignment of power dynamics in medicine, aligning with Foucault's notion that power is continuously negotiated and redefined within social interactions.

Understanding the nuances of the current stage of the physician-patient relationship provides a foundational basis for this book's comprehensive examination of key concepts related to physician's conduct and civil liability in the context of AI. This understanding is essential for analysing the evolution of contractual duties and physician responsibilities within the ethical and civil spheres, as they have adapted to the growing emphasis on patient autonomy, informed consent, and collaborative decision-making in modern medical practice.

2.1.1 Medical Service Contracts Under Brazilian Law

Medical service contracts are legal agreements that establish the conditions under which medical or healthcare services are provided by a professional, clinic, hospital, or other healthcare entity to a contracting party, which may be an individual, a company, or a public entity. These contracts are essential for defining the rights, duties, and responsibilities of the parties involved, ensuring legal certainty for both sides and compliance with applicable regulations.

According to Ronsevald and Braga Netto (2021), the provision of medical services is a legal transaction whereby one party, in exchange for remuneration, utilises the specialised services of the other party. In other words, it involves an obligation to perform, assumed by one party (the service provider or executor), which consists of carrying out medical activities that benefit the other party (the service recipient or requester), in return for compensation.

The consequences of applying the Brazilian Consumer Code (Law No. 8,078/1990) to contracts between physician and patient are extensive, as Miragem (2007) explains. First, this law establishes several basic consumer rights, including the right to life, health, and safety (Article 6, I), the right to information (Article 6, III), the right to effective prevention and redress of damages (Article 6, VI), and the facilitation of legal defence (Article 6, VIII). These provisions grant the consumer-patient, who has suffered harm due to substandard medical services, a favourable regime regarding the liability of physicians as well as hospital and clinic institutions.

Medical service contracts have the following characteristics: (a) bilateral—it creates rights and obligations for both parties; (b) synallagmatic—it presupposes a balance between performance and counterperformance; (c) onerous—it involves reciprocal sacrifices and benefits, with the remuneration of the service provider being inherent to the contract; (d) personal (*intuitu personae*)—it prohibits the unilateral transfer of service execution or the right to services to another party; and (e) consensual and informal—it can be concluded by mutual agreement, without formalities, allowing for tacit consent expressed through the parties' behaviour, particularly when the provider demonstrates their intention to perform through their actions (Tepedino et al. 2021).

Every obligational relationship arises and develops with a view toward proper performance. An obligation is a process (Couto e Silva 2006), culminating in fulfilment. In the context of a bilateral and onerous contract, the provision of medical services establishes reciprocal obligations and duties, marked by the presence of an obligational synallagma, where the contracting patient and the contracted physician are mutual creditors and debtors (Farias and Rosenvald 2021). Consequently, there are legal duties (duties of conduct) imposed on both contracting parties, applicable at three stages—before treatment begins, during the treatment, and after the therapy/treatment has concluded. These duties may derive from the parties' agreements, the principle of good faith, or the specific circumstances of the contract and the nature of the relationship itself.

According to Kfouri Neto (2024), the physician (service provider) is subject to: (a) the obligation to perform medical services with the required efficiency and diligence, in accordance with bioethical principles and the *leges artis* of the profession, in order to formulate diagnoses, prognoses, and/or treatments; and (b) the duty to maintain confidentiality regarding the patient's medical conditions, alongside other duties of conduct, such as the duty of disclosure. On the other hand, the patient (service recipient) is bound by the following obligations: (a) to pay the agreed remuneration within the terms and period arranged with the physician; and (b) to provide the minimum conditions necessary for the physician's protection and work, sharing all relevant information with the physician that may assist in the development of the patient's clinical history.

In the specific context of medical service contracts, it is important to recognise that such arrangements are *sui generis*, owing to the significant element of *alea* (risk or uncertainty) inherent in medical treatment. The unpredictable nature of illnesses, combined with the highly individualised responses of human physiology, makes the precise determination of outcomes impossible.

Therefore, the obligation undertaken by the physician, as the service provider, is an obligation of *means*, as it is not tied to a guaranteed result. The physician cannot ensure the attainment of the outcome desired by the patient but is instead bound to diligently employ the appropriate means to achieve the intended goal—these means, therefore, form the core of the physician's obligation (Kfouri Neto 2024).

In medical practice, harmful outcomes sometimes occur independently of any causal involvement by the physicians. Here, *therapeutic alea* applies, as the patient's pathological condition, which the treatment aimed to alleviate or cure, may deteriorate even under the care of a highly diligent physician. Although medical practice seeks to alleviate illness and improve patient health, it is inherently bound to a high level of risk, given the *alea* associated with the individuality and unpredictability of human physiological responses. This uncertainty persists even in simple treatments, and advancements in medicine do not eliminate the random, unpredictable nature of medical science (Kfouri Neto 2022; Dantas 2024).

Some adverse events arise from endogenous causes, attributable to the patient's bodily reactions, varying degrees of drug efficacy, unpredictable factors inherent to treatment, or even as a result of idiosyncratic factors, congenital weaknesses, or the underlying illness itself. Harm resulting from a medical act is not necessarily due to negligence. A physician may treat two oncology patients of the same age, with similar clinical conditions and the same type of cancer, administering identical treatment to both, yet one may survive while the other does not.

The complexity of the human body and the inevitable influence of external factors render *therapeutic alea* an inseparable attribute of medical practice. In this regard, Lopez (2004) argues that the physician always operates within a zone of inherent risk, as each person is unique, and individual reactions to the same treatment can vary and remain fundamentally unpredictable.

Thus, it is unjustifiable to impose all of these risks and uncertainties solely on the physician. The professional is not bound by an obligation to deliver a specific outcome (such as a cure) but is instead required to fulfil a duty of diligence and attentiveness, acting in accordance with the prevailing standards of knowledge in their field, which they are expected to maintain and continuously update (Rosenvald and Braga Netto 2020). Indeed, one of the greatest challenges facing judges is the assessment of negligence. As previously noted, the physician cannot be held accountable for all inherent risks in their practice. In this regard, França (2021) aptly cautions that not every adverse outcome in individual or collective healthcare equates to medical error.

It is important to highlight that, although the physician is not obligated to cure or to achieve a specific favourable outcome, the obligational relationship is not a static or uniform construct, as Clovis V. do Couto e Silva (2006) explains. Rather, it is a dynamic reality, shaped by a sequence of actions undertaken by both parties, each fulfilling their respective obligations and duties (whether primary or ancillary), all directed towards a particular goal. In this context, Fachin (2012) is categorical about the nature of contractual dynamics in contemporary law, asserting that concepts of movement, circulation, and process have become essential to this new understanding—both internal and external—of the legal relationship.

Thus, within the structure of the physician-patient relationship, there exists a bundle of obligations and duties, understood from the perspective of a dynamic and complex obligational relationship. It is *dynamic* because it develops through various phases—before, during, and after medical treatment, with potential transformations in its content. It is *complex*, as it does not establish a single, unified bond; rather, within the same obligational process, numerous duties arise, each defined by the overarching purpose of the relationship in question (França 2021).

The obligational relationship cannot be detached from its purpose-driven dimension, as this ultimately determines its intended outcome and trajectory. On one side, good faith propels the obligational process, while on the other, purpose directs it (Couto e Silva 2006).

Understanding the physician's obligation as a process leads us to conclude that it is the physician's role to apply the techniques available in the field of medicine, with diligent attention to the treatment required by the patient. However, if all reasonable efforts ultimately prove unsuccessful and, for example, the patient passes away, the physician may not be held liable, as fault is not presumed merely by virtue of the failure to achieve a cure. The intended outcome, to some extent, also forms part of the obligation of means, considering that the goal is inseparable from the contract made with the physician. The *process* of obligation is directly linked to its sources (how duties arise) and the development of the relationship itself.

Considering the reflections above, it is concluded that the physician's duty is to carry out all possible actions with diligence, scientific rigour, and technical responsibility, while providing the patient with loyal, complete, and accessible information regarding the diagnosis, prognosis, therapeutic alternatives, and associated risks. Fulfilment of the contract resides in acting diligently and in compliance with specific contractual duties of conduct—before, during, and after a given treatment or surgical procedure, for example.

Over recent decades, the need for contracting parties to adopt honest and integral conduct in entering into contracts has become increasingly reaffirmed. Thus, rather than merely questioning whether there was an intent to act in good faith, the focus has shifted to examining whether the actions undertaken by the contracting parties were transparent and met the conduct standards that qualify the general clause of objective good faith in postmodern society.

2.1.2 A Proposed Classification of Physicians' Duties of Conduct in Brazil

In Brazil there are professional duties of conduct in medicine that may extend beyond the fulfilment of the primary obligation, effectively existing as independent duties. Due to this particular characteristic, these duties can be invoked independently of the main service provided. From this perspective, the medical service contract, when interpreted and shaped by the Constitutionalisation of Civil Law, encompasses six primary duties of physician's conduct, as outlined in the comparative Table 2.2.

Table 2.2 Comparative table created by the author of this book, based on the studies of the following scholars: Nilo (2020), França (2021), Fachin (2006), Cordeiro (2017), and Kfouri Neto (2024)

Physician's duties of conduct	
Duty of information	(I) Duty of information, disclosure and explanation
	(II) Duty of documentation and confidentiality/secrecy
Duty of loyalty	(III) Duty of cooperation and loyalty *stricto sensu*
	(IV) Duty to refrain from abuse or misuse of power
Duty of protection	(V) Duty of up-to-date knowledge
	(VI) Duty of care and vigilance

Before engaging in a detailed analysis of physician's conduct duties, it is essential to outline a few preliminary considerations regarding contemporary contract theory in Brazil.

It is essential that the study of contracts—especially when considering the *existential nature* of the physician-patient contractual relationship (Bizelli 2018)—goes beyond a dogmatic analysis of its structural elements, prioritising a functional perspective that recognises the contract as a tool for achieving specific practical objectives that reflect the exercise of contractual autonomy. Each type of contract, as regulated by the legislator, should be analysed from a functional perspective, with a focus on the intended purpose, so that the parties' interests are realised through the applicable contractual framework (Nalin 2008).

Furthermore, the contract should be understood as a *means* to realise values beyond merely an *agreement of wills*; it must, above all, be interpreted under the principles of objective good faith and its contemporary derivatives—transparency, trust, and equity—which reinforce the constitutional desire for a contract that is both solidaristic and socially just. Thus, the contract's significance extends beyond the contracting parties to encompass the broader social environment and context, taking on a social function in favour of contractual justice. According to the insights of Hironaka (2014), the contract between the contracting parties has, in recent decades, become a contract that demands a greater ethical and political commitment from each participant, expanding its influence far beyond the mere *synallagma*.

In the book *On Contracts: A Postmodern Concept* (2008), Paulo Nalin highlights the need to formulate contracts aligned with constitutional principles in Brazil, advocating for a rethinking of contractual principles and duties under the premise that the contract is a solidary, complex relationship. Following the civil-constitutional methodology, Civil Law norms must be validated, interpreted, and applied in alignment with constitutional values and principles, which serve as criteria for harmonising the legal system. Moreover, the Constitutionalisation of Civil Law requires that constitutional norms be considered not only as a hermeneutic rule but also as a rule of conduct that impacts the content of legal situations and promotes their functionality.

In light of constitutional legality, where human dignity is a foundational value of the legal order, it is imperative to align patrimonial legal situations with existential ones. Since the 1988 Brazilian Constitution, a reinterpretation of ancillary contractual duties has been undertaken, particularly in contracts for medical services, as this work will seek to demonstrate.

In the last decades, the importance of contractual good faith is growing exponentially in Brazil, driven by a revision of the general Theory of Obligations, influenced by new jurisprudential and doctrinal trends, largely motivated by the Constitutionalisation of private law. Duties arising from good faith are organised according to varying degrees of intensity, depending on the nature of the legal acts to which they relate (Ehrhardt Júnior 2014).

In Brazilian Contract Law, the concept of *good faith* plays a central role in shaping not only the primary obligations established in a contractual agreement, but also additional, implicit duties known as *ancillary obligations* or *collateral duties*. These duties arise directly from the principle of objective good faith, which is enshrined in the Brazilian Civil Code (Law No 10,406/2002—Article 422). Unlike in some other legal systems, where good faith may primarily serve as a subjective standard reflecting the parties' intentions or honesty, in Brazil, objective good faith operates as a normative standard. It imposes a duty of ethical and cooperative behaviour on all contracting parties throughout the lifecycle of a contract—during its formation, execution, and even post-performance.

The ancillary duties deriving from objective good faith include duties such as information, cooperation, and loyalty. For example, a party is required to disclose relevant information to the other party, act in a manner that facilitates the fulfilment of the contract and avoid actions that could harm the legitimate expectations of the other party. These duties exist independently of the contract's express terms and are enforceable under Brazilian law.

This approach represents a broader and more proactive interpretation of contractual duties compared to some legal systems. It ensures that contracts are performed in a manner consistent with ethical standards and mutual trust, reflecting a deeper concern with fairness and equity in contractual relationships. Violations of these ancillary duties, even if the primary obligation is fulfilled, may result in civil liability for damages or the termination of the contract. This highlights the importance of objective good faith as a mechanism for fostering justice and balance within Brazilian Contract Law.

Objective good faith, in its current conception, was introduced into Brazilian law by the Consumer Code (Law No. 8,078/1990), with express reference in Articles 4, III, and 51, IV. The Civil Code (Law No. 10,406/2002) subsequently incorporated objective good faith as a standard of conduct imposed upon contracting parties (Article 422), and further provides that legal transactions must be interpreted in accordance with good faith (Article 113).

Brazilian legal doctrine has systematically and methodically classified objective good faith according to the three functions it serves within the Brazilian legal system: (i) as a hermeneutic canon for integrating legal transactions (interpretative function); (ii) as a norm limiting the exercise of subjective rights (control function); and (iii) as a rule establishing or creating ancillary duties alongside the primary obligation (integrative function). This final function will be analysed in detail throughout this book. Good faith, as a general principle of obligations with its integrative/creative function of establishing collateral or general duties of conduct within legal relationships, has been rigorously examined by Brazilian jurists in recent decades (Ehrhardt Júnior 2014).

However, Nalin, Venazzi and Copi (2021) highlight that contemporary constitutional Civil Law has undergone significant transformation since the promulgation of the Brazilian Constitution in 1988, differing markedly in both its methodology and the theoretical nuances governing private institutions. The movement for the Constitutionalisation of Civil Law in Brazil, influenced by the Italian scholar Perlingieri (2006), has sparked numerous studies and debates since the inception of the Brazilian Federal Constitution.

More than three decades later, however, Brazilian society is certainly not the same as in 1988, and the great constitutional ideals of that era no longer fully align with the work of the constituent assembly. It is also worth noting that, as Rodrigues Júnior (2019) argues, constitutionalisation is far from being a consensual concept and remains lacking an objective (and objectifiable) content, in other words, without an operational concept of the constitutionalisation of law.

In this context, Paulo Nalin advocates for reflections on private law through the lens of what he called the *Post-Constitutionalisation of Civil Law* (2021)—a concept he introduced—which is the perspective adopted by this book. From this viewpoint, by establishing objective parameters and criteria for a functional perspective on private law, the aim is to pursue a more refined methodological rigour and to reinforce constitutional axiological vectors, especially in light of attempts at regression within postmodern society. In this respect, the Constitution is understood in its prospective dimension—as a period of consolidating Civil Law within constitutional legality—meaning a phase following the constitutionalisation of Civil Law that does not supersede it, but rather complements it in response to emerging social demands.

Thus, it becomes essential, for instance, to reframe private autonomy and the entire process of fulfilling contractual duties within the physician-patient relationship to align with the new reality of *Person-Centred Medicine*. This will be explained in further detail later in this book.

This is a *Constitutional Civil Law for the future*, as the aim is not to view the challenges presented as immutable proposals to be followed as unassailable doctrines, but rather as constructive prompts toward a forward-looking framework for a Civil Law and a Republican Constitution that together can address the complexities and paradoxes of a civil society advancing boldly into the twenty-first century (Fachin 2021). The guiding principles and duties of Contract Theory undergo re-evaluations over time, adapting them to the historical and social context in which the contracting parties operate.

As discussed in an earlier section of this book, there was a period when the concept of broad freedom to act prevailed, with the physician viewed as a *divine figure* and later as a wise authority who knew what was best for the patient (medical paternalism). However, over time, regulatory standards for the physician emerged, underscoring the principle that medical practice entails a set of duties and obligations to which the professional is bound.

In this *Post-Constitutionalisation context of Civil Law*, it must be acknowledged that the patient's decision-making autonomy in their healthcare does not carry the same understanding as it did at the time of the Constitution's enactment. Indeed, the principles of autonomy and human dignity themselves have undergone substantial reinterpretation over the past three decades.

As Farias and Rosenvald (2021) assert, duties of conduct are subject to constant change over time and across contexts, as their application must align with the specific contract's purpose as assessed in each case. It is both necessary and urgent to adjust interpretative parameters, reinterpreting the ancillary duties in these contracts to ensure the effective protection of constitutional values within the legal relationship between physician and patient.

It is important to note that contractual duties of conduct, arising from the principle of objective good faith in contracts, have been extensively categorised by Brazilian legal scholars. For the purposes of this work, we begin with the typology offered by the Portuguese professor Cordeiro (2017), who classifies these as ancillary duties of disclosure, loyalty, and protection. Subsequently, we proceed to a more detailed subclassification of these physician's duties of conduct, based on specialised studies in Brazilian Medical Law, particularly the work of Kfouri Neto (2024) and França (2021).

The contractual duties arising from the principle of good faith are referred to in legal doctrine as ancillary, secondary, collateral, accessory, or instrumental duties. These are obligations imposed on both the contracting and the contracted parties. They are not directly aimed at fulfilling the main obligation or primary duties but rather relate to the proper management of the contractual relationship, ensuring the overall satisfaction of the interests at stake. These duties focus on achieving a common purpose within the complex nature of the contractual relationship, aiming to safeguard the mutual interests involved in the obligation.

The principle of good faith operates within contract integration through three major duties: the duty of information, the duty of loyalty, and the duty of protection. As emphasised by Guia da Silva (2019) and Martins-Costa (2019), the primary purpose of these ancillary duties of conduct is to promote the specific contractual purpose, ensuring proper performance in line with the functional approach that underpins contemporary Civil Law.

It is important to emphasise that in the physician-patient relationship, these duties often overlap with the primary obligation itself, which is to care for and treat the patient with a minimum standard of diligence. This core obligation frequently encompasses these ancillary duties, as the responsibility to provide proper care inherently involves upholding duties of disclosure, loyalty, and protection. As such, these secondary duties are not easily separated from the main obligation to safeguard the patient's health and well-being.

2.2 A Detailed Analysis of Duties Related to Disclosure, Loyalty, and Protection in Brazil

The duty of information requires the parties to mutually inform each other of all relevant aspects concerning the contractual relationship. This includes the duty to disclosure, warn, clarify, and advise. The duty of loyalty, meanwhile, obliges the parties to refrain from any behaviour that could distort the purpose of the contract or unbalance the reciprocal obligations agreed upon. Finally, the duty of protection involves safeguarding the other party from risks of harm to their person or property throughout the duration of the contractual relationship. This duty can be imposed in a negative form (abstaining from harm) or in a positive form (taking action to prevent or minimise damage).

These duties govern the contractual relationship from its inception to its conclusion, encompassing all stages, from preliminary negotiations to the post-contractual phase. Building on this foundation, a detailed analysis will be conducted of the subclassification of these duties of conduct (*standards*), as redefined within the framework of the Constitutionalisation of Civil Law and the Person-Centred Medicine approach.

These standards are essential as they establish a framework of trust, cooperation, and safety within the physician-patient relationship, ensuring that the rights and obligations of both parties are upheld. In the following sections, each of these duties of conduct—disclosure, loyalty, and protection—will be examined in detail to clarify their practical applications and significance according to Brazilian doctrine and case law.

2.2.1 *The Duty of Disclosure and the Reinterpretation of Informed Consent*

As previously discussed, the duty of information comprises: (I) Duty of information, disclosure and explanation; and (II) Duty of documentation and confidentiality/secrecy. Regarding topic I, it is initially worth emphasising that the duty of information, disclosure and explanation are closely connected to the process of obtaining the patient's informed consent, as will be further explained below.

In Brazil, the legal basis for patient self-determination in medical care is derived from general rights enshrined in the 1988 Federal Constitution of Brazil, particularly concerning freedom and the inviolability of privacy. Regarding the right to freedom, Article 5, subsection II, guarantees that no one shall be compelled to do or refrain from doing anything except by virtue of law. This principle grants the patient the freedom to make decisions regarding their own body and health. It protects the patient's ability to select treatments, to accept or refuse procedures, and to make informed choices about medical care. Freedom is essential to patient autonomy, as it enables the patient to be the central figure in decisions concerning their health.

The right to the inviolability of privacy, set forth in Article 5, subsection X, guarantees the rights to privacy and intimacy, including the protection of personal information, particularly medical information. The right to privacy means that the patient has the right to keep their health information confidential and to control access to it. This right reinforces patient autonomy by ensuring that they may determine who has access to sensitive information concerning their health history and body. Therefore, these constitutional rights are fundamental to patient autonomy, which encompasses the right to make free and informed decisions about one's own body and health.

Bodily self-determination, encapsulated to a certain extent by the concept of *consent*, introduces into Civil Law, and specifically into Medical Law, the notion of the horizontal effect of fundamental rights. This concept refers to the application of constitutional rights—such as dignity, privacy, and equality—not only in relations between the State and individuals but also in relations between private parties. In Medical Law, this means that a patient's rights must be respected by healthcare providers, ensuring that private individuals or institutions uphold these fundamental rights within their interactions.

As discussed in a previous subsection of this book chapter, the relationship between physician and patient was traditionally a civil relationship marked by inequality. However, once the patient's vulnerability is recognised, and a demand for substantive equality between them arises, the fundamental rights enshrined in the 1988 Constitution of Brazil come to bear on the situation of the patient, thereby granting them a sphere of self-determination to exercise autonomy over their body for the purposes of medical interventions.

The notion of patient consent and freedom to choose medical treatments distinctly embodies the general principle of human protection in Medical Law; it represents an evident instance of the positive application of fundamental rights, as it enables an individual to freely develop their personality through personal bodily choices. In other words, a person's right to undergo or refuse medical treatment is integral to the development of their personality, constituting a fundamental right that provides mechanisms for enhancing the dignity of both life and death.

Alvez and Schaefer (2022) assert that the human body (as an element of personhood) should be considered through a post-metaphysical concept of the *person*, that is, as an element shaping personal identity and as an instrument for realising one's own identity. The authors argue that this premise is essential for understanding the scope of bodily rights, as self-determination (the capacity to make choices and assume responsibility for them) should be considered in light of the values that constitute personhood itself and how these values interact with the body and autonomy in pursuit of self-realisation. It is from this understanding that the physician should receive and respect their patient's expressions of will.

With regard to the regulation of patient self-determination and consent, although there is no specific legislation on the matter in Brazil, provisions (either explicit or implicit) are found within various statutes. The Brazilian Civil Code enshrines the principle of autonomy, as stated in Article 15: "No one may be compelled to undergo medical treatment or surgical intervention involving risk to life". Additionally, the Brazilian Consumer Code establishes duties of information and transparency.

Article 6, subsection III, mandates "clear and adequate information regarding different products and services, including correct specifications on quantity, characteristics, composition, quality, applicable taxes, and price, as well as information on associated risks"; and Article 46 provides that "contracts governing consumer relations shall not bind consumers if they have not been given the opportunity to be informed of their content in advance, or if the instruments are drafted in such a way as to obscure their meaning and scope". Furthermore, Article 30 highlights that the duty of information in consumer relations forms part of the primary obligation through compulsory contractual integration, as the supplier's offer constitutes a binding legal commitment.

It is worth clarifying that contracts established between physician and patient in Brazil are considered *consumer contracts*, thereby falling under the specific legislation of the Brazilian Consumer Protection Code (*Código de Defesa do Consumidor*—CDC). This classification arises because, according to the legislation, consumer relations are those in which a consumer is the end recipient of a service or product, while a supplier provides the service or product habitually. The CDC provides consumer protection in cases of services which, by their nature, place the consumer in a position of vulnerability, as with medical services, given the technical complexity involved. In this context, the patient is regarded as the consumer, being the final recipient of the medical service, and the healthcare professional is deemed the supplier, particularly when the medical activity is conducted on a habitual basis and involves remuneration. Medical services are compensated, even indirectly (for instance, when payment is made through a health plan), thus establishing a commercial relationship that falls within the scope of the CDC.

Furthermore, whether in private or public services provided through the Unified Health System (Sistema Único de Saúde—SUS), Brazil's Organic Health Law (Law No. 8,080/1990) mandates that medical actions and services (both public and private) must uphold individuals' autonomy in safeguarding their physical and moral integrity (Article 7, section II). Ministry of Health Ordinance No. 1,820/2009 stipulates that all individuals must have their values, culture, and rights respected in their interactions with health services, ensuring free, voluntary, and informed consent (Article 5, section V).

Sectoral legislation addressing these matters is also important, including: Law No. 10,216/2001 (Articles 4 and 6), which provides for the protection and rights of individuals with mental health disorders and reorients the mental health care model; Law No. 9,263/1996 (Article 10, paragraphs 1 and 6), which governs family planning; and Law No. 9,434/1997 (Article 9, caput, paragraphs 4 and 8), which regulates the removal of organs, tissues, and body parts for transplantation and treatment purposes. These various laws enshrine provisions about patient autonomy and the right to informed consent.

In the ethical sphere, deontological principles issued by the Federal Council of Medicine in Brazil (Conselho Federal de Medicina—CFM) recognise patient self-determination, emphasising freedom and dignity, while also legitimising the medical practice of intervening in another's body. The duty to provide information is likewise derived from the Code of Medical Ethics, which stipulates in Article 22 that a physician must not "fail to obtain the patient's or their legal representative's consent after providing clarification regarding the procedure to be performed, except in cases of imminent risk of death". Numerous other provisions throughout the document underscore the importance of respecting and valuing patient autonomy in medical care.

In addition, the Federal Council of Medicine (CFM) has issued several deontological norms that deserve particular attention: (i) Recommendation No. 1/2016, which addresses the process of obtaining free and informed consent in medical care; (ii) Resolution No. 2,174/2018, which regulates the practice of anaesthetic procedures; (iii) Resolution No. 2,294/2021, which pertains to assisted reproduction techniques; (iv) Resolution No. 1,605/2000, which governs access to medical records; and (v) Resolution No. 2,232/2019, which establishes ethical guidelines on therapeutic refusal by patients and conscientious objection in the physician-patient relationship. All these norms include provisions on patient consent, and in cases of violation, the physician may be held accountable under the ethical penalties established by the Federal Council of Medicine.

Concerning Recommendation No. 01/2016 issued by the Federal Council of Medicine in Brazil (CFM), it is important to highlight its essential guidelines for the process of obtaining free and informed consent in medical care. The document advises physicians on the necessity of clearly informing patients about their diagnosis, treatment options, risks, benefits, and the potential consequences of each approach.

The Recommendation underscores that consent must be obtained properly, following comprehensive explanations, allowing patients to make an informed and conscious decision. It further emphasises the importance of individualising consent, suggesting that the document should be tailored to the specific circumstances of each case and the patient's capacity for understanding. Moreover, the CFM advises that consent should always be viewed as an ongoing process, revisited throughout the course of treatment, particularly in cases where significant changes occur in the patient's condition or the therapeutic plan.

Having established these initial premises regarding the legal and ethical framework supporting patient self-determination and informed consent, attention now turns to a comprehensive examination of judicial rulings and prevailing doctrinal interpretations on the subject in Brazil.

According to the prevailing judicial and doctrinal understanding in Brazil (Kfouri Neto 2024; França 2021; Dantas 2024), a physician's duty to inform the patient extends beyond a mere ancillary contractual obligation. Unlike other duties of conduct discussed in this book, it is readily identifiable as an independent damage, forming part of the physician's primary obligation to respect the patient's self-determination in healthcare decisions. This duty carries an existential dimension, linked to the patient's right to the free development of their personality, as previously explained.

The Brazilian Superior Court of Justice (Special Appeal No. 1.144.840/SP, adjudicated on 20 March 2012) has held that the right to information serves to ensure that consumers can make informed choices, thereby aligning their expectations with the actual benefits of the product or service. This principle reflects what is commonly referred to as *qualified consent*. Under this framework, the requirement set out in Article 6(III) of the Brazilian Consumer Code is only fulfilled when the information provided to consumers meets the criteria of *adequacy*. Adequate information is defined as being simultaneously complete, comprehensible, and useful. Moreover, the provision prohibits the dilution of genuinely relevant communication through the use of fragmented, redundant, or otherwise unhelpful information that offers no practical value to the patient-consumer.

In practical terms, informed consent arises as a consequence of the physician's duty to inform. Patient consent constitutes a legal act of a *sui generis* nature. According to Soares (2021), it involves permission granted to the physician to act upon the patient's legal sphere concerning rights exclusively inherent to the individual, arising from an informational and decisional process that unfolds to a greater or lesser extent, depending on the circumstances of the case. If the physician fails to provide complete and comprehensible information, the patient's consent may be deemed flawed or invalid, potentially resulting in civil or ethical liability for the healthcare professional (Soares 2021; Sá and Naves 2021).

It is worth noting that Kfouri Neto (2024) explains that the evolution of the doctrine of informed consent worldwide can be divided into two major phases, which have also influenced the Brazilian context, particularly in relation to recent judicial decisions and doctrinal understanding.

The first phase emerged in the post-Second World War period, during which the indispensability of individuals' voluntary consent in medical experiments was established (the *Collegial Model* of the physician-patient relationship). Subsequently, the second phase introduced the concept of informed and explicit consent, characterised by qualified consent (the *Contractual Model*). This phase emphasises that mere provision of information is insufficient; such information must be complete, clear, and precise.

In the United Kingdom, the landmark Scottish case of *Montgomery v. Lanarkshire Health Board*, adjudicated in 2015, exemplifies this second phase of the doctrine. It marks a departure from the paternalistic approach, establishing clear rules on the physician's duty to inform patients about treatment risks to meet the criteria of informed consent. The judicial reasoning in this case will be analysed in detail in Sect. 2.3.

Following this line of reasoning, a landmark decision adjudicated in 2018 by the Brazilian Superior Court of Justice (Special Appeal No. 1.540.580/DF) established that generic consent (*blanket consent*) or consent obtained through standardised forms is invalid and must be clearly individualised. This ruling represents a significant milestone in Brazilian jurisprudence, emphasising that information provided to patients must be tailored to the specific circumstances of each case and the individual needs of each patient. Information alone is not sufficient; it must, above all, be clear, tailored to the recipient, and presented in a comprehensible and accessible manner. In other words, the physician's explanation must be thorough and adapted to the intellectual and cultural level of the patient (Nalin 2008).

Rosenvald and Braga Netto (2020) emphasise that the duty to inform with loyalty and transparency has significantly strengthened over the past decades. It is no longer acceptable, as it was in the past, to keep patients in a state of ignorance regarding their health, choices, and options. Physicians and patients must act—each within their respective responsibilities—with prudence and good faith. More broadly, it is expected that physicians, before, during, and after consultations, surgeries, or treatments, act in accordance with objective good faith, the duty of care, and cooperation.

As Schaefer (2010) observes, the physician-patient relationship can no longer rest on a foundation of unrealistic expectations and satisfactions that will never materialise, particularly when such expectations are built on so-called *benevolent falsehoods*. Patients must be empowered to exercise their right to freedom by autonomously determining their treatment, whether by choosing among the options presented or declining all of them. In this context, *qualified consent* becomes essential, requiring consideration of the legal interests involved as well as the individual values and preferences of each patient.

The duty of truthfulness in obtaining patient consent is essential. A physician is not entitled, based on their subjective perspective, to decide what should or should not be disclosed to the patient. For example, the concept of the so-called *benevolent lie* finds no support in law. The physician-patient relationship must instead be defined by the patients' autonomy to decide what information they wish to receive and to whom it may be disclosed (Schaefer 2010).

In urgent or emergency situations, the duty to inform may be relativised. Patients may be unable to express their will, and contacting their representatives or verifying any prior directives regarding medical treatment might be impossible. In such cases, physicians are expected to act according to established protocols. However, if a patient's wishes become known, either through express communication or advance directives, these cannot be disregarded under the utilitarian argument that saving the patient's life is the only option (Alvez and Schaefer 2022).

Additionally, in exceptional circumstances, physicians may act immediately without patient consent or legal authorisation under the concept of therapeutic privilege. When faced with imminent danger to life or irreversible harm, the urgency to preserve life or physical integrity justifies immediate medical intervention. In such cases, the physician's actions are shielded by legal provisions, such as the *state of necessity* and the *regular exercise of a recognised right*, outlined in Articles 23 of the Brazilian Penal Law and 188 of the Brazilian Civil Code. These exclude the illicitness of the act and presume the patient's consent, eliminating civil or penal liability (Godinho 2023).

Kfouri Neto (2024) highlights significant issues with generic consent forms, noting that such documents may inadvertently serve as evidence of flaws in the consent process, ultimately causing harm to the patient. For example, pre-drafted templates with vague, imprecise, or poorly constructed language can lead to serious misunderstandings. These forms might permit any physician within a service to perform a surgical procedure, rather than limiting the intervention to the specific physician who obtained the consent and provided the relevant explanations.

Additionally, overly rigid documents that present blanket permissions or refusals, lack sufficient detail, or use one-sided language fail to fulfil the essential purpose of informed consent. Such deficiencies render the forms ineffective, as they do not provide patients with the clear, personalised, and case-specific information necessary for making informed decisions about their treatment.

Consider, in this regard, an excerpt from a decision by the Court of Justice of Paraná, rendered by Appellate Judge Clayton Maranhão in his capacity as the reporting judge, during which I had the opportunity to serve as his legal advisor:

> It should be emphasised that the informed consent form submitted in the case file is not deemed valid, as it constitutes blanket consent, which should have been clearly individualised to the patient's circumstances. The form should have outlined the specificities, benefits, and risks of the carpal tunnel decompression surgery – such as the foreseeable risk of ulnar nerve impairment, which was experienced by the patient. (...) While the surgical procedure in question is technically indicated for releasing the carpal tunnel via a small incision in the wrist, and although the patient was exposed to an inherent surgical risk, it is evident that the physician utilised a standardised form to obtain consent. As a result, there is no evidence that the patient underwent a genuine prior informational and decisional process (Civil Appeal No. 0003343-28.2020.8.16.0019, adjudicated on 18 July 2022).

Regarding the annullability of generic consent forms, Soares (2021) highlights that, pursuant to Article 46 of the Brazilian Consumer Code, consent may be rendered voidable if the patient did not have prior knowledge of its content or if its wording is drafted in such a way as to preclude understanding. In principle, the use of a form containing general and standardised provisions, where the content is unilaterally and pre-emptively set for a broad category of patients in similar conditions of care, is not prohibited.

However, the criterion determining the admissibility of such a document is the patient's cognoscibility, that is, whether the patient was afforded a genuine opportunity to undergo an adequate prior informative phase and an effective decision-making process. In other words, when a judge is presented with a generic document in litigation, the burden falls on the physician to provide other evidence demonstrating that the patient was informed of a specific risk that materialised and was given the opportunity for information and clarification. In practice, though, this often proves to be an enormous challenge.

According to the testimony of physicians regarding their experience in obtaining patient consent, the most challenging aspect for them is determining the precise extent of information that must be provided regarding the risks to be disclosed. In light of this, Brazilian legal doctrine and case law have established that it is essential to consider the gradation of risks, and the levels of complexity involved in medical care within the context of consent to medical intervention. As articulated by legal scholars, the more severe the risk, the greater the obligation to inform and to obtain the patient's fully informed consent (Kfouri Neto 2024; Soares 2021).

Currently, many physicians in Brazil already rely on legal counsel, wherein lawyers draft consent forms in accordance with the understanding that there is a duty to communicate *significant risks*—those which a physician knows or ought to know are important and relevant to the reasonable person placed in the same circumstances as the patient.

This is known as the *Theory of Significant Risks*, which defines a risk as *significant* based on four (4) key criteria: (1) the therapeutic necessity of the intervention; (2) the frequency of the risk (statistical occurrence); (3) its severity; and (4) the patient's characteristics or behaviour. The *therapeutic necessity* criterion operates on the principle that the greater the necessity of the intervention, the more flexible the obligation to inform may be. Regarding the *frequency of risk*, the principle is that the more frequent the occurrence of the risk, the greater the duty to provide information. The criterion of *severity* establishes that the severity of a risk, even if infrequent, imposes a duty to disclose it. Minor risks, however, do not require disclosure.

It is noteworthy that, although the gradation of risks has been advocated in judicial decisions and legal scholarship in Brazil only in recent years, the same theory has been supported in Portugal for at least two decades by authors such as Pereira (2004). In Brazil, Martins-Costa (2019) argues that it is reasonable to limit the duty to inform to frequent risks and severe risks that are typically foreseeable—commonly referred to as significant risks—while excluding exceptional risks from its scope. Significant risks are those which the physician knows or ought to know are important and relevant to a reasonable person placed in the same circumstances as the patient required to consent.

According to Soares (2021), the specific risks of an intervention or treatment must be disclosed, even when they are statistically insignificant. In this regard, one might consider the risk of tetraplegia in spinal surgery, the risk of spontaneous reversal of ducts following a vasectomy, or the risk of complications in cataract surgery that could result in blindness.

Some scholars argue for distinguishing the scope of the duty to inform and clarify between therapeutic and diagnostic interventions. In diagnostic procedures, there is a heightened duty of disclosure (qualified consent), as patients may face risks without immediately obtaining therapeutic benefits (Kfouri Neto 2024). Similarly, this view is shared in Portugal, as noted by Pereira (2015), who emphasises the greater informational duty in diagnostic interventions. This is due to the potential severity of side effects and risks associated with certain tests and examinations. Even where statistical evidence justifies such procedures, individuals must be free to decide, consciously and autonomously, whether to undergo such intrusions into their physical integrity.

Moreover, another significant debate in Brazilian legal scholarship concerns the notion that excessive information, though intended to inform, can lead to misinformation when patients are unable to assimilate the content provided by physicians, as highlighted by Mascarenhas and Bahia (2022). Hyperinformation undermines informed consent, as patients often cannot process the overwhelming volume of data. This renders consent neither free nor rational, resembling the superficial *I have read and agree* practice commonly encountered in digital environments, such as software installations or terms of service agreements, where users routinely accept terms without fully understanding or even reading them.

Sometimes physicians tend to overinform, fearing liability for informational negligence, as courts frequently penalise underinformation but rarely excessive disclosure. This results in a deluge of information that overwhelms patients, who then agree passively, compromising their autonomy. The lack of clear guidelines on the appropriate level of disclosure perpetuates this issue, with physicians opting for overinformation to shield themselves from potential legal disputes, even at the expense of the patient's rights.

This highlights the growing importance of engaging specialised legal counsel to guide physicians on what information should be disclosed and how to effectively communicate it. Legal advisors can help establish a balanced approach, ensuring that the patient receives essential and comprehensible information without being overwhelmed, thereby protecting both the patient's autonomy and the physician from undue liability.

In Brazil, this practice is referred to as *Preventive Medical Law*, which focuses on proactively addressing legal risks associated with medical practice. It involves advising healthcare professionals on compliance with legal and ethical standards, drafting clear and effective consent forms, and providing guidance on patient communication to minimise disputes. By anticipating potential legal challenges, *Preventive Medical Law* aims to create a safer environment for both patients and physicians, reducing the likelihood of litigation while ensuring respect for patient rights and professional responsibilities.

It is important to emphasize that, as mentioned before, consent obtained by the medical team must be procedural, evolving over the course of treatment and being renewed as the case progresses. In no other service relationship is the consensual agreement between the parties so repeatedly renewed, step by step over time, as in the medical service contract (Nilo 2020; Kfouri Neto 2024; Dantas 2024). Thus, it is insufficient for a physician merely to provide information to the patient in order to fulfil their duty to inform. The right to information cannot be reduced to a one-time act coinciding with the moment the patient gives consent. Simply providing a consent form for the patient to sign does not satisfy the duty of disclosure. As noted, it is essential to adhere to the proper informational and decision-making process, meaning professional diligence throughout the entire informed consent and decision-making procedure.

This scenario represents a reinterpretation of the patient's private autonomy and self-determination, reframed through the lens of the *Post-Constitutionalisation of Brazilian Civil Code*, which integrates constitutional principles into Civil Law obligations.

In light of the key discussions surrounding patient consent in Brazil, it is essential to consider the alignment of the current period of Post-Constitutionalisation of Civil Law with the model of Person-Centred Medicine. As outlined at the beginning of this chapter, this scenario demands a more rigorous practical application, requiring the development of objective standards and criteria for a functional perspective on Medical Law. Specifically, in analysing the private autonomy of the patient, there is a heightened focus on methodological precision and the reinforcement of constitutional axiological principles, particularly in response to the challenges and potential regressions present in postmodern society.

In the framework of Person-Centred Medicine, the current stage of the doctor-patient relationship is understood as having shifted from an authoritarian and hierarchical model to a democratic and horizontal one. Greater emphasis is placed on clinical communication skills, seen as a continuous process of interaction between the healthcare professional and the patient. This approach prioritises the individual characteristics and values of each patient, ensuring that these factors are meaningfully incorporated into the decision-making process.

Finally, it is worth noting that scientific studies indicate significant impacts from the implementation of effective clinical communication in patient care. These include improved health outcomes, higher quality of care, and greater (and more appropriate) adherence to medical treatments. According to scientific research, the use of clinical and interpersonal communication skills during consultations does not result in longer appointments. Evidence demonstrates that consultations with effective, patient-centred communication do not take more time than others (Campos et al. 2021).

Albuquerque and Antunes (2021) mention a 2018 Brazilian study revealing that physicians listen to patients describe their health conditions for an average of only 11 seconds before interrupting. Reports of physicians failing to listen to patients are recurrent, often leading to feelings of isolation among patients. The failure to listen to patient complaints can result in unnecessary tests, diagnostic errors, and negative experiences, such as withdrawal and confusion on the part of patients.

In Brazil, the teaching of clinical and interpersonal communication skills to medical students is explicitly provided for under Resolution No. 3/2014 of the Brazilian Association of Higher Education Institutions. Additionally, as mentioned before, the importance of patient communication is evident in various provisions throughout the Brazilian Medical Code of Ethics (Resolution CFM No. 2.217/2018).

Effective communication is a cornerstone of high-quality, humanised medical practice, serving as a continuous process of interaction between healthcare professionals and patients (or their legal representatives). By integrating the individual characteristics and values of each patient, this approach fosters mutual understanding of diagnoses, prognoses, and therapeutic alternatives. This dynamic exemplifies the *Contractual Model* of the doctor-patient relationship—extensively discussed in an earlier subsection of this chapter—, where effective communication not only enhances interaction but also mitigates the risks of litigation over medical errors (Martins and Barros 2022).

In Brazil, there is a deeply entrenched culture of litigiousness, which often results in nearly all conflicts being brought before the courts, primarily due to ineffective communication between physicians and patients. Such issues arise not only during clinical consultations but also in the aftermath of adverse events, where the absence of proper disclosure and apologies exacerbates disputes.

However, efforts are currently underway to mitigate this litigious environment, supported by the National Council of Justice (*Conselho Nacional de Justiça*—CNJ).

This initiatives, aimed at promoting early-stage mediation and shifting the focus from adversarial proceedings to constructive dialogue, are likely to become increasingly visible and impactful over the coming years.

Regarding the second duty of information, there is the duty of documentation and confidentiality/secrecy. It is important to distinguish between a *secret*, which denotes information that must not be disclosed, and *confidentiality*, which refers to the safeguard that ensures such information remains secret. Physicians, as necessary confidants entrusted with matters inspiring trust, are subject to a duty of confidentiality. This duty is not merely an ethical obligation enshrined in the Brazilian Code of Medical Ethics but also constitutes a legal requirement or contractual obligation.

Physicians are required to maintain medical records contemporaneously with the provision of treatment. Physicians have a duty to prepare clinical records in accordance with Article 87 of the Brazilian Code of Medical Ethics (CEM – Resolution No. 2,217/2018). These records consist of a standardised and organised set of documents, including a permanent multidisciplinary health report. The clinical record serves as a historical document of physician's conduct and is one of the principal means of evidence in clinical practice, as the information recorded therein is presumed to be accurate.

Under Article 1 of Resolution No. 1,638/2002 of the Federal Council of Medicine, the information, signs, and images documented in medical records are derived from "facts, events, and situations concerning the patient's health and the care provided, possessing legal, confidential, and scientific characteristics, enabling communication among members of the multidisciplinary team and ensuring the continuity of care provided to the individual". Any corrections or additions to medical records are permissible only if the exact moment when the modification was made is expressly identified.

The records must contain all clinical data necessary for "the proper management of the case, to be completed during each evaluation in chronological order, including the date, time, signature, and the physician's registration number with the Regional Medical Council" (Article 87, § 1, CEM). A breach of this duty may result in ethical liability, as it constitutes a violation of the standards set forth in the Code of Medical Ethics, potentially subjecting the physician to disciplinary proceedings and sanctions imposed by the relevant professional regulatory body.

This duty of documentation has also repercussions in the civil sphere. In a landmark case decided in 2021 by the Brazilian Superior Court of Justice (Special Appeal No. 1.698.726/RJ), it was recognised that a physician's deliberate failure to adequately complete medical records not only breaches ethical obligations but also proves a lack of care and insufficient monitoring of the patient. The court emphasised that such conduct constitutes a failure to fulfil the duties inherent to the physician, which, if properly observed, "could have led to a different outcome" or, at the very least, demonstrated that "all expected and possible diligence had been employed, even if the harmful event was unavoidable".

The court further underscored that "the duty to record, in addition to its ethical connotation, constitutes a legal obligation". This obligation arises not only from the prohibitions enshrined in the Code of Medical Ethics (CEM) but also from "legal duties set forth in Law No. 12,843/2013, which governs the practice of medicine and, under Article 2, mandates practitioners to act with the utmost diligence and to apply the full extent of their professional capabilities". Additionally, the duty to document arises from the contractual good faith, highlighting its indispensable role in ensuring trust and accountability within the physician-patient relationship.

It is also important to note that, pursuant to Article 88 of the CEM, a physician is prohibited from denying a patient—or, if the patient is unable, their legal representative—access to their medical records or withholding a copy when requested.

Amid numerous controversies surrounding administrative requests for access to the medical records of deceased patients, the Federal Council of Medicine issued Recommendation CFM No. 03/2014. It regulates the release of medical and hospital records of deceased patients, authorising their provision to spouses and legitimate successors of the deceased, except in cases where the patient explicitly objected to the disclosure of their medical records after death (Article 1). In the civil sphere, the refusal to provide access to these documents may result in compensation for moral damages, as established by Statement No. 66 of the Third Health Law Conference held by the National Council of Justice in 2019.

On the other hand, physicians are bound by a duty of confidentiality, which prohibits them from disclosing to third parties any information regarding a patient contained in their medical records, test results, progress notes, or reports. On the subject of medical confidentiality, the Hippocratic Oath provides a meaningful illustration: "Whatever I see or hear in the course of my practice or in daily life, which ought not to be spoken of, I will keep secret".

The obligation to safeguard patient information is firmly established in the Code of Professional Ethics and regulations issued by the Brazilian Ministry of Health. Medical confidentiality, according França (2021), is "the obligation of silence imposed on physicians regarding facts they become aware of exclusively in the exercise of their professional activities, which are not imperative to disclose". In the same vein, Kfouri Neto (2024) explains that physicians have a duty "not to reveal facts learned through their profession that pertain to the private sphere of the patient". Accordingly, medical records and files must be preserved, and if they contain confidential information, access is limited solely to the attending physicians and the patients themselves.

Furthermore, the confidentiality of medical data is closely tied to the recognition of the right to informational self-determination. Physicians have a specific duty of care in handling such data, classified as sensitive under the Brazilian General Data Protection Law (LGPD) (Article 11, Section I). This duty includes ensuring transparency and providing clear information about which patient data will be processed, the purpose of such processing (principle of purpose limitation), and with whom the data will be shared (Faleiros Júnior 2019).

A breach of medical confidentiality constitutes a violation of the constitutional rights to privacy and intimacy (Article 5, Section X, of the Brazilian Federal Constitution) and may be characterised as a defect in the provision of medical or hospital services under Article 14 of the Brazilian Consumer Code. Both physicians and hospitals are responsible for safeguarding medical records and ensuring their non-disclosure.

From a legal perspective, the disclosure of confidential information about a patient's health is considered *damage in re ipsa* under Brazilian jurisprudence. This means that there is no requirement to prove non-material harm, as the mere act of disclosing sensitive health-related documents inherently constitutes the damage. The breach, therefore, gives rise to liability irrespective of evidence of specific harm, reinforcing the paramount importance of preserving sensitive health data and patient confidentiality – as well as the legal repercussions of failing to do so.

For example, in Civil Appeal No. 1000365-55.2020.8.26.0125, decided in 2021 by the São Paulo Court of Justice, the court reaffirmed that the unauthorised disclosure of a patient's medical information constitutes a breach of confidentiality and a violation of the patient's rights to privacy and intimacy. The decision emphasised that such a breach is classified as *damage in re ipsa*, where the harm is presumed and does not require proof of specific extrapatrimonial damages. This case serves as a precedent, illustrating the legal consequences of violating the duty of medical confidentiality and the strict liability imposed on healthcare providers in such situations.

However, it is important to note that professional confidentiality, while a guiding principle of the doctor-patient relationship, cannot be regarded as absolute. As Schaefer (2010) argues, while the scope of confidentiality continues to expand, certain circumstances arise that limit the extent of this duty to remain silent. Exceptions to the prohibition on disclosing medical records include the express authorisation of the patient (or their legal representative), compliance with a judicial order (legal obligation), and the need to present a defence in judicial or administrative proceedings, such as ethical-professional hearings involving the physician or healthcare professional and institution. This interpretation was affirmed in Civil Appeal No. 70077883106, decided in 2018 by the Rio Grande do Sul Court of Justice.

Furthermore, confidentiality may be breached for just cause, such as when disclosing information about a serious and transmissible disease is necessary to protect the life and health of third parties. These exceptions illustrate that while confidentiality is fundamental, it must sometimes yield to other competing legal and ethical considerations.

2.2.2 *Duties Related to Loyalty and Protection*

In the contractual relationship between physician and patient, the *duty of loyalty* in its broad sense is particularly significant, encompassing the (i) *duty of cooperation and loyalty stricto sensu* and the (ii) *duty to refrain from abuse or misuse of power.* Regarding item I, it is important to emphasise that the *duty to cooperate* is not restricted to a passive obligation to refrain from hindering the performance of contractual obligations. Instead, intersubjective collaboration may take an active form, such as when the parties mutually facilitate the fulfilment of obligations through the provision of documents or the performance of auxiliary tasks (Farias and Rosenvald 2021).

Cooperation between the parties is essential in the physician-patient contract and is demonstrated through the bilateral exchange of adequate information (Nilo 2020). When evaluating the conduct of the parties, the patient has a duty to cooperate by providing the physician with accurate details of their medical history, general habits, or other relevant factors necessary for a proper diagnosis or therapeutic recommendation. Consider a situation where a patient is a smoker but fails to disclose this information to the physician. The patient undergoes surgery, and the healing process is significantly impaired due to infected scars. In such a case, the physician cannot be held liable for failing to detail the specific risks associated with performing medical procedures on smokers, as the patient, when questioned, withheld this crucial information, thereby breaching their contractual duty of cooperation.

Throughout the legal relationship established between the patient and the physician, collaboration between the parties is essential to ensure the proper implementation of treatment. Regarding good faith and the duty of cooperation in contractual relations, the teachings of Tomasevicius Filho (2020, pp. 311–314) are particularly relevant:

> Observance of the duty of cooperation facilitates the formation, conclusion, and execution of contracts. Many contractual conflicts can be resolved. If cooperation is possible even between enemies in a war, there is all the more reason for the harmonisation of contractual interests through the duty of cooperation. By imposing cooperation between the parties, the principle of good faith prevents both from acting in bad faith, thereby preserving their relationship. (…) The principle of good faith – understood as a legal institution – enables the necessary conditions for cooperation to arise, for instance, through duties of consistency and disclosure. This increases the predictability of the other party's behaviour, providing individuals with better conditions for making decisions. (…) Based on the rules governing cooperation, it can be concluded that good faith requires an initiative to cooperate, prohibiting conduct that hinders the fulfilment of the other party's obligations and contributing to the maximisation of the benefits and utility that the transaction seeks to provide.

Consider, additionally, the case of a cancer patient who fails to provide the physician with previous medical test results or disclose that he has already undergone treatment with another professional for the same type of cancer. In this scenario, the oncological treatment itself may be compromised, as the physician remains unaware that the patient is dealing with a recurrence of the disease. This information is crucial for the physician to properly assess the patient's clinical condition and advise them on the most appropriate therapeutic options. As Nilo (2020) aptly notes, in the performance of a *treatment contract* – that is, a contract for the provision of medical services –, it is of little use for the physician to provide all necessary information for the patient to make a free and informed decision if the patient does not contribute truthful, accurate, and timely information to assist the physician in the diagnostic process and therapeutic approach.

From the perspective of the physician's role in fostering collaboration, it is crucial for the professional to maintain open dialogue and ensure that the patient has received all the necessary information to form a well-informed decision and, more importantly, that this information has been fully understood. When information and comprehension are lacking, as noted by Araújo and Fernandes (2021), there is an increased tendency for the relationship to result in legal disputes. Indeed, as mentioned before, a significant portion of lawsuits involving physicians and patients worldwide stems from failures in fulfilling the duty to inform, whether due to errors on the part of the physician or misunderstandings by the patient.

The *duty of loyalty* is intrinsically connected to the *duty of cooperation*, forming a foundational element of good faith in legal relationships. Under the doctrine of objective good faith, individuals are required to adhere to standards of integrity and honesty in their conduct. This duty is not merely a subjective expectation but rather an objective model of behaviour that reflects societal norms of fairness and ethical responsibility. In essence, the duty of loyalty demands that each person align their actions with a recognised social archetype—one that embodies the qualities of honesty, probity, and loyalty. It imposes both an obligation and a responsibility to act as a reasonable, upright individual would in similar circumstances. By adhering to this standard, parties in a legal or contractual relationship not only fulfil their duties but also contribute to building trust and fostering cooperative and equitable interactions (Nunes 2019; Reale 2003; Miragem 2007).

Regarding the *duty of loyalty* in contractual relations, the insights of Nunes (2019) are particularly noteworthy:

> In consumer legal relationships, the parameters of loyalty and honesty aim to establish balance between the parties—not economic balance, as some might suggest, but rather balance in contractual positions. This is because, within the complex of rights and duties of the parties, consumer relations typically involve an imbalance of power. Thus, when referring to objective good faith, one envisions faithful and loyal behaviour from each contracting party to ensure mutual respect. It is a principle designed to guarantee conduct free from abuse, obstruction, or harm, fostering cooperation to achieve the intended purpose of the contract and fulfil the interests of both parties.

This perspective highlights how the duty of loyalty, rooted in the principle of objective good faith, serves to mitigate power imbalances in consumer contracts, ensuring fairness and cooperation throughout the contractual relationship. Reale (2003, pp. 11–13) emphasises that:

> Objective good faith is characterised as a normative standard of loyal behaviour. Conduct, according to objective good faith, is thus understood as synonymous with public honesty. Understood in this way, good faith requires that individual or collective behaviour – whether in court or outside it – be assessed within the concrete set of circumstances of each case. (…) This is because what is at stake is the principle of trust: trust in the lawmakers and in those who draft agreements, and trust in the firm intent of their recipients to fulfil, without evasion or delay, what has been legislated or agreed upon.

Reale's perspective underscores that objective good faith is not merely an abstract concept but a practical principle that governs behaviour in legal and contractual relationships. It demands honesty and loyalty in actions, fostering trust both in the creation and performance of laws and agreements.

Contractual loyalty takes on particular significance in contract for medical services, where trust is regarded as one of the most critical principles. This is especially true given the presumption of the patient's hyper-vulnerability and the inherently trust-based nature of the relationship. The importance of trust is further highlighted in Portugal, where the *Theory of Trust* has been the subject of scholarly debate. Manuel A. Carneiro da Frada (2015) explains that the decision of one party to enter into a contract, as well as the terms of that contract, often hinges on the representations and expectations generated by the other party.

In medical service contract, the interplay between the duty of conduct derived from good faith and the protection of (reasonable) expectations is closely tied to the obligation to inform. This duty encompasses clear communication about the patient's condition, potential therapeutic measures, available alternatives, and possible effects. It reflects the broader principle of loyalty, where the physician must not only provide accurate and transparent information but also ensure that the patient's expectations are aligned with what can reasonably be achieved (Miragem 2007; Kfouri Neto 2024).

Such obligations are essential to maintaining the balance and integrity of the physician-patient relationship, ensuring that decisions are based on mutual trust and informed consent. By grounding the contractual relationship in these principles, both parties are better positioned to avoid misunderstandings and conflicts, fostering a collaborative approach to achieving the best possible outcomes.

Thus, it becomes evident that the duty of information and the duty of loyalty are closely intertwined. The discussion leans more towards the duty of loyalty when the physician not only fails to inform but also engages in active behaviour that creates false expectations of success regarding a specific medical intervention.

In such cases, the breach transcends a mere omission of information, as it involves conduct that undermines the trust inherent in the physician-patient relationship. By fostering unrealistic expectations, the physician compromises the patient's ability to make an informed and autonomous decision, violating both ethical and legal standards of medical practice. This breach of loyalty can lead to significant consequences, including damage to the patient's trust and an increased likelihood of legal disputes.

Finally, it is worth reflecting on the evolving nature of the duty of medical loyalty in the Digital Age in recent years. The standards governing the advertising practices of medical professionals have undergone significant transformation, particularly in the field of aesthetics, where the promotion of medical services on social media has become widespread. In many such online postings, physicians often project an ideal of beauty or therapeutic possibilities that are highly subjective, frequently showcasing results from previous patients. This practice can create an impression of guaranteed certainty in achieving outcomes that, depending on the patient, may be uncertain or even unattainable.

In this context, some Brazilian scholars argue that a breach of this duty of loyalty could give rise to an *obligation of result*, as it instils in the patient a legitimate expectation that a specific outcome will be replicated (Nogaroli and Mascarenhas 2022; Romeiro et al. 2022). Medical advertising that violates the duty of loyalty is subject to the deontological rules established by the Federal Council of Medicine (Resolution CFM No. 2.336/2023). Furthermore, any abusive advertising may also be scrutinised under Civil Law in accordance with the Brazilian Consumer Protection Code (CDC).

The law prohibits misleading and abusive advertising (Articles 6(IV), 30, 31, 35, 36, and 38 of the CDC). Non-compliance with these provisions may result in sanctions under Articles 56, 60, 67, 68, and 69 of the CDC. These regulations reinforce the importance of aligning medical advertising practices with ethical standards and legal obligations, ensuring that patients are not misled by unrealistic promises or deceptive promotional tactics.

The duty of loyalty *lato sensu* also encompasses the *duty to refrain from abuse or misuse of power*. In this regard, a physician's conduct must avoid any semblance of rashness, untimeliness, or imprudence. Overstepping therapeutic boundaries or resorting to overly risky measures constitutes a misuse of power, which must be unequivocally condemned. As França (2021) asserts, any particularly bold or innovative professional action, undertaken without the scope of informed consent, must be justified and legitimised by an imperative need to intervene.

A physician fails in their duty to refrain from abuse when, for example, they proceed hastily with surgery, bypass the essential participation of an anaesthetist throughout the procedure, or delegate complex medical tasks to technical staff or medical students (França 2021). Similarly, a misuse of power occurs when a physician conducts experiments on humans without therapeutic necessity, thereby endangering their life and health.

Nonetheless, as França (2021, pp. 273–274) cautions, "this does not mean that the future needs of humanity should be deprived of the advantages of scientific progress and the active participation of researchers". This highlights the critical balance between advancing medical innovation and adhering to ethical and legal responsibilities, ensuring that all actions remain firmly rooted in the patient's best interests while upholding the principles of trust, prudence, and accountability.

The duty to avoid abuse is compromised when vanity leads the physician to opt for *boldness*, abandoning conventional practice in favour of adopting a newly developed, unproven, or overly audacious technique to showcase an unusual professional ability. On this matter, Aguiar Dias is unequivocal (2006): "the physician has no right to conduct medical experiments on the human body unless compelled by the necessity to combat a condition that poses a serious threat to the patient". It is essential to prioritise patient safety and well-being over personal ambition or professional recognition, ensuring that medical decisions are guided by necessity and evidence-based practice rather than by a desire for notoriety.

In this context, it is important to note that, according to the jurisprudence of the Brazilian Superior Court of Justice, there is a clear distinction between experimental treatment and innovative treatment, which the last one involves the use of technology through modern equipment or techniques. This distinction is reflected in a 2013 decision (Special Appeal No. 1.320.805/SP), which involved a case of robot-assisted surgery: "experimental treatment is one for which there is no medical-scientific proof of efficacy, as opposed to a procedure that, although performed with modern equipment, is recognised by science and selected by the physician as the most appropriate method to preserve the patient's physical integrity and ensure their full recovery". The Superior Court recognised the substantial body of medical-scientific evidence supporting the use of robotic assistance in surgical procedures, particularly the efficacy of laparoscopic radical prostatectomy as essential to preventing the metastasis of the neoplasm in this patient's specific case. Accordingly, the health insurance provider was ordered to cover the costs of the procedure performed with robotic assistance.

This judicial interpretation highlights the need to carefully differentiate between untested experimental methods and scientifically validated innovative approaches, ensuring that patients receive treatments grounded in recognised medical standards.

Furthermore, rulings from the Court of Justice of the State of Paraná have examined a physician's conduct when performing a procedure (Civil Appeal No. 0023638-48.2017.8.16.0001, decided on 11 July 2022) or prescribing medication (Criminal Appeal No. 0066631-70.2021.8.16.0000, decided on 27 November 2021) using techniques prohibited by the Federal Council of Medicine. Both decisions emphasise that, in such cases, "not even the patient's consent is effective," as "reckless experimentation that turns the patient into a test subject cannot be tolerated. However, this does not mean restricting the freedom of professionals to explore new scientific methods [provided they have been scientifically proven effective]".

The physician's freedom to act is framed by best practices and the principles of medical ethics. Aguiar Dias (2006) asserts that while physicians have the right to innovate and even employ treatments by analogy, their attempts must be conscientious and scrupulously guided by scientific principles. They cannot involve purely random experiments, as the human body is not raw material for experimentation, not even in the purely scientific domain.

Medical treatment must adhere to the standards generally recognised at the time the treatment is provided. In other words, physician's conduct should align with the prevailing paradigm of knowledge adopted by the medical community at the time the contract is formed. The physician's salutary freedom of action, as emphasised by Facchini Neto and Soares (2021), depends on a necessary anchoring in science—specifically, evidence-based medicine—as well as adherence to relevant regulatory requirements. This ensures that innovation remains grounded in scientific rigour and ethical responsibility.

Even if the patient is duly informed about the surgical procedure to which they will be subjected, their consent, while present, becomes invalid. This is because a patient's consent is not considered acceptable for professional acts that do not constitute best practices. As Soares (2021) argues, it is not legitimate to consent to acts that are not technically recognised or scientifically supported. Therefore, when follow-up research confirms the ineffectiveness of certain treatments or procedures, the physician's actions lose their scientific basis and may result in medical liability. This underscores the principle that medical practice must always align with evidence-based standards to ensure both ethical and legal compliance.

These rulings underscore the delicate balance between safeguarding patient rights and fostering scientific progress, highlighting that medical innovation must consistently align with established ethical and legal standards.

Finally, attention turns to the analysis of the duty of protection in the physician-patient contractual relationship, which can be divided into two key components: (i) the duty of up-to-date knowledge and (ii) the duty of care and vigilance.

The duty of protection within the medical services agreement explicitly encompasses the obligation to maintain up-to-date knowledge and skills, as provided in the Brazilian Code of Medical Ethics (CME – Resolution CFM No. 2.217/2018). Among the fundamental principles of medical practice (Chapter I, Clause V), it is stated that medical professionals are responsible for "continuously enhancing their knowledge and using the best of scientific progress for the benefit of patients and society". Additionally, under Article 32, it is expressly prohibited for physicians to "fail to use all available means for the promotion of health and the prevention, diagnosis, and treatment of diseases that are scientifically recognised and within their reach, in favour of the patient".

The obligation to maintain up-to-date knowledge and skills is frequently examined in cases concerning medical malpractice, particularly lack of skill, which is characterised by the failure to observe technical standards or professional unpreparedness (França 2021).

Physicians are obligated to remain current with developments in the profession through continuous medical education, which should be viewed not merely as a right but also as a professional obligation. It is essential to assess this obligation within the specific circumstances of each case, considering factors such as the workplace setting, available resources, the physician's professional profile, the state of scientific knowledge, the patient's overall condition, and the complexity and significance of the medical act performed.

As will be addressed throughout this book, physicians' obligation to stay updated is intrinsically linked to the evolving nature of medical science and the rapid pace of technological advancements in healthcare. Innovations such as artificial intelligence (AI), robotic surgery, and personalised medicine require not only technical proficiency but also ethical awareness and a commitment to integrating these tools responsibly into clinical practice. This dynamic environment highlights the critical importance of continuous medical education as a cornerstone of patient safety and the provision of evidence-based care.

From a legal standpoint, failure to fulfil the obligation to maintain up-to-date knowledge may constitute a breach of professional duty, particularly when such failure results in harm to a patient. Brazilian courts have increasingly recognised that adhering to outdated practices or neglecting to adopt available and established advancements may constitute medical negligence. This recognition emphasises the dual responsibility of the individual physician to pursue ongoing education and the healthcare institution to provide access to adequate training and resources, enabling physicians to meet this essential standard.

The assessment of this obligation requires a nuanced and case-specific analysis. Considerations such as the physician's area of expertise, the accessibility of continuing education opportunities, and the availability of resources in the specific practice environment are all relevant. For instance, a general practitioner operating in a resource-limited rural setting may encounter different obstacles compared to a specialist working in a technologically advanced urban hospital. Such contextual analysis ensures that the obligation remains equitable while upholding a high standard of diligence and professional competence.

Turning to the final duty of conduct expected of physicians, attention must be directed to the *duty of care and vigilance*. This contractual duty is breached when a physician fails to respond to a patient's call or neglects required visits (Aguiar Dias 2006). It arises from the trust-based relationship between physician and patient, obligating the doctor to safeguard the patient's health with dignity and prudence, ensuring that care is provided, especially in urgent or emergency situations where no other qualified physician is available. Nonetheless, the physician is entitled to withdraw from care when the professional relationship becomes untenable, provided adequate prior notice is given.

With respect to the duty of vigilance, emphasis is placed on the physician's responsibility to attentively monitor the progression of a patient's clinical condition. This includes recommending a timely transfer to a hospital with better facilities when necessary (Kfouri Neto 2024). In addition, the duty extends to ensuring proper guidance and follow-up care during the postoperative period. França (2021) has stated that a physician breaches the duty of vigilance by failing to address the specific demands of each circumstance. Such failures may arise through patient abandonment, unjustified treatment restrictions, or delays in necessary referrals.

Conversely, compliance with the duty of care is observed when physicians adhere to established clinical protocols and guidelines as standards of professional conduct. Any deviation from these standards, unless adequately justified, creates a presumption of breach of contractual obligations. In jurisdictions such as Brazil and Portugal, non-compliance with established professional norms is considered *prima facie* evidence of negligence (Pereira 2015).

The duty of care, encompassing the obligation to preserve life, prohibits the use of methods intended to accelerate death, even at the patient's or their legal representative's request. On the other hand, breaches of this duty may also arise through the wrongful prolongation of life, such as a failure to recommend palliative care in cases involving irreversible or terminal conditions (Dadalto 2022; Sá and Moureira 2015).

It is also relevant to acknowledge that a physician may refuse to provide care by invoking the right to conscientious objection, a principle grounded in professional ethics. This right allows physicians to abstain from actions that conflict with their moral, ethical, religious, or personal beliefs, without the need to disclose the specific reasons behind their refusal.

Milagres (2010) has noted that the trust inherent in the doctor-patient relationship permits physicians to decline care that violates personal values. Just as patients have the right to choose their healthcare provider, the physician is not obliged to render services that conflict with their conscience, except in cases of urgency or emergency, the absence of another professional, or where refusal would harm the patient's health. In such circumstances, a failure to act may constitute a breach of the duty of care.

An interesting Brazilian case concerning the debate about duty of care and conscientious objection occurred during the COVID-19 pandemic. A patient requested the prescription of a so-called "COVID kit" for prophylactic treatment, offering to sign any necessary consent forms. The attending physician, citing the absence of clinical indications for the disease and a lack of scientific evidence supporting the treatment, declined the request. The patient subsequently threatened legal action and published a social media post naming the physician and linking to an article titled "COVID-19 deaths in Brazil may reach 88,300 in August", implying that such deaths were attributable to doctors' refusal to prescribe off-label medications.

Legal action was initiated by the physician in 2021 before the Small Claims Court of the city of Santos, under the jurisdiction of the São Paulo Court of Justice, Judgment No. 1010084-11.2020.8.26.0562, seeking the permanent removal of the publication.

The court ruled in favour of the physician and ordered the patient to pay compensation for moral damages. The judgment affirmed the physician's authority to determine the appropriate course of treatment, establishing that the patient cannot impose personal beliefs on the medical opinion. While patients retain the right to seek second opinions or alternative consultations, no circumstances justify compelling a physician to act against their professional and ethical standards.

Regarding the *duty of care*, the classic teachings of Miranda and Cavalcante (1954) highlight the importance of recognising that a higher standard of diligence is typically expected from professionals in specialised fields: the negligence of a specialist lawyer, for example, must be assessed more rigorously than that of a generalist. The same principle applies to physicians, engineers, architects, and other professionals whose fields permit specialisation.

This view has been endorsed in 2001 by Brazil's Superior Court of Justice in a landmark judgment (Special Appeal No. 316.283/PR) delivered by the late Minister Ruy Rosado de Aguiar, which distinguished the standard of diligence required of resident doctors compared to their supervising physicians: "the assertion that all doctors are equal under the law is not supported, as individual circumstances and the context of professional activity must always be considered".

Resident doctors are general practitioners undergoing training to specialise in specific fields. Miragem (2007) has argued that standards of technical competence must reflect the professional's level of expertise, with higher expectations for specialists than for generalists. Thus, residents should be afforded greater leniency, and the same standard of care should not be applied to them as to supervising physicians (Kfouri Neto 2024).

As further noted by Kfouri Neto (2022), residents, as doctors in training, should not be placed in situations for which they are unprepared. Consequently, when evaluating the duty of care and diligence, Machado and Vianna (2022) emphasise the need to assess each case individually, considering the professional levels involved—whether academic, resident, or specialist—and, where appropriate, mitigating liability according to the degree of fault.

2.2.3 *Professional Accountability and Legal Consequences of Breaching Duties, with Focus on Informed Consent*

The violation of any of the six duties of physician's conduct arising from the principle of contractual good faith, as discussed in the previous subchapter of this book, carries consequences established by law. In the civil sphere, liability is governed by the provisions of the Brazilian Civil and Consumer Codes; in the ethical sphere, responsibility is determined in accordance with the Brazilian Code of Medical Ethics.

As mentioned before, Brazilian legal doctrine on Medical Law frequently explores the principle of good faith and the corresponding duties of physician's conduct, such as loyalty, disclosure, cooperation, and professional development. However, it often neglects to address in greater detail the legal implications of breaches of these duties.

The exception is the duty of information, which is no longer regarded merely as an ancillary obligation but is widely recognised as an independent source of liability. This duty constitutes an integral part of the physician's primary obligation to uphold the patient's right to self-determination and carries an existential dimension, as discussed in the preceding section of this book.

For a physician to be held civilly liable for failing to obtain a patient's informed consent, Kfouri Neto (2024) emphasises that an evident causal relationship must be established between the lack of (or incorrect) information provided and the harm suffered. In this context, the damage must directly result from the deficient or absent information, with a causal nexus linking the two. The physician may be held liable for moral damages if they failed to warn the patient of a specific risk that subsequently materialised. Such damages are awarded to compensate for the infringement of the patient's right to self-determination.

Dantas (2024) further clarifies that, in establishing causation, the patient must demonstrate that the harm stems from a risk about which the patient should have been informed, enabling them to make an informed decision about accepting or declining the treatment. However, if the harm that the patient would have suffered by refusing the treatment outweighed the harm resulting from the intervention, the lack of information becomes immaterial (Kfouri Neto 2024).

It must be shown that a reasonable person, when properly informed, would have refused the treatment. Compensation is not justified if, under the same circumstances and with the same information, another reasonable person would have agreed to undergo the therapy. Dantas (2024) also underscores the importance of judicial analysis in distinguishing between two critical issues: the absence of adequate information and the causal link to the harm suffered by the patient. The judgment must clearly delineate the origin of the claim for damages, ensuring that the basis for compensation is well-defined.

By contrast, breaches of other ancillary duties or duties of conduct also warrant careful legal analysis. The position defended in this book is that such breaches must be subject to a subjective assessment, as will be demonstrated below.

Physician's liability is defined as an act or omission involving negligence, recklessness, or lack of competence in fulfilling obligations relating to diagnosis, prognosis, or treatment. With respect to civil liability in medical practice, Kfouri Neto (2024) asserts that fault remains an essential element for establishing liability. The imposition of strict liability within the physician is, as a matter of principle, untenable. Even in cases involving alleged breaches of ancillary or conduct-related duties, strict liability would undermine the personal and trust-based nature of the doctor-patient relationship, which is central to the practice of medicine.

Furthermore, *duties of conduct take on a qualified nature within the contractual relationship between physician and patient*, often approaching the status of primary obligations. For instance, with regard to the duties of loyalty (abstention from abusive practices) and protection (up-to-date knowledge), the following scenarios may be considered:

(i) A physician uses forceps to facilitate the passage of a baby's head through the vaginal canal or employs the Kristeller manoeuvre (applying pressure on the mother's abdomen to push the baby out); or
(ii) A healthcare professional performs a particular treatment and successfully cures the patient but employs an excessively painful and invasive technique, despite the availability of more modern and less distressing alternatives in medical science that could achieve the same result.

In both cases, it becomes apparent that performance was rendered in an unsatisfactory manner, violating instrumental duties of loyalty, protection, and professional development, all of which are closely connected to the diligent fulfilment of the primary obligation (whether conducting the delivery or administering medical treatment).

In a traditional private relationship, it is often easier to delineate between the content of a primary obligation and ancillary obligations. However, in the physician-patient relationship, secondary duties take on a qualified form and are inextricably linked to, and at times indistinguishable from, the principal obligation itself. For example, while confidentiality might be merely advisable in the context of a commercial merger negotiation, it is a fundamental presumption in the physician-patient relationship.

It becomes evident in both cases that, although the primary medical objective was technically achieved—whether facilitating childbirth or effecting a cure—the manner in which performance was rendered was unsatisfactory. This resulted in breaches of ancillary duties of loyalty, protection, and professional development. These duties, while formally classified as accessory obligations, are intrinsically connected to the diligent execution of the principal obligation, whether conducting the delivery or administering treatment. Indeed, within the physician-patient relationship, the distinction between primary and secondary obligations becomes increasingly blurred. Unlike in ordinary contractual relationships—where accessory duties may serve a merely supportive role—medical duties of conduct assume a qualified, and at times, autonomous character. They are inextricably linked to the very purpose of the contract, which is not merely the technical delivery of a service but the comprehensive safeguarding of the patient's health, dignity, and well-being. This re-interpretation of physician's duties of conduct is grounded in the framework of *Person-Centred Medicine*, where the patient's individual needs and dignity are at the core of medical practice.

It is necessary to recognise that the needs of contemporary society require differentiated protection for patrimonial and existential situations, as they are grounded in distinct underlying principles. In this context, Bizelli (2018) and Basan (2020) explain that the evolution of contractual models has given rise to the concept of fundamental rights within private relationships. As Soares (2021) asserts, the medical service contract constitutes an *existential agreement.*

In contracts for the provision of medical services, as will be explored in detail in the next chapter of this book, negligence constitutes the legal basis for the professional's liability. Consequently, it is argued that breaches of duties of conduct must be assessed subjectively too, as mandated by law under § 4 of Article 14 of the Brazilian Consumer Code. Failure to adhere to this principle risks undermining the viability of the medical profession and depersonalising the physician-patient relationship.

It is also important to note that in cases where proven negligence arises from not fulfilling the principal obligation (acting diligently in diagnosis, prognosis, or treatment), Brazilian courts have traditionally refrained from conducting a detailed analysis of ancillary duties. However, a gradual shift in this approach can now be observed. Breaches of physician's duties of conduct (such as loyalty, trust, cooperation, and vigilance) are increasingly being considered as relevant factors in judicial reasoning, particularly as a criterion for aggravating liability and increasing awards for non-pecuniary damages.

This consideration would align with the assessment of the degree of professional fault in the second phase of the so-called *bifurcated method of damage quantification* applied by Brazilian courts. In this context, it is relevant to take into account that the professional was not only negligent but also failed to comply with ancillary duties (Maranhão and Nogaroli 2022). As an example, a notable Brazilian case decided by the Court of Justice of the State of Paraná in 2022 (Civil Appeal No. 0023638-48.2017.8.16.0001) illustrates this principle. In this judgment, in which I had the opportunity to serve as a judicial assistant to the reporting appellate judge, the court upheld the physician's liability for negligence commited during a treatment period involving three bariatric surgeries.

In the quantification of damages, the physician's conduct was evaluated based on the high degree of professional fault demonstrated. The surgeries were performed using a technique prohibited by the Federal Council of Medicine (CFM), which carries a high risk of complications (a violation of the duty of care). The technique was repeated on two occasions despite the patient's unfavourable health condition and her expressed desire to reverse the procedure (a violation of the duty to refrain from abuse of authority or misuse of power). Furthermore, the physician failed to inform the patient about the CFM's prohibition of the technique and the associated risks (a violation of the duty of disclosure).

The Court also considered the physician's misconduct in presenting the procedure to the patient as having a primarily aesthetic purpose, coupled with promises of weight loss and the simultaneous performance of aesthetic surgeries alongside the bariatric procedure. Additionally, it noted the physician's repeated appearances in the media, engaging in sensationalist advertising and promoting the method through celebrity endorsements. This created false expectations and misled the patient into continuing with the technique even after she had requested its reversal (a violation of the duty of loyalty).

The evaluation of the physician's conduct in this case led the Paraná Court of Justice to reject the defendant's request to reduce the compensation awarded. The judgment explicitly addressed the numerous breaches of physician's duties of conduct arising from contractual good faith and highlighted that the awarded damages, in principle, should have been recalibrated to reflect the specific circumstances of the case. The court further emphasised the pedagogical function of moral damages in such instances. Had the claimant appealed, the damages would have been significantly increased, given the gravity and extent of the violations committed by the physician.

2.3 European Law on Patient Consent: Jurisprudential and Doctrinal Perspectives

The evolving doctor-patient relationship within the Brazilian legal framework, as explored in Sects. 2.1 and 2.2, has been profoundly influenced by European legal systems. This influence is particularly evident in the new paradigms surrounding patient autonomy and informed consent. These concepts, rooted in European jurisprudence, have shaped the understanding of patient rights and the duties of healthcare professionals, providing a comparative backdrop for analysing global developments in Medical Law.

This subchapter aims to provide a broad overview of how informed consent is understood within European Medical Law. It does so primarily by examining key judicial decisions that exemplify and reinforce the principles discussed thus far, demonstrating the evolution of global legal doctrine concerning this topic. Such an approach not only highlights the influence of landmark cases but also underscores the universal trend towards prioritising the patient's right to self-determination in healthcare decisions.

In parallel with the global phenomena explored in the previous subchapters, the growing emphasis on *patient autonomy* has also gained *worldwide prominence*, aligned with a *broader cultural shift towards consumerism*. This trend is evident across various legal systems and healthcare models. In the United States, the concept of *patients as consumers* was initially introduced by medical economists as early as the 1930s (Mold 2015). However, it was not until the 1960s that this notion gained widespread acceptance. In Europe, the trend towards the *marketisation of healthcare* became more pronounced in the 1980s (Shutzberg 2021). These developments coincided with the rise of an individualistic framework of autonomy, heavily influenced by Kantian principles of self-governance and self-reliance. The primary aim was to shield patients from the paternalistic tendencies of traditional medical practice, which often placed them at a significant disadvantage when negotiating with healthcare professionals wielding superior expertise and power.

Over the decades, there has been an increasing recognition of patient rights, supported by numerous patient advocacy organisations. These groups championed the principle that the patient—or *consumer*—must remain at the core of healthcare systems (Mold 2010; Van der Zeijden 2000). Today, the *integration of a consumer-focused framework into healthcare systems* is evident across all European Union Member States, where it is now considered a foundational aspect of EU health law (Hervey and McHale 2015).

The shift towards this consumeristic and individualistic healthcare model is perhaps best encapsulated by the UK Supreme Court's decision in *Montgomery v. Lanarkshire Health Board* (2015). The Supreme Court held that healthcare providers must disclose all material risks associated with medical treatment, tailored to the specific circumstances and preferences of each patient. As analysed by Sandip Talukdar in the article *Ensuring Risk Awareness of Vulnerable Patients in the Post-Montgomery Era* (2020), the judgement marks a decisive shift away from paternalistic models of care, embracing a patient-centred approach that prioritises autonomy and informed decision-making.

The case itself arose when Nadine Montgomery, a diabetic patient, was not informed of the increased risk of shoulder dystocia associated with natural delivery—a condition where the baby's shoulders become stuck during vaginal delivery, which can result in severe complications, including injuries to both the baby and the mother.

Despite the known risks associated with diabetes in pregnancy, Montgomery's doctor chose not to inform her, believing that discussing the risk might lead her to opt for a Caesarean section (C-section), which the doctor deemed unnecessary. Montgomery proceeded with a natural delivery, during which shoulder dystocia occurred, resulting in permanent injuries to her child, including cerebral palsy. The patient argued that had she been informed of the increased risk, she would have chosen to undergo a C-section, thereby avoiding the complication and the resulting injuries to her child.

The UK Supreme Court ruled in favour of Montgomery, marking a significant shift in Medical Law regarding informed consent. The court firmly established that a medical professional's duty of care extends beyond mere clinical expertise to include the full disclosure of material risks associated with treatment options—particularly those that could influence a patient's decision-making process. The concept of *material risk* was clarified as one that a reasonable patient in the same position would likely consider significant. The court emphasised that doctors must take into account the individual circumstances of the patient, including their values, preferences, and concerns.

The court recognised that patients are no longer mere passive recipients of care but are active agents endowed with rights, making informed decisions based on comprehensive information. This recognition aligns with broader global trends that *frame patients as consumers capable of exercising choice*, a perspective that has significantly influenced the development of healthcare systems.

This shift from a paternalistic framework, in which doctors unilaterally determined what was *best* for patients, to a model that *empowers individuals to assess their own risks and benefits*, is emblematic of a broader cultural transformation in healthcare. The impact of this case law extends beyond the UK, reflecting global trends towards patient autonomy and consumerism in healthcare systems, where patients are viewed not only as beneficiaries of care but as individuals capable of making critical, informed choices about their own health.

In the last years, this consumer-centric dynamic is particularly evident in transnational contexts, such as medical tourism and the free movement of patients within the EU. As noted by Pattinson (2017), Medical Law must now consider the growing consumerism of patients, the associated phenomena of medical tourism, and the impact of market forces. In this context, the *commodification of healthcare intertwines consumerism and care*, with patients not only asserting their rights but also engaging in a buyer-seller relationship. Although this paradigm represents an extreme form of consumerism, it underscores the profound transformation of the doctor–patient relationship in recent decades. Now the key question is how these shifts will adapt and evolve with the incorporation of artificial intelligence into healthcare practices, as will be investigated in the next Chapters of this book.

In conclusion, the European approach to informed consent, as exemplified by the Montgomery case and its aftermath, demonstrates a commitment to safeguarding patient autonomy in an increasingly complex healthcare environment. This shift reflects broader global trends, from the rise of consumerism to the challenges posed by emerging technologies, offering valuable insights for the future of Medical Law.

Regarding regulation, within the European Union framework, the explicit recognition of the right to informed consent is enshrined in the Charter of Fundamental Rights of the European Union (2000). Prior to this, the European Parliament had adopted the European Charter of Patients' Rights (1984), which outlined a set of rights aimed at safeguarding individuals undergoing medical treatment. The Oviedo Convention (1997) further cemented the principle of informed consent as a prerequisite for medical interventions, highlighting the need to respect human dignity in healthcare. Later, the European Charter of Patients' Rights (2002), drafted by the Active Citizenship Network, was positively received by the European Economic and Social Committee, which issued its Opinion on Patients' Rights (2008). The Patients' Rights in Cross-Border Healthcare Directive (2011) safeguarded access to clear information on treatment options and risks for patients seeking care across Member States. The EU Clinical Trials Regulation (2014) reinforced this right within the context of medical research, mandating transparent and comprehensive information for participants. Similarly, the General Data Protection Regulation (2016) addressed informed consent in relation to the processing of sensitive health data, ensuring autonomy and the right to withdraw consent. Together, these instruments underscore the European Union's commitment to a robust, patient-centred healthcare framework that prioritises transparency, autonomy, and dignity.

Building on these European-level frameworks, the analysis now shifts to national documents and case law from EU Member States, starting with France. Within the French context, it is notable that in 2010, the Chambre Civile of the Cour de Cassation, the highest judicial body in civil matters, delivered a landmark ruling on the issue of informed consent in healthcare (*First Civil Chamber, Decision of 3 June 2010, Case No. 09-13.591*). This judgment established that the failure to provide adequate information to a patient constitutes an autonomous harm, even in the absence of concrete damage to the patient's health. The decision reinforced the importance of informed consent as a fundamental right linked to human dignity.

The case involved a patient who claimed not to have received sufficient information about the risks and alternatives of a medical procedure. Although there was no direct harm to their health, the patient argued that the lack of informed consent violated their fundamental rights. The central issue was whether the lack of sufficient medical information could be recognised as harm in itself or whether it was necessary to demonstrate actual harm to health to justify compensation.

The Cour de Cassation ruled that "the non-compliance with the duty of information causes harm to the person to whom the information was legally owed, which, under Article 1382 of the French Civil Code, the judge cannot leave without compensation". This judgment explicitly establishes that it is unnecessary to prove concrete physical or psychological damage to justify reparation for the breach of the duty to inform. The violation of the patient's right to be informed constitutes an autonomous harm, grounded in the principles of human dignity and the right to self-determination.

The court highlighted that the patient's dignity, which includes their ability to make autonomous decisions regarding their body and health, forms the cornerstone of informed consent. This duty is not merely a technical obligation for healthcare professionals but a fundamental right protecting the patient's autonomy. Consequently, the absence of informed consent—regardless of whether any physical or psychological harm occurred—was deemed sufficient to warrant compensation, reinforcing the legal and ethical importance of transparency in medical practice.

The decision was innovative because it diverged from the predominant French jurisprudence at the time. In many previous cases, French courts had decided that the absence of informed consent would only lead to compensation if there was actual harm to the patient's health, prioritising a direct causal link between the lack of information and the harm suffered. By recognising the absence of informed consent as independent harm, the Cour de Cassation expanded legal protection for patients and affirmed that the right to information is essential for the exercise of valid consent. The violation of this right, on its own, gave rise to the need for compensation, irrespective of any medical consequences.

The legal foundation for the decision was rooted in fundamental principles of French law, such as Article 16-3 of the Civil Code, which enshrines respect for the integrity of the human body and stipulates that medical interventions may only be carried out with the free and informed consent of the patient. Additionally, human dignity, recognised as a general principle of French law and an essential cornerstone of its legal framework, was central to justifying the recognition of autonomous harm.

Although progressive, the decision sparked debates among academics and legal professionals. Some argued that it strengthened patients' rights by placing human dignity and self-determination at the heart of the doctor-patient relationship, while also promoting greater accountability for healthcare professionals in fulfilling their informational duties. On the other hand, criticisms were raised regarding the potential increase in litigation, which could impose a disproportionate burden on medical professionals, as well as the difficulty of justifying financial compensation in the absence of material or physical harm.

The French decision reflects broader European trends, such as those observed in the United Kingdom, where informed consent is also treated as a fundamental right. Cases like Montgomery v Lanarkshire Health Board (2015) emphasise the duty of doctors to provide clear and personalised information about risks, prioritising the autonomy of the patient. However, the recognition of autonomous harm without impact on health has not yet been widely established in the UK.

The greater prominence of the Montgomery decision compared to the French ruling of 2010 can be attributed to factors such as the common law system, which allows judicial precedents to influence jurisdictions globally, whereas the French ruling is limited to its civil law framework. Furthermore, Montgomery repositioned the patient as the central figure in decisions regarding their healthcare, breaking away from the previous physician-centred standard and imposing a more rigorous duty to disclose relevant risks, which attracted significant attention in the medical and legal fields worldwide. The compelling personal narrative of the Montgomery case also generated greater public empathy and recognition.

Conversely, the French decision is significant for its recognition of human dignity as a fundamental right, establishing that the absence of informed consent constitutes autonomous harm even in the absence of damage to health. However, its lower visibility outside France reflects the more technical and abstract context of its reasoning and the lack of an immediate practical impact comparable to that of Montgomery.

Nevertheless, both cases represent advances in the protection of patients' rights, albeit with distinct approaches and repercussions. As mentioned above, The 2010 ruling by the Cour de Cassation was a significant step forward in safeguarding patients' rights in France. It reaffirmed informed consent as a cornerstone of human dignity and an essential obligation in medical practice, even in the absence of harm to the patient's health. This judgment remains a milestone in the evolution of jurisprudence on medical liability and human rights, consolidating self-determination as a fundamental element in the doctor-patient relationship.

On a broader European scale, numerous countries have implemented legislation addressing the duty to inform, with significant examples including recent regulatory advancements in France, Italy, Spain, and Belgium. These laws often reflect the influence of broader European norms, such as those enshrined in the European Convention on Human Rights and the Council of Europe's Convention on Human Rights and Biomedicine (Oviedo Convention). There is a shared commitment across European jurisdictions to fostering transparency, empowering patient autonomy, and embedding these principles as integral elements of contemporary Medical Law.

According to Pereira (2015), a *system of opt-out* or *presumed consent* is in force in several European countries, with different nuances, including Portugal, Spain, France, Italy, Austria, Belgium, among others. Within the European Union, in 2010, 24 countries had implemented some form of presumed consent (opt-out). Presumed consent means that, in specific situations, individuals are assumed to have agreed to certain medical interventions, unless they have explicitly stated otherwise, often through formal registration of their refusal. Conversely, Anglo-Saxon and Germanic countries, influenced by Protestant traditions that emphasise individualism and explicit consent (where actions require clear and affirmative agreement), generally adopt *opt-in systems*. This is the case in the United Kingdom, Germany, the United States, and some Scandinavian countries, where explicit consent is required even for the use of a cadaver.

Another interesting issue is that, in the context of European Civil Law countries, the principles surrounding the burden of proof in cases involving informed consent reflect the prevailing approach to patient autonomy and medical liability. As Pereira (2015) highlights, in jurisdictions such as Austria, Germany, France, Belgium, Italy, Portugal, and Spain, the burden of proof regarding the disclosure of information rests with the medical professional.

It is worth noting that this principle also applies in Brazil, where the burden of proof similarly lies with the healthcare provider. This responsibility is grounded in the recognition that medical treatment, as an interference with the patient's physical integrity, requires valid and informed consent to be legally and ethically justified. By imposing this burden, the legal systems of these jurisdictions ensure that healthcare providers demonstrate they have fulfilled their duty to adequately inform patients, enabling autonomous decision-making and safeguarding patients' rights. In Brazil, however, there is a growing application of the concept of *dynamic burden of proof* (*carga dinâmica do ônus da prova*), which assigns the burden to the party best positioned to provide the necessary evidence. This approach has been codified in Article 373, §1° of the 2015 Brazilian Code of Civil Procedure, allowing judges to allocate the evidentiary burden dynamically based on the circumstances of the case.

Under Spanish domestic law, the Basic Law 41/2002, enacted in 2002, stands out as the key legislation governing patient autonomy and establishing rights and obligations concerning clinical information and documentation (hereinafter referred to as the *Patients' Rights Law* or PRL). This legislation was introduced to address several deficiencies in the earlier General Health Law 14/1986 (GHL), particularly in areas such as informed consent, access to health information, and the regulation of clinical documentation, including the management of medical records and associated materials.

As articulated in Article 1, the PRL seeks to regulate the rights and responsibilities of patients, healthcare users, medical professionals, and public healthcare institutions, specifically in matters concerning patient autonomy and access to clinical information. The law aims to provide a comprehensive framework to safeguard these rights during healthcare interventions. While Article 10 of the GHL previously recognised certain patient rights in relation to public health authorities, these provisions were deemed inadequate due to evolving societal attitudes towards patient autonomy and a growing emphasis on the need for clarity, enforceability, and effective protection of such rights. This shift has been reinforced by both national and international legal developments, most notably the Council of Europe's Convention on Human Rights and Biomedicine (CHRB), adopted in 1997 and ratified by Spain in 2000.

The CHRB represents a milestone in the protection of patients' rights, as noted by Requejo (2003). It not only establishes a shared framework for safeguarding human dignity and individual rights in the fields of biology and medicine but also constitutes the first binding international legal instrument in this domain. The ratification of the CHRB necessitated reforms in Spanish healthcare legislation, as several provisions of the GHL conflicted with its principles, and certain rights enshrined in the CHRB, such as informed consent and the right to privacy, were previously unaddressed in Spanish law.

Chapter 2 of the PRL explicitly codifies the right to receive health information. Article 4.1 states that "patients, as part of any medical intervention, have the right to be informed of all relevant details concerning their health, subject to legal exceptions". Additionally, "as a general rule, this information shall be conveyed verbally, with corresponding documentation entered into the patient's clinical record".

In line with expert opinions and established jurisprudence (Ortega et al. 2004), the PRL sets verbal communication as the default mode for providing health information and obtaining informed consent, except in cases involving surgical procedures, invasive diagnostic methods, or interventions presenting significant and predictable risks or adverse consequences for the patient's health. Furthermore, informed consent is not required in situations where: (i) non-intervention would pose a risk to public health; or (ii) an urgent, life-threatening condition precludes the possibility of obtaining authorisation.

By aligning Spanish healthcare law with the principles of the CHRB, the PRL underscores the essentiality of patient autonomy and informed consent. This law not only fills critical gaps left by earlier legislation but also reinforces the legal and ethical duties of medical professionals, ensuring greater transparency, accountability, and respect for patients' rights in the provision of healthcare services.

In 2019, the Spanish legal scholar Manuel Ortiz Fernández, in his article *The Civil Liability in the Health Field Derived from the Informed Consent*, analysed a paradigmatic Spanish decision that demonstrates the evolving understanding of informed consent in the country. The Supreme Court (STS), in its ruling of 26 May 2015 (*EDJ 2015/86912, Cassation Appeal 2548/2013*), provided a detailed and authoritative examination of the principles underpinning informed consent and its violation. It was emphasised that:

> Regarding the lack or absence of informed consent, this Court has repeatedly recalled that such a violation of the right to informed consent constitutes in itself or by itself an infraction of the *lex artis ad hoc*, which infringes the patient's right to self-determination by preventing them from choosing, with knowledge and in accordance with their own interests and preferences, among the various vital options available to them.

When examining this decision, Ortiz Fernández (2019) and Barceló-Doménech (2018) highlight that, in modern practice, two types of *lex artis* can be identified: the *traditional lex artis*, associated with proper curative medical practice, and the *new lex artis*, which relates to informed consent.

From this landmark judgment, the Spanish Supreme Court has consistently interpreted that *the duty to inform is an essential element of the lex artis* in the practice of medicine and is encompassed within the obligations assumed by the physician. The obligation to provide information and to obtain consent is regarded as an integral component of medical practice, such that its omission may give rise to a right to compensation in favour of the patient, regardless of whether the medical intervention itself was performed correctly or not (Barceló-Doménech 2018).

As observed, the duties of medical professionals have evolved and are no longer confined to the correct execution of treatments, interventions, or the provision of necessary care to patients. Instead, they also include the obligation to inform patients and obtain their consent before administering any health-related procedure. According to Galán Cortés (2024), the physician is under a duty to inform the patient of the diagnosis and prognosis of their condition, the method (means) and the purpose of the medical treatment, the existing therapeutic options or alternatives available in their particular case, as well as the certain and potential consequences thereof, and all other circumstances which may reasonably influence the patient's decision, including, among these, any possible lack of resources at the healthcare centre where the patient is located, and the consequences that a refusal of treatment might entail for the patient's health.

Therefore, the traditional *lex artis* centred on curative medical practice must now encompass the additional responsibilities linked to informed consent. The evaluation of a medical professional's conduct thus involves *two distinct stages*. The first stage examines the medical activity itself, determining whether it meets the standard of care expected in the profession. The second stage assesses whether the professional fulfilled their duties of information and consent (Ortiz Fernández 2019).

In many cases, this first stage—evaluating how the medical intervention was carried out—is essential to compare it with the information provided and the consent obtained. This allows for a determination of whether the healthcare professional's initial explanation, which the patient authorised, corresponds to the procedure ultimately performed. Consequently, different scenarios may arise: those where only one of the *lex artis* obligations is violated, and *others where both are breached, which may lead to cumulative claims for liability* (Ortiz Fernández 2019).

In the same context, regarding patient consent, it is worth making additional brief considerations about the legal framework in France. According to the French legal scholar Baccino (2013), an error may be technical (e.g., damage to an organ following surgery where there was no anatomical anomaly). Such technical errors may also occur at the diagnostic stage (e.g., prescribing an X-ray of the skull when medical literature clearly recommends a CT scan or MRI in certain cases of cranial trauma) or during post-operative check-ups or general examinations (e.g., a patient falling from a surgical table).

On the other hand, according Baccino, errors may also arise in a situation referred to as a breach of the *duty to humanity*, such as the *failure to inform or obtain the consent* of the patient. In this regard, the information provided to patients must be clear, intelligible, and honest, ensuring that patients receive an explanation that they can understand.

Nevertheless, even in situations where patients have not provided consent, or where proof of consent has not been duly recorded by the physician - as became a legal obligation following the *Loi Kouchner* (Law of 4 March 2002)—, it is understood that if patients had no viable alternative due to the severity of their health condition, the offence of bodily harm is not constituted.

Furthermore, French courts acknowledge the possibility of compensating for damages not directly linked to medical techniques or practices but stemming from the fact that patients, for instance, are deprived of the opportunity to choose the less hazardous treatment or to refuse surgery due to the absence of information provided by the physician. However, in cases of urgency or severe health conditions, the *principle of the loss of the possibility of refusing medical care* is upheld.

Returning to the discussion on the context in Spain, another paradigmatic case concerning informed consent is *Reyes Jimenez v. Spain* (8 March 2022, Case no. 57020/18, European Court of Human Rights)—that highlights the importance of understanding consent as an ongoing process, requiring specific agreement for each medical procedure performed.

Luis Reyes Jimenez, a six-year-old child, was diagnosed with a brain tumour at the University Hospital of Murcia, Spain. In 2009, he underwent three surgeries. While the third surgery, deemed an emergency, was carried out with valid written consent from his parents, the second operation—conducted almost a month after the first—was performed without obtaining proper written consent. Following these medical interventions, Luis's health deteriorated severely, leaving him in a state of total dependency, unable to move, communicate, or perform basic bodily functions. His parents initiated administrative and judicial proceedings, alleging a failure to obtain informed consent; however, Spanish courts, including the Constitutional Court, dismissed their claims on the grounds of lacking constitutional relevance.

The case was subsequently brought before the European Court of Human Rights (ECtHR), which ruled that the Spanish courts had failed to correctly apply national legislation governing informed consent. Spanish law, specifically Law 41/2002, mandates that each medical procedure must be preceded by written informed consent, except in urgent, life-threatening situations. The ECtHR found that the second surgery, conducted without written consent, did not meet the criteria for *urgency*, as it was performed weeks after the first operation and at a time when the child's health had further declined.

Moreover, the Court emphasised that informed consent must provide clear and comprehensive information about the procedure and its associated risks, in line with the Oviedo Convention on Human Rights and Biomedicine. By failing to adhere to these legal requirements, Spain was found to have violated Article 8 of the European Convention on Human Rights, which protects the right to private life and physical integrity. This judgment underscores the vital importance of compliance with informed consent laws to safeguard patient autonomy and dignity, even in complex medical circumstances.

In this line, under Portuguese domestic law, Article 25 of the Constitution of the Republic guarantees the right to personal integrity, declaring that "the moral and physical integrity of individuals is inviolable". Complementing this, Article 26, paragraph 1, enshrines the right to the free development of personality, while paragraph 3 protects the "personal dignity and genetic identity of the human being, particularly in the creation, development, and use of technologies, as well as in scientific experimentation". Together, these provisions underscore the moral and physical integrity of individuals and their right to self-determination, serving as fundamental expressions of the overarching principle of Human Dignity, as articulated in Article 1 of the Constitution.

In the realm of civil law, Article 70 of the Portuguese Civil Code recognises the general right to personality, providing a strong legal basis for the protection of individual rights. Within the contractual context, certain legal scholars argue that the principle of good faith underpins the physician's duty to inform, even in cases involving an unfavourable prognosis. This interpretation reinforces both the ethical and legal imperatives to uphold transparency and respect for patient autonomy in the physician-patient relationship.

The Health Framework Law, codified in Law No. 95/2019, of 4 September, further strengthens the right of patients to be informed. Under Base 2, paragraph 1, subsection e, this law explicitly provides that individuals are entitled "to be adequately, accessibly, objectively, comprehensively, and intelligibly informed about their situation, the purpose, nature, possible alternatives, benefits, and risks of proposed interventions, as well as the likely evolution of their condition under the planned care regime". This updated provision expands upon the earlier framework (Law No. 48/90, of 24 August) and aligns with modern principles of patient autonomy and dignity.

Additionally, the Portuguese Medical Association's Code of Ethics formalises the duty to inform, as stipulated in Article 38, which obligates medical professionals to ensure that patients fully understand their treatment options and the consequences of refusing care. This ethical obligation is independent of any formal contractual relationship, highlighting its central importance to medical practice and the respect for patient rights.

There is also Guideline No. 015/2013 of the Portuguese Directorate-General of Health, which addresses the requirement for informed consent to be freely given, clarified, and documented in writing. As noted by Pereira (2017), this guideline has driven a greater implementation of the practice of obtaining written consent from patients in the context of medical interventions, particularly in medico-surgical procedures. This regulatory measure underscores the importance of formalising the informed consent process, ensuring that healthcare practices adhere to legal and ethical standards while safeguarding patients' autonomy and rights.

Pereira (2017) explains that the current Portuguese jurisprudential understanding regarding civil liability for breaches of the duty to inform the patient is presently guided by the Judgment of 2 June 2015 (rapporteur Clara Sottomayor) of the

Supreme Court of Justice, which marked the first time the Court held a physician liable for failing to obtain informed consent—whereas in previous decisions, although the right to informed consent had been expressly recognised, the defendants were ultimately acquitted. In summary, the judgment of the Portuguese Supreme Court of Justice represents a milestone in jurisprudence by consolidating civil liability for breaches of informed consent. This decision not only reaffirms the patient's right to self-determination and freedom but also recognises the obligation to compensate for both non-pecuniary and pecuniary damages resulting from a failure in the duty to inform. Accordingly, as explained by Pereira (2017), compensation may be awarded not only for non-pecuniary damages resulting from the violation of the patient's right to autonomy and freedom but also for breaches of their physical integrity—and, in certain circumstances, even of the right to life—as well as for pecuniary damages linked to the worsening of the patient's health condition. Consequently, the amount of compensation awarded in claims for breaches of informed consent may be as substantial as that awarded in cases of medical negligence.

The legal doctrine surrounding patient consent in Portugal reflects a rich and nuanced understanding of the balance between medical duties and patient autonomy. Several Portuguese scholars have explored the essential components and boundaries of informed consent, shedding light on its multifaceted nature.

According to Rodrigues (2001), informed consent encompasses multiple duties on the part of the physician, beyond the mere adherence to the *leges artis* of their profession. The doctor must respect the patient, which translates into the duties to inform, confirm understanding, and obtain consent. These layers highlight that informed consent is not a singular act but rather a *continuous process* aimed at ensuring the patient's comprehension and voluntary agreement to medical intervention.

Cordeiro (2017) further refines this perspective by emphasising the dynamic nature of the physician's duty to inform. He identifies the realm of medical service contracts as particularly fertile ground for examining this duty. Cordeiro explains that the scope of a doctor's explanatory duties is limited to the typical effects of prescribed therapies and does not extend to every conceivable outcome. This scope is influenced by the patient's intelligence, knowledge, and the specifics of the case, underscoring the need for a personalised approach to information delivery.

Pereira (2004) points out that while obtaining the patient's signature on a consent form may serve as evidence of diligent medical practice, such documentation does not equate to the fulfilment of the physician's duty to inform. Pereira asserts that information is merely one aspect of informed consent, distinguishing the act of providing information from the broader duty to ensure that the patient's consent is truly informed, voluntary, and reflective of their understanding.

Adding further depth to this discussion, Azevedo (2019) stresses that informed consent is a holistic process requiring active communication between doctor and patient. For the patient to truly exercise their right to consent, the physician must first provide comprehensive information about the diagnosis, risks, prognosis, and treatment alternatives. Subsequently, the doctor must engage in dialogue to assess the patient's understanding and cognitive grasp of this information. Azevedo argues that this iterative process is indispensable for the validity of consent. Without adequate comprehension, the duty to inform remains unfulfilled. She also underscores the profound ethical and legal dimensions of informed consent, describing it as a mechanism through which patients assert their autonomy and self-determination, reinforcing their dignity in the medical context.

Collectively, these Portuguese scholars emphasise that informed consent is not a mere formality but a fundamental component of the doctor-patient relationship, which occurs as a process involving multiple acts by both the physician and the patient. It embodies the principles of autonomy, dignity, and respect, serving as a cornerstone of modern medical ethics and legal duties in Portugal.

One of the most significant debates in European countries regarding patient consent concerns the scope and depth of the information to be disclosed. Central to this discussion is the obligation to inform patients about serious risks associated with medical interventions, even when such risks are rare.

This issue lies at the intersection of medical ethics, patient autonomy, and civil liability, giving rise to complex legal questions. Informed consent, while universally recognised as a fundamental principle, has sparked differing approaches in legal doctrine and jurisprudence across Europe. Two main perspectives have emerged on this matter, reflecting the diversity of legal and cultural frameworks within the continent.

The first, considered more stringent, requires physicians to disclose all highly serious risks, such as death, paralysis, or severe disability that may impede the ability to work, regardless of how rare these risks may be. This perspective has been firmly established in French jurisprudence.

In contrast, a more moderate approach has been adopted in jurisdictions like Spain and Belgium, where the duty to disclose is limited to serious risks that are common or foreseeable. Spanish law, for example, refers to risks related to the patient's personal or professional circumstances and those that are statistically probable under normal conditions. Similarly, Belgian law restricts the obligation to *normally foreseeable risks*, focusing on those that can reasonably be anticipated given the nature of the intervention.

Historically, as observed during the discussions presented earlier in this Chapter, medical ethics in the nineteenth century discouraged the disclosure of risks to patients. At that time, the prevailing view was that such information could unduly alarm or discourage patients from pursuing necessary treatment, and physicians were often encouraged to withhold details that might lead to a rejection of medical interventions. However, contemporary ethical standards have shifted significantly. In the modern era, respect for patient autonomy demands transparency, requiring that patients be fully informed of the advantages, disadvantages, and uncertainties of any proposed treatment. This evolution reflects broader changes in both medical ethics and the legal framework governing the doctor–patient relationship.

One of the most contentious aspects of informed consent remains the communication of risks, which continues to raise complex questions in legal and medical practice. Recent developments have given rise to what is known as the *Theory of*

Significant Risks, which has even influenced Brazilian law, being referenced in judicial decisions and Brazilian legal doctrine, as previously discussed in this book. In Portugal, the theory has gained significant prominence, particularly through the seminal teachings of Pereira (2004).

According to the Portuguese legal scholar, in a brief comparative law overview regarding the duty to disclose risks, it can be concluded that in several Civil Law countries (such as Italy, the Netherlands, and Spain), only foreseeable and serious risks must be disclosed. For example, in Belgium, regarding the risks of a treatment, Belgian courts apply the theory of normal and reasonably foreseeable risks. This means that a doctor is not required to inform the patient about serious but exceptional risks or minor but frequent risks.

In the other hand, in countries that apply the Theory of Significant Risks, such as Portugal, physicians are obligated to disclose risks that are deemed significant. Significant risks are those that the physician knows or reasonably should know are important and relevant to the patient's decision-making process. This approach prioritises the patient's autonomy by ensuring they are informed about risks that could influence their consent to a proposed medical procedure or treatment.

According to the Portuguese framework, such risks are evaluated based on several factors, including the therapeutic necessity of the intervention, the statistical likelihood of the risk occurring, the severity of the potential harm, and the specific circumstances or behaviour of the patient. Additionally, *the novelty of a treatment or procedure* plays a significant role, with higher standards of disclosure required for innovative or experimental methods due to their inherent uncertainty (Pereira 2004).

The severity of a risk, even if its likelihood is low, often imposes a duty of disclosure. While foreseeable serious risks are widely acknowledged as falling within the scope of a physician's obligation to inform, rare but grave risks may also require disclosure, especially if withholding such information could undermine the patient's autonomy.

French courts, for example, initially held that only frequent and foreseeable risks needed to be disclosed, as informing patients of rare risks was deemed unnecessary and potentially distressing. However, this position has evolved over recent decades.

In 1998, the Cour de Cassation ruled that failing to disclose serious risks, even if hypothetical or of exceptional rarity, constitutes a breach of the physician's duty. The court clarified that unless the patient explicitly refuses to be informed or exceptional circumstances such as emergencies render disclosure impractical, physicians must provide clear, accurate, and appropriate information about all serious risks associated with the proposed treatment.

This position was further reinforced by the Conseil d'État in 2000, which ruled that exceptional risks must also be disclosed if their severity could influence the patient's decision-making process. The court stated that when medical procedures involve risks of death or severe disability, patients must have the opportunity to give informed consent. Such information may only be withheld in cases of urgent necessity, impossibility, or the patient's explicit refusal to be informed. Even then, the exceptional nature of a risk does not automatically exempt physicians from their duty to inform.

This heightened duty of disclosure has significantly increased the potential for medical liability, placing greater pressure on healthcare providers, both in private clinics and public hospitals. In Germany, for example, it is widely recognised that patients have the right to be informed of the gravest risks associated with a particular intervention, even if these risks are rare. Laufs and Kern (1984), leading German legal scholars, argue that physicians must disclose rare risks if they are specific to the intervention in question and could result in serious harm to the patient's life.

These developments reflect an overarching shift in medical ethics and law, emphasising the importance of transparency and the patient's right to make informed decisions. Physicians are increasingly required to communicate not only foreseeable risks but also rare or hypothetical risks when their severity warrants such disclosure. This evolution underscores the centrality of informed consent as both a legal and ethical imperative, ensuring that patients retain autonomy and control over decisions affecting their health and well-being.

More recently, as explained by the Portuguese legal scholar Pereira (2004), the *novelty of the treatment or procedure* stands as a critical factor in determining the scope and content of the information that must be disclosed to the patient. When a therapeutic or diagnostic intervention is relatively new, the inherent uncertainty surrounding its risks, benefits, and outcomes necessitates a higher standard of disclosure. This is because recent or experimental treatments often lack the extensive empirical data that more established methods provide, making it essential for patients to be fully informed about the potential uncertainties and limitations involved. In such cases, physicians are expected to exercise greater rigour in their duty to inform. This elevated standard reflects the ethical and legal emphasis on patient autonomy, particularly in situations where the novelty of the treatment introduces an additional layer of complexity to the decision-making process.

Based on the discussions throughout this Chapter, several important conclusions can be drawn. The ethical and legal evolution of the physician-patient relationship underscores the profound influence of European legal frameworks on the Brazilian legal system, particularly in shaping approaches to patient autonomy and self-determination.

Landmark cases such as *Montgomery v. Lanarkshire Health Board* in the United Kingdom and pivotal decisions by the French Cour de Cassation have been instrumental in this transformation. These rulings established that the duty to inform is not merely a procedural formality, but a fundamental obligation tied to the ethical and legal imperative of respecting patient autonomy. By emphasising the comprehensive and personalised disclosure of material risks, these decisions have embedded informed consent as a cornerstone of modern medical practice, ensuring that patients are equipped to make informed decisions about their healthcare.

Additionally, a landmark decision by the Spanish Supreme Court redefined the concept of *lex artis*, distinguishing between its traditional application to the technical quality of medical procedures and a new dimension focused on the duty to inform. The court held that a failure to provide adequate information constitutes a *breach of the lex artis of information*, irrespective of whether the medical intervention itself was technically sound. This ruling highlighted informed consent as an independent legal obligation, underscoring its fundamental role in safeguarding patient self-determination and dignity.

A particularly notable influence on Brazilian legal doctrine has also been the Portuguese framework concerning the *Theory of Significant Risks*. As observed, this approach emphasises the obligation to disclose not only common and foreseeable risks but also rare risks if their severity could significantly affect the patient's decision-making process. Developed in Portuguese legal scholarship and case law, this principle has guided Brazilian courts in recognising the nuanced nature of the physician's duty to inform, ensuring that it is tailored to the specific circumstances, needs, and preferences of the patient.

All these developments in European jurisprudence and legal thought have profoundly shaped Brazilian legal doctrine and jurisprudence. By fostering greater transparency, accountability, and respect for individual decision-making, these advancements have redefined the physician-patient relationship and the medical services contract. As healthcare systems continue to evolve, these principles will remain vital in addressing new challenges, including those arising from the incorporation of artificial intelligence and other emerging technologies into medical practice—as will be examined in the next chapters of this book.

References

Aguiar Dias J (2006) Da Responsabilidade Civil. 11th ed. Rio de Janeiro: Renovar

Albuquerque A, Antunes CMTB (2021) Tomada de decisão compartilhada na saúde: aproximações e distanciamentos entre a ajuda decisional e os apoios de tomada de decisão. Cadernos Ibero-Americanos de Direito Sanitário 10(1):203–223

Alvez HM, Schaefer F (2022) Protocolos na Medicina de emergência e o respeito às diretivas antecipadas de saúde. In: Kfouri Neto M, Nogaroli R (eds) Debates Contemporâneos em direito médico e da saúde, 2nd edn. Thomson Reuters Brazil, São Paulo

Araújo ATM, Fernandes LS (2021) Liberdade decisória do médico e compreensão pelo paciente: o dever recíproco de informação como pressuposto fundamental. Cad Ibero-amer Dir Sanit 10(1):149–164

Azevedo FM (2019) O consentimento informado silenciado na esfera da telemedicina. Cadernos da Lex Medicinae II 4:253–262

Baccino E (2013) Medical responsibility and liability in France. In: Ferrara SD (ed) Malpractice and medical liability. European State of the Art and Guidelines. Springer Berlin Heidelberg, Berlin

Balint M (2000) The Doctor, His Patient and the Illness. 2nd ed. Philadelphia: Churchill Livingstone

Barceló-Doménech J (2018) Consentimiento informado y responsabilidad médica. Actualidad Jurídica Iberoamericana 8

Basan AP (2020) Contratos existenciais: hermenêutica à luz dos direitos fundamentais. LAECC, Uberlândia

Bizelli RF (2018) Contrato existencial: evolução dos modelos contratuais. Lumen Juris Rio de Janeiro

Campos CFC, Leão J, Dohms M (2021) Comunicação clínica efetiva. In: Dohms M, Gusso G (eds) Comunicação clínica: aperfeiçoando os encontros em saúde. Artmed, Porto Alegre

Cordeiro AM (2017) Da boa-fé no Direito Civil. Almedina, Coimbra

Cortés JCG (2024) Responsabilidad Civil Médica, 9th edn. Civitas, Navarra.
Couto e Silva CV (2006) A Obrigação como Processo. Rio de Janeiro: Editora FGV
Dadalto L (2022) Testamento vital, 6th edn. Foco, Indaiatuba
Dantas E (2024) Direito Médico, 6th edn. Juspodivm, Salvador
Durand G (2005) Introduction générale à la bioéthique: histoire, concepts et outils. Les Editions Fides, Montreal
Ehrhardt Júnior M (2014) Responsabilidade civil pelo inadimplemento da boa-fé. Fórum, Belo Horizonte
Facchini Neto E, Soares FR (2021) Liberdade de prescrição e responsabilidade médica: quando a liberdade se converte em responsabilidade? Available via Migalhas de Responsabilidade Civil. https://www.migalhas.com.br/coluna/migalhas-de-responsabilidade-civil/345630/liberdade-de-prescricao-e-responsabilidade-medica
Fachin LE (2006) Estatuto jurídico do patrimônio mínimo, 2nd edn. Renovar, Rio de Janeiro
Fachin LE (2012) A relação obrigacional e responsabilidade solidária em contrato. Soluções práticas de direito – pareceres. Revista dos Tribunais 1:137–156
Fachin LE (2021) Forword. In: Nalin P, Copi LM, Pavan VO (eds) Pós-Constitucionalização do Direito Civil: novas perspectivas do direito civil na constituição prospectiva. Toth, Londrina
Faleiros Júnior JLM (2019) A tutela jurídica dos dados pessoais sensíveis à luz da Lei Geral de Proteção de Dados. In: Faleiros Júnior JLM, Longhi JVR (eds) Estudos essenciais de direito digital. LAECC, Uberlândia
Farias CC, Rosenvald N (2021) Curso de direito civil: contratos – teoria geral e contratos em espécie, vol 4, 11th edn, JusPodivm, Salvador
Fitzharris L (2017) The Butchering Art: Joseph Lister's Quest to Transform the Grisly World of Victorian Medicine. Scientific American, New York. Portuguese edition: Fitzharris L (2019) Medicina dos Horrores: a história de Joseph Lister, o homem que revolucionou o apavorante mundo das cirurgias do século XIX (trans. unidentified). Intrínseca, Rio de Janeiro.
Foucault M (1977) Discipline and punish: the birth of the prison (trans: Sheridan A). Pantheon Books, New York
Foucault M (1978) The history of sexuality: an introduction (trans: Hurley R). Pantheon Books, New York
França GV (2021) Direito Médico. 17th ed. Rio de Janeiro: Forense
Fürst H (2023) Teoria do Biodireito. Letramento, Belo Horizonte
Godinho AM (2023) A responsabilidade civil dos profissionais de saúde pelo dano derivado do desrespeito à autonomia dos pacientes. Available via Migalhas de Responsabilidade Civil. https://www.migalhas.com.br/coluna/migalhas-de-responsabilidade-civil/383886/responsabilidade-pelo-dano-do-desrespeito-a-autonomia-dos-pacientes
Guia da Silva R (2019) Inadimplemento e violação positiva do contrato: aspectos da aplicação da boa-fé objetiva no direito brasileiro. In: Terra TMV, Konder CN, Guedes GSC (eds) Princípios contratuais aplicados: boa-fé, função social e equilíbrio contratual à luz da jurisprudência. Foco, Indaiatuba
Herring J (2020) Medical Law and Ethics. 8th ed. Oxford: Oxford University Press
Hervey TK, McHale JV (2015) European Union health law. European Union Health Law: Themes and Implications, 30–70
Hironaka GMFN (2014) Principiologia contratual e a valoração ética no Código Civil Brasileiro. Civilistica.com 3(1):1–11
Kfouri Neto M (2022) Responsabilidade civil dos hospitais, 5th edn. Thomson Reuters Brazil, São Paulo
Kfouri Neto M (2024) Responsabilidade civil do medico, 12th edn. Thomson Reuters Brazil, São Paulo
Laufs A, Kern B-R (1984) Die ärztliche Aufklärungspflicht. Unter besonderer Berücksichtigung der richterlichen Spruchpraxis. Springer-Verlag, Berlin
Lifton RJ (1986) The Nazi Doctors: medical killing and the psychology of genocide. Basic Books, New York

Lopez TA (2004) O dano estético: responsabilidade civil, 3rd edn. Thomson Reuters Brazil, São Paulo
Machado YAF, Vianna JRA (2022) Necessidade de equalização da responsabilidade civil do médico residente. In: Kfouri Neto M, Nogaroli R (eds) Debates Contemporâneos em direito médico e da saúde, 2nd edn. Thomson Reuters Brazil, São Paulo
Maranhão C, Nogaroli R (2022) O método bifásico como critério de quantificação dos danos morais e estéticos decorrentes da atividade médica na jurisprudência do TJ/PR. In: Kfouri Neto M, Nogaroli R (eds) Debates Contemporâneos em direito médico e da saúde, 2nd edn. Thomson Reuters Brazil, São Paulo
Martins MW, Barros JPL (2022) Mediação de conflitos na área da saúde: uma análise de direito comparado. In: Kfouri Neto M, Nogaroli R (eds) Debates Contemporâneos em direito médico e da saúde, 2nd edn. Thomson Reuters Brazil, São Paulo
Martins-Costa J (2019) A boa-fé no direito privado. Critérios para a sua aplicação, 2nd edn. Saraiva Educação, São Paulo
Mascarenhas IL, Bahia SJC (2022) O exercício da medicina defensiva enquanto reação às decisões judiciais: o papel do judiciário na construção de uma postura ética no exercício médico. Revista de Direito do Consumidor 141:339–355
Mezzich JE (2011) The Geneva Conferences and the emergence of the international network for person-centered medicine. J Eval Clin Pract 17(2):333–336
Milagres MO (2010) Proteção da confiança nas relações médicas. Revista de Direito Privado 44:298–315
Miragem B (2007) Responsabilidade civil médica no direito brasileiro. Revista de Direito do Consumidor 63:52–91
Miranda P, Cavalcante F (1954) Tratado de Direito Privado, vol 11. Borsoi, Rio de Janeiro
Mold A (2010) Patient groups and the construction of the patient-consumer in Britain: an historical overview. J Soc Policy 39(4):505–521
Mold A (2015) Making British patients into consumers. Lancet 385(9975):1286–1287
Nalin P (2008) Do contrato: conceito pós-moderno (em busca de sua formulação na perspectiva civil-constitucional), 2nd edn. Juruá, Curitiba
Nalin P, Venazzi K, Copi LM (2021) Introdução sobre a metodologia civil constitucional e a sua pós-constitucionalização. In: Nalin P, Copi LM, Pavan VO (eds) Pós-Constitucionalização do Direito Civil: novas perspectivas do direito civil na constituição prospectiva. Toth, Londrina
Nilo AT (2020) Direito médico: o contrato de tratamento no direito brasileiro. Juruá, Curitiba
Nogaroli R, Mascarenhas IL (2022) Ser visto para ser lembrado: a publicidade médica em redes sociais como desencadeadora de responsabilidade civil. Available via Migalhas de Responsabilidade Civil, 24 maio 2022. Disponível em: https://www.migalhas.com.br/coluna/migalhas-de-responsabilidade-civil/366566/publicidade-medica-em-redes-sociais-como-responsabilidade-civil
Nunes R (2019) A boa-fé objetiva como paradigma da conduta na sociedade capitalista contemporânea. Revista dos Tribunais 1000:327–333
Ortega CG, Murillo VC, Barrios JA (2004) Patient autonomy and information and clinical documentation-related rights within the context of Spanish Law 41/2002. Revista espanola de salud publica 78(4):469–479
Ortiz Fernández M (2019) La responsabilidad civil en el ámbito sanitario derivada del consentimiento informado. Actualidad Jurídica Iberoamericana 10:548–565
Pattinson SD (2017) Medical law and ethics, 5th edn. Sweet & Maxwell, London
Pereira AGD (2004) O consentimento informado na relação médico-paciente. Estudo de direito civil. Coimbra Publisher, Coimbra
Pereira AGD (2015) Direito dos pacientes e responsabilidade médica. Coimbra Publisher, Coimbra
Pereira AGD (2017) O consentimento informado em portugal: breves notas. Revista Eletrônica da Faculdade de Direito de Franca 12(2):23–36

Perlingieri P (2006) Il diritto civile nella legalità costituzionale. Edizioni Scientifiche Italiane, Napoli. Portuguese edition: Perlingieri P (2008) O direito civil na legalidade constitucional (trans: De Cicco MC) Rio de Janeiro: Renovar
Reale M (2003) A boa-fé no Código Civil. Revista de Direito Bancário e do Mercado de Capitais 21:11–13
Requejo MT (2003) Legal Analysis of the Spanish Basic Law 41/2002 on the autonomy of the patient and the rights and obligations with regard to clinical information and documentation. Eur J Health Law 10(3):257–269
Rodrigues JV (2001) O consentimento informado para o acto médico. Elementos para o estudo da manifestação de vontade do paciente. Coimbra Publisher, Coimbra
Rodrigues Júnior OL (2019) Direito civil contemporâneo: estatuto epistemológico, Constituição e direitos fundamentais. Forense Universitária, Rio de Janeiro
Romeiro DA, Mascarenhas IL, Godinho AM (2022) Descumprimento da ética médica em publicidade: impactos na responsabilidade civil. Revista Bioética 30(1):27–35
Ronsevald N, Braga Netto F (2021) Código civil comentado, 2nd edn. JusPodivm, Salvador
Rosenvald N, Braga Netto FP (2020) Responsabilidade civil na área médica. In: Braga Netto FP, César Silva M (eds) Direito privado e contemporaneidade. Foco, Indaiatuba
Sá MFF, Moureira DL (2015) Autonomia para morrer, 2nd edn. Fórum, Belo Horizonte
Sá MFF, Naves BTO (2021) Bioética e biodireito, 5th edn. Foco, Indaiatuba
Sandman L, Munthe C (2009) Shared decision-making and patient autonomy. Theor Med Bioethics 30:289–310
Sandman L, Munthe C (2010) Shared decision making, paternalism and patient choice. Health Care Anal 18:60–84
Schermer M (2002) The Different Faces of Autonomy: Patient Autonomy in Ethical Theory and Hospital Practice. Dordrecht: Springer Nature BV
Schaefer F (2010) Proteção de dados de saúde na sociedade de informação. A busca do equilíbrio entre privacidade e interesse social. Juruá, Curitiba
Shutzberg M (2021) The doctor as parent, partner, provider… or comrade? Distribution of power in past and present models of the doctor–patient relationship. Health Care Anal 29:231–248
Soares FR (2021) Consentimento do paciente no direito médico: validade, interpretação e responsabilidade. Foco, Indaiatuba
Stewart M, Roter D (eds) (1989) Communicating with medical patients. Sage Publications, London
Stewart M et al (2013) Patient-centered medicine: transforming the clinical method, 3rd edn. Radcliffe Publishing, London
Talukdar S (2020) Ensuring risk awareness of vulnerable patients in the post-Montgomery era: treading a fine line. Health Care Anal 28(3):283–298
Tepedino G, Konder CN, Bandeira PG (2021) Fundamentos do Direito Civil. Contratos, vol 3, 2nd edn. Forense, São Paulo
Thomasma DD, Bergsma J (2000) Autonomy and clinical medicine. Renewing the health professional relation with the patient. Kluwer Academic Publishers, Dordrecht
Tomasevicius Filho E (2020) O princípio da boa-fé no direito civil. Almedina Brasil, São Paulo
Van der Zeijden A (2000) The patient rights movement in Europe. Pharmacoeconomics 18:7–13
Vasconcelos C (2020) Direito médico e bioética: história da judicialização da relação médico-paciente. Lumen Juris, Rio de Janeiro
Veatch RM (1972) Models for ethical medicine in a revolutionary age. What physician-patient roles foster the most ethical relationship? Hastings Center Rep 2(3):5–7
Wittgenstein L (1953) Philosophical investigations. Basil Blackwell, Oxford

Chapter 3
Civil Liability in Healthcare

3.1 Spheres of Medical Liability: Civil, Criminal, and Ethical

A doctor who fails to provide adequate care in Brazil may face liability across three distinct spheres: administrative (ethical), criminal, and civil. This tripartite division is rooted in the specific legal frameworks and codes governing each area, ensuring comprehensive accountability for professional misconduct or negligence.

i) Administrative liability pertains to breaches of ethical standards as outlined by the Federal Council of Medicine (*Conselho Federal de Medicina*—CFM) and Regional Medical Councils (*Conselhos Regionais de Medicina*—CRMs). These bodies regulate the professional conduct of physicians, ensuring adherence to the Brazilian Code of Medical Ethics (*Código de Ética Médica*—CEM). Violations—such as failing to obtain informed consent, disrespecting patient confidentiality, refusing to provide emergency care when capable, charging for unnecessary procedures, falsifying medical records, or abandoning treatment without just cause –, can lead to sanctions ranging from warnings to the suspension or revocation of the medical licence.
ii) Criminal liability arises under Brazilian law when a physician's actions or omissions constitute a crime, such as negligent homicide or fraud in medical practice. These offences are prosecuted under the Brazilian Penal Code (*Código Penal Brasileiro*—CP) and adjudicated by the Judiciary. Criminal proceedings aim to determine culpability and impose penalties, which may include imprisonment or fines. The classification of medical conduct as a crime is reserved for actions or omissions of sufficient gravity to warrant the attention of the penal system, whose purpose is both repressive and preventive. For example, gross medical negligence resulting in death may be classified as a criminal offence if it demonstrates recklessness or lack of due diligence. In such cases, the judiciary evaluates the evidence, determines whether the legal limits for criminal

R. Nogaroli, *Medical Liability and Artificial Intelligence*,
https://doi.org/10.1007/978-3-031-94306-5_3

liability are met, and imposes appropriate sanctions based on the severity of the misconduct.

iii) In the civil sphere, liability arises from claims for damages under the Brazilian Civil Code (*Código Civil Brasileiro*—CC), Articles 186 and 927, and the Brazilian Consumer Protection Code (*Código de Defesa do Consumidor*—CDC), Article 14, § 4°. These provisions establish the physician's obligation to compensate victims for harm caused by negligent acts. Article 186 (CC) defines civil liability as arising from any act or omission that causes harm to another due to negligence. Article 927 (CC) establishes the obligation to repair damages caused by unlawful acts. Article 14, §4° (CDC) specifically addresses the liability of professionals, stating that service providers, such as physicians, are liable for damages caused by the provision of defective or negligent services, except when they can prove there was no fault.

Affected patients or their families may initiate legal proceedings in the Judiciary to seek compensation by proving that the doctor breached their duty of care and caused harm. Civil courts evaluate these claims to determine whether the physician's conduct was negligent or improper, and if so, to establish the extent of the harm caused. Compensation may include reparations for medical expenses, loss of earnings, and moral damages. The judiciary's role is to ensure the appropriate allocation of liability and remedy for the harm suffered.

In Brazil, as explained above, a single instance of inadequate care can trigger liability across all three spheres. In summary, the distinction between these three forms of liability lies in the legislative framework: ethical violations are determined in accordance with the Code of Medical Ethics; criminal liability arises solely from acts defined as crimes under the Brazilian Penal Code; and civil liability applies to acts falling within the parameters established by the Civil Code. It is worth emphasising that, while these spheres may overlap in substance, they involve separate processes, procedures, and sanctions.

For example, a doctor who refuses to attend to a critically ill patient in an emergency situation, despite being capable of providing assistance, exemplifies inadequate medical conduct. This omission can trigger liability across the administrative, criminal, and civil spheres, as follows:

i) Ethical liability: Article 7 (CEM) explicitly prohibits a doctor from failing to attend to patients in emergency and urgent care settings when it is their duty to do so. The refusal to act in such circumstances breaches the ethical obligation to prioritise patient health and safety. Ethical responsibility is directly linked to the regulation of the individual by their peers, with a technical and scientific character. This is initially investigated exclusively by CRMs' members through an inquiry, which may or may not result in an ethical-professional process adjudicated by the CFM. The sanctions imposed for a violation of Article 7 may include: i.I) a formal warning or reprimand; i.II) temporary suspension of the medical licence; i.III) permanent revocation of the licence, in severe cases of misconduct or repeated violations. These measures aim to uphold the ethical standards of the profession and ensure public trust in healthcare services.

ii) Criminal liability: the refusal to provide emergency care may constitute a criminal offence under Article 135 (CP), which criminalises the act of *failure to render assistance*. This article stipulates that: ii.I) any individual who fails to assist a person in danger, when assistance is possible without significant personal risk, commits a criminal offence punishable by detention (1–6 months) or a fine; ii.II) if the refusal results in serious injury or death, the penalties may be aggravated under Articles 121 (homicide) or 129 (bodily harm) if gross negligence or recklessness is proven. In the context of medical practice, the professional duty heightens their obligation to act, making such omissions particularly egregious under criminal law.

iii) Civil liability: in the civil sphere, the affected patient or their family may file a claim for damages and must prove: iii.I) duty of care: the doctor had a professional and ethical obligation to assist; iii.II) breach of duty: the refusal to provide emergency care constituted negligence; iii.III) causation: the omission directly resulted in harm to the patient, such as worsened health outcomes or death. Compensation may cover medical expenses incurred due to delayed treatment, moral damages for emotional distress or psychological suffering, and financial losses suffered by the patient or their dependents.

This example illustrates how a single act of negligence—failing to provide emergency care—can result in liability across all three spheres.

It is important note that the principles of Bioethics—autonomy, beneficence, non-maleficence, and justice—serve as foundational ethical guidelines in medical practice. These principles aim to balance patient rights, medical obligations, and broader societal interests. Violations of these principles have repercussions across administrative, civil, and criminal spheres, depending on the specific circumstances of the case.

To consider another scenario, suppose a doctor carries out a surgical procedure on a patient without obtaining the informed consent, even though the surgery was not an emergency. Subsequently, the patient discovers that alternative, less invasive treatment options were available but were not disclosed. This conduct constitutes a breach of the bioethical principle of the patient's autonomy, as it disregards the entitlement to actively participate in decisions concerning the own care. Such conduct may lead to liability across the administrative, criminal, and civil spheres in the following manner:

i) Ethical liability: Article 22 (CEM) explicitly requires doctors to obtain informed consent from patients before performing procedures, except in emergency situations where consent is not feasible. This duty reflects the fundamental bioethical principle of respect patient autonomy. In this scenario, the physician's failure to inform the patient about the procedure and alternative options constitutes an ethical violation.

ii) Criminal liability: performing a medical procedure without informed consent may constitute a criminal offence. Article 129 (CP) criminalises bodily harm, which can include medical interventions performed without consent, except in emergencies. The unauthorised procedure could be classified as bodily harm by omission of consent, particularly if the patient experiences unnecessary physical harm or adverse effects. If the procedure results in severe injury or is considered a gross violation of the patient's rights, the penalties may be aggravated.

iii) Civil liability: in the civil sphere, the patient may file a claim for damages under Articles 186 and 927 (CC), and Article 14, §4° (CDC). The plaintiff would need to prove the following: iii.I) duty of care: the physician had a professional obligation to explain the procedure and obtain informed consent; iii.II) breach of duty: the failure to inform the patient and obtain consent constituted *informational negligence*; iii.III) causation: the lack of consent is directly linked to harm, which does not constitute a negligence on the part of the doctor, but could be avoided if the patient had been informed of the risk of the adverse event and chosen not to be undergo the treatment.

It is important to note that, due to their distinct nature, these spheres of responsibility must be addressed autonomously, reflecting the *principle of independence*. This principle applies even though it is not absolute, given the overriding effect of a final criminal judgement when it renders a *categorical finding*, whether positive or negative, regarding the facts, their unlawfulness, and the identity of the perpetrator. Such a judgement creates *res judicata* within the civil and disciplinary domains.

While these processes are interrelated, they are not interdependent, as explicitly provided in Article 935 of the 2002 Brazilian Civil Code (CC) and Article 7 of the 2022 Brazilian Code of Professional Ethical Procedure (*Código de Processo Ético-Profissional*—CPEP). Nevertheless, in Brazil, despite the formal independence of the administrative, criminal, and civil spheres, in practice, decisions made by medical councils, including the Federal Council of Medicine (CFM) and the Regional Medical Councils (CRMs), often serve as crucial support in judicial proceedings (Oliveira and Dantas 2022).

Ethical-professional procedures conducted by these councils involve detailed evaluations by medical inspectors with specialised expertise in assessing complex medical cases. These assessments provide a level of technical scrutiny and objectivity that is more difficult to replicate within the judiciary. In medical liability cases, judges and parties frequently rely on these administrative findings to address the technical challenges inherent in analysing medical evidence. Decisions issued by the councils, which incorporate evaluations conducted by professionals with extensive medical knowledge, are often used not only to supplement judicial reasoning but also, in some instances, to replace the need for independent expert evidence. This reliance highlights the importance of council evaluations in cases that require nuanced medical expertise.

Over the past decade, in Brazil, the use of ethical decisions as borrowed evidence in civil and criminal cases has become a widespread practice. Judicial decisions referencing council rulings have increased significantly (Oliveira and Mascarenhas 2024). The technical evaluations provided in ethical-professional procedures—conducted by the CFM and CRMs—play a decisive role in cases involving conflicting expert opinions or intricate medical issues. In this regard, the following decisions from Brazilian courts are noteworthy: Court of Justice of the State of Paraná, Appeal

No. 0001964–14.2018.8.16.0119, adjudicated on 2 July 2021, and Appeal No. 0024214–59.2009.8.16.0021, adjudicated on 4 April 2019. Similarly, Court of Justice of the State of São Paulo, Appeal No. 0000826–52.2012.8.26.0213, adjudicated on 12 December 2021.

The expediency of administrative proceedings conducted by the CFM and CRMs makes their findings particularly valuable, as they are often incorporated into judicial rulings before they become final, offering technical clarity and an impartial foundation for decision-making. These evaluations not only reinforce judicial reasoning but also illustrate the practical interdependence of administrative, civil, and criminal domains in medical liability cases, despite their formal separation.

3.1.1 Medical Malpractice Cases Under the Brazilian Legal System

According to the Brazilian National Council of Justice (CNJ), in 2024 there were 801,720 lawsuits concerning Medical and Health Law pending judgment in Brazil. Of these, approximately 497,000 are related to the public healthcare system (Sistema Único de Saúde – SUS), while 318,000 involve the supplementary (private) healthcare sector. In 2024 alone, 306,000 new lawsuits were filed, and by June 2024, 264,000 cases had been adjudicated, representing nearly 33% of the total caseload. The majority of these claims arise from allegations of medical malpractice, involving supposed acts of negligence, recklessness, or professional incompetence committed by physicians, other healthcare professionals, or healthcare institutions. The most common harms reported in these cases include diagnostic errors, medication-related mistakes—such as errors in prescribing, dispensing, or administering drugs—surgical errors resulting from deviations from accepted standards of care, and hospital-acquired infections. Specialists point out that, beyond the issues directly related to the quality and safety of healthcare services, this significant surge in litigation also reflects a systemic failure of regulatory bodies and health institutions to provide effective, timely, and adequate responses to the population's demands, which, in turn, contributes to the escalation of judicialisation in the healthcare sector.

The judicialization of healthcare in Brazil underscores the extent to which the assessment of medical liability for adverse events suffered by patients has become a recurring and highly relevant issue before the Brazilian Judiciary. As previously discussed, medical liability is subjective and based on fault, in accordance with Articles 927 and 951 of the Brazilian Civil Code (CC) and Article 14, § 4, of the Brazilian Consumer Protection Code (CDC). It is necessary to prove the professional's culpable conduct to establish liability. When evaluating medical fault, the judge must consider the following question: "Would a prudent doctor, placed in the same external circumstances, have acted in the same manner as the person responsible for the harm?". Broadly speaking, medical fault consists of a deviation from the standard of conduct aligned with the codes and protocols prescribed for medical practice. In such cases, the professional does not intend to harm the patient but causes damage due to negligent action (Kfouri Neto 2024; Tepedino 2006).

Article 951 (CC) provides that compensation is owed by any person who, in the exercise of professional activity, through negligence, recklessness, or lack of skill, causes the death of a patient, aggravates their condition, causes an injury, or renders them unable to work. Thus, medical fault is classified into the categories of negligence, recklessness, and lack of skill. In practice, liability is established in the same manner, and for the purposes of this work, these categories will be grouped under the umbrella term "negligence." Nevertheless, to illustrate the conceptual distinctions proposed in Brazilian legal doctrine, a more detailed analysis of each category follows.

Negligence refers to an omission on the part of the doctor to exercise due care and attention, as required by common experience or the standards of medical practice. It is the opposite of diligence. Rosenvald and Braga Netto (2020) illustrate this concept: "A surgical instrument left inside a patient's body is a notarised signature of negligence". Other examples of negligent conduct include failure to provide an accurate diagnosis due to superficial examination; operating on the wrong limb; mismanagement of medical records and test results; delays in referring a patient to a specialist; or postponing necessary surgical intervention.

Recklessness, by contrast, involves a positive act of fault. The professional engages in unjustified or hasty actions without exercising caution. Recklessness is characterised by imprudence and lack of reflection. Examples of medical recklessness include: an anaesthetist administering simultaneous anaesthetics to multiple patients; a doctor performing a high-risk surgical procedure without ensuring availability of an intensive care unit (ICU) bed; or a professional rushing through a complex surgical procedure in 30 min, when it would typically require 2 h given its intricacy.

Lack of skill refers to a deficiency in the technical knowledge or practical preparedness necessary for the task. For instance, a gynaecologist who, without proper qualifications in plastic surgery, undertakes cosmetic procedures, would be considered unskilled. Similarly, an obstetrician who, during a caesarean section, inadvertently cuts the patient's bladder, or who mishandles forceps during delivery, causing cranial trauma to the newborn, exemplifies a lack of skill (Kfouri Neto 2024).

Consider, for instance, a case of harm sustained by a patient undergoing robot-assisted surgery. Medical unskilfulness may be demonstrated through technical inadequacy or insufficient training in the use of robotic platforms. Furthermore, harm could also result from negligent conduct, such as an undue delay in converting a robotic procedure to open surgery when the robotic system malfunctions during the operation.

Once the physician's fault is established, the hospital is held jointly liable (pursuant to Articles 932, item III, 933, and 942, sole paragraph, of the Brazilian Civil Code). This is known as the *Theory of Mitigated Objective Liability*, under which the hospital is objectively liable for damages caused to the patient, provided that the professional's fault is first demonstrated.

Conversely, if the doctor has no employment or agency relationship with the hospital and merely rents the facility to perform a procedure, the obligation to compensate cannot be imputed to the hospital. In such cases, liability is exclusively attributable to the professional. This position is supported by a decision of the Superior Court of Justice: Special Appeal No. 1,832,371/MG, adjudicated on 22 June 2021.

Regarding medical liability in the context of diagnostic errors a topic that will form a significant focus of the discussions in this book—it is essential to emphasise that the judge's role is not to evaluate the diagnostic error itself but rather to determine whether the professional acted negligently in the diagnostic process. Diagnostic errors can, therefore, be classified as *excusable* or *inexcusable*.

On this matter, Fernanda Schaefer (2002, p. 66) insightfully observes: "Diagnostic errors can be divided into avoidable [excusable] and unavoidable [inexcusable]. They are unavoidable when they result from the inherent limitations of medicine; for instance, there are numerous diseases that have yet to be catalogued, and many whose causes remain unknown. Technological advances are sometimes insufficient to ensure an accurate diagnosis. Such errors do not constitute gross faults and, therefore, are not punishable".

As a general rule, diagnostic errors are excusable unless they are gross. Liability arises when the diagnostic error is one that a prudent professional, operating under the same circumstances, would not have committed. The analysis requires determining whether the physician employed all reasonable and available means to investigate the illness, including preliminary examinations, radiological imaging, and laboratory tests (Miguel Kfouri Neto 2024).

If the physician conducts a comprehensive examination of the patient, utilising all the tools and techniques at their disposal, but still makes an error in diagnosis, he or she will not be held liable. Medicine is not a field where infallibility can be demanded, nor is absolute precision a realistic expectation. However, when the diagnostic error is gross—demonstrating an unacceptable level of ignorance or negligence—it becomes culpable, thereby giving rise to medical liability.

Gross diagnostic errors may arise from various causes, including: (i) conducting a superficial examination of the patient; (ii) displaying inexcusable ignorance of fundamental medical knowledge; (iii) failing to utilise diagnostic tools and resources available to the professional; (iv) disregarding obvious symptoms that required further testing to accurately determine the clinical condition.

It is important to recognise that holding professionals accountable for gross diagnostic errors is not intended to impose an unrealistic standard of perfection but to ensure that the trust placed in medical practitioners is upheld. This approach protects patients' rights while encouraging adherence to established protocols and the continuous improvement of diagnostic practices. By balancing the need for accountability with the inherent challenges of medical science, the law seeks to safeguard the quality and reliability of healthcare services.

It is important to note that when a patient receives an incorrect or delayed medical diagnosis and subsequently dies, there are circumstances where, despite the professional not directly causing the ultimate harm—death—their conduct may have reduced the patient's probability of recovery or survival. In such cases, Brazilian legal doctrine and jurisprudence recognise the applicability of the so-called *Loss of a Chance Theory* (Peteffi da Silva 2013; Gondim 2010; Kfouri Neto 2024; Uscocovich and Santos 2023).

This theory, originally developed in French legal doctrine, conceptualises the lost opportunity itself as a distinct and compensable harm. It has since been adopted in Brazil and has been increasingly applied in the medical field over the past decades. Under this framework, compensation may be awarded when a patient's diminished probability of survival or recovery, attributable to medical negligence, constitutes a measurable loss, even if a direct causal link between the negligent act and the ultimate harm cannot be conclusively established. The *lost chance* is therefore treated as an autonomous form of harm, separate from the final outcome.

3.1.2 Concurrence of Causes and Exclusions of Causality in the Healthcare Sector

To assess medical civil liability in the context of an adverse event involving a patient, it is necessary to determine the efficient cause of the harm and identify the party to whom the duty of indemnification is attributed—whether the physician, the nursing team, the hospital, and/or the manufacturer of a medical product or device. Before delving into this analysis, it is essential to highlight some key aspects related to causation, contributory factors, and exonerating circumstances in civil liability. One of the most complex points in such disputes is identifying which events can be considered decisive in producing a harmful outcome in healthcare services.

Causation refers to the legal connection established between antecedent conduct or activity and the harm caused, for the purpose of assigning the duty to compensate. It serves as a criterion for determining the extent to which an action or omission contributed to the occurrence of harm, thereby defining the scope of compensation owed by the wrongdoer to the victim (Carpes 2016). Causation is a fundamental prerequisite for the attribution of civil liability; to disregard it would render the concept of liability arbitrary and akin to "a game of chance, a blind lottery" (Farias et al. 2021, pp. 464–465).

Article 944 of the Brazilian Civil Code (CC) stipulates that "compensation is measured by the extent of the harm". Establishing the scope of compensation requires a causal analysis to ascertain both *who* is liable to indemnify and *what* is subject to indemnification. Causation serves two primary functions: firstly, it allows the imposition of liability on the party whose behaviour—whether by fault or risk inherent in their activity—constituted the efficient cause of the harm; secondly, it defines the extent of the damage and the degree of reparation required.

In cases where there are two or more proven instances of fault—attributable to both the patient-victim and the defendant (physician and/or hospital)—liability for the damages will be shared between them, and compensation may be reduced, though not entirely excluded. This phenomenon, referred to as *plural causation*, is addressed in Article 945 (CC). It arises when "various causative factors of the harm can be attributed to different parties or when there is a concurrence between one party's actions and an external force, such as force majeure, or the victim's own conduct" (Farias et al. 2021, pp. 466).

Contributory causes arise when two or more factors collectively lead to a result that would not have occurred independently of each other (Carpes 2016). It is important to note that multiple causation does not exclude the causal link but rather distributes liability among the different causative factors. The victim's participation does not eliminate the agent's responsibility but may mitigate it.

In cases where multiple parties contribute to the harm, medical-hospital liability may be assessed through the application of the *Theory of Direct and Immediate Causation*, which attributes liability to the conduct that qualifies as a *conditio sine qua non* of the final result. Additionally, the *Sub-theory of Causal Necessity* may be applied, aligning Article 403 (CC) with the principle of proportionality. According to Schreiber (2007) and Tepedino (2001), this interpretation understands *direct and immediate damage* as requiring a necessity-based relationship between the agent's conduct and the harm, even if such effects are indirect.

Legal doctrine teaches that the *Sub-theory of Causal Necessity* moves beyond the rigidity of the *Theory of Direct and Immediate Causation* by evaluating the specific context in which the parties were situated. This approach ultimately determines whether the harm was necessarily justified by the agent's conduct, that is, whether it was a certain consequence of the unlawful act (Farias et al. 2021).

The civil liability system is guided by the *principle of full reparation of harm*—Article 944 (CC). However, certain contextual limitations to this principle are permitted, leading to a reduction in compensation. The primary example is the general clause of equitable reduction of indemnification (Article 944, sole paragraph, CC). According to Sanseverino (2011), the court is vested with the duty to conduct an equitable assessment based on three factors: (i) the severity of the fault; (ii) the extent of the harm; and (iii) any excessive disproportionality between the fault and the harm. Causation, therefore, not only serves as a prerequisite for liability but also functions as a measure of the obligation to indemnify, influencing the allocation of responsibility among the liable parties.

Articles 944, sole paragraph, and 945 of the CC address the analysis of fault gradation and the patient's behaviour, weighing the degree and potential concurrence of faults to proportionately define the extent of damage compensation. The existence of proven fault, regardless of its degree, grants the injured party the right to compensation. However, in cases of excessive disproportionality between the gravity of the fault and the harm, the court may *equitably reduce* the compensation. Indemnification is thus proportionate to the degree of fault, whether minimal, light, or grave.

The equitable reduction of compensation, as noted by Ronsevald and Braga Netto (2021), does not apply unless it is established that the harm is disproportionate to the fault, which must also not be light or minimal. Such an assessment requires an examination of the average diligence demanded by the case and the objective circumstances of the event, including time and location. The authors emphasize that equitable reduction is not merely a matter of judicial discretion but constitutes a substantive right of the liable party, contingent upon meeting these prerequisites.

For instance, a lower degree of fault may be observed in medical practice during the chaotic circumstances of the early stages of the COVID-19 pandemic. Rosenvald and Clemente (2021) underscore the importance of considering the *mitigation of medical liability* within objective parameters during the pandemic, highlighting the modulation of diligence standards over time as knowledge of the disease and its treatment evolved. In the initial phase of 2020, a doctor misdiagnosing COVID-19 under conditions of excessive workload and limited reliability of rapid tests may initially be regarded as minimally culpable (Nalin and Nogaroli 2021). However, as circumstances evolved and medical understanding increased, the same conduct during a later stage of the pandemic could no longer be deemed minimally culpable (Kfouri Neto and Nogaroli 2022). This progression underscores the dynamic nature of medical liability, where the evaluation of fault must account for the evolving standards of care and the contextual challenges faced by professionals during unprecedented public health crises.

Moreover, Brazilian jurisprudence includes cases in which, when quantifying damages, the professional is not held liable for the harmful event itself but for the breach of the patient's right to information, as discussed in the previous chapter of this book. For example, the Paraná State Court of Justice, in Civil Appeal No. 0003343–28.2020.8.16.0019, adjudicated on 18 July 2022, recognised the duty to compensate for informational negligence. In this case, the indemnity for the absence or inadequacy of informed consent was not calculated based on the harm caused, as it would be if the harm were directly attributable to the professional's negligence, recklessness, or lack of skill. Instead, it was measured by the probability that the patient, if properly informed, would not have consented to the treatment or procedure. As noted by Kfouri Neto (2019) and Reis (2019), compensation in such cases should be equitably reduced to a level lower than that awarded for harm directly caused by the professional's fault.

Particular attention must be paid to cases involving *contributory fault* or *exclusive fault* on the part of the patient. Examples include failure to adhere to prescribed post-surgical care, such as exposing the healing area to sunlight, engaging in physical activity prematurely, neglecting to change dressings, failing to use prescribed compression garments, or not taking medications or applying topical treatments as directed. It is possible for the professional to act negligently while the patient simultaneously contributes to an unsatisfactory outcome following medical intervention.

However, in Brazilian courts — as is likely the case in any jurisdiction worldwide — , recognising the concurrence of causes, that is, the interaction between the patient's conduct and the actions of the physician and/or the hospital's activities in producing a harmful event, presents significant practical challenges in the adjudication of medical legal claims. Such complexity arises primarily from three key factors : (i) challenges in proving causation through evidence (ii) concurrent causes arising at distinct moments; and (iii) the rupture of the causal link due to therapeutic risk.

(*First reason*) There is a substantial evidentiary difficulty faced by the judge in assessing the concurrence of causes in medical practice. This challenge stems from the inherent complexity of proving that a specific action—or inaction—on the part of the patient significantly contributed to the adverse outcome, alongside the actions of the physician or/and the medical institution. For instance, consider a scenario where a professional is required to demonstrate that a patient failed to adhere to postoperative instructions, such as using prescribed medication. Proving both the occurrence of noncompliance and its causal relationship to the negative health outcome demands not only detailed factual evidence but also expert testimony to establish the degree of influence such noncompliance had on the overall result.

This evidentiary burden becomes even more pronounced in cases involving complex medical scenarios, where multiple factors, both endogenous (related to the patient's health or biological condition) and exogenous (arising from the medical conduct), interact in producing the harm. In practice, the difficulty lies in isolating and quantifying the relative contribution of each factor within the intricate chain of events, which often involves significant medical and legal uncertainty.

Moreover, there are situations in which Brazilian courts recognise that a delay or gross diagnostic error by a medical professional deprives the patient of a chance of cure or survival. However, such circumstances do not involve concurrence of causes; rather, they concern professional conduct that serves as a determining factor in the loss of a chance for a favourable outcome.

For example, consider an oncology patient who receives an erroneous diagnosis—arising from gross negligence in the anamnesis or the request for medical tests—undergoes unsuccessful treatment, and later consults another physician, who provides a correct cancer diagnosis. Although treatment is initiated, the patient subsequently passes away. In this scenario, it is impossible to determine the extent to which the actions of the first physician contributed to the patient's death. However, despite the fact that the physician did not directly cause the final harm, their conduct reduced the probability of cure or survival. This reflects the application of the already mentioned *Loss of a Chance Theory* in the medical field.

It is worth noting that this theory aligns with the current state of civil liability worldwide, which demonstrates a tendency toward the erosion of traditional filters for compensation by softening the rigidity of the causal link concept. Kfouri Neto et al. (2022, p. 308) observes that, in the ever-changing dynamics of the modern world, new risks emerge constantly, and, in this context, damages cannot be left uncompensated. Consequently, efforts have been made to develop "mechanisms to ensure compensation at all costs, sometimes disregarding the concept of fault, sometimes extending the notion of causation, or establishing compensation funds to guarantee redress for all those harmed".

Thus, evidentiary challenges not only hinder the recognition of concurrence of causes in medical practice but also underscore the broader shift in civil liability from a rigid causal framework to a more flexible and inclusive model of compensation. This development reflects an increasing emphasis on fairness and justice in addressing harm, particularly in complex cases where traditional notions of causation fail to adequately capture the realities of modern medical practice.

(*Second reason*) The rare recognition of concurrence of causes in Medical Law by Brazilian courts arises from the uncommon occurrence of multiple causes materialising simultaneously. For example, in traffic accidents, there is an immediacy of two or more contributing factors, enabling the proportional allocation of liability for the damage caused. Consider a collision between two vehicles where the driver of one car ignores a right-of-way sign and collides with a motorcycle travelling at excessive speed, incompatible with the road conditions.

In such a case, the Paraná State Court of Justice adjudicated a similar matter, concluding that the reckless actions of both drivers contributed to the collision (Civil Appeal No. 0054922–16.2013.8.16.0001, decided on 25 June 2020). While the imprudent manoeuvre of the car driver was a significant factor, the motorcyclist's excessive speed also played a role, as the severity of the collision would not have reached the same magnitude without it. Accordingly, the court apportioned liability at 70% to the car driver and 30% to the motorcyclist, with compensation awarded in these proportions.

Thus, in cases involving multiple causes, two key aspects must be examined: (i) whether both actions genuinely contributed to the damage; and (ii) if so, determining the proportional contribution of each party to the resulting harm.

By contrast, in medical practice, multiple causes tend to occur successively over time (successive causality), encompassing consultations, diagnostic procedures, and treatments that often extend over long periods. As a result, it is exceedingly difficult to determine to what extent a specific act by the patient or the medical professional adequately contributed to the harmful outcome.

Typically, in such disputes, the patient's conduct is found to be the sole cause of the harm, thereby severing the causal link and exonerating the defendant (whether physician or hospital) from liability. This scenario differs from cases of contributory causation, where liability is proportionally shared. In these situations, the patient's actions are recognised as the determining cause of the harm, thereby excluding any responsibility on the part of the healthcare provider.

Common examples of exclusive patient fault that the Brazilian courts frequently identify as exculpatory causes include abandoning prescribed treatment, hiding true symptoms, and failing to follow postoperative care instructions. To constitute an exclusive cause, the patient's behaviour must independently result in the harm suffered, without any contributory fault by the medical professional.

In this regard, Miragem (2007) offers an instructive analysis of how exclusive patient fault breaks the causal link:

> The exculpatory hypothesis must be unequivocally demonstrated, particularly from the perspective of causation, as this fact must independently result in the harm without any contributory fault by the medical professional or breach of the duty of care. For instance, the Superior Court of Justice has recognised a hospital's liability for the suicide of a cancer patient who had expressed suicidal intent while hospitalised, a fact known to the attending physician. In this case, the hospital's liability arose from its failure to take measures to prevent the patient from carrying out their intentions. Thus, exculpatory causes of liability are not based on the greater or lesser degree of fault on the consumer's part but on the exclusive fault of the patient, which must be interpreted restrictively given the extreme vulnerability they face due to illness or the psychological strain of undergoing medical treatment.

Several recent cases illustrate these ideas. In 2022, the São Paulo State Court of Justice ruled in Civil Appeal No. 0002349–61.2008.8.26.0562, involving a patient who abandoned postoperative care following breast implant surgery. Expert evidence showed that the poor aesthetic result was unrelated to technical inadequacy but rather to the premature abandonment of prescribed treatment and follow-up. The physician recommended additional surgery to remove the implant due to compromised healing and a diagnosis of extrusion (an inherent risk), but the patient failed to attend the scheduled consultation, instead seeking treatment from another professional.

In another 2022 case (Civil Appeal No. 1102765–62.2019.8.26.0100), the same court ruled on a patient who suffered a bathroom fall while hospitalised. Despite the hospital's duty of care and safety, it was proven that the fall did not result from negligence by the staff, as the patient, who was lucid, refused professional assistance during bathing despite being informed of the risk. In this case, the patient's exclusive fault detached the causal link, absolving the hospital of liability.

A further exculpatory cause in medical-hospital liability may be the fault of a third party. For example, in a decision by the Paraná State Court of Justice (Civil Appeal No. 0000555–62.2001.8.16.0001, ruled in 2019), a paediatric patient suffered cardiac arrest due to respiratory obstruction caused by aspirated gastric contents. The forensic report concluded that the medical staff had appropriately performed resuscitation measures and that the patient's mother had fed the child regurgitated food before the anaesthesia, contrary to the nursing staff's explicit instructions for pre-anaesthetic fasting. Consequently, the court found no causal link between the medical services and the harm, recognising the third party's actions as the exculpatory cause.

This analysis highlights how, in Medical Law, the evaluation of causation often deviates from the straightforward simultaneity seen in other contexts, such as traffic accidents. Instead, medical causation typically involves successive interactions over time, making it particularly challenging to establish proportional liability or concurrence of multiple causes. Where exclusive fault by the patient or a third party is identified, the causal link is broken, reinforcing the principle that compensation must rest on a robust and demonstrable nexus between conduct and harm.

(*Third reason*) Finally, the third reason that complicates the recognition of concurrence of causes in medical law is that the patient's inherent physiological responses—known as therapeutic risk—often sever the causal link between the medical conduct and the harmful event.

Therapeutic risk refers to the unpredictable, individualised reactions of a patient's body to medical interventions, which may include surgeries, treatments, or medications. These reactions are not attributable to any fault or negligence on the part of the healthcare provider but are instead inherent to the patient's biological characteristics or the inherent risks of medical procedures. As such, these physiological responses can act as independent factors that interrupt the causal chain, making it difficult to assign liability to the medical professional.

For instance, a patient undergoing a surgical procedure may develop an unexpected allergic reaction to anaesthesia, despite all appropriate preoperative tests and precautions having been taken by the medical team. Similarly, a patient may experience postoperative complications, such as an infection or poor wound healing, despite adherence to best medical practices. In these situations, the harm is not the result of substandard care but arises from the patient's unique biological response to the treatment or procedure.

Courts often grapple with the challenge of determining whether the harmful outcome was predominantly caused by medical error or whether it was an unavoidable result of therapeutic risk. In many cases, the therapeutic risk serves to break the causal link, absolving the medical professional of liability because the harm could not have been reasonably foreseen or prevented.

This difficulty is further exacerbated by the complex nature of medical evidence, which requires expert testimony to distinguish between harm caused by medical conduct and harm resulting from therapeutic risk. Without clear evidence of fault, the courts are unlikely to recognise concurrence of causes, as the presence of an inherent risk eliminates the proportional allocation of liability.

Thus, the unpredictable and often uncontrollable nature of therapeutic risks represents a significant barrier to recognising concurrence of causes in medical law. These risks underscore the importance of establishing a robust causal link as a prerequisite for attributing liability, while simultaneously highlighting the limits of medical science in predicting or controlling the outcomes of every medical intervention.

3.2 Allocation of Civil Liability Among Physicians, Hospitals, and Manufacturers

In addition to the physician's individual responsibility, it is essential to consider the broader ecosystem of civil liability that underpins medical practice in Brazil. When a harmful event occurs involving a patient, the potential liabilities must be assessed within this ecosystem, which includes not only physicians but also nurses, healthcare institutions, and the manufacturers or suppliers of medical devices.

In this context, in claims for compensation, Brazilian courts determine the outcome of cases based on the regime of civil liability applicable to the specific circumstances of the case. Medical services provided within the public sector, under the Unified Health System (*Sistema Único de Saúde*—SUS), are subject to the administrative risk theory, as established by Article 37, paragraph 6, of the Brazilian Federal Constitution. Under this framework, the state assumes objective liability for damages caused by public healthcare services, irrespective of fault.

However, the determination of fault on the part of individual healthcare professionals is deferred to regressive actions, which may be filed by healthcare service providers against the individual agents responsible for the patient's care. This principle was affirmed in Topic 940 adjudicated by the Federal Supreme Court (*Supremo Tribunal Federal*—STF), which provides the legal basis for such proceedings.

A second regime of objective liability applies to private healthcare services, including those rendered by private providers or under health insurance plans. This regime is governed by the Brazilian Civil Code and, more specifically, the Consumer Code, which establishes the consumer's basic rights to prevention and full compensation for damages arising from services and products available in the marketplace.

In this context, liability arises under the product or service defect theory, codified in Article 14 of Brazilian Consumer Protection Code (*Código de Defesa do Consumidor*—CDC). This provision encompasses two distinct forms of liability:

i) *subjective personal liability* (Article 14, paragraph 4): this applies specifically to liberal professionals, such as physicians, whose liability is dependent on evidence of fault or negligence. Unlike institutions, liberal professionals are not held to strict liability because their work often involves subjective assessments and complex decision-making processes, where outcomes cannot be absolutely guaranteed due to the existence of therapeutic risk. For a physician to be held liable under this provision, the claimant must demonstrate that the harm resulted from a breach of duty, such as failure to meet the standard of care expected in the circumstances, or acts of recklessness, negligence, or incompetence.
ii) *objective liability* (Article 14, caput): this applies to service providers, such as hospitals, clinics, or healthcare institutions, which are held strictly liable for damages caused by defective services, irrespective of fault. In this context, liability extends to *extramedical services*, such as accommodation, meals, the comfort of the facilities, patient transportation within the hospital premises, and the maintenance and regular functioning of equipment. These services are typically performed by auxiliary staff under the direction of the hospital administration. A defect in any of these areas that causes harm to the patient establishes liability on the part of the hospital, without the need to prove negligence.

In a case adjudicated by the Paraná State Court of Justice (Civil Appeal No. 0021106–53.2017.8.16.0017, decided on 28 June 2021), a patient sustained second-degree burns on her buttocks following a surgical procedure conducted at a hospital. Despite the procedure itself being performed without complications, the burns emerged several days later and were ultimately attributed to an electric current transmitted through the surgical table. The expert evidence established that the burns were not caused by any aspect of the surgery itself but rather by a failure in the hospital's equipment.

The court ruled that the hospital was objectively liable for the harm, as the damage stemmed from the defective functioning of its facilities—specifically, the surgical table—and not from any fault on the part of the medical team. This decision highlights the expansive scope of hospital liability, which encompasses not only direct medical services but also the proper maintenance and operation of the equipment and infrastructure required to deliver safe care.

This distinction ensures a nuanced approach to liability within the healthcare sector, recognising the inherent differences between the institutional responsibilities of service providers and the professional obligations of individual practitioners.

While hospitals are accountable for structural and systemic failures, including defects in the ancillary services and equipment they provide, physicians are evaluated on the basis of their individual conduct and adherence to professional standards in the delivery of care. This dual framework seeks to balance the rights of patients to full compensation with the practical realities of medical practice and institutional operation.

This comprehensive framework of civil liability within the healthcare sector lays the foundation for a deeper examination of how liability is allocated when adverse events involve medical technologies. With the increasing integration of advanced devices and innovative treatments into medical practice, questions of responsibility become even more complex. Whether it is a malfunctioning medical device, improper usage by a professional, or failure to provide adequate information about risks, the interplay between human and technological factors introduces unique challenges to the attribution of liability. The next section delves into the specific legal considerations surrounding medical technologies, highlighting their role in patient care and the corresponding obligations of physicians, institutions, and manufacturers.

3.2.1 Adverse Events Involving Medical Technologies

The introduction of technological innovations in healthcare has significantly increased the complexity of analysing causation, particularly in determining the efficient cause of harm suffered by patients. Frequently, disputes arise concerning liability exclusions and the so-called *unknown risks* or *development risks* (also referred to as *unknowable risks*). These risks typically arise in situations where a product or technology is later found to cause harm that could not have been predicted using the scientific or technical knowledge available at the time of its development. Accordingly, this Subchapter and the next aim to provide a concise analysis of these issues. First, an analysis is conducted of the possible adverse events that may arise in this context.

Medical devices, a product of technological advancement, began to emerge in the first half of the nineteenth century. However, the most significant developments have occurred over the last 50 years and continue to progress rapidly. These devices—incorporating a wide range of technologies—have quickly become an essential part of healthcare, playing a pivotal role in various activities undertaken by healthcare professionals. Their integration has facilitated diagnostic and therapeutic efforts, increasing the efficiency and precision of medical interventions.

According to the World Health Organisation (WHO), a *medical device* is defined as any instrument, apparatus, machine, implant, diagnostic equipment, software, or other material that achieves its primary intended purpose not through pharmacological, immunological, or metabolic means. Such devices serve several purposes, including: (i) diagnosing, preventing, monitoring, treating, or alleviating injury or disease; (ii) investigating, replacing, modifying, or supporting anatomy or a physiological process; (iii) analysing in vitro samples derived from the human body to provide information for diagnostic, monitoring, or screening purposes, or determining compatibility with potential recipients of blood, tissues, or organs.

Since the 1980s, there has been a worldwide marked increase in the use of medical devices for patient care, particularly continuous monitoring systems for cardiovascular parameters, such as heart rate, cardiac output, and blood pressure. Advances in technology have made ventilators, renal dialysis machines, and neonatal incubators commonplace in hospital settings. Between 1980 and 2000, the variety of medical devices on the market grew exponentially. Hospitals widely adopted CT scanners and MRI units, and surgeons began offering patients various medical devices for the replacement of limbs or body parts (Gaev 2004).

From 2000 to 2020, robotic medical devices became a crucial aspect of healthcare. These include a wide range of assistive devices for individuals with functional disabilities. Additionally, the concept of medical devices integrated with information systems or web-based platforms emerged, revolutionising surgical procedures. It is estimated that robotic platforms have enabled minimally invasive surgeries for more than eight million patients worldwide.

Globally, approximately 1.5 million different medical devices are currently available on the consumer market, according to WHO data. In Brazil, around 10,000 medical devices were registered, as reported by the National Health Surveillance Agency (Anvisa) in 2022. Additionally, the Brazilian medical device and in vitro diagnostics market was valued at USD 15.4 billion in 2023, reflecting an average annual growth of 11.6% between 2018 and 2023.

In comparison, the European Union medical technology sector is significantly larger, with total trade (imports and exports) in medical products amounting to approximately €123 billion in 2019, according to the European Parliament. In European countries, more than 500,000 types of medical devices and in vitro diagnostics (IVDs) were available in 2024, according to European Comission. Examples of medical devices are sticking plasters, contact lenses, X-ray machines, pacemakers, breast implants, software apps and hip replacements. IVDs are used to perform tests on samples, and examples include HIV blood tests, pregnancy tests and blood sugar monitoring systems for diabetics.

The benefits of medical devices enhanced by computational technology are numerous and transformative. They have improved diagnostic accuracy, increased the efficiency of medical interventions, advanced health condition monitoring, facilitated the development of new medicines, and generally enhanced the safety of healthcare practices. However, technological innovations also introduce new risks.

For instance, robotic-assisted surgeries have prompted numerous claims in the United States, the country where the Da Vinci surgical robot was developed. These cases, often referred to as *finger-pointing cases* (Mclean 2007, 2008; Mclean and Waxman 2010), revolve around the question of liability in adverse events during robotic-assisted surgeries.

Central to these disputes is determining who should bear responsibility for harm caused to patients: the physician or the equipment manufacturer. Physicians and hospitals often claim that the harm resulted from a defect in the robot itself, thereby placing liability on the manufacturer. Conversely, manufacturers argue that the harm arose from medical malpractice or improper maintenance and calibration of the robot by hospital staff.

In 2017, a breakthrough innovation emerged with the development of the *dVLogger*, a type of *black box* integrated into the *Da Vinci surgical robot*. This device records video and metadata during surgeries, capturing the positioning of instruments and the surgeon's operation of the robot (Hung et al. 2018). This technology facilitates the identification of critical factors during surgery. For example, it can reveal whether the robot issued an alert or error message that the surgeon ignored, choosing to proceed with the procedure (medical liability). Alternatively, it can identify malfunctions in the robot itself, such as an unexpected movement attributable to a product defect, poor maintenance (hospital liability), or incorrect calibration or sterilisation of robotic instruments by hospital staff (hospital liability) (Kfouri Neto and Nogaroli 2022).

In the landmark American case of *Zarick v. Intuitive Surgical*, adjudicated by the Civil Jury of the California State Court in 2016, it was alleged that a patient suffered severe harm following robotic surgery due to a defect in the *tip cover accessory*. This component, designed to cover the tip of surgical scissors and prevent electrical discharge, developed microfissures during the procedure. These small cracks allowed electrical current to pass into surrounding tissues and organs outside the surgical field—an issue undetectable by the surgeon during the operation. When surgical robots were initially introduced to the US market in the 2000s, this defect had not been identified. However, following numerous injuries linked to the accessory, a recall was issued in 2012, as it became evident that the tip cover was prone to developing microfissures, leading to burns in tissues and organs (Alemzadeh et al. 2016).

These incidents highlight the complex interplay between innovation and risk in the medical device industry. Just as robotic surgery has raised questions about liability and product safety, adverse events in radiotherapy treatments further exemplify the potential dangers posed by insufficient testing, software defects, and weak regulatory oversight, demonstrating the urgent need for robust safety and accountability measures across all medical technologies.

Adverse events involving medical devices have also been exemplified by two paradigmatic cases in radiotherapy treatment, which underscore the risks and fatalities associated with software bugs, insufficient product testing prior to market approval, and inadequate systems for post-market accident reporting and investigation.

Between 1985 and 1987, at least six incidents were reported in which patients received massive overdoses of radiation from the Canadian radiotherapy machine *Therac-25*, resulting in deaths or severe injuries. The overdoses, sometimes hundreds of times greater than intended, were attributed to software failures. Operators believed they were administering a low-energy beam but instead delivered a megavolt beam. In other instances, overdoses were repeated because the machine's display incorrectly showed that no dose had been delivered (Baase 2008).

Approximately 15 years later, between 2000 and 2001, around 20 patients were injured, and 5 died, due to excessive radiation exposure from the *Cobalt-60* device at Panama's National Oncology Institute (International Atomic Energy Agency 2001). Unlike the modern *Therac-25*, the *Cobalt-60* was an outdated, overused device with inadequate maintenance. Its software was a post-sale programme provided by Multidata Systems, as the hospital claimed it could not afford the costs charged by the device's manufacturer, Theratronics. Some radiologists left the institution due to the lack of maintenance, while those who remained unsuccessfully requested action from hospital administrators (Lake 2010).

At one point, the medical team devised an allegedly *more efficient method* for aligning the shields that defined the radiation target. Although this method was not included in the device manual, it *appeared to be effective*. However, aligning the shields in a specific sequence triggered an obscure software bug that caused patients to receive excessive radiation. Due to the hospital's workload and lack of oversight by clinical management, this practice continued for 7 months before the World Health Organisation became aware of the situation and dispatched a team of experts to investigate the case.

From these incidents involving medical technologies, significant conclusions can be drawn. Despite the technological advancements of medical devices, which ostensibly reduce adverse events in healthcare, any risk that materialises must be thoroughly investigated to establish the liability of the manufacturer as the primary responsible party for defective products. In exceptional cases, liability may also extend to medical professionals who continue to use an evidently defective device, breaching duties of vigilance grounded in the principle of good faith.

The discussion regarding the subjective liability of medical professionals when using outdated or defective medical technologies will be addressed in greater detail later in this book, particularly in the chapter on medical duties of care in AI systems. In the paragraphs that follow, however, the focus remains on the objective liability of manufacturers for defective medical devices.

As Rosenvald (2022) clarifies, there is an important distinguish between *unknown risks* or *unknowable risks*. Unknown risks are those of which the defendant, or a class of similarly situated persons, is unaware. In contrast, unknowable risks pertain to dangers that no reasonable person in the defendant's position could have foreseen. Hogg (2016) further refines this distinction: an unknown risk involves a lack of factual knowledge specific to the defendant, while an unknowable risk is one that no individual, given the circumstances, could reasonably anticipate. This differentiation underscores the importance of assessing liability based on both subjective and objective standards of foreseeability.

According to Wesendonck (2015), unknowable risks occur when a product that is considered safe at the time of its design, based on the technical and scientific knowledge then available, later proves to have defects that could not have been foreseen. These risks emerge only with the passage of time and the development of new investigative techniques or scientific advancements that reveal previously undetectable flaws.

For instance, consider the introduction of certain medical implants, such as early-generation metal-on-metal hip replacements. At the time of their approval, these devices were heralded as innovative solutions for joint replacement, and their safety was supported by the best available testing methods. However, years after their widespread adoption, patients began experiencing serious complications, including tissue damage and elevated metal ion levels in the bloodstream. These issues, linked to the wear and tear of the implant, were unknowable at the time of design and approval, as the necessary long-term data and diagnostic tools were unavailable. Nowadays, advances in biomaterials—particularly the widespread use of highly cross-linked polyethylene and ceramic components—have significantly reduced these risks, providing greater biocompatibility, lower wear rates, and improved long-term safety for patients undergoing hip replacement surgeries.

This example illustrates the principle that unknowable risks are inherently tied to the evolving nature of science and technology. Such risks challenge both manufacturers and regulators to anticipate potential flaws, even when the limits of contemporary knowledge seem to provide a comprehensive safety assessment.

3.2.2 Accountability and Unknowable Risks in Medical Devices

In the context of Tort Law, accountability for *unknowable risks* (also known as development risks) associated with medical devices presents a complex interplay between technological innovation, patient safety, and legal responsibility. Medical devices, which range from diagnostic tools to implantable technologies, are subject to rigorous regulatory frameworks designed to ensure their safety and efficacy. However, even the most advanced oversight mechanisms cannot entirely eliminate the emergence of unforeseen risks, particularly in the rapidly evolving field of medical technology.

Manufacturers are held to high standards in ensuring the safety of their products. This duty includes thorough pre-market testing, compliance with regulatory requirements, and post-market surveillance. While no device can be entirely free of risk, manufacturers must demonstrate that they have taken all reasonable measures to mitigate potential harm. Moreover, the duty to inform becomes critical. Manufacturers are obligated to provide clear, accurate, and comprehensive warnings about known risks and instructions for safe use. Failure to disclose known or reasonably foreseeable risks constitutes a breach of this duty and may lead to liability. Despite these extensive obligations, unknowable risks present a unique challenge to manufacturers.

Unknowable risks arise due to the inherent complexity of medical devices, which often rely on cutting-edge science, intricate engineering, and their interaction with unique human biological systems. These factors introduce uncertainties that may only surface after a device has been widely deployed in real-world conditions, beyond the controlled environment of clinical trials.

For instance, consider a pacemaker, a sophisticated medical device designed to regulate heart rhythm. During controlled clinical trials, the pacemaker might demonstrate excellent performance and safety, adhering to the highest standards of scientific and technical knowledge. However, once the device is used in diverse real-world conditions, unforeseen complications might emerge. These could include rare interactions with medications, unanticipated malfunctions under specific environmental conditions (e.g., exposure to electromagnetic interference), or even unexpected biological responses in a small subset of patients.

Such risks challenge traditional legal notions of defect and liability because they are not discoverable at the time of production, even with the most advanced knowledge and rigorous testing available. This scenario raises complex questions in Tort Law. Should the manufacturer be held liable for a defect that was unknowable at the time the product was developed? Different legal systems approach this issue differently.

In Brazilian legal system, the question of who should bear the burden of unknowable risks associated with a product—the supplier or the consumer—has given rise to two opposing legal doctrines. This debate centres on the *allocation of accountability* within the framework of Tort Law and is closely tied to principles of fairness, risk distribution, and public policy. The issue is particularly challenging in cases where a product, deemed safe at the time of its design and market release, later causes harm due to risks that were unforeseeable under the prevailing technical and scientific knowledge.

One perspective argues that the supplier, as the party profiting from the product, should bear the responsibility for unknowable risks. This view aligns with the *principle of strict liability*, commonly found in Tort Law, which holds manufacturers accountable for defective products regardless of fault. Proponents of this approach contend that assigning liability to suppliers incentivises them to invest in rigorous safety measures and ensures a fair distribution of risks between parties with unequal access to information and resources.

Conversely, others argue that holding suppliers liable for unknowable risks imposes an undue burden, potentially stifling innovation and discouraging the development of beneficial products. This perspective emphasises the importance of *foreseeability* in establishing liability, suggesting that consumers must accept a degree of risk inherent in using any product. Under this approach, liability would only arise if the manufacturer failed to meet the standards of care reasonably expected at the time of design and production.

This debate is not unique to Brazilian law. In Europe, similar discussions have taken place within the context of product liability under the EU Product Liability Directive. Directive 85/374/EEC provided for strict liability but allowed manufacturers to invoke the development risks defence, exempting them from liability for unknowable risks. This exemption aimed to strike a balance between protecting consumers and fostering innovation by ensuring that manufacturers were not held liable for risks genuinely unforeseeable at the time of market entry. However, this defence has been a source of controversy, and with the repeal of Directive 85/374/EEC and its recent replacement by Directive 2024/2853, this debate has been revisited (see Sect. 4.2.2 of this book), reflecting the need for legislative reform to better address the complexities of modern technologies, particularly in rapidly evolving fields such as artificial intelligence.

The allocation of liability for unknowable risks remains a contentious and evolving area of law, both in Brazil and internationally. It requires a careful balance between safeguarding public health, encouraging technological progress, and ensuring equitable risk distribution. Further analysis and debate are crucial to navigating this intricate legal terrain.

In Brazil, Article 12, paragraph 1, of the Brazilian Consumer Protection Code (*Código de Defesa do Consumidor*—CDC) states that a product is deemed defective if it "fails to offer the safety that may legitimately be expected from it, considering the relevant circumstances, including: I – its presentation; II – the use and risks reasonably expected from it; III – the time when it was placed on the market". Conversely, paragraph 2 clarifies that a product is not considered defective "merely because a better-quality product has been subsequently placed on the market".

At first glance, one might mistakenly conclude that a manufacturer of a medical device sued in court could rely on the argument that the product, when introduced into the market, possessed sufficient safety based on the best technology and scientific knowledge available at the time, thereby excluding liability. However, the prevailing Brazilian doctrinal stance supports the view that manufacturers are always subject to strict liability, even in cases involving unknowable risks. As Marcelo Calixto (2004, p. 246) argues, "it dispenses with any inquiry into conduct or the foreseeability or unforeseeability of risks, reinforcing the product's defective nature since, it has failed to meet a legitimate expectation of safety".

Moreover, Calixto (2004) asserts that even when a risk was unknowable to both the manufacturer and the consumer and is only discovered later, the manufacturer remains liable because the legitimate expectation of safe use has been violated. This scenario differs from the rule in Article 12, paragraph 2, of the CDC, where the risks of the product have been disclosed to consumers, who cannot then claim ignorance. If the manufacturer fails to disclose a known risk, their liability for defective information is established.

This approach is grounded in the principle of consumer protection enshrined in the Brazilian Consumer Code, which prioritises the safety and well-being of consumers over the unforeseeability of certain risks. Under this framework, manufacturers are held accountable for harm caused by their products, regardless of whether the defect could have been anticipated based on the state of scientific or technical knowledge at the time of production. The rationale is that the manufacturer, as the party introducing the product to the market and benefiting from its use, is in the best position to bear the costs of such risks, thereby ensuring that consumers are not left unprotected.

This strict liability regime also reflects broader public policy considerations, aiming to incentivise manufacturers to adopt the highest possible safety standards, invest in post-market surveillance, and develop mechanisms for continuous product improvement. By placing the burden of unknowable risks on manufacturers, Brazilian law seeks to reinforce the principle of fairness in risk allocation and uphold the trust between consumers and the marketplace.

The concept of *defect*, according to Rosenvald (2020), requires modernisation to be understood as a *failure to meet a general duty of safety*, i.e., the standard of safety expected in relation to specific technologies. The degree of care demanded of suppliers varies according to the concrete circumstances, as Soares (2019) explains, noting that the required level of safety "increases in proportion to the risk involved in the provision of products or services and their intended recipient". Lopez (2008, p. 41) further reinforces this principle, asserting that "the duty of safety is now a general principle within society and, especially, within commercial transactions, particularly those involving consumers".

By introducing a medical device into the market, the manufacturer assumes the risks—both foreseeable and unforeseeable—associated with its use. This principle is reflected in the strict liability framework of Article 931 of the Brazilian Civil Code, which states: "individual entrepreneurs and companies are liable, irrespective of fault, for damages caused by products placed into circulation". It is crucial to emphasise that this provision does not adopt the *Theory of Integral Risk*, which would impose an absolute duty to compensate even in the presence of an exculpatory causal factor.

Instead, Article 931 adheres to the Theory of Aggravated Strict Liability, which applies when the offender engages in commercial activities that present inherent risks of significant harm. As Rosenvald (2021, p. 950) explains, "facts that previously excluded liability due to their classification as external fortuitous events gradually, with jurisprudential evolution, come to be regarded as internal fortuitous events". These internal events are considered inherent to the product or its operation, thereby falling within the scope of the manufacturer's liability.

For medical devices, internal fortuitous events include defects or failures intrinsic to the product, such as: (i) design defects: Errors in the conceptualisation of the device, making it unsafe even when properly manufactured; (ii) manufacturing defects: Faults arising during production, causing specific units to deviate from intended specifications; (iii) maintenance-related issues: Failures in providing clear instructions for proper maintenance, calibration, or use. Such events are considered internal because they are tied to the manufacturer's responsibility to ensure the product meets safety standards throughout its lifecycle.

Conversely, exculpatory causes (external fortuitous events) that could exclude the manufacturer's liability include: (i) improper use by the consumer or third party: For example, if a medical device is used in a manner expressly prohibited by the instructions; (ii) intervention by an external force: Such as an unforeseeable and extraordinary event like a natural disaster damaging the device; (iii) tampering or unauthorised modifications: Situations where a third party alters the device in a way that compromises its safety or functionality.

This distinction reinforces the idea that while manufacturers are strictly liable for risks internal to the device, their liability is not absolute. Exculpatory causes that are external to the manufacturing process or operation of the device can interrupt the causal link and preclude liability.

Given the circumstances described, the legal framework in Brazil, as outlined in Article 931 of the Civil Code, imposes strict liability on manufacturers for damages caused by products they place on the market, irrespective of fault. This principle ensures that the burden of unknowable risks does not fall on the patient, who is in a position of vulnerability. Instead, such risks are treated as inherent to the business activity of the manufacturer, recognising that the benefits of placing medical devices on the market come with an assumption of responsibility for potential harm.

This approach aligns with the *precautionary principle*, which mandates that uncertainties about risks should not excuse inaction. While unknowable risks might not eliminate liability, they prompt a broader inquiry into whether the manufacturer adequately managed known risks and adhered to high standards of care in product development and monitoring. In today's risk society, with increasingly complex and sophisticated products, the major challenge, as Lopez (2010) argues, is how to demand, and consequently sanction, risk creators who fail to adequately manage both known dangers (principle of prevention) and potential risks (principle of precaution).

Healthcare providers have a duty to ensure that devices are used appropriately and according to guidelines. Regulatory agencies also play a critical role by establishing robust oversight mechanisms, conducting post-market evaluations, and facilitating transparency about adverse events. Together, these efforts create a network of shared responsibility that prioritises patient safety without stifling innovation.

From an ethical perspective, holding manufacturers accountable for unknowable risks reflects the broader societal expectation that those who create potential hazards must also manage them responsibly. This expectation becomes particularly acute in the field of medical technology, where the stakes often involve life and death. Legally, the doctrine of legitimate expectation plays a pivotal role, emphasising that patients and healthcare providers rely on the implicit assurance of safety when utilising medical devices.

As will be further examined in this book, the rapid pace of innovation in medical technology presents significant challenges in addressing accountability for unknowable risks. The growing integration of artificial intelligence and interconnected systems into medical devices amplifies the range of potential hazards, including cybersecurity breaches, algorithmic biases, and unforeseen interactions between devices. These developments necessitate a proactive approach from legal systems, which must evolve to accommodate these emerging risks. Striking a delicate balance between encouraging technological advancement and safeguarding public safety remains a critical objective in this evolving landscape.

Over the past decades, legal scholars have focused extensively on the analysis of possible sanctions for non-compliance with the principles of precaution and prevention in the distribution of defective products. These issues will be explored in greater depth in the following chapters. For now, the present chapter highlights the role Tort Law must play, from a polyfunctional perspective, within the legal system. As

Perlingieri (2006) aptly warns, "the legal order must do everything to prevent damage and enable the effective realisation of existential situations".

Accountability for unknowable risks in medical devices represents a critical intersection of law, ethics, and technology. By imposing strict liability on manufacturers, the legal framework in Brazil ensures that patients are not left to bear the burden of unforeseen harm. However, this accountability must be complemented by proactive risk management, transparent communication, and coordinated efforts among all stakeholders in the healthcare ecosystem. As the field of medical technology continues to evolve, the principles of precaution and prevention will remain central to addressing the challenges posed by unknowable risks.

3.3 Legal Frameworks on Liability for Medical Negligence in European Countries

Defining a common framework for European legislative systems in the context of medical liability is a challenging task. These legal systems are notably diverse and do not consistently adopt similar approaches. The primary challenge lies in recognising the variety of historical and socio-cultural contexts, as well as political and institutional transformations, that characterise each nation.

An initial step in establishing comparisons, distinctions, and similarities among these systems often involves categorising countries according to their legal traditions: those following the *Romano-Germanic Civil Law system* (typical of most continental European nations) and those adhering to the *Anglo-Saxon Common Law system* (characteristic of England and former colonies of the British Empire, such as Ireland). A subsequent layer of analysis could explore the varying levels of judicial discretion in interpreting and applying the rules governing medical liability.

In England, the legal framework demonstrates a limited reliance on regulatory instruments, with judicial decisions holding significant weight and authority. British judges adhere to the *ratio decidendi* of precedents, namely the legal principles established in prior judgments. Innovations in judicial decisions are relatively rare, occurring only in exceptional circumstances, such as through *overruling* or *distinguishing*. Within the realm of medical liability, this reliance on judicial interpretation over statutory law highlights the centrality of precedent when adjudicating cases of medical negligence.

In recent years, however, a significant convergence between the judicial decisions and legal frameworks of Civil Law and Common Law systems has been observed on a global scale. This trend extends beyond the European context, as demonstrated by Brazil, where the 2015 Code of Civil Procedure introduced a structured system of judicial precedents. This reform aimed to foster legal certainty and promote jurisprudential uniformity, aligning aspects of the Brazilian legal system more closely with Common Law traditions. Such developments illustrate the increasing interplay between these historically distinct legal systems, eroding the rigid boundaries that once separated them.

Moreover, Italy, for example, operates within the Civil Law tradition yet provides an illustrative case where judges frequently transcend their traditional role as mere appliers of the law. Instead, they often assume the position of interpreters or even "creators" of legal norms, particularly in cases where the existing legal framework is silent or insufficient.

As a result, an analysis solely reliant on the traditional distinction between Civil Law and Common Law systems is inadequate for a comprehensive and comparative examination of medical liability regimes across European countries. The growing interconnection and cross-influence between these traditions call for a broader approach that considers shared principles and evolving jurisprudential trends.

A significant distinction in medical civil liability claims across European jurisdictions concerns the legal characterisation of the doctor-patient relationship. In certain legal systems, this relationship is deemed contractual, whereas in others it is characterised as extracontractual. In Italy, Law No. 24/2017 (commonly referred to as the Gelli Law) established a dual framework, enabling the doctor-patient relationship to be classified as either contractual or extracontractual, depending on the specific circumstances of each case. This distinction will be examined in greater detail later in this Subchapter.

In Spain, medical practitioners are held civilly liable for fault (medical negligence), provided a causal link is established between the negligent act and the resulting harm. Liability may arise under Tort Law (*responsabilidad aquiliana*) as per Article 1.902 of the Spanish Civil Code or from a breach of contractual obligations under Article 1.101. In both cases, the responsible party is obliged to compensate for damages unless exonerating factors eliminate such liability. Although distinctions exist between contractual and extracontractual liability, the underlying principle of fault remains unified. In both cases, courts assess whether the conduct deviated from the standard expected under the *lex artis ad hoc* and whether causation is established.

Liability in Spanish medical malpractice cases may be either contractual or extracontractual. Contractual liability stems from the failure to fulfil obligations arising from an agreement, typically seen in private medical care. In such cases, a contractual relationship is established between the healthcare professional and the patient, obligating the former to provide treatment with due diligence and the latter to pay for the services rendered.

According to the Spanish legal scholar Julio César Galán Cortés in his work *Responsabilidad Civil Médica* (Cortés 2024), the physician assumes an obligation of activity, diligence, and prudence, aligned with the current state of medical science. This constitutes an obligation of means, as the desired outcome is influenced by randomness and factors beyond the professional's control. Medicine is inherently an inexact science. As Galán Cortés highlights, the obligation is fulfilled when the practitioner provides care in accordance with the *lex artis* (rules of the profession) during the diagnostic, therapeutic, and recovery phases, as expected of an ordinary professional. The duty is performed even if the patient is not cured, as healing is the aim but not the legal content of the obligation. Thus, the analysis of fault is essential to determine a lack of diligence. It identifies whether the practitioner failed to meet the required standard, providing the basis for liability where harm arises.

As Galán Cortés explains (2024), the origins of the distinction between obligations of means and obligations was in France and gained prominence through the landmark *Mercier Decision* (*Arrêt Mercier*—Mercier v. Dr. Nicolas), issued by the Cour de Cassation, Civil Chamber 1, on 20 May 1936. The case concerned a medical treatment involving X-rays administered by Dr. Nicolas to a patient suffering from a nasal condition. The treatment caused radiodermatitis on the mucous membranes of the patient's face. X-ray treatment, particularly in the 1930s, was known for its potential adverse effects, such as radiodermatitis, which refers to inflammation and damage to the skin caused by excessive exposure to ionising radiation (radiodermatitis, a condition involving inflammation and damage to the skin due to excessive exposure to ionising radiation). Such effects were inherent to the technology available at the time, even when used correctly. In this context, radiodermatitis was not caused by error or negligence but rather resulted from the necessary use of the procedure to treat the nasal condition.

The patient brought legal action against the professional, arguing that the harm resulted from improper care. This situation provided an opportunity for the French courts to define the nature of the medical professional's legal obligation to their patient. The decision marked a turning point by establishing the legal nature of the relationship between physician and patient. The court classified the physician's obligation as one of *means* rather than result. It held that "the contract concluded between the physician and the patient imposes on the former the obligation of providing diligent, informed, and prudent care".

The Mercier Decision made it evident that a physician does not guarantee a cure but is required to deliver careful and attentive treatment, in accordance with the current state of medical science. This ruling established the principle of diligence as the cornerstone of medical liability and became a reference point in Medical Law.

Moreover, a few decades later, French jurisprudence has defined the concept of *therapeutic risk* (*alea terapéutico*) as the occurrence of an accidental risk inherent to medical practice that is beyond the control of the physician and arises without any fault on their part. This principle was affirmed in several decisions by the Cour de Cassation, such as the ruling of 8 November 2000, Civil Chamber 1. The court held that the consequences of such unavoidable risks do not fall within the obligations assumed by the physician in their relationship with the patient. As long as the medical professional has acted in accordance with the *lex artis* (professional standards), they cannot be held liable for damages resulting from such risks, which are intrinsic to medical procedures and cannot be prevented, even with the utmost diligence.

Another interesting issue is that, in recent decades, the European legal landscape offers numerous examples of jurisprudential innovations designed to address procedural imbalances between doctors and patients, particularly concerning the burden of proving medical fault. Patients are often perceived as occupying a weaker position, given the significant challenges they face in substantiating claims of medical error.

To address this disparity, French courts have developed mechanisms that diverge from the general principles of contractual liability. These include practices such as the *judicial reversal* and *dynamic distribution of the burden of proof*, and doctrines that ease the causation requirement, such as *faute virtuelle*, *présomption de faute*, *causalité virtuelle*, *présomption de causalité*, and *perte d'une chance*. In Spanish jurisprudence, in cases involving disproportionate harm, courts have acknowledged the application of *presumptive negligence doctrines*, such as the *res ipsa loquitur rule*. This doctrine, referenced by the Supreme Court decisions, allows a presumption of negligence when an atypical result—one not ordinarily occurring without fault—arises, and the harm originates within the sphere of the physician's actions, even if the precise details are unknown.

Together, these developments illustrate a dynamic and evolving approach to medical liability within and beyond Europe, one that reflects the growing need for fairness, procedural balance, and legal adaptability in addressing the complexities of modern healthcare systems.

In the last two decades, it is worth highlighting the significant interest of the European Union in *promoting alternative dispute resolution mechanisms in the healthcare sector*, particularly in light of the increasing number of claims related to medical malpractice. Directive 2008/52/EC of 21 May 2008, concerning civil and commercial mediation, though not specifically addressing medical liability, emphasises the importance of access to justice and encourages the use of extrajudicial procedures.

This directive has influenced the legal systems of Member States. In Italy, for instance, as will be discussed later, the Gelli Law (2017) requires that, prior to initiating a medical malpractice claim directly before the judiciary, parties must first undergo a mediation procedure or, alternatively, a preliminary process involving technical consultancy (*consulenza tecnica preventiva*). In this preliminary stage, an expert evaluation of the alleged malpractice is conducted, with the aim of facilitating conciliation between the parties.

Regarding the debate about the legal nature of medical liability in cases of medical malpractice, whether assessed objectively (strict liability) or based on the determination of fault, the Council of the European Communities (the predecessor of today's Council of the European Union) proposed a directive, published on 18 January 1991, suggesting the potential adoption of a strict liability model for the provision of medical services within the European Union. This proposal stemmed from the pressing need to address significant transformations observed in the healthcare sector in the last decades.

These transformations included a shift in the practice of liberal professions, particularly in the medical field, from the traditional model of independent, individual practice to more collaborative and institutionalised frameworks. Under the individual model, medical practitioners operated autonomously, assuming direct responsibility for their professional decisions and actions. In contrast, the emergence of group practices, partnerships, and larger organisational entities has redefined the structure and dynamics of service delivery.

This evolution in professional practice was alleged to necessitate a corresponding adjustment in liability rules. Some argued that traditional fault-based systems, which emphasise individual culpability, were increasingly inadequate for addressing the impersonal and collective nature of modern professional service delivery. Instead, it was suggested that there was a growing need for liability rules that better reflected the organisational and institutional characteristics of healthcare systems. Proponents of this view contended that such rules would align more effectively with the notion of professional services as a public good, prioritising patient safety and systemic accountability rather than focusing solely on the actions of individual practitioners.

However, the Council of the European Communities' proposal encountered strong resistance from medical associations and the legal community. One of the primary concerns was the reversal of the burden of proof, which was seen as a measure that would substantially increase pressure on healthcare professionals, compelling them to prove their innocence even in inherently complex and high-risk situations. This model was criticised for promoting *defensive medicine*, whereby practitioners might prioritise unnecessary treatments or diagnostic procedures solely to mitigate potential legal actions. Furthermore, medical organisations raised concerns about the financial implications of such an approach, particularly the expected increase in the costs of medical professional liability insurance.

The legal community across European countries also voiced objections, questioning the compatibility of the proposed model with traditional principles of justice upheld across Member States, many of which adhere to fault-based liability regimes. Additional challenges arose concerning the harmonisation of national legal frameworks. Medical liability is governed by diverse systems within individual countries, and the imposition of a uniform model was deemed overly complex and unnecessary, particularly in light of the principle of subsidiarity.

Although the 1991 proposal was never adopted, it underscored a growing expectation for enhanced patient protection and the modernisation of liability regimes. Nevertheless, the introduction of a model akin to strict liability for medical services remains a contentious issue, reflecting the inherent tension between the imperative of ensuring patient safety and the need to preserve the medical profession's viability under balanced conditions.

In 2011, *Directive 2011/24/EU* of the European Parliament and of the Council was implemented, mandating that "Member States should ensure that mechanisms for the protection of patients and for seeking remedies in the event of harm are in place for healthcare provided on their territory and that they are appropriate to the nature and extent of the risk. However, it should be for the Member State to determine the nature and modalities of such a mechanism".

Accordingly, in cases of medical error resulting in harm to a patient's health, life, physical integrity, or safety, the injured party must rely on specific legal mechanisms established by each Member State to restore their legal position to the *status quo ante* prior to the harm. A comparative analysis of European legal systems reveals that, in most countries, there is no specific legislation governing medical liability. Medical errors are generally assessed under the general principles of civil and criminal law and, in certain cases, administrative law.

As mentioned before, traditionally, establishing fault remains the primary criterion for compensation in cases of medical liability. In most European jurisdictions, compensation is contingent upon proving fault, typically through evidence of negligence. However, a minority of jurisdictions have adopted *no-fault compensation systems*, while a very small number operate under a hybrid approach. In these hybrid systems, fault-based compensation remains the standard legal route, but supplementary schemes have been developed to address instances where injured patients might otherwise go uncompensated.

According to a study published by the European Commission (Study on Patients' Rights in the European Union - Mapping Exercise—2016), there are two principal models for compensating harm in the context of medical liability. The key distinction among Member States lies in the legal basis for claims: (1) *the fault-based system*, which requires proof of fault as the foundation for liability, and (2) *the no-fault system*, inspired by the concept of enterprise risk in healthcare, which permits compensation without establishing fault. The majority of European legal systems align with the first category (fault-based system).

No-Fault systems are characterised by their focus on the socialisation of medical risk and the simplification of claims procedures, particularly regarding the burden of proof. Under such systems, patients are not required to prove a healthcare provider's fault but must establish a direct causal link between the medical intervention and the harm suffered. An additional aim of these systems is to reduce legal costs by employing administrative compensation mechanisms. They are frequently paired with mandatory professional insurance schemes designed to limit litigation and facilitate indemnity payments.

The choice between fault-based and no-fault systems ultimately depends on the strategic and financial priorities of the State. Implementing a no-fault compensation system, for example, requires significant financial resources. Healthcare, much like other enterprise activities, inherently carries a margin of risk, exposing hospitals to the possibility of adverse events. In this context, risk is understood as the likelihood of such events occurring, and the approach to compensation reflects how each State manages these inherent uncertainties.

The French legal system represents one of the most intricate contexts for discussions regarding civil liability in the healthcare sector, particularly due to the coexistence of rules derived from Administrative Law and Private Law. The applicability of either framework depends on the public or private nature of the hospital where the alleged medical error occurred. If the hospital is public, procedural rules of Administrative Law apply; conversely, in private entities, the procedural rules of Private Law govern such matters.

For decades, French legal doctrine on medical civil liability has been marked by diverse proposals for legislative reform. A portion of scholars advocated for the establishment of a common compensation fund, abandoning fault-based civil liability in favour of addressing the issue on a different basis. This would involve creating an insurance mechanism, subscribed to by both physicians and hospitals, to cover all abnormal outcomes of medical treatments and surgical procedures.

On the other hand, some legal theorists argued for the retention of general rules on civil liability, while framing medical obligations as obligations of result. For a significant period, France experienced a marked intensification of physicians' civil liability. Medical obligations increasingly leaned towards obligations of result. At times, fault was presumed; at other times, physicians were held liable even when the causal link was uncertain. This was particularly evident in cases where the courts applied the notion of *loss of a chance of cure or survival* (*perte d'une chance de survie ou guérison*). French legal thought in this area has significantly influenced litigation in various European countries and beyond, including Brazil.

Regarding the judicial evaluation of professional diligence by French courts, Baccino (2013) explains that physicians' obligations are understood as requiring the provision of the *most appropriate* treatment. This ensures patients receive therapies that are recognised as effective and aimed at improving health, based on established medical knowledge. Preventive measures undertaken by physicians, according to medical standards, should not expose patients to risks disproportionate to the expected benefits. Physicians are not bound to guarantee outcomes but are required to act in the best interest of their patients at a given time, using treatments that a *reasonably competent physician* would provide.

When civil liability claims against physicians began to emerge with greater frequency in France from the 1930s onward, the courts adopted the well-known classification by René Demogue, as disseminated by Henri and Léon Mazeaud and André Tunc, to assess medical fault. This classification distinguishes between obligations of means (*obligations de moyens*) and obligations of result (*obligations de résultat*). These concepts, however, were not entirely novel; earlier mentions can be found in German legal scholarship (Franz Bernhoff and Hermann Fischer), French legal doctrine (Jean Domat and Marcel Planiol), and Roman law. In French jurisprudence, this distinction was first recognised in a landmark decision, by the Cour de Cassation in 1936, as discussed in great detail earlier.

Demogue, in his *Traité des obligations en général* (Demogue 1923), asserted:

> A physician assumes an obligation of means, not of result. They are not liable if the patient does not recover. The physician merely promises attentive care, and it is up to the patient to prove the physician's fault and the causal relationship between that fault and the harmful outcome (death, etc.). By exception, if a physician who has undertaken to provide care fails to do so, they become fully liable for the resulting harm.

Although this classification has been widely embraced in legal doctrine and jurisprudence worldwide, it has never been formally codified and thus is absent from any legislative framework or codification.

Furthermore, in classical French jurisprudence, the concept of *loss of a chance* (*perte de chance*) allows a victim to claim compensation from the party whose fault deprived them of an opportunity to secure a specific benefit. Crucially, compensation is awarded for the lost chance itself rather than the final harm. This theory has been adapted to the medical field under the doctrine of *perte de chance de survie ou de guérison* (*loss of a chance of survival or recovery*), shifting the focus from the ultimate harm to the causation of the lost opportunity.

This approach holds particularly significance in medical liability cases, where establishing a direct causal link between a physician's conduct and the ultimate harm suffered by the patient is often inherently complex. By allowing compensation for the lost of a chance, the doctrine acknowledges the intrinsic uncertainty of medical outcomes while ensuring that patients are not left without recourse where negligence has diminished their prospects of survival or recovery. It has become an indispensable legal tool for addressing situations where the harm is probabilistic rather than certain, effectively bridging gaps in traditional causation requirements and offering a fairer framework for the allocation of liability in complex clinical contexts.

Article 1240 of the French Civil Code, previously designated as Article 1382 before the reform of obligations law effective from 1 October 2016, enshrines the principle of liability for personal acts (*responsabilité du fait personnel*). It provides: "any act of a person that causes harm to another obliges the one at fault to provide reparation".

This provision establishes that whenever an individual's fault causes harm (*dommage*) to a third party, the responsible party is obligated to compensate the victim. Originally included in the 1804 Civil Code, known as the Code Napoléon, article 1382 drew upon the classical theory of extra-contractual liability, which is solely fault-based. This theory, widely propagated by jurists such as Domat and Pothier, laid the foundation for the model of reparation for harm caused by wrongful acts, profoundly influencing modern legal systems.

In the specific context of medical civil liability, the need to safeguard patients' rights and ensure the quality of the healthcare system led to the enactment of the *Loi Kouchner* on 4 March 2002 (Law No. 303 on Patients' Rights and the Quality of the Health System). This law introduced specific provisions on medical liability and brought significant innovations to French law, including:

(i) the consolidation of the no-fault system (système sans faute), which allows compensation for certain medical injuries even in the absence of fault on the part of the healthcare professional, creating a more efficient and less adversarial process for victims;
(ii) the creation of a new national solidarity fund for compensation (*Office National d'Indemnisation des Accidents Médicaux*—ONIAM), established to provide redress for medical injuries caused by risks not attributable to the fault of a specific individual;
(iii) the definition of the concept of *aléa thérapeutique*, which refers to injuries that occur during medical treatment and are unavoidable, even when the highest standard of care is observed;
(iv) the introduction of *mandatory liability insurance* for all practising physicians and healthcare institutions operating within French territory, ensuring that patients are compensated under all circumstances; and

(v) the establishment of Regional Conciliation Committees (*Commissions Régionales de Conciliation et d'Indemnisation*—CRCI), which facilitate alternative dispute resolution for conflicts related to medical injuries.

These reforms reflect a significant shift in the French legal framework, balancing the need for patient protection with the realities of medical practice, while fostering a more equitable system of compensation and accountability. The innovations introduced by the Loi Kouchner brought significant amendments to the *Code de Santé Publique* (Public Health Code of 1953), aligning it with contemporary demands and enhancing legal certainty within the French healthcare system.

By adopting a *hybrid model of civil liability* that combines both no-fault and fault-based systems, the legislation aimed to strike a balance between safeguarding patients' rights and ensuring accountability for medical negligence or malpractice, while also facilitating compensation for harm that is unavoidable. The law also strengthened the obligation for physicians to provide clear, comprehensible, and honest information, and made the formal documentation of patients' informed consent mandatory.

Article 1240 of the French Civil Code remained a cornerstone for civil liability under French law, complemented by the reforms introduced by the Loi Kouchner. These changes have solidified France's position as a global benchmark in the regulation of medical liability. Notably, the Loi Kouchner reaffirmed the primacy of the fault-based system, yet explicitly acknowledged the existence of harm arising from *aléa thérapeutique* (therapeutic risks). Article 1142, paragraph 1, of the French Public Health Code, as amended by Article 98 of Law No. 303/2002, stipulates that physicians and healthcare institutions are liable for adverse events associated with medical treatments (including prevention, care, and diagnosis) only when medical fault is established.

However, the second paragraph of the same provision introduces a compensation mechanism that does not require proof of professional fault. This is rooted in the principle of *national solidarity* (socialisation of risks) and applies to cases where, following medical intervention, the patient sustains a disability exceeding 25% or is rendered incapable of working for a period of at least 6 months. In such instances, there is no medical error; rather, the harm results from adverse events linked to *aléa thérapeutique*. This legislative approach simultaneously addresses the most severe cases of harm caused by unknown factors and those arising from hospital-acquired infections, providing compensation under the framework of national solidarity.

Claims related to injuries caused by *aléa thérapeutique* are adjudicated by the National Office for the Compensation of Medical Accidents, Iatrogenic Conditions, and Nosocomial Infections (*Office Nationale d'Indemnisation des Accidents Médicaux, des Affections Iatrogènes et des Infections Nosocomiales*—ONIAM), an entity created specifically to administer the Public Compensation Fund.

In summary, when a patient suffers harm, they have two distinct avenues to seek compensation, depending on whether the harm resulted from *aléa thérapeutique* or medical fault. For harm arising from *aléa thérapeutique* (where the patient experiences a disability exceeding 25%), compensation is payable upon demonstrating a causal link between the alleged harm and the healthcare professional's actions, without the need to establish fault. This no-fault compensation system operates where there is no medical negligence (the adverse event is attributed to the inherent risks of medical treatment) and also applies to cases involving hospital-acquired infections. In these situations, establishing a causal nexus between the medical intervention and the harm suffices to trigger compensation.

Beyond the two compensation systems outlined—the fault-based system and the no-fault compensation system—the 2002 Law introduces a *preventive conciliation procedure* under Article 1142, paragraph 14, designed to filter patient claims and prevent their escalation into legal disputes. To this end, Regional Conciliation and Compensation Commissions (*Commissions régionales de conciliation et d'indemnisation*—CRCI) were established pursuant to Article 1142, paragraph 5. These commissions standardise the compensation procedure, regardless of whether the healthcare institution involved is public or private.

The CRCIs are tasked with assessing, through an internal review process, the legitimacy of a patient's claim for compensation, including whether the harm resulted from medical fault or *aléa thérapeutique*. Ultimately, the Commission must issue a key determination: (i) whether there is medical or institutional fault (in which case compensation is typically paid by the relevant insurer); (ii) whether the harm involves a disability exceeding 25% and arises from *aléa thérapeutique*, in which case compensation is provided by ONIAM under the principle of "national solidarity"; and (iii) whether no compensable harm occurred.

Following this determination, a compensation proposal is submitted to the insurer (or ONIAM in cases of No-Fault liability), subject to mandatory review within 4 months, as stipulated in Article 1142, paragraph 14. If conciliation cannot be achieved, the patient retains the right to pursue compensation through traditional judicial or administrative channels, depending on whether the healthcare institution involved is public or private.

Having outlined these brief observations on the French legislative framework governing medical civil liability, it is pertinent to consider that, as noted by Watson and Kottenhagen (2018), the French experience serves as an instructive example of how a no-fault system can be integrated within a traditionally fault-based civil liability framework. However, the authors caution that this approach carries the risk of gradually generating an increasingly complex and fragmented web of rules web of rules—at times inconsistent—by incorporating divergent liability principles applicable to different categories of patients.

Watson and Kottenhagen (2018) further observe that, despite the significant increase in both the complexity and volume of medical procedures in France—and the probably corresponding rise in medical accidents—litigation rates have not grown at a comparable pace over recent decades. They attribute this phenomenon to the fact that medical malpractice cases are first submitted to, and largely resolved by, the CRCI. This indicates that an extrajudicial dispute resolution system can function effectively as a viable and patient-friendly alternative to court-based remedies, complementing traditional judicial pathways for compensation.

Shifting the focus of analysis to the Italian context, fault constitutes as the basis for civil liability. This is evident from Article 2043 of the Italian Civil Code, which states: "any intentional or negligent act that causes unjust harm to another obliges the person who committed the act to compensate for the damage". Article 1227 provides for a reduction in compensation, proportionate to the degree of fault, when the injured party has also contributed to the causation of the damage. The following article explicitly establishes liability for acts committed by auxiliaries, except where otherwise agreed, encompassing both intentional and negligent acts of such persons. Specifically, regarding medical liability, the application of these basic principles is remarkably similar to the model adopted in Brazil.

A topic that has been frequently debated in Italy is the significant rise in medical malpractice litigation over recent decades. A 2018 Report (*Studio sull'andamento del rischio da medical malpractice nella sanità italiana pubblica e private*) examined 42 public healthcare providers and documented 20,947 healthcare incidents between 2004 and 2016 (Cascini et al. 2020). The analysis revealed a median cost exceeding €88,000 per incident, amounting to a total financial impact of over €900 million on the Italian healthcare system during the analysed period, creating substantial financial pressure on healthcare providers and insurers.

Physicians, seeking to minimise the risk of becoming the target of legal claims, significantly altered their practices by adopting a highly *defensive approach to treatment*. This often involved taking arguably unnecessary precautions or avoiding treatments that, although potentially in the best interest of the patient, could lead to future legal disputes or claims. According to Panella et al. (2017), defensive medical practices have, for many years, accounted for approximately 10% of the expenditures of the Italian National Health System. Medical civil liability has thus become a persistent topic of debate in Italian health policy and a significant concern for the nation's economy.

In response to this growing crisis, Italy enacted Law No. 24/2017, commonly referred to as the *Gelli Law*. This legislation was designed to establish a better structure regulation for the medical malpractice cases. It established a comprehensive framework for the professional liability insurance market in the healthcare sector and introduced various provisions governing medical liability (its nature and scope) and mechanisms for compensation. The primary objectives of the Italian Parliament were to monitor medical malpractice cases, implement preventive measures, and reduce the incidence of litigation.

Article 8 of the Gelli Law aims to minimise judicial claims involving medical malpractice by requiring that such claims first undergo either: (i) an attempt to resolve the dispute through a mediation body or (ii) a *pre-judicial* technical evaluation (expert assessment). In the latter case, the insurer must either offer a settlement to the claimant or provide reasons for declining to do so. If the insurer refuses to agree to an extrajudicial settlement and the patient subsequently obtains a favourable judicial decision, the presiding judge is required to forward a copy of the judgment to IVASS (the Italian Insurance Supervisory Authority) for the potential imposition of sanctions against the insurer.

Article 10 of the law prescribes that all hospitals—and, more broadly, all public or private entities providing medical services—must obtain professional liability insurance covering harm caused to third parties (arising from the acts of their physicians or other healthcare professionals) or implement a similar alternative, such as self-insurance. Insurance coverage is also obligatory for physicians practicing in public or private entities but on a private/contractual basis. According to Article 11, all professional liability insurance policies issued after the enactment of the Gelli Law must provide retroactive coverage for incidents occurring within the 10 years preceding the policy's inssurance.

Patients are entitled to bring claims directly against the insurer of the hospital or physician (Article 12). However, in the absence of insurance coverage, patients may turn to the Guarantee Fund (a fund for damages arising from medical liability), which ensures compensation for harm caused by medical errors. This fund is also accessible when insurance coverage is insufficient to fully compensate the patient or if the insurer is insolvent or under compulsory administration (Article 14).

Regarding the assessment of medical liability, Article 7 of the Gelli Law establishes two forms of liability, depending on the legal nature of the relationship between the patient and the healthcare provider: contractual or non-contractual. As a result, different rules concerning the burden of proof and the limitation period apply based on the legal basis of the relationship. In summary, a physician's liability is determined by the nature of their relationship with the patient: a direct relationship with a private-practice physician establishes contractual liability, while an indirect relationship—where the professional is an employee of a hospital—gives rise to non-contractual liability.

As mentioned before, under Italian law, medical malpractice claims can no longer be filed directly in court. Instead, claimants are required to first pursue either mediation or a preliminary procedure involving technical consultancy (*consulenza tecnica preventiva*). This process evaluates the alleged medical liability and aims to foster reconciliation between the parties before formal litigation. The Gelli-Bianco Law reinforces this approach through the implementation of Preventive Technical Assessments (PTAs) under Article 696 bis of the Code of Civil Procedure. PTAs are designed to encourage early dispute resolution, minimise adversarial litigation, and streamline the determination of liability in medical cases.

This emphasis on extrajudicial resolution aligns with broader European trends in medical liability. For example, French law, under the 2002 Loi Kouchner, also mandates that physicians and hospitals obtain professional liability insurance and promotes dispute resolution through non-judicial mechanisms before judicial proceedings are initiated. Both frameworks aim to balance patient protection with the mitigation of systemic pressures on healthcare providers, reducing defensive practices while ensuring accountability and compensation for harm.

In Portugal, Article 483 of the Portuguese Civil Code establishes the general principle of civil liability for medical practitioners: "1. Anyone who, with intent or mere negligence, unlawfully violates the rights of another or any legal provision designed to protect the interests of others shall be obliged to compensate the injured party for the damages resulting from the violation. 2. There is only an obligation to compensate regardless of fault in cases specified by law". Article 487 further addresses the concept of fault: "1. It is for the injured party to prove the fault of the wrongdoer, except where there is a legal presumption of fault. 2. Fault is assessed, in the absence of other legal criteria, by the diligence of a good father of the family, in view of the circumstances of each case".

Thus, in the Portuguese context, fault is assessed according to an *abstract standard*, considering both the degree of diligence and care, as well as the professional competence of the individual. As explained by Pereira (2015), the assessment of fault in Article 487 adopts an objective approach, following the *theory of abstract fault*, specifically fault as a deficiency in conduct. Fault is therefore not limited to deficiencies in will—such as negligence, carelessness, or rashness—but also includes deficiencies in skill or aptitude, such as incompetence or incapacity. The degree of diligence required is that of a *bonus pater familias*—a person who is reasonably prudent, judicious, and vigilant. In medical practice, this translates to a physician who is ordinarily careful, diligent, and knowledgeable, equipped with the physical, intellectual, and emotional capacity to perform the tasks they undertake.

This assessment is moderated by the distinction between obligations of means and obligations of result. As mentioned before, in medical practice, the physician typically assumes an obligation of means, meaning they do not guarantee a specific result (such as a cure) but must exercise due diligence and care in treating the patient. The inherent uncertainties of medicine, including the inability to fully control causal processes or predict individual physiological responses, mean that medical outcomes are not guaranteed. From a Portuguese legal perspective, this categorization has also become increasingly significant.

Regarding the causation and burden of proof in medical malpractice cases, Figueiredo Dias and Monteiro (1984) highlight the principle of *adequate causation*. Under this principle, the burden of proof lies with the plaintiff, who must demonstrate causality and prove that the best possible care was not provided, resulting in harm. Judges may rely on *judicial presumptions* (Articles 349 and 351 of the Portuguese Civil Code), drawing inferences from known facts to establish unknown ones, inspired by principles of logic, probability, or human intuition.

When harm occurs that, based on medical experience, is typically attributable to negligent treatment, negligence may be presumed. However, the physician has the opportunity to provide exculpatory evidence to rebut this presumption. The use of such presumptions, which resemble the *prima facie* concept in German law and the Anglo-Saxon doctrine of *res ipsa loquitur*, must be applied with caution, given the need for robust and authentic evidence (Pereira 2015).

In summary, the legislative and doctrinal approach to medical liability in Portugal aligns closely with the Brazilian framework. Both systems adopt similar principles regarding fault, causation, and the evidentiary burdens placed on the injured party and the accused practitioner. Moreover, the distinctions between obligations of means and result provide a nuanced framework that balances the inherent uncertainties of medical practice with the need for diligence and accountability.

Finally, regarding the context of the United Kingdom, as a country rooted in the Common Law tradition, its legal system is primarily based on judicial precedents rather than codified statutes. This means that court decisions play a central role in shaping and interpreting the law, with judges relying on principles established in prior cases to resolve disputes. In contrast to Civil Law systems, which derive from codified rules (such as the French or Brazilian Civil Codes), Common Law evolves through case law, creating a dynamic and adaptable legal framework.

The absence of a general principle of civil liability, such as Article 1382 of the French Civil Code of 1804 or Article 186 of the Brazilian Civil Code of 2002, reflects this approach. Instead, the UK developed the concept of *damage reparation through writs*—judicial actions available to victims of civil wrongs (torts), designed to provide compensation for harm suffered. This reliance on case law has given rise to a practical and case-specific body of doctrine, particularly in the area of medical malpractice.

Medical malpractice in the UK is governed primarily by principles of medical negligence, with liability assessed through judicial precedents. Two *key legal tests*, the *Bolam test* and the *Bolitho test*, form the cornerstone of this framework. The Bolam test, derived from the landmark case *Bolam v. Friern Hospital Management Committee* (1957), evaluates whether a physician's conduct aligns with a practice accepted as proper by a responsible body of medical opinion within the relevant field. If the professional's actions are supported by such a body, they are generally not considered negligent, even if other opinions within the medical community might disagree. This test relies heavily on the prevailing practices and standards within the medical profession, providing a degree of deference to professional judgment (Brazier and Miola 2000).

More recently, the *Bolitho test*, established in *Bolitho v. City and Hackney Health Authority* (1998), refines the Bolam test by introducing an additional requirement for logical justification. While the Bolam test focuses on whether a body of medical opinion supports the professional's actions, the Bolitho test allows courts to scrutinise whether that opinion withstands rational analysis. In other words, even if a practice is widely accepted within the medical community, it may still be deemed negligent if it cannot be logically or reasonably justified in the concrete case evaluated. The Bolitho test ensures that *blind reliance* on professional opinion is avoided, adding a safeguard to protect patients from potentially flawed medical practices.

According to UK Courts' decision, to establish a claim for medical negligence, four elements must be proven. The first is the *duty of care*, which arises from the professional relationship between the healthcare provider and the patient. This duty is codified in guidelines such as the *General Medical Council's (GMC) Good Medical Practice*, which includes obligations like obtaining informed consent. The second element is a *breach of that duty*, demonstrated by showing that the professional failed to meet the standard of a reasonably competent practitioner in their field. Third, *causation* must be established, proving that the breach directly caused or materially contributed to the patient's harm. Finally, the claimant must demonstrate *damages*, such as physical injury, psychological harm, or financial loss, resulting from the negligence.

In this sense, the Bolam and Bolitho tests work together to assess whether a healthcare professional has breached their duty of care. The *Bolam test* provides a foundational standard by deferring to medical consensus, recognising the complexities of medical judgment. However, the *Bolitho test* introduces a critical check, ensuring that such consensus is not followed blindly but is subjected to logical scrutiny. Together, these tests create a balanced framework that respects professional autonomy while safeguarding patient welfare, offering a fair and adaptable approach to resolving claims of medical negligence (Elgujja and Elgujja 2021).

Considering all that has been discussed throughout this Chapter, it is important to emphasise that the element of fault stands at the core of disputes involving medical liability, whether in Brazil or across European legal systems. It is also essential to clarify that the purpose here was not to provide an exhaustive analysis or an in-depth examination of each European legal system. Rather, the intention was to offer a general overview, focusing on contemporary trends in medical malpractice cases and comparative aspects relevant to the central theme of this book.

All jurisdictions grapple with the challenge of assessing negligence and attributing liability in complex medical contexts, reflecting shared concerns about justice, patient safety, and accountability. This chapter has provided a comparative overview of these frameworks, examining the Brazilian approach to medical malpractice, the concurrence of causes, and the allocation of responsibility among healthcare providers, institutions, and manufacturers. Similarly, it has explored how European jurisdictions address medical negligence, highlighting commonalities and distinctions that enrich our understanding of these legal systems.

This comparative analysis underscores the significance of understanding how different jurisdictions establish the conditions for medical liability, which serves as the foundation for the book's multi-jurisdictional approach. By exploring these diverse perspectives, this work aims to provide insights into the principles and mechanisms that govern medical liability globally, setting the stage for discussions about the integration of medical technologies and artificial intelligence in subsequent chapters.

The investigation into fault-based liability in traditional medical contexts is a necessary precursor to the broader discussions that will follow. The next chapters will address the duties of care owed by medical professionals and the challenges of determining fault when advanced technologies, including artificial intelligence, are involved. These scenarios demand a nuanced understanding of how liability is allocated, particularly in cases where the interplay between human judgment and technological systems raises novel legal and ethical questions.

By bridging the comparative analysis presented here with forward-looking debates about medical technologies and AI, this book seeks to contribute to the development of legal frameworks that uphold fairness and accountability while adapting to the complexities of modern healthcare. The themes introduced in this chapter serve as a basis for exploring the evolving role of fault in medical liability as technology reshapes the practice of medicine.

References

Alemzadeh H et al (2016) Adverse events in robotic surgery: a retrospective study of 14 years of FDA data. PLoS One 11(4):e0151470

Baase S (2008) A gift of fire: social, legal, and ethical issues for computing and the internet, 3rd edn. Pearson, New York

Baccino E (2013) Medical responsibility and liability in France. In: Ferrara SD (ed) Malpractice and medical liability. European state of the art and guidelines. Springer, Berlin

Brazier M, Miola J (2000) Bye–bye Bolam: a medical litigation revolution? Med Law Rev 8(1):85–114

Calixto MJ (2004) A responsabilidade civil do fornecedor de produtos pelos riscos do desenvolvimento. Renovar, Rio de Janeiro

Carpes AT (2016) A prova do nexo de causalidade na responsabilidade civil. Thomson Reuters Brazil, São Paulo

Cascini F et al (2020) Patient safety and medical liability in Italy. Eur Secur 26(1):34–38

Cortés JCG (2024) Responsabilidad Civil Médica, 9th edn. Civitas, Navarra

Demogue R (1923) Traite des obligations En general. Effets des obligations, vol. II, tome VI. Librairie Arthur, Paris

Elgujja AA, Elgujja AA (2021) To what extent are healthcare professionals immune from professional negligence: a review of the bolam and bolitho cases. https://papers.ssrn.com/sol3/papers.cfm?abstract_id=3973837

Farias CC, Rosenvald N, Braga Netto FP (2021) Curso de direito civil: responsabilidade civil, vol 3, 8th edn. JusPodivm, Salvador

Figueiredo Dias J, Monteiro JS (1984) Responsabilidade médica em Portugal. Boletim do Ministério da Justiça 332

Gaev JA (2004) Technology in health care. In: Dyro J (ed) Clinical engineering handbook. Elsevier, San Diego

Gondim GG (2010) A reparação civil na teoria da perda de uma chance. Master's thesis, Federal University of Paraná (Brazil). https://hdl.handle.net/1884/23451

Hogg MA (2016) Liability for unknown risks: a common law perspective. J Eur Tort Law 7(2):113–142

Hung AJ et al (2018) Development and validation of objective performance metrics for robot-assisted radical prostatectomy: a pilot study. J Urol 199(1):296–304

International Atomic Energy Agency (2001) Investigation of an accidental exposure of radiotherapy patients in Panama. https://www-pub.iaea.org/MTCD/publications/PDF/Pub1114_scr.pdf

Kfouri Neto M (2019) A quantificação do dano na ausência de consentimento livre e esclarecido do paciente. Revista IBERC 2(1):1–21

Kfouri Neto M (2024) Responsabilidade civil do médico, 12th edn. Thomson Reuters Brazil, São Paulo

Kfouri Neto M, Nogaroli R (2022) Estudo comparatístico da responsabilidade civil do médico, hospital e fabricante na cirurgia assistida por robô. In: Kfouri Neto M, Nogaroli R (eds) Debates Contemporâneos em direito médico e da saúde, 2nd edn. Thomson Reuters Brazil, São Paulo

Kfouri Neto M, Dantas E, Nogaroli R (2022) Medidas extraordinárias para tempos excepcionais: da necessidade de um olhar diferenciado sobre a responsabilidade civil dos médicos na linha de frente do combate à Covid-19. In: Kfouri Neto M, Nogaroli R (eds) Debates Contemporâneos em direito médico e da saúde, 2nd edn. Thomson Reuters Brazil, São Paulo

Lake M (2010) Epic failures: 11 infamous software bugs celebrate 'debugging day' by remembering these monster problems from the past. Available via Computer World. https://www.computerworld.com/article/2515483/epic-failures-11-infamous-software-bugs.html?page=6

Lopez TA (2008) Nexo causal e produtos potencialmente nocivos: a experiência brasileira do tabaco. Quartier Latin, São Paulo

Lopez TA (2010) Princípio da precaução e evolução da responsabilidade civil. Quartier Latin, São Paulo
Mclean TR (2007) The complexity of litigation associated with robotic surgery and cybersurgery. Int J Med Robotics Comp Assisted Surg 3(1):23–29
Mclean TR (2008) Principle of robotic surgery litigation in the United States. Clinical Risk 14(5):179–181
Mclean TR, Waxman S (2010) Robotic surgery litigation. J Mech Eng Sci 224(7):1539–1545
Miragem B (2007) Responsabilidade civil médica no direito brasileiro. Revista de Direito do Consumidor 16(63):52–91
Nalin P, Nogaroli R (2021) Responsabilidade civil do médico na telemedicina durante a pandemia da Covid-19 no Brasil: a necessidade de um novo olhar para a aferição da culpa médica e da violação do dever de informação. In: Pinho AC (ed) Discussões sobre direito na era digital. GZ, Rio de Janeiro
Oliveira MTRA, Dantas E (2022) Processos ético-profissionais dos médicos: aspectos gerais e influência nas decisões judiciais. In: Kfouri Neto M, Nogaroli R (eds) Debates Contemporâneos em direito médico e da saúde, 2nd edn. Thomson Reuters Brazil, São Paulo
Oliveira MTRA, Mascarenhas IL (2024) A crescente influência dos processos ético-profissionais de médicos nas decisões judiciais. In: Kfouri Neto M, Nogaroli R (eds) Direito Médico e Bioética: Decisões Paradigmáticas. Foco, Indaiatuba
Panella M et al (2017) Prevalence and costs of defensive medicine: a national survey of Italian physicians. J Health Services Res 22(4):211–217
Pereira AGD (2015) Direito dos pacientes e responsabilidade médica. Coimbra Publisher, Coimbra
Perlingieri P (2006) Il diritto civile nella legalità costituzionale. Edizioni Scientifiche Italiane, Napoli. Portuguese edition: Perlingieri P (2008) O direito civil na legalidade constitucional (trans: De Cicco MC) Rio de Janeiro: Renovar
Peteffi da Silva R (2013) Responsabilidade civil pela perda da chance, 3rd edn. Atlas, São Paulo
Reis C (2019) Dano moral. Thomson Reuters Brazil, São Paulo
Ronsevald N, Braga Netto F (2021) Código civil comentado, 2nd edn. JusPodivm, Salvador
Rosenvald N (2020) Foundations of civil liability in the face of the challenges of new technologies. Online lecture delivered at the meeting of the research group in Philosophy of Private Law, Federal University of Rio Grande do Sul (Brazil), on May 28, 2020. https://www.facebook.com/filosofiadpufrg
Rosenvald N (2022) O direito civil em movimento: desafios contemporâneos, 4th edn. JusPodivm, São Paulo
Rosenvald N, Braga Netto FP (2020) Responsabilidade civil na área médica. In: Braga Netto FP, César Silva M (eds) Direito privado e contemporaneidade. Foco, Indaiatuba
Rosenvald N, Clemente GT (2021) Desafios para a responsabilidade civil médica na 2ª era da Covid-19. Available via Migalhas de Responsabilidade Civil. https://www.migalhas.com.br/depeso/344495/desafios-para-a-responsabilidade-civil-medica-na-2-era-da-covid-19
Rosenvald N, Pereira AGD, Doménech JB (2021) Proteção jurídica dos profissionais de saúde envolvidos no atendimento em contexto da pandemia da COVID-19. Cadernos Ibero-Americanos de Direito Sanitário 10(2):151–182
Sanseverino PTV (2011) Princípio da reparação integral. Indenização no Código Civil. Saraiva, São Paulo
Schaefer F (2002) Responsabilidade civil do médico e erro de diagnóstico. Juruá, Curitiba
Schreiber A (2007) Novos paradigmas da responsabilidade civil. Da erosão dos filtros da reparação à diluição dos danos. Atlas, São Paulo
Soares FR (2019) Veículos autônomos e responsabilidade por acidentes: trajetos possíveis e desejáveis no direito civil brasileiro. In: Rosenvald N, Dresch RFV, Wesendonck T (eds) Responsabilidade civil: novos riscos. Foco, Indaiatuba
Tepedino G (2001) Notas sobre o nexo de causalidade. Revista Trimestral de Direito Civil 6:3–20

Tepedino G (2006) A responsabilidade médica na experiência brasileira contemporânea. Temas de Direito Civil 2:83–122

Uscocovich CM, Santos RB (2023) A perda de uma chance no direito médico e a jurisprudência do Superior Tribunal de Justiça. Civilisticacom 12(3):1–31

Watson K, Kottenhagen R (2018) Patients' rights, medical error and harmonisation of compensation mechanisms in Europe. Eur J Health Law 25(1):1–23

Wesendonck T (2015) O regime da responsabilidade civil pelo fato dos produtos postos em circulação. Livraria do Advogado, Curitiba

Chapter 4
Ethical and Legal Aspects of Artificial Intelligence (AI) in Medical Service Contracts

4.1 The Emergence of AI in Clinical Decision-Making Worldwide

Deciding which patient data to collect and analyse, determining the appropriate examinations to request, interpreting and integrating this information to derive diagnostic conclusions, and proposing suitable treatments constitute the fundamental stages of the *clinical decision-making process*. Were a physician required to summarise the diagnostic decision-making process, he or she would likely articulate it as follows:

> First, I conduct the anamnesis, gathering case facts through a conversation with the patient, medical history, physical examination, and laboratory tests. Next, I assess the significance of each symptom presented. Certain health data may be of primary importance, while others may hold lesser relevance for the diagnosis. Subsequently, I compile a list of all potential diseases that the specific case might resemble, ranking them according to their likelihood based on the patient's dataset. In cases of uncertainty between two or more conditions, I request additional examinations to clarify the clinical picture. Furthermore, I may consult scientific studies to substantiate my diagnostic conclusions.

This description, though a simplified representation, effectively illustrates the dynamics of the medical diagnostic process and the manner in which patient health data are employed to reach clinical conclusions.

Staying up-to-date with the latest advancements presents a significant challenge in the current era of continuous information flow, especially for physicians, who must contend with an overwhelming volume of medical literature to remain informed in their specialties. A 2004 study by Brian Alper et al. highlighted this issue, estimating that keeping pace with medical publications would require over 600 h per month—an expectation that makes it practically unfeasible to balance professional responsibilities with basic needs such as eating and sleeping. Although more recent data quantifying this effort are not available, the exponential growth of scientific information is evident. For instance, a 2021 report by the American Heart

R. Nogaroli, *Medical Liability and Artificial Intelligence*,
https://doi.org/10.1007/978-3-031-94306-5_4

Association revealed that the number of articles featuring the term *stroke* increased fivefold between 2000 and 2020 (Salim et al. 2020). These findings highlight the considerable difficulties faced by physicians in staying informed about the constant advancements in medical science.

According to a 2021 study, physicians typically have an average of only 5 h per week available for professional development. This limited availability results in a significant delay in the assimilation of new knowledge, thereby creating an ever-widening gap between the outcomes achieved by leading scientific research centres and the reality of clinical practice (Jie et al. 2021).

Consequently, there is an increasingly urgent need for innovative tools to bridge this knowledge gap, enabling healthcare professionals to make decisions that are both efficient and grounded in robust evidence. In the domain of clinical diagnosis, artificial intelligence (AI) emerges as a transformative solution, offering the potential to significantly enhance diagnostic accuracy and expedite the identification of diseases. By harnessing the capacity to process vast quantities of health data, AI systems can uncover patterns and correlations with a degree of precision unattainable through traditional methods. Furthermore, these systems are capable of integrating disparate sources of information, such as electronic health records, medical imaging, and genomic data, thus facilitating a more comprehensive and timely approach to patient care. Such advancements not only improve individual clinical outcomes but also hold promise for addressing broader public health challenges by streamlining resource allocation and supporting preventive medicine initiatives.

It is worth noting an interesting fact: contrary to popular belief, scientific research into the use of automated systems to support medical practice is not a recent development. As Harry Truman once remarked, *the only thing new in the world is the history you do not know*.

In 1959, scientists Robert Ledley and Lee Lusted proposed, in their article entitled *Reasoning Foundations of Medical Diagnosis,* the development of *expert systems* that would utilise computational power and electronic health data to support physicians in clinical decision-making. The researchers from George Washington University envisioned a future where the implementation of technology would bring about two principal consequences: a significant portion of physicians' tasks would become automated, and various human errors could be avoided. Several decades later, the digitalisation of the healthcare sector and advancements in technology—particularly the increased computational power and the ability to store large volumes of electronic data in the cloud—gradually enabled the development of software with AI algorithms designed to assist medical practice.

This same vision also inspired concrete developments on the other side of the Atlantic. In the early 1970s, the London Hospital in Whitechapel developed a mechanical system known as the Survival Predictor, designed to assist doctors in estimating the probability of recovery for patients in comas. The device compared brain activity measurements from the current patient with historical data stored in its memory, indicating whether the prognosis aligned with "survive" or "irreversible brain damage." Although the final decision always remained with physicians, this system represents one of the earliest attempts to incorporate automated decision-making tools into clinical practice—an analogue precursor to the AI-based systems that would emerge in subsequent decades. By the late 1970s, Stanford University (USA) launched the *SUMEX-AIM Project*, becoming one of the first institutions in the world to initiate a programme dedicated to research on AI applications for solving problems in the healthcare sector. In addition to developing AI systems to assist in diagnoses, prognoses, and treatment recommendations, the project also gave rise to the so-called *AI Handbook Project*, aimed at creating academic materials to explain fundamental AI concepts and principles, thereby fostering a more effective and appropriate integration of these technologies into clinical practice. This evolution in thought appears strikingly similar to contemporary debates, does it not?

In light of this, if ideas and reflections concerning the potential role of AI in healthcare are not groundbreaking, then why has there been such a considerable delay in achieving meaningful progress in the development, implementation, and dissemination of these technologies across clinics and hospitals?

Historically, the advancement of AI in medicine remained stagnant for an extended period, primarily because, despite the conceptual and theoretical developments, the essential prerequisites for the effective functioning of AI algorithms were largely absent throughout the majority of the twentieth century. This stagnation was due, in part, to the lack of sufficient computational power, inadequate data storage solutions, and the limited availability of digital biomedical datasets, which are fundamental for the development and refinement of AI systems.

This paradigm began to shift progressively as the healthcare sector underwent a transformative process of digitalisation. This movement facilitated the generation of vast quantities of structured and unstructured biomedical data, enabling more effective algorithmic training and development (Topol et al. 2022). Moreover, significant advancements in cloud computing and increased computational capacity allowed for the efficient processing and analysis of these datasets, providing the technical infrastructure necessary to support AI-based innovations.

Concurrently, the adoption and diffusion of AI in global clinical practice were catalysed by the mounting pressures on healthcare systems worldwide. Over recent decades, these systems have faced unprecedented demands, including ageing populations, rising healthcare costs, and workforce shortages. The integration of advanced technological tools has been pursued as a means to enhance the efficiency and precision of healthcare delivery while streamlining medical and hospital operations.

Furthermore, the collective efforts of hospitals, academic research centres, and technology startups have intensified, reflecting a shared objective to improve access to high-quality care, optimise clinical outcomes, and reduce operational costs. This concerted movement has not only fostered innovation but has also created an environment characterised by heightened enthusiasm—perhaps even a degree of *hype*—surrounding the transformative potential of emerging digital technologies in the healthcare landscape.

Currently, there are AI systems designed for healthcare data management that encompass the entire patient journey within a hospital setting. These systems operate from the moment of patient admission, through diagnostic evaluation, to the prescription of appropriate medication and even the anticipation of the patient's response to treatment. Such systems leverage advanced algorithms to integrate and analyse data from diverse sources, including electronic health records, laboratory results, imaging studies, and genomic information. This holistic approach not only streamlines clinical workflows but also enhances the accuracy of diagnoses and the personalisation of treatment plans.

Additionally, these technologies have the potential to predict adverse drug reactions and optimise therapeutic outcomes, thereby contributing to improved patient safety and the overall quality of care. By automating and refining complex medical processes, these AI-driven solutions aim to address inefficiencies in traditional healthcare systems, reduce clinical errors, and support healthcare professionals in making more informed and timely decisions.

Over the past two decades, the field of medical imaging in the healthcare sector has undergone a profound transformation, driven by the integration of AI algorithms. These advancements enable the precise and rapid diagnosis of a wide range of diseases through the analysis of imaging modalities such as magnetic resonance imaging (MRI), computed tomography (CT), and radiography (Topol 2019). AI-powered systems in medical imaging employ techniques such as machine learning and deep learning to identify patterns and abnormalities within complex datasets, often with accuracy levels comparable to, or exceeding, those of human radiologists. These technologies are particularly effective in detecting conditions like tumours, fractures, cardiovascular anomalies, and pulmonary diseases, significantly reducing diagnostic delays and improving treatment outcomes (Buijs et al. 2024).

Moreover, the implementation of AI in imaging workflows has the potential to optimise radiologists' productivity by automating repetitive tasks, prioritising cases based on urgency, and minimising the likelihood of diagnostic errors. Such innovations not only enhance clinical decision-making but also contribute to a more efficient allocation of healthcare resources, addressing the growing demand for high-quality imaging services (Brady et al. 2024).

Furthermore, according to Nordlinger et al. (2020), the use of automated decision-making systems is particularly prominent in the field of oncology. These algorithms are capable of detecting subtle or fine details in medical images that are imperceptible to the human eye. Even in cases where image resolution is poor, AI systems can identify missing data and enhance image quality, thereby facilitating more accurate diagnoses. Additionally, AI can predict future outcomes based on the analysis of current images, offering a proactive approach to patient care.

Predictive analytics also serve as a critical tool in evaluating responses to chemotherapy treatments. Traditionally, tumour response to chemotherapy has been estimated using approximate measurements of tumour diameter. However, autonomous systems provide advanced capabilities for modelling and simulating tumour growth processes, enabling the prediction of individual tumour responses to specific treatments. These innovations hold immense potential for tailoring therapeutic strategies to each patient's unique circumstances.

In this context, one notable example is *Watson for Oncology*, a technology developed by IBM in the United States. This AI system analyses biomedical data from a patient's medical records and cross-references it with its extensive database, which contains millions of medical evidences, scientific articles, and clinical studies. By doing so, the AI presents potential treatment options for cancer patients, organised and classified by levels of confidence.

The primary aim of *Watson for Oncology* is to assist physicians in navigating the complex interplay of patient symptoms, laboratory data, and imaging results to arrive at potential clinical diagnoses and treatment options. Ultimately, the physician remains responsible for evaluating the insights provided by the AI and determining the most appropriate treatment plan for the patient. Since its introduction in 2017, *Watson for Oncology* has been adopted in numerous hospitals worldwide.

It is also worth emphasising the current trend at the intersection of genomics and artificial intelligence, which is leading to a new era of *Precision Medicine* or *Personalised Medicine*. This approach has the potential to revolutionise cancer treatment by offering more precise and individualised insights into the disease (Shaban-Nejad and Michalowski 2020). Genomic testing can identify specific genetic mutations that influence the effectiveness of certain treatments. In parallel, AI algorithms analyse these genomic data in conjunction with other clinical variables—such as patient age, family history, and disease stage—to support physicians in determining the most appropriate treatment plan for each individual, tailored to the genetic profile of their tumour.

Eric Topol, in his book *Deep Medicine: How Artificial Intelligence Can Make Healthcare Human Again* (Topol 2019), highlights numerous scientific studies demonstrating the ability of AI to diagnose certain types of skin cancer or identify specific cardiac rhythm abnormalities as effectively as, and in some cases potentially better than, dermatologists and cardiologists. These findings underscore the growing potential of AI to complement and enhance clinical expertise across diverse medical specialties.

Furthermore, there are algorithms trained on extensive biomedical databases containing thousands of ophthalmological examinations. These algorithms are capable of assessing risk factors and, using detailed images of a patient's fundus and retina, diagnosing conditions with greater precision or even predicting future cardiovascular diseases. This capability represents a significant step forward in preventive medicine, enabling earlier interventions and improved patient outcomes (Rudnicka et al. 2022; Poplin et al. 2018).

AI's ability to integrate vast datasets from multiple medical disciplines, coupled with its capacity for pattern recognition, highlights its transformative role in reshaping diagnostic practices. By providing rapid, accurate assessments, AI tools not only assist clinicians but also hold the promise of reducing diagnostic errors and addressing disparities in access to specialist care.

Just as in the mid-twentieth century, the exciting promise of how automated systems can revolutionise the healthcare sector persists today. However, as technology advances and its adoption expands across numerous healthcare institutions, some of the same concerns raised decades ago remain unresolved. These include critical issues such as algorithmic accuracy and bias, patient privacy, the ethical and legal accountability of physicians, and the regulation of these technologies. Additionally, ongoing debates about the potential displacement of physicians by technology continue to provoke significant discourse.

While these concerns are far from new, they are no less pressing and undoubtedly require collective societal effort to address effectively. We stand at a pivotal moment, as the adoption of AI in clinical decision-making accelerates at an unprecedented pace.

Understanding how these technologies function, how they should be implemented and evaluated, where they excel and where they fall short, as well as the benefits and consequences of their use, are all fundamental questions that demand thoughtful consideration. These questions are not only critical for the medical field but also for the legal domain, as both are intrinsically intertwined in navigating the challenges posed by AI.

In light of this, and to focus the legal discussion of technological innovations within the scope of this book, the following sections will present practical applications of AI to support medical decision-making. Subsequently, an analysis of the risks and the resulting ethical-legal impacts will be provided, with particular emphasis on ethical principles, professional duties of care, and medical liability.

4.1.1 Applications of Artificial Intelligence in Brazilian and European Medical Practice

Over the past two decades, particularly in recent years, public policies and targeted funding initiatives across Europe have been instrumental in promoting the adoption of AI within the healthcare sector. Various governments and international organisations, including the World Health Organisation (WHO) and the European Commission, have recognised the transformative potential of AI to improve patient outcomes and enhance the efficiency of healthcare systems (van Noordt et al. 2023).

The European Commission has established funding programmes to support research and development in AI across multiple sectors. Such policies aim not only to drive technological progress but also to ensure ethical AI applications in healthcare by addressing crucial issues such as data security, patient privacy, and algorithmic transparency. These funding frameworks and policy supports collectively encourage innovation while upholding the rights and welfare of patients within the evolving digital health landscape.

In Brazil, until recently, much of this technological innovation was applied primarily in large private medical centres. However, since 2020, there has been a marked trend towards the broader dissemination of AI-based systems, driven in part by the Covid-19 pandemic, which accelerated this new reality globally, including in developing and underdeveloped countries. In the Brazilian context, the government, through the Unified Health System (SUS), has actively promoted public-private partnerships to establish AI initiatives within the healthcare sector.

The SUS Digital Programme, part of Brazil's health digitisation strategy, seeks to modernise healthcare within SUS through a comprehensive digital transformation approach. Key objectives of the programme include promoting interoperability and improving digital infrastructure to facilitate a cohesive digital ecosystem across the healthcare network. Below are the primary components of the SUS Digital Programme:

- *National Maturity Index in Digital* Health (Índice Nacional de Maturidade em Saúde Digital—INMSD): This index is used to measure, monitor, and evaluate digital maturity within healthcare services, providing metrics essential for assessing progress in digital transformation.
- *Digitalisation of the SUS and adoption of interoperable electronic health records* (EHRs): The programme emphasises implementing EHR systems that comply with interoperability standards, ensuring seamless data sharing and coordination across healthcare providers.
- *Enhancement of infrastructure for digital systems and connectivity*: By improving digital infrastructure, the SUS aims to support the reliable operation of digital health tools, expanding the reach of digital services to more remote and underserved areas.
- *Digital health ecosystem development*: This involves fostering open innovation and building a collaborative network of healthcare providers, technology developers, and other stakeholders. The programme envisions a connected ecosystem that supports patient-centred care and enables data-driven healthcare advancements.

By integrating tools such as telemedicine, artificial intelligence, and data analytics, the *SUS Digital Programme* enhances the quality, efficiency, and accessibility of healthcare services across Brazil. This initiative aligns with global digital health trends and is designed to meet the evolving healthcare needs of the Brazilian population through a robust technological framework.

In recent years, a wide range of AI-driven systems has been developed and approved across Brazil and Europe for application in hospitals and clinics. For the purpose of clarity and academic discussion, these innovations can be categorised into two big groups, as detailed in the Table 4.1.

Table 4.1 This table was created by the author to summarise and categorise the main groups of AI-driven technologies currently being developed and implemented in healthcare settings, which are particularly relevant to the discussions in this book

Group	Description
1. *AI-Powered Softwares for Biomedical Data and Medical Imaging Analysis*	AI-powered software designed to analyse biomedical data and medical images, supporting critical tasks such as patient triage, diagnosis, and prognosis. These tools enhance precision and streamline clinical workflows, improving efficiency and decision-making in healthcare settings.
2. *Platforms, Smartphones, IoT Devices, and Wearable Technologies for Patient Monitoring*	Mobile technologies and wearable devices engineered to monitor patients and assist in risk assessment. By collecting real-time health data, these tools enable continuous monitoring, early detection of potential complications, and timely interventions, particularly for chronic conditions and post-operative care.

The rapid advancement and integration of artificial intelligence into medical practice have transformed healthcare delivery in both Brazil and Europe. As outlined above, AI technologies have been strategically categorised into two key groups, each addressing critical areas such as diagnostic accuracy, patient monitoring, personalised care, and risk management. This classification offers a comprehensive framework for understanding the diverse functionalities and applications of AI in healthcare. Building upon this foundation, the following discussion will explore practical case studies that showcase the utilisation of these AI systems within Brazilian and European healthcare contexts. These examples will offer valuable insights into the tangible impact of AI innovations, highlighting their capacity to improve clinical outcomes, optimise healthcare processes, and shape the future trajectory of medical practice.

Group 1: AI-Powered Software for Biomedical Data and Medical Imaging Analysis

Artificial intelligence (AI) has become a cornerstone in modern healthcare, transforming the diagnosis, treatment, and management of complex medical conditions. By leveraging vast datasets and advanced algorithms, AI systems enhance diagnostic precision, streamline workflows, and improve accessibility, particularly in underserved regions where specialist care is limited. From chronic conditions such as diabetic retinopathy to acute emergencies like ischaemic strokes, AI-driven technologies are addressing critical healthcare challenges and improving patient outcomes.

DeepMind Health, a subsidiary of Alphabet Inc. based in London, has established itself as a leader in AI applications for healthcare. Originally recognised for groundbreaking achievements in AI research, such as AlphaGo, DeepMind transitioned to healthcare by partnering with leading institutions to tackle pressing medical challenges. Its flagship projects include collaborations with the National Health Service (NHS) in the United Kingdom, where it developed *Streams*, an app designed to assist clinicians in identifying and managing acute kidney injury (AKI). By integrating real-time patient data with predictive algorithms, Streams has demonstrated the ability to improve diagnostic speed and accuracy, optimising hospital workflows and enhancing patient safety.

DeepMind Health has also made significant strides in medical imaging and oncology. Its partnership with Moorfields Eye Hospital in London led to the creation of AI algorithms capable of analysing retinal scans to detect eye diseases such as macular degeneration and diabetic retinopathy with human-level accuracy or better. Additionally, the company developed an autonomous system to support radiation therapy planning for prostate cancer, which uses advanced algorithms to analyse patient data and recommend precise dosage plans. These innovations exemplify the transformative potential of AI in improving diagnostic precision, streamlining complex decision-making processes, and advancing personalised medicine by tailoring treatments to individual patients' genetic and physiological profiles.

The integration of artificial intelligence (AI) into healthcare systems has revolutionised the diagnosis and management of complex conditions, particularly in underserved regions with limited access to medical specialists. Diabetic retinopathy, a leading cause of vision loss among individuals with diabetes, presents a critical challenge due to the necessity of early detection and timely intervention. Every year, over 60,000 people go blind from diabetic retinopathy, and with a growing lack of doctors and a complex healthcare system, getting patients the right care is harder than ever.

AI systems such as IDx-DR, now known as *LumineticsCore*, the first FDA-cleared autonomous AI technology that can detect diabetic retinopathy at the point of care, have emerged as transformative tools in addressing this issue, offering innovative solutions to enhance diagnostic precision and accessibility. It is an AI-powered system designed to detect diabetic retinopathy by analysing retinal images captured during routine eye examinations. It's technology that is able to provide rapid results that previously would have taken days, hours, or multiple appointments. It is validated to detect the same biomarkers that a doctor would use to diagnose disease. Using a camera that is simple to operate, *LumineticsCore* can analyze these biomarkers and provide an autonomous diagnosis.

This medical technology uses machine learning algorithms trained on vast datasets to identify early signs of the condition, such as microaneurysms, haemorrhages, and other retinal abnormalities. Importantly, *LumineticsCore* operates autonomously, generating reliable diagnostic results without the need for input from an ophthalmologist or other specialist. This feature makes it particularly valuable in primary care settings, enabling general practitioners and optometrists to screen patients effectively and refer those requiring specialist care.

This AI system has been the subject of several pivotal studies evaluating its efficacy. A landmark clinical trial in 2018, involving 900 subjects across 10 primary care sites in the U.S., demonstrated that *LumineticsCore* achieved a sensitivity of 87% and a specificity of 90%, meeting all pre-specified superiority endpoints (Abràmoff et al. 2018). Additionally, a recent 2024 study (Riotto et al. 2024) conducted at the Jules Gonin Eye Hospital in Lausanne, Switzerland, compared the diagnostic accuracy of *LumineticsCore* to human graders. The results indicated that while negative results provided by the system can be trusted, *LumineticsCore* consistently overestimated diabetic retinopathy stages. The study concluded that fundus images classified as 'mild DR' or greater by the AI system should always be reviewed by a specialist to confirm the diagnosis. This insight underscores the importance of integrating clinical oversight into the use of autonomous AI systems.

LumineticsCore is currently utilised in various healthcare institutions across Europe, including hospitals and clinics in the United Kingdom, Germany, and the Netherlands. By streamlining the detection process, the system reduces diagnostic delays, facilitates early treatment, and significantly mitigates the risk of severe complications such as blindness. As the prevalence of diabetes continues to rise globally, tools like *LumineticsCore* play a vital role in ensuring timely, equitable, and effective management of diabetic retinopathy, ultimately improving patient outcomes and quality of life.

As artificial intelligence continues to demonstrate its transformative potential in healthcare, another compelling application lies in the realm of stroke management.

While tools like LumineticsCore are revolutionising the detection and management of diabetic retinopathy, addressing a global rise in chronic conditions, AI is also making significant strides in acute care settings.

One notable example is the *Viz.ai LVO system*, a groundbreaking platform designed to enhance the diagnosis and treatment of large vessel occlusions (LVOs), a severe and life-threatening type of ischaemic stroke. This innovation underscores how AI can not only improve outcomes in chronic disease management but also play a pivotal role in urgent, high-stakes medical scenarios where time is of the essence.

Viz.ai LVO leverages advanced AI algorithms to analyse CT angiograms, automatically detecting LVOs with high precision and immediately alerting healthcare teams to take prompt action. Once a CT angiogram is uploaded, the system scans the image for signs of occlusion and flags potential cases within minutes, sending notifications directly to specialists via a secure mobile or desktop application. This instant communication ensures that neurologists, radiologists, and stroke teams are informed simultaneously, enabling rapid decision-making. By significantly reducing the time between imaging and treatment, Viz.ai LVO addresses one of the most critical factors in stroke care—*time*. For stroke patients, every minute of delay equates to the loss of millions of brain cells, making this technology a lifesaving innovation.

This AI system has been validated through multiple clinical studies that highlight its accuracy and effectiveness in real-world settings. A key trial demonstrated the system's ability to detect LVOs with a sensitivity of 92% and specificity of 89%, rivalling the performance of human radiologists (Yahav-Dovrat et al. 2021). The system has been approved by regulatory bodies, including the FDA in the United States and CE certification in Europe, underscoring its compliance with stringent safety and efficacy standards. Currently, Viz.ai LVO is being implemented in leading hospitals across Europe and North America, where it has been integrated into stroke care pathways to streamline diagnosis and improve coordination among medical teams.

The adoption of Viz.ai LVO exemplifies the transformative potential of AI in healthcare. By addressing bottlenecks in traditional workflows and enhancing the efficiency of stroke diagnosis, this platform not only improves patient outcomes but also reduces the burden on overstretched healthcare systems. As AI continues to advance, systems like Viz.ai LVO set a benchmark for integrating innovative technologies into clinical practice, ensuring timely and effective care for stroke patients worldwide.

Moreover, considering that early cancer detection is critical in improving survival rates and enhancing patient outcomes, AI also has emerged as a powerful tool in achieving this goal. The *Paige Prostate Detect System* is a groundbreaking AI-driven software designed to assist pathologists in identifying prostate cancer with remarkable precision and efficiency. Developed by Paige, a leading company in AI applications for pathology, the software leverages advanced algorithms trained on vast datasets of digitised pathology slides. By analysing prostate biopsy images,

Paige Prostate Detect offers unparalleled diagnostic accuracy and speed, ultimately transforming the workflow of oncology diagnostics and improving patient outcomes.

The AI system has achieved regulatory approval in multiple regions, including the United States (FDA approval), Europe (CE-IVD certification), and Brazil (ANVISA approval). This global adoption underscores the system's compliance with rigorous safety and efficacy standards, positioning it as a valuable tool in the fight against cancer worldwide. In Brazil, it is being implemented at the *Oncoclínicas Precision Medicine Laboratory*, marking the first institution in the country to effectively utilise AI for prostate cancer diagnostics.

In Europe, the system is currently being evaluated in clinical settings within the United Kingdom. Notably, three NHS (National Health Service) hospitals—North Bristol NHS Trust Southmead Hospital, University Hospitals Coventry and Warwickshire NHS Trust, and Oxford University NHS Foundation Trust—are assessing the Paige Prostate Suite as part of the ARTICULATE PRO study. This initiative, led by the University of Oxford, aims to explore the potential of AI technology to enhance cancer diagnostics across England. The study evaluates how the Paige Prostate Suite impacts clinical decision-making, pathology service delivery, and resource utilisation in real-world settings.

The system integrates seamlessly into the oncological diagnostic process, encompassing laboratory information management systems (LIMS), digital pathology scanners, and web-based digital pathology viewers. Paige Prostate Detect's algorithm is capable of categorising biopsy samples into two classifications: initial (no further investigation required) and suspicious (necessitating additional immunohistochemical and/or histological analysis). This prioritisation enables pathologists to focus their attention on cases requiring further scrutiny, thereby enhancing diagnostic precision.

Studies published in the *Journal of Pathology* (Medeiros da Silva et al. 2021) highlight the transformative potential of Paige Prostate Detect. The system can reduce the turnaround time for diagnostic results by up to 65.5%, significantly expediting treatment planning. Furthermore, it mitigates variability in histopathological diagnoses, increases sensitivity in detecting microscopic lesions that may be overlooked by the human eye, and enhances overall accuracy. By streamlining the diagnostic workflow, Paige Prostate Detect not only accelerates the release of pathology reports but also provides critical support in identifying and addressing complex cancer cases.

The adoption of Paige Prostate Detect also illustrates the transformative role of AI in modern oncology. By combining advanced technology with pathologists' expertise, this innovative system ensures that patients receive timely and accurate diagnoses, paving the way for personalised and effective treatment strategies.

It is worth noting that, in Brazil, the shortage of pathologists, particularly in remote and underserved regions, poses a significant challenge to the accurate analysis and reporting of biopsies, a crucial step in diagnosing and treating various diseases. Histological image analysis is essential for determining disease activity and chronicity, especially in renal conditions, and for guiding treatment decisions and prognoses. To address these challenges, AI systems have the potential to improve accuracy and precision in lesion identification and classification, providing critical support to the diagnostic process.

In this context, the PathoSpotter Project, initiated in 2014, has spearheaded advancements in digital pathology in Brazil. The project focuses on developing AI systems for automated recognition in nephrology, particularly for classifying renal lesions such as glomerular sclerosis, hypercellularity, and membrane thickening. Achieving an accuracy rate between 88.3% and 95.73%, PathoSpotter enhances the diagnostic workflow by allowing users to upload histological images and receive automated reports (Oliveira et al. 2022). Each new image processed further refines the system's algorithmic precision. Although still in development, PathoSpotter is poised to revolutionise nephrology diagnostics, making advanced technology accessible nationwide. This AI system is the product of a decade-long collaboration between the Federal University of Bahia, Fiocruz Bahia, and the State University of Feira de Santana, and it was recognised in 2023 with the fifth DASA-Veja Medicine Award in the Diagnostic Medicine category.

In 2024, the Albert Einstein Hospital, one of Brazil's leading healthcare institutions in technological solutions, has been at the forefront of developing AI algorithms for detecting rare diseases and tropical diseases such as leishmaniasis. These initiatives, supported by the Brazilian Ministry of Health, are envisioned to be integrated into the country's public healthcare system (*Sistema Único de Saúde*—SUS). By leveraging AI, these projects aim to enhance diagnostic accuracy and ensure timely treatment, especially in underserved regions where such technologies could have a transformative impact.

Additionally, the same hospital, in collaboration with AstraZeneca, has established a Centre of Excellence for the Diagnosis and Treatment of Thrombotic Microangiopathies. This initiative focuses on expediting the identification of this rare and often life-threatening condition, which is frequently diagnosed in advanced stages due to delays in detection. The centre's goal is to facilitate early diagnosis, enabling prompt intervention and improved clinical outcomes. There is also an expectation to expand this model to the SUS, thereby increasing access to innovative diagnostic technologies and improving the treatment of rare diseases for a broader segment of the population.

These efforts exemplify the growing role of AI and public-private partnerships in advancing healthcare in Brazil. By addressing challenges in the diagnosis and management of both common and rare diseases, such initiatives have the potential to redefine care delivery and set new benchmarks for integrating cutting-edge technology into public health systems.

As evidenced by the aforementioned examples of automated decision-making systems, medical imaging is an invaluable resource for the analysis and diagnosis of diseases. However, in Brazil, significant challenges persist, including the lack of standardised protocols for collecting diagnostic tests and the absence of a universal framework for data storage and access. Consequently, many healthcare institutions, particularly within the public healthcare system (SUS), often delete diagnostic tests over time, which exacerbates delays in obtaining accurate diagnoses. Additionally, there is a notable shortage of specialised physicians, such as radiologists and dermatologists, particularly in underserved regions.

In this context, the *Image Bank and Algorithms Project* (BCIM_IA) emerges as a promising initiative with the potential to revolutionise Brazil's healthcare sector. This project aims to create a unified platform for storing and analysing medical imaging conducted within the SUS. Developed by scientists at the Albert Einstein Hospital in São Paulo as part of the Institutional Development Support Programme of the Unified Health System (PROADI-SUS), in collaboration with the Ministry of Health, the initiative is currently undergoing validation. The goal is to enable medical imaging to be securely stored and analysed using AI algorithms, thereby enhancing diagnostic accuracy and efficiency.

The PROADI-SUS, established in 2009, is a pivotal programme designed to improve the SUS through projects focusing on human resource training, research, technology evaluation and implementation, management, and specialised care as required by the Ministry of Health. It currently comprises six non-profit hospitals renowned for their medical and managerial excellence: Oswaldo Cruz German Hospital, Portuguese Beneficence Hospital of São Paulo, HCor—Heart Hospital, Albert Einstein Israelite Hospital, Moinhos de Vento Hospital, and Syrian-Lebanese Hospital. These institutions, exempt from tax obligations, allocate their resources to support projects in areas such as hospital management optimisation, technological development, and improvements in diagnostics and treatment delivery.

Since its inception in 2019, the *BCIM_IA Project*, coordinated by the Albert Einstein Hospital, has brought together a multidisciplinary team of researchers, physicians, data scientists, developers, and other collaborators. The project focuses on developing and refining AI models to detect abnormalities and diagnostic findings. Initial priorities include identifying tuberculosis in chest X-rays, volumetric changes in cranial CT scans, and malignant skin lesions using dermatoscopic and photographic images. Thus far, three algorithms have been developed: one for detecting tuberculosis in chest radiographs, another for identifying brain infections caused by the Zika virus in cranial CT scans, and a third for analysing skin photographs to detect melanoma, an aggressive form of skin cancer.

Although these algorithms have not yet been tested in clinical settings, preliminary analyses indicate a diagnostic accuracy rate of 95%. The algorithms still require clinical validation before they can be integrated into medical practice. In its initial phase, the project has benefited from international partnerships, notably with Stanford University (USA), a worldwide leading institution in AI and imaging diagnostic innovations. These collaborations underscore the project's potential to elevate diagnostic capabilities in Brazil and set a precedent for the global adoption of AI in public healthcare systems.

Group 2: Platforms, Smartphones, IoT Devices, and Wearable Technologies for Patient Monitoring

In recent years, the global healthcare landscape has witnessed the development of numerous big data and artificial intelligence (AI) solutions, integrated into smartphone applications and wearable devices. These innovations aim to manage medication, monitor physical and mental health, and track diet and exercise. Such technologies are particularly beneficial for individuals living with chronic conditions, including asthma, diabetes, cancer, cardiovascular diseases, and mental illnesses, which are among the most pressing global health challenges.

Several companies have pioneered the creation of sophisticated technologies and algorithms capable of collecting and analysing vital signs, heart rate, temperature, mood, cognition, and physical activity. For instance, one of the primary challenges faced by individuals with diabetes is maintaining stable blood glucose levels. Leveraging these emerging digital technologies, patients can now continuously monitor their glucose levels. In real time, AI algorithms analyse the data, enabling healthcare professionals to make informed therapeutic decisions, such as adjusting insulin dosages or recommending dietary interventions.

In Brazil, 2022 marked a significant milestone with the approval by ANVISA of a new AI-based insulin infusion pump designed to prevent hypo- and hyperglycaemia autonomously. This advanced device, worn around the waist and connected to the abdominal area via a cannula, delivers insulin continuously throughout the day, making adjustments every 5 min to ensure precise blood glucose control. The system includes a smart sensor that transmits insulin data to the pump via Bluetooth and to a mobile application, allowing patients to monitor their glucose levels and manage insulin administration through their smartphones. Developed by the multinational Medtronic, the *MiniMed 780G System* has also been introduced in European markets. However, in Brazil, the widespread adoption of this technology faces significant barriers due to its high cost.

Eric Topol, in his seminal works on the future of medicine (2013, 2015, 2019), highlights an emerging era of democratised healthcare access and a transformative shift in the doctor-patient relationship. He describes this development as "the new era of patient engagement," wherein patients assume an active and continuous role in providing biomedical data to inform clinical decisions, effectively becoming "data-gatherers." This model redefines the doctor-patient relationship from a sporadic interaction into an ongoing process, a transition that has been greatly facilitated by the advent of wearable technologies.

Artificial intelligence (AI) is also transforming cardiac care, addressing critical issues like arrhythmias, which affect over 20 million people in Brazil and cause more than 320,000 sudden deaths annually, according to the Brazilian Society of Cardiac Arrhythmias (SOBRAC). In collaboration with the Heart Institute (InCor), Lenovo developed the TRAdA (Remote Assisted Monitoring of Arrhythmia—*Telemonitoramento Remoto Assistido de Arritmia*) platform in 2024. This AI-driven system remotely monitors heart rhythms using wearable devices and an AI algorithm. With a user-friendly interface, TRAdA sends real-time alerts to patients and healthcare teams, enabling faster and more effective diagnoses, particularly during the critical 72-h period following cardiac surgery when complications are most likely to occur.

The TRAdA platform underwent rigorous clinical validation at InCor, including trials involving 253 participants and a final proof-of-concept study with 51 post-surgical cardiovascular patients. The AI algorithm analyses cardiac signals to detect conditions such as atrial fibrillation, sending timely alerts to dedicated medical teams. This capability has proven crucial in preventing severe complications, as highlighted by cases where early alerts helped avoid emergencies and reduced healthcare costs. Developed over 3 years, with 70% of the time dedicated to training the AI model, TRAdA also allows patients to report symptoms, providing valuable data for medical teams. By combining cutting-edge AI with practical telemonitoring, TRAdA exemplifies the potential of technology to enhance patient outcomes and optimise healthcare delivery.

A similar AI-driven system in the cardiology is the *Kardia 12L ECG System*, a handheld 12-lead ECG device powered by the FDA-cleared KAI 12L AI technology, which was approved by the FDA in United States in 2024. This system is capable of detecting 35 cardiac conditions, including acute myocardial infarction and other life-threatening issues, using a streamlined leadset that simplifies the traditionally cumbersome ECG process. Compact and battery-operated, the *Kardia 12L* weighs only 0.3 pounds and is designed for use in a variety of healthcare settings, including rural and under-resourced areas. The AI-powered algorithm can identify various irregularities, including atrial fibrillation, bradycardia, and tachycardia, enabling early detection and timely intervention. Its innovative design and accessibility have made it a valuable tool for empowering patients and enhancing the efficiency of cardiac care. By offering rapid, accurate diagnostics in a highly portable format, it represents a breakthrough in making advanced cardiac monitoring more accessible and efficient.

In Europe, wearable devices and smartphone applications have become integral to modern healthcare, leveraging artificial intelligence (AI) and big data to address chronic and acute health conditions. Among the numerous innovations in this space, two notable examples are the *FreeStyle Libre 2 system* for diabetes management and *MySense*, a remote monitoring platform for older adults. These devices exemplify how technology is reshaping patient care, providing real-time data to enhance decision-making, prevent complications, and improve quality of life.

The *FreeStyle Libre 2 system*, developed by Abbott, is a wearable device designed to assist individuals with diabetes in continuously monitoring glucose levels. By utilising a small sensor worn on the back of the upper arm, the system provides real-time readings, eliminating the need for frequent finger-prick tests. Data collected by the device is transmitted to a smartphone application, enabling users and healthcare professionals to monitor trends, set alerts for hypo- or hyperglycaemia, and adjust insulin dosages or dietary plans accordingly. Widely adopted across Europe, the FreeStyle Libre has been praised for its accuracy and ability to empower patients in managing their condition effectively, while reducing the burden on healthcare systems. Everyone with type 1 diabetes in the UK is entitled to flash glucose sensing or continuous glucose monitoring (CGM) on the NHS.

Another significant innovation is *MySense*, a UK-based AI-powered platform designed to remotely monitor the health and well-being of older adults. MySense integrates data from wearable devices and home sensors to track key health metrics such as heart rate, temperature, hydration, and physical activity. It picks up around 17,000 data points per day per individual supported, and these come from a wearable device, a bed sensor and passive sensors located in specific places across the home.

By analysing this data in real time, the *MySense* platform detects deviations from an individual's baseline health patterns and alerts caregivers or healthcare professionals to potential issues, such as falls, dehydration, or early signs of illness. This technology not only enhances the safety and independence of older adults but also provides valuable insights to healthcare providers, enabling early interventions that can prevent hospitalisations.

Philips, a Dutch company, has developed the *HealthSuite Digital Platform* to integrate data from wearable devices, home sensors, and clinical records. This platform is widely used across Europe for managing chronic conditions like chronic obstructive pulmonary disease (COPD) and heart failure. It allows clinicians to monitor patients remotely, providing real-time updates on their health and enabling timely interventions, particularly for those in remote or underserved areas.

Neuroelectrics, a Spanish company, specialises in wearable devices for neurological monitoring and therapy. Their technologies, such as the Starstim system, combine non-invasive electrical stimulation with EEG monitoring, supported by AI-driven data analysis to optimise treatment protocols. This integration of artificial intelligence and neurotechnology reflects a growing trend in recent years, aiming to personalise therapies for conditions like epilepsy, chronic pain, and depression. Neurotechnologies are increasingly being adopted in clinical trials and therapeutic settings across Europe.

The *Eversense XL* is a long-term continuous glucose monitoring system designed for patients with diabetes. It features a small sensor implanted under the skin that can continuously monitor blood glucose levels for up to 180 days. Data is transmitted to a smartphone app via a wearable transmitter, allowing real-time glucose tracking and alerts for hypo- or hyperglycaemia. This device is CE-marked and widely adopted in Europe for its reliability and convenience.

BioPatch is a small, lightweight wearable sensor used for continuous monitoring of vital signs such as heart rate, respiratory rate, and temperature. The device is widely implemented in European hospitals and care facilities, enabling remote monitoring of patients' post-surgery or with chronic illnesses. Data from the BioPatch is sent to a centralised system, allowing healthcare providers to track patient health remotely and intervene when necessary.

These wearable devices represent the diverse applications of AI and digital health technologies in Europe, addressing chronic diseases, post-operative care, and general wellness. They demonstrate how wearable devices are improving healthcare accessibility, personalising treatment plans, and empowering patients to take an active role in their health management. These technologies bridge gaps in care, promote proactive health management, and exemplify the shift towards more personalised, patient-centred approaches in modern medicine.

In the context of AI systems for hospital risk management, Brazil has emerged as a leader with the implementation of *Laura Robot*, a pioneering cognitive technology approved by ANVISA. This system mines clinical data from hospitalised patients to assist in the timely identification of clinical deterioration. By collecting real-time data such as vital signs, medical history, electronic health records, test results, and treatment information, *Laura Robot* effectively identifies potential health risks or signs of clinical decline. Operating cyclically, the system analyses each patient and applies predefined care protocols that can be customised by the healthcare institution. Alerts are generated to flag anomalies in vital signs or test results, with the information accessible via a mobile app for medical teams. Patients are ranked by risk classification, enabling professionals to prioritise care and improve efficiency.

Initially developed in 2014 to address sepsis-related mortality, *Laura Robot* expanded its application during the Covid-19 pandemic to include patient triage and monitoring for coronavirus symptoms. The AI system assessed risk profiles to determine whether in-person medical attention was required. Over time, its utility grew to encompass other critical conditions, such as cardiac, hypertensive, and diabetic patients requiring constant monitoring. The technology has been adopted by health insurance providers nationwide, with several municipalities partnering with the Instituto Laura to integrate the system into the Unified Health System (SUS). These initiatives underscore the transformative potential of AI in enhancing public health infrastructure and care delivery.

Beyond patient monitoring, AI has also revolutionised hospital resource management and risk administration in Brazil. A prominent example is the AI-powered system established in 2018 at the Albert Einstein Israelite Hospital, which features a control room dedicated to predicting bed occupancy. This system processes patient information from triage to final medical evaluations, enabling the hospital to predict daily occupancy and reserve beds in advance. Upon a patient's arrival, their complaints and electronic medical records are analysed by algorithms to determine whether they should be attended to by a specialist or general practitioner. The system evaluates the likelihood of hospitalisation at four key stages: during triage, after initial medical assessment, following test results, and after a final medical review. These predictive capabilities ensure efficient resource allocation and improved patient care (Lottenberg et al. 2019).

The hospital's *Centralised Monitoring and Assistance Unit* (*Central de Monitoramento Assistencial*—CMOA) further enhances patient outcomes by continuously updating algorithms with real-time biometric, test, and medical data. Monitoring approximately 150 predefined indicators, the AI system issues alerts when thresholds are met, such as significant delays in administering pain medication. Alerts displayed on large CMOA panels prompt direct action from medical teams, improving response times and reducing risks associated with extended hospital stays. Significant impacts have been observed in emergency care, surgical centres, and specialised departments such as Oncology and Haematology. This integration of AI into hospital operations exemplifies the profound impact of digital innovation on improving healthcare efficiency and patient safety.

Nowadays, the broader digital revolution in Brazil is particularly evident in renowned hospitals located in major urban centres, where digital tools such as tablets have become integral to medical routines, enabling instant access to electronic health records, medication information, and patient procedures. This digital transformation extends beyond individual hospitals to encompass integrated care, bed management, and diagnostic services, modernising laboratories and imaging centres.

The examples of AI applications in Brazil and Europe discussed in this section represent only a glimpse of the extensive advancements currently underway in healthcare technology. The growing number of startups, research centres, and healthcare institutions investing in innovation underscores Brazil's position as South America's largest digital health market and a global leader alongside Europe in generating transformative healthcare technologies. This progressive landscape highlights the pivotal role of AI in shaping the future of healthcare, enabling more efficient, precise, and patient-centred care delivery worldwide.

4.1.2 Key Risks and Challenges in the Implementation of Algorithms in Medicine

The risks associated with Artificial Intelligence (AI) have provoked significant global concern, particularly in light of incidents involving autonomous vehicles. For instance, in 2021, two occupants of a Tesla Model S tragically lost their lives, allegedly due to the vehicle's failure to navigate a curve on a winding road, which resulted in a collision with a tree and subsequent fire. Neither victim was seated in the driver's position, and the vehicle was reportedly operating in autopilot mode. In 2023, another Tesla Model S collided with a fire truck, causing a fatal accident. This marked the 17th fatal incident reported by the company since 2021.

Autonomous vehicles, while promising to reduce accidents attributed to human error—such as inattention, fatigue, or negligence—also introduce potential hazards stemming from inherent technological risks. These risks include flawed algorithmic programming, algorithmic fallibility, sensor malfunctions, system vulnerabilities to hacking, and the emergence of unpredictable behaviours derived from machine learning processes. Furthermore, reports from 2019 highlighted that autonomous vehicles equipped with *LiDAR technology*—relying on light reflection from surrounding objects—demonstrated a higher propensity to strike Black pedestrians, thereby exposing a discriminatory bias within the algorithm's programming (Faleiros Júnior 2021).

In the healthcare sector, AI systems face some crisis of credibility. This is particularly pronounced due to the risks associated with the implementation of AI in clinical practice, including a relevant degree of fallibility, the potential for discriminatory outcomes and decisions influenced by significant biases (Obermeyer et al. 2019).

Recent scientific studies have highlighted a significant degree of fallibility in algorithms employed in the medical field after their deployment in the market (Ross 2021b). This issue is particularly concerning for algorithms used in clinical practice to assist with diagnoses and treatment recommendations. For instance, systems like *Watson for Oncology* claim an accuracy rate of 90%, leaving a notable 10% margin for error.

On the other hand, AI algorithms are being tested as decision-support tools in recommending *palliative care*. However, these systems exhibit a significantly high degree of imprecision. For example, the Jvion CORE algorithm has approximately a 40% probability that patients flagged as being at *high risk of death* will indeed pass away in the subsequent month. This indicates an algorithmic fallibility rate of 60% (Robbins 2020). For this reason, Topol (2019) asserts that, until more accurate models of such algorithms—referred to as *AI Dying Algorithms*—are developed, uncertainties persist regarding the role AI can play in the context of palliative care.

While such accuracy levels may appear impressive, they underscore the critical need to address the remaining degree of fallibility, which can have profound implications in a clinical context. Even a small margin of error can lead to misdiagnoses, inappropriate treatment plans, or delayed interventions, particularly in high-stakes scenarios where patient outcomes depend on timely and accurate decision-making.

The evaluation of AI systems in healthcare requires rigorous scrutiny to ensure their accuracy and reliability when transitioning from controlled preclinical studies to real-world clinical applications. While preclinical studies often demonstrate high performance, real-world scenarios introduce variables such as patient diversity, imaging quality, and clinical workflow differences that can significantly affect outcomes. This underscores the importance of validating AI systems through robust methodologies, such as randomised controlled trials (RCTs), to ensure they meet the high standards necessary for clinical use.

The EchoGo system, developed by Ultromics and originating from the University of Oxford, exemplifies this need for stringent evaluation. Designed to assist in diagnosing coronary artery disease, this AI-powered platform leverages advanced algorithms to analyse stress echocardiography scans, automating image interpretation to provide quicker and more standardised results. Initially heralded as a groundbreaking tool with an accuracy rate of 90%, EchoGo aimed to streamline workflows and improve diagnostic precision in clinical settings. However, recent findings from the PROTEUS trial, presented at the European Society of Cardiology (ESC) Congress 2024 in London, UK, held between 30 August and 2 September, offer a more complex perspective on the system's capabilities (Barrie 2024).

The trial, conducted across multiple UK hospitals with over 2300 patients, marked the first randomised controlled trial (RCT) evaluating EchoGo's use in stress echocardiography, a diagnostic procedure that demands significant expertise. The study revealed an accuracy rate of 70% for the AI-augmented approach in triaging patients for invasive coronary angiograms, lower than the 90% reported in preclinical studies. This discrepancy highlights the differences between controlled and real-world testing environments. Preclinical studies use standardised, high-quality datasets under ideal conditions, optimising performance but not accounting for real-world variability. RCTs introduce diverse patient populations, varying image quality, and operational complexities, providing a more realistic measure of effectiveness.

The PROTEUS trial highlights the necessity of rigorous evaluation to bridge the gap between AI performance in idealised preclinical settings and the complexities of real-world clinical practice. While the findings revealed areas for improvement, they also demonstrated EchoGo's potential to support less experienced clinicians and assist in challenging diagnostic scenarios. This underscores the importance of ongoing refinement and validation to ensure that AI tools not only meet technical benchmarks but also reliably enhance decision-making and patient outcomes in diverse healthcare environments.

Another critical issue surrounding AI in healthcare, exemplified by *Watson for Oncology*, is the reliance on limited and narrowly focused training data, which can lead to recommendations poorly suited to the diverse realities of global and local healthcare contexts, ultimately undermining the system's applicability and eroding trust among clinicians and patients.

IBM Watson was introduced to the world in 2011 when it achieved a historic milestone by defeating human champions on the television game show Jeopardy! This success showcased the potential of AI to process and analyse vast amounts of information with remarkable speed and accuracy. Following this achievement, IBM sought to leverage Watson's capabilities in real-world applications, identifying healthcare as a prime area of focus.

In 2012, the company partnered with *Memorial Sloan Kettering Cancer Centre* to develop *Watson for Oncology*, an AI-driven platform designed to assist oncologists in diagnosing and recommending treatment plans for cancer patients. By synthesising clinical guidelines, peer-reviewed literature, and patient records, the AI system aimed to deliver evidence-based treatment recommendations within seconds. This initiative was marketed as a revolutionary tool to bridge the gap between cutting-edge research and clinical practice, promising to enhance personalised care, improve patient outcomes, and expand access to oncology expertise globally.

Watson for Oncology was launched by IBM with the promise of revolutionising cancer care through artificial intelligence. Its aim was to assist oncologists by providing evidence-based treatment recommendations derived from analysing vast datasets of clinical guidelines, medical literature, and patient records. It was envisioned a tool capable of improving patient outcomes, bridging knowledge gaps, and expanding access to quality care, particularly in underserved regions. However, despite initial optimism, the project faced significant challenges and was ultimately discontinued in 2023, marking a $4 billion failure for IBM.

The system was designed to offer several benefits: (1) streamlining clinical decision-making by processing vast amounts of data quickly and delivering treatment recommendations in seconds; (2) providing personalised care by tailoring treatments to individual patients based on their genetic profiles and clinical history; (3) bridging knowledge gaps by keeping clinicians informed of the latest research and emerging treatment protocols; and (4) addressing healthcare disparities by allowing access to world-class expertise in regions with limited specialist availability.

Despite these ambitious goals, the AI system encountered significant issues that ultimately led to its downfall: (1) the system overrelied on limited training data, predominantly from the Memorial Sloan Kettering Cancer Centre, which made its recommendations poorly suited to global or local healthcare contexts; (2) it occasionally provided inaccurate or unsafe suggestions, undermining trust among clinicians and patients; (3) IBM's marketing of Watson exaggerated its capabilities, creating unrealistic expectations that led to widespread criticism when the system failed to deliver; (4) physicians found the interface disruptive and difficult to integrate into their workflows; and (5) moreover, Watson's inability to adapt to local treatment guidelines, drug availability, and healthcare infrastructure further limited its applicability in diverse settings.

The failure of *Watson for Oncology* underscores critical lessons for future AI projects in healthcare. Developers must prioritise diverse training data from multiple institutions worldwide to ensure global relevance and practical application. Moreover, iterative development processes involving clinicians are essential to align the system with real-world needs, while transparent communication about the system's capabilities and limitations is crucial for maintaining stakeholder trust. Ethical oversight should also be implemented to safeguard data integrity, ensure transparency in marketing, and protect patient safety. Finally, AI systems must be designed with local adaptability to accommodate variations in regional healthcare guidelines, infrastructure, and resources.

Ultimately, the case of IBM *Watson for Oncology* demonstrates the complexities of applying AI in high-stakes medical fields. While the technology held significant promise, its implementation fell short due to overambition, inadequate validation, and misalignment with clinical realities. Moving forward, these lessons can guide the development of more effective, ethical, and impactful AI solutions that truly enhance healthcare outcomes.

The *American Medical Association*, in a recent publication discussed the primary challenges in integrating this technology into healthcare, underscoring the risks of discrimination and algorithmic biases (Crigger et al. 2022). Below is an excerpt from this study:

> (…) the recent example of an algorithm that used historical health care spending as a proxy for illness severity to predict an individual's future health needs and establish their eligibility for additional services. This method excluded many Black patients from disease management programs, effectively expanding long-standing racial inequities in access to care (…) it is appropriate to draw attention briefly to the potential for bias in the design, operation, or deployment of adaptive systems in clinical settings. Algorithms trained on electronic health records (EHRs), as most currently are, risk building into the model itself whatever flaws exist in the record: EHRs capture information only from individuals who have access to care and whose data are captured electronically; data are not uniformly structured across EHRs; and the majority of data in EHRs reflect information captured *downstream* of human judgments, with the risk that the model will replicate human cognitive errors. Moreover, well-intended efforts to correct for possible bias in training data can have unintended consequences, as is the case when *race-corrected* algorithms direct resources away from patients from minoritized populations rather than provide equitable personalized care.
>
> Efforts to build fair adaptive models must meet challenges of mathematically defining *fairness* in the first place, and of determining just what trade-offs between fairness and model performance are acceptable. Beyond these challenges, even algorithms that are, hypothetically, *fair* out of the box may become *biased* over time when they are deployed in contexts different from those in which they were created, or when they learn from pervasive, ongoing, and uncorrected biases in the broader health care system. Models may be followed uncritically, or be implemented only in certain settings such that they disproportionately benefit individuals who are already experiencing privilege of one sort or another.

> Finally, they may preferentially select or encourage outcomes that do not reflect the interests of individual patients or the community (...) Equity issues arise when the data set used to train an algorithm excludes or underrepresents historically marginalized and minoritized patient populations, failing to account for significant differences in experience or outcomes associated with patient identity. The design of the algorithm itself might exacerbate inequities if proxies or assumptions are based in historical discrimination and injustices, as illustrated by the disease management algorithm cited above.

The study underscores the critical need for comprehensive ethical and regulatory frameworks to govern the integration of AI into healthcare, ensuring adherence to the principles of *equity* and *non-discrimination*. To foster *trustworthiness*—defined as dependability and deserving of confidence—AI systems in healthcare must be developed, validated, implemented, and monitored using rigorous, standardised processes grounded in ethical considerations and a commitment to equity. Without these essential safeguards, the adoption of AI technologies risks perpetuating systemic inequalities, compounding existing disparities, and eroding trust in their application within clinical settings.

Another study, conducted by the *University of Cambridge* in England, revealed that the vast majority of algorithms used in the healthcare sector worldwide are trained on small, single-source datasets with limited population diversity. For instance, of the 161 AI products approved by the FDA in the United States till 2021, only 73 publicly disclosed the amount of data used to validate the product, and of those, merely 7 specified the racial composition of their study populations (Ross 2021a).

The failure to test AI models on data from diverse sources—a process known as *external validation*—is a frequent shortcoming in studies published in leading medical journals globally. This often results in algorithms that appear highly accurate in controlled studies but fail to perform at the same level when applied to real-world variables involving different patient types across various locations.

In this context, it has been argued that Black women with breast cancer are more likely to receive delayed diagnoses from existing predictive algorithms on the market, as these are often trained on populations with few or no Black individuals (Ledford 2019). Nonetheless, it must be emphasised that incorporating clinical data from diverse populations during the programming of algorithms is indispensable, given the significant variations in how diseases manifest across different racial groups. As mentioned before, recent studies have confirmed that *Watson for Oncology* exhibits certain limitations in its database used for algorithm training, leading to significant discrepancies in accuracy and consistency when this AI system is deployed in other countries (Jie et al. 2021). This is attributable to the fact that White, Mixed-race, and Black individuals display significant differences in sensitivity and tolerance to specific chemotherapeutic drugs, resulting in clinical guidelines that vary according to the specific characteristics of each country and region.

It is worth emphasising that achieving more appropriate data for healthcare within the technological arsenal requires looking beyond the sheer volume of data needed to programme an algorithm. Without adequate racial representation, proper external validation, appropriate data handling, and other critical factors, significant risks arise for the companies developing AI technologies. These risks include negative impacts on patients' lives, financial losses, and potential legal actions.

It is noteworthy that this complexity in handling sensitive data and training AI systems in the healthcare sector is exemplified by IBM's recent exit from the healthcare market. In January 2022, IBM sold its *Watson Health* assets to Francisco Partners. This platform, developed in 2015, was designed to offer various AI solutions for healthcare, including the aforementioned *Watson for Oncology*. This scenario highlights the demanding need for careful supervision in the development and deployment of AI in healthcare, ensuring that these technologies serve to enhance care equitably and responsibly while mitigating risks to patients and providers alike.

Beyond the specific challenges outlined above, additional inherent risks associated with AI systems merit closer examination. Pasquale (2015) identifies the *black box problem*, whereby algorithms generate outcomes without providing a transparent explanation of their decision-making processes. Ford and Price (2016) expand on this concern, cautioning against the proliferation of *black box medicine*. This term refers to the increasing reliance on opaque algorithms to discern patterns in patient data, which are then used to generate diagnoses, predict health risks, or recommend medication dosages—often without clear accountability or interpretability.

An illustrative example of this issue is the development of *Deep Patient* in 2015 by a group of American scientists. This AI software, trained on a dataset comprising approximately 700,000 electronic medical records, demonstrated remarkable capabilities in predicting future illnesses, such as schizophrenia, diabetes, and cancer (Miotto et al. 2016). However, despite its apparent success in anticipating these diagnoses, the machine learning processes underpinning its predictions remains a mystery to researchers. The inability to explain how the AI arrived at its conclusions underscores the opacity inherent in such systems.

This highlights the growing sophistication of algorithms that arrive at conclusions which are often inexplicable, even to their creators or users. The lack of transparency in how such decisions are reached poses significant challenges, particularly in fields like medicine, where the stakes are high. The inability to understand the reasoning behind algorithmic decisions not only undermines trust in these systems but also raises critical questions about their reliability and accountability. As algorithms evolve to perform increasingly complex tasks, this opacity remains a persistent and troubling issue, requiring robust mechanisms for validation, oversight, and interpretability.

Another striking example pertains to an experiment conducted at the *University of California's Department of Computer Science*, where a student developed an algorithm to classify images of huskies and wolves (UCI Beall Applied Innovation 2017). The algorithm achieved a high degree of accuracy in distinguishing between the two animals. However, subsequent analyses revealed that the algorithm was not, in fact, identifying specific features of the animals but was instead relying on the presence of snow in the background of the photographs to label images as wolves. This case exemplifies the risks of poorly designed AI, which can produce superficially impressive results while failing to address the intended problem.

Now consider the potential consequences of a poorly programmed or flawed AI system in high-stakes scenarios such as the diagnosis of COVID-19 during the pandemic. In several countries, AI was deployed to identify patients infected with the virus. If such algorithms were improperly designed or exhibited any degree of fallibility, the ramifications could have been catastrophic. The inability to ascertain how an algorithm arrives at a particular outcome is especially concerning in healthcare, where decisions often involve life-or-death situations.

These examples highlight the imperative for vigilance in implementing AI within the healthcare sector. Rigorous validation processes, robust ethical oversight, and a steadfast commitment to transparency are essential to ensure that AI systems contribute to improved care while minimising risks to patient safety and preserving trust among clinicians and patients. Without such safeguards, the potential for unintended consequences could undermine the very advancements these technologies seek to achieve. In this sense, Maranhão et al. (2024) emphasise the importance of transparency in advanced technologies, as it facilitates the contestation of both automated decisions and those based on machine-generated recommendations. Furthermore, the authors assert that transparency is essential for detecting biases in models or data, ensuring compliance with privacy and data protection standards, assessing accuracy, and safeguarding system integrity against failures.

Another critical consideration is the self-improving capability of algorithms, which can lead to unforeseen outcomes not anticipated by their programmers or direct users, such as hospitals, clinics, healthcare professionals, and patients (Brag 2020). A noteworthy example illustrating this concern is the experiment conducted in 2002 by scientists at the Magna Science Adventure Centre in England. In this experiment, two robots were placed in an arena to simulate a scenario involving *predators* and *prey*. The objective was to investigate whether AI could leverage machine learning to enhance its performance and develop novel techniques for hunting and self-defence. Unexpectedly, one of the robots adopted an unanticipated behaviour: it discovered an exit in the arena wall, ventured into the car park, and was subsequently struck by a vehicle (Čerka et al. 2015). The disastrous outcome of the English experiment serves as a stark warning regarding the self-learning capabilities of technology and the associated risks of producing unintended and potentially harmful results.

The two aforementioned examples—one involving an AI system ostensibly designed to classify huskies and wolves, and the other simulating a predator-prey scenario—also underscore the critical importance of robust mechanisms for the approval, commercialisation, and post-market surveillance of such autonomous devices, particularly in the healthcare sector. These cases highlight the need for a comprehensive and reflective approach to ensure that these technologies are not only effective but also safe, predictable, and aligned with the ethical principles governing their use. Without stringent oversight, the integration of AI into critical domains such as healthcare risks yielding consequences that could undermine its intended benefits.

Moreover, there is a considerable risk that AI algorithms may be used to support medical decision-making without patients' knowledge. This has drawn significant criticism, as patients are often neither informed nor asked to provide consent for the use of certain technological tools in their care (Robbins and Brodwin 2020). Some physicians have adopted an overtly paternalistic stance, asserting that their expertise in the *legis artis* of the medical profession absolves them from the need to disclose all the resources employed in the clinical decision-making process.

However, it is crucial to consider the historical evolution of the doctor-patient relationship, particularly the current *Contractual Model* discussed earlier in this book, which departs from the paternalism of the past. The contractual framework emphasises patient autonomy and informed consent as foundational principles, underscoring the ethical obligation to involve patients transparently in decisions regarding their care, including the use of AI technologies.

Additionally, it must be considered that AI-driven systems require extensive user information and data to achieve optimal functionality. This dependence highlights that the risks associated with AI in medicine are inherently linked to fundamental issues concerning the sensitivity of transmitted data. Particular attention must therefore be paid to safeguarding data confidentiality and patient privacy, as the increased circulation, connection, and coordination of structured sensitive personal data amplify the risks of data breaches and improper handling.

According to Brent Mittelstadt, author of the 2021 report *The Impact of Artificial Intelligence on the Doctor-Patient Relationship*, prepared for the *Council of Europe*, innovation in the healthcare sector poses significant threats to privacy and confidentiality in two primary ways. First, there may be heightened pressure to repurpose and grant third-party access to patient data and electronic health records for the testing and development of AI systems. Second, healthcare professionals may be encouraged to prescribe additional tests and analyses, not for their clinical value but for their utility in training or testing algorithms.

Such practices have implications not only in terms of escalating healthcare costs but also in exposing patients to unnecessary risks, including data breaches or other privacy violations (Mittelstadt and Floridi 2016). The interplay between innovation and ethical responsibility thus necessitates robust safeguards to ensure that advancements in AI technology do not come at the expense of patient trust and privacy.

In light of the issues discussed in this subchapter concerning the potential risks associated with implementing AI algorithms in medical practice, it can be concluded that there is a *tripartite semantic dimension of algorithmic opacity*, particularly relevant to medicine: (I) epistemic opacity; (II) opacity by non-disclosure; and (III) explanatory opacity. This classification was originally proposed by the author of this book in collaboration with José Faleiros Júnior in the work *Ethical challenges of artificial intelligence in medicine and the triple semantic dimensions of algorithmic opacity with its repercussions to patient consent and medical liability* (Nogaroli and Faleiros Júnior 2023).

Epistemic opacity arises from the inherent complexity of data processing by algorithms, meaning that the opacity stems from the healthcare professional's inability to fully understand how the AI system operates. The lack of in-depth knowledge among clinicians about the benefits and risks of each technology may lead to suboptimal outcomes for patients. This is because medical professionals may fail to discern which tools add value to their practice or how to effectively integrate AI into clinical workflows. A deeper understanding of the limitations of automated decision-making would enable healthcare professionals to make better-informed decisions, thus avoiding overly simplistic or reductive approaches and preventing patients from becoming *hostages* to decisions wrongly rendered by *algorithmic black boxes*.

Opacity by non-disclosure refers to the considerable risk of algorithms being used to support medical decision-making without the patient's awareness or consent (disclosure). This type of algorithmic opacity does not pertain to the intrinsic characteristics of AI systems but rather to the risks posed to the patient's informational self-determination. It arises from the manner in which medical decisions are made, and health data is handled, often without the patient's knowledge—either during the medical intervention or after a potentially harmful event.

Finally, *explanatory opacity* relates to the evolving doctrine of informed consent, as discussed in an earlier chapter. In this context, a physician might disclose that an AI algorithm was used to support a clinical evaluation but fail to explain the functionality of the technology in terms comprehensible to the patient.

The tripartite semantic dimension of algorithmic opacity has a significant and direct impact on the assessment of medical civil liability and the doctrine of informed consent. These subjects will be explored in greater depth in Chap. 5 of this book, through an analysis of practical cases.

Finally, it is pertinent to address the specific risks associated with a groundbreaking new technology that promises to revolutionise various sectors, including healthcare, in ways unprecedented in human history: generative pre-trained transformers (GPTs), exemplified by ChatGPT.

Since its release in late November 2022, ChatGPT has garnered significant media attention, amassing approximately 100 million active users within just 3 months. Developed by OpenAI, ChatGPT operates as a generative pre-trained transformer—a general-purpose large language model (LLM) designed to execute a wide array of natural language processing tasks. By analysing vast datasets of textual and linguistic information, it identifies patterns and relationships to generate content.

Unlike *conventional AI*—such as *expert systems* programmed to perform specific tasks—generative AI can create apparent novel and unexpected outputs, including text, images, music, or even video. Trained on vast amounts of unstructured text data from the internet, it predicts the next word in a sentence with remarkable accuracy. At its launch in November 2022, ChatGPT was among the largest AI models ever created, incorporating hundreds of gigabytes of online text data. Users can interact with the platform to receive answers to a wide variety of questions, request essays on particular topics, or even generate music and poetry.

In the healthcare sector, ChatGPT represents a significant advancement over traditional search engines or online symptom checkers. In a country as vast and diverse as Brazil, such tools could be especially valuable for individuals living in remote or underserved areas with limited access to healthcare.

On 29 March 2023, neurosurgeons from three American hospitals published a study (Ali 2023) confirming that ChatGPT-3 and ChatGPT-4 achieved passing scores on the neurosurgical residency examination, with success rates of 73.4% and

83.4%, respectively. In February 2023, another study (Kung et al. 2023) found that ChatGPT-3 correctly answered 60% of the questions on the United States Medical Licensing Examination (USMLE). Both studies focused on the potential of AI to support medical education and clinical decision-making.

In March 2023, ChatGPT transitioned from the text-only GPT-3.5 model to GPT-4, which is multimodal, capable of interpreting text, images, and even video. This opens new possibilities for healthcare applications, moving beyond traditional single-model AI systems designed for tasks such as analysing medical images, monitoring heart rhythms, or predicting outcomes from electronic health records.

The GPT-4 model—more accurate and with greater technical knowledge than its predecessor—has shown remarkable capacity to synthesise medical knowledge without specific pre-training in medicine. In *The AI Revolution in Medicine: GPT-4 and Beyond*, Lee et al. (2023) highlight how GPT-4 accurately assessed a rare medical condition, occurring at a frequency of just 1 in one million people, based on biomedical data and symptoms. This underscores the immense potential of AI when trained with biomedical content.

To illustrate ChatGPT's potential in medical triage and diagnosis, the author of this book conducted a test by posing the following question:

> My 70-year-old father is experiencing nausea and vomiting. The right side of his body is becoming weak, and he is struggling to speak and comprehend language. His symptoms began with mild slurred speech but progressed over several minutes to severe difficulty speaking and paralysis of his right arm. What could be causing his symptoms?

The AI system provided the following response:

> The symptoms described suggest a possible stroke (also known as a cerebrovascular accident or CVA). It is important to seek medical attention immediately, as time is critical in treating this condition. A stroke can occur due to a blockage or rupture in a blood vessel in the brain, resulting in a lack of oxygen and nutrients to brain cells, causing symptoms such as muscle weakness, difficulty speaking, understanding language, nausea, and vomiting. If your father is exhibiting these symptoms, call an ambulance or take him to the nearest hospital immediately. The sooner treatment begins, the better the chances of recovery and minimising brain damage.

This response demonstrates ChatGPT's potential to assist in patient triage based on symptoms, medical history, and other factors. Such tools could facilitate earlier identification of health problems and timely referral for appropriate medical care.

Another striking example of ChatGPT's capabilities occurred in the United States in 2023, involving a 4-year-old boy who had spent 3 years consulting with 17 different doctors, none of whom could provide a definitive diagnosis. In a desperate attempt to find answers, the boy's mother compiled all his medical records and clinical data and input them into ChatGPT. The AI suggested a diagnosis of tethered cord syndrome, a rare condition that was subsequently confirmed by a paediatric neurosurgeon. Following the correct diagnosis, the child's clinical condition improved significantly after receiving appropriate treatment.

These two examples illustrate the remarkable potential of ChatGPT to accelerate complex diagnoses, integrate fragmented information, and propose more precise approaches. However, this application raises questions about the inherent risks of generative AI and whether its algorithmic outputs can be trusted.

Despite its potential, ChatGPT carries significant risks that warrant careful examination: (i) *bias and stereotypes*: the algorithm is trained on vast datasets reflecting human language and behaviour, which means it can reproduce and amplify societal biases and stereotypes; (ii) *misinformation and fake references*: ChatGPT has been documented generating plausible-sounding but false information, including fabricated bibliographic references, raising concerns about its reliability; (iii) *imprecise comprehension of limitations*: many users lack a proper understanding of ChatGPT's limitations, particularly its algorithmic inaccuracies, which may lead to misplaced trust in its outputs.

A study published in March 2023 (Ariyaratne et al. 2023) highlighted the frequent provision of false bibliographic sources by ChatGPT, particularly in a medical context. This raises concerns about the potential harm of disseminating inaccurate medical information, especially to users without specialised training, who might perceive the outputs as authoritative.

One of the most pressing challenges in deploying this technology in healthcare lies in the validation of its outputs. In 2023, a journalistic report in Brazil revealed that Microsoft's search engine Bing, following its integration with ChatGPT, erroneously linked the name of a Brazilian doctor to over 100 cases of sexual harassment.

The doctor in question was one of the officials responsible for investigating complaints against medical professionals at Regional Medical Council of São Paulo. In an interview, he stated that, since 2011, there had been more than 100 ongoing investigations in São Paulo related to cases of sexual harassment. However, Bing's AI misinterpreted this information. The system mistakenly concluded that the number of complaints mentioned in the news article referred to accusations against the doctor himself, rather than the cases he was investigating concerning other professionals. This error led the doctor to file a lawsuit against Microsoft in the seventh Civil Court of Bauru, seeking R$ 60,000 in compensation for moral damages.

This case highlights the broader issue of generative AI systems, like ChatGPT, producing information that is factually incorrect or non-existent. To mitigate these risks, it is essential that such technology is deployed under the supervision of qualified professionals, particularly in high-stakes contexts like healthcare. Supervision ensures that outputs are accurate and adapted to specific needs. Furthermore, robust data protection measures and strict adherence to patient privacy are imperative to minimise potential harm.

The rapid progress of ChatGPT and the broader race to develop increasingly intelligent generative AI tools reached a critical juncture in 2023. An open letter, signed by over 1300 scientists, technologists, and academics—including figures such as Elon Musk and Steve Wozniak—called for a 6-month pause on the development of AI systems more powerful than GPT-4 (Future of Life Institute 2023). The letter expressed deep concerns about the societal and existential risks posed by generative AI.

While some experts criticised the letter for its catastrophic tone and speculative scenarios, it underscores the urgent need for better AI regulation and the application of ethical principles tailored to specific sectors. It is essential to shift the focus from speculative fears about AI to addressing the tangible risks posed by existing and near-term technologies.

Merely pausing advanced AI experiments will not achieve responsible, human-centric, and ethically sound technological development. Instead, transparent, well-documented systems must be implemented as part of robust governance frameworks. Collaborative efforts among governments, industry, and institutions are essential to mitigate risks—both known and unforeseen—associated with AI technologies. Only through coordinated research, regulation, and oversight can AI's transformative potential be realised in a manner that benefits society without compromising safety, trust, or accountability.

4.2 Ethics and Regulation of Artificial Intelligence in Europe

Throughout human history, technological progress has acted as a driving force for the evolution of tort law in common law jurisdictions and civil liability systems in civil law frameworks worldwide. The advent of railways and motor vehicles, for instance, introduced heightened risks of harm to individuals and property, often occurring without direct fault. This necessitated the creation of legal mechanisms to ensure fair compensation for victims, prompting the adoption of strict liability regimes. These frameworks reflected the principle that those engaging in inherently hazardous activities should bear responsibility for resulting damages, regardless of negligence.

Today, post-modern society faces a similar challenge—perhaps one with even greater significance than those posed by earlier advancements. The current AI-driven technological revolution is distinct from any prior industrial revolution due to its unparalleled pace, global reach, and the intricate interplay of advancements in fields such as artificial intelligence, biotechnology, and automation. As Schwab (2017) aptly observes, this convergence of technologies is reshaping industries, economies, and societal norms on an unprecedented scale and complexity.

According to Schwab, the *Fourth Industrial Revolution* represents a transformative period marked by groundbreaking developments in AI and other advanced technologies. These innovations are prompting the legal community—and society at large—to reconsider the adequacy of existing civil liability frameworks. Should entirely new legal systems be devised to address these emerging challenges, or can existing legal principles and rules be adapted to meet the demands of this new era?

In the field of medicine, as previously discussed, AI algorithms hold immense potential to enhance patient care by enabling more accurate and effective diagnoses and prognoses. However, these technologies also introduce significant challenges to the healthcare sector, particularly concerning the risks associated with imprecise, biased, or improperly utilised algorithms, as well as decision-making processes that lack transparency. These issues raise critical questions regarding the regulation of AI in healthcare and pose a recurring concern: how will the legal systems of different countries effectively manage harm arising in the context of AI-assisted healthcare?

Within the domain of civil liability, intense debate persists within the legal community, with no consensus yet reached regarding the necessity for new mechanisms to address harm caused by autonomous systems. The European Union has assumed a leading role in publishing guidelines for potential liability regimes applicable to automated decision-making systems, which will be briefly examined in this chapter.

In determining the appropriate civil liability regime, European documents highlight the importance of assessing the degree of autonomy of AI systems and their categorisation as either *high-risk* or *medium/low-risk* technologies. As a complementary and alternative approach to traditional liability mechanisms, the *principles of solidarity* and *risk management* gain notable prominence, along with proposals for establishing *compensation funds* and mandatory insurance schemes.

This intersection of technological innovation and legal adaptation underscores the need for robust frameworks capable of balancing the benefits of AI with the imperative of ensuring accountability and fairness in the face of emerging risks. As Schwab (2017) eloquently notes, the transformative nature of the *Fourth Industrial Revolution* demands the need to embrace creative and forward-thinking solutions that integrate ethical, social, and legal considerations into the very fabric of this new technological age.

In Brazil, a commission composed of distinguished legal scholars, including Juliano Maranhão and Filipe Medon, was established in 2023. Following extensive deliberations, public hearings, and seminars involving experts and both national and international representatives, the commission prepared a draft bill aimed at regulating artificial intelligence within the country. Consequently, on 10 December 2024, the Federal Senate approved Bill No. 2338, which is currently under consideration and awaiting review and voting by the Chamber of Deputies. This initiative represents a significant endeavour to establish a Legal Framework for AI in Brazil, heavily influenced by the debates conducted within the European Union concerning the AI Act.

The American Medical Association, in a recent publication addressing the challenges of AI in the healthcare sector, argues that the oversight and regulation of AI systems in medicine worldwide should be risk-based, considering both potential harms and benefits. This approach involves a range of factors, including but not limited to: (i) intended and reasonably expected uses; (ii) evidence of safety, efficacy, and fairness; (iii) potential for discrimination; (iv) level of automation and degree of transparency; and (v) other conditions related to the implementation of the technology (Crigger et al. 2022).

Globally, States have been progressing slowly in making legislative interventions in the field of artificial intelligence. Consequently, the role of international organisations in setting guidelines and principles—non-binding instruments known as *soft law*—has become increasingly significant. This gap between innovation and regulation has underscored the necessity for collaborative solutions, creating more opportunities for the development of soft laws.

Approximately 100 proposals outlining ethical principles for artificial intelligence have been developed over the past decade worldwide (Chinese Academy of Sciences 2022; Zeng et al. 2019). According to the European Commission, *AI Ethics* is a subfield of applied ethics focusing on the ethical challenges posed by the development, deployment, and use of artificial intelligence, aiming to assess how AI can either enhance or pose risks to human quality of life, autonomy, and freedom within a democratic society.

A mapping study published by the *Berkman Klein Center for Internet & Society* at Harvard University (Fjeld et al. 2020) identified eight core ethical principles frequently adopted in recent guidelines: privacy; accountability; safety and security; transparency and explainability; fairness and non-discrimination; human oversight of technology; professional responsibility; and the promotion of human values.

These principles are also featured in the OECD (*Organisation for Economic Co-operation and Development*) Principles on Artificial Intelligence, adopted in 2019 by various countries. In Brazil, they influenced the 2021 *Brazilian Artificial Intelligence Strategy*, established under Ordinance No. 4617 by the Ministry of Science, Technology and Innovations.

The global landscape of ethical principles and soft laws is significantly enriched by the *Ethics Guidelines for Trustworthy AI* issued by the European Commission in 2019. This document establishes a comprehensive framework to ensure that AI systems are lawful, complying with applicable laws; ethical, respecting fundamental rights and values; and robust, both technically and socially. There are overarching principles operationalised through seven key requirements: human agency and oversight; technical robustness and safety; privacy and data governance; transparency; diversity and non-discrimination; societal and environmental well-being; and accountability. By fostering trust through adherence to these principles, the guidelines advocate for a balanced approach that harmonises innovation with ethical safeguards, ensuring the responsible development and deployment of AI systems.

4.2.1 Ethical Principles of AI in Medicine and Their Impact on Physician's Duties of Conduct

The integration of artificial intelligence (AI) into healthcare presents a landscape of immense opportunities and challenges, necessitating a balanced approach that combines technological innovation with ethical and professional accountability. A recent study conducted by the American Medical Association (AMA 2023), involving over 1000 physicians, reveals a growing enthusiasm among medical professionals for the potential of AI in improving diagnostic accuracy and operational efficiency. Notably, 65% of respondents identified benefits to the use of AI in their practices, with 72% seeing its greatest promise in supporting diagnosis and 69% in optimising workflow. However, physicians expressed significant concerns about the potential impact of AI on patient privacy (41%) and the patient-physician relationship (39%), with 41% of respondents reporting equal levels of excitement and apprehension about the adoption of AI in healthcare.

These findings highlight the critical importance of educating physicians on the ethical principles underpinning AI's use in medicine, equipping them to navigate both the opportunities and the complexities associated with this transformative technology. Luciano Floridi, in his seminal work *The Ethics of Artificial Intelligence: Principles, Challenges, and Opportunities* (2023), underscores the necessity of an ethical strategy that transcends mere legal compliance. He argues that adherence to legal norms is a baseline requirement but insufficient for achieving a *Good AI Society*. Floridi advocates for an *ethical approach* characterised by proactive evaluation, development, incentivisation, and support of ethical AI practices. Among his 20 recommendations, the 18th specifically calls for the *establishment of self-regulatory codes of conduct for AI-related professions*, akin to those governing socially sensitive fields such as medicine and law.

This recommendation envisions the certification of ethical AI through trust labels, fostering public understanding of and demand for ethically designed AI systems. Such instruments would ensure transparency, promote trust, and mitigate the risks of attention manipulation and other unethical practices. By *embedding these principles into medical education and fostering a culture of ethical reflection*, physicians can be empowered to use AI not merely as a tool for efficiency but as a means of enhancing the quality of care, preserving patient dignity, and reinforcing the foundational values of the patient-physician relationship.

In 2021, the World Health Organisation (WHO) published its first global report on the *Ethics and Governance of Artificial Intelligence for Health*, following 2 years of extensive research and consultations with numerous experts worldwide. This document is addressed to all individuals involved in the development, use, or impact of AI, encompassing companies, institutions, organisations, professionals and civil society. The report outlines six guiding ethical principles for AI: (1) protecting human autonomy; (2) ensuring transparency, explainability, and intelligibility; (3) promoting AI that is responsive and sustainable; (4) ensuring inclusiveness and equity; (5) promoting human well-being, safety, and the public interest; and (6) fostering responsibility and accountability [data-informed duties]. It is noteworthy that each of these six principles elucidated by the WHO highlights the ethical and legal impact of technology on the physician-patient relationship, maintaining a close connection with the professional duties of conduct in the twenty-first century.

This discussion warrants a parenthesis to demonstrate that the foundation for redefining physicians' duties of conduct in the implementation of AI systems is firmly rooted in Gregório Robles's Communicational Theory of Law. This theory underscores the need for a dynamic interaction between ethical and juridical imperatives and the evolving technological landscape, emphasising the importance of justice and accountability in contemporary medical practice.

Gregorio Robles Morchón, in his work *La Justicia En Los Jueces. Dos Ensayos De Teoría Comunicacional Del Derecho* (2009), contends that law should be understood as a social phenomenon shaped by processes of communication and interpretation. His approach, rooted in the *Communicational Theory of Law*, examines how law is communicated, interpreted, and legitimised within society, highlighting the crucial role of interaction among the various actors in the legal system and the impact of these communications on the perception of justice. Within this framework, the author explores how judges interpret and apply the concept of *justice* in their decisions, portraying it as a dynamic ideal, influenced by the social, cultural, and legal contexts in which it is situated.

Robles views law as a channel of communication among the diverse participants in the legal system, including judges, lawyers, legislators, and citizens. Law is more than a static collection of norms; it is an interactive process that communicates values and shapes social behaviour. This model is predicated on three key elements: first, law conveys norms and values, serving as a guide for social conduct; second, judicial decisions function as communicative acts that not only resolve specific disputes but also articulate to society what is considered just and appropriate; and third, law retains its communicative function only when it is comprehensible and perceived as legitimate.

For Robles, justice is not a universal or immutable concept but a value that adapts to the realities in which judges operate. Judicial interpretation does not occur in isolation but is influenced by factors such as culture, morality, and societal demands. Consequently, judicial decisions must effectively communicate justice to society. A failure to achieve this perception risks undermining the legitimacy of law as a normative system.

In the context of medical law and artificial intelligence (AI) applied to healthcare, this communicational perspective assumes particular relevance in addressing the ethical and legal dilemmas arising from technological advancements. For instance, consider a hospital employing AI technology for cancer diagnosis without disclosing its use to the patient. In the event of a diagnostic failure, the judiciary would need to acknowledge the breach of the duty to inform, emphasising in its decision the critical importance of transparency in preserving the patient's autonomy and self-determination.

Furthermore, the concept of consent has evolved significantly from its traditional understanding; the relationship between physician and patient must now involve a true communicational process—a mutual exchange in which both parties speak and listen simultaneously. This reciprocal interaction signifies a revaluation of values, reshaping the duty to inform in light of new societal expectations and the ethical principles of AI. The duty to inform, traditionally understood as a mere obligation to convey information, must be expanded to incorporate these ethical principles, requiring explanation and justification. Physicians must not only disclose their use of AI but also explain and justify its functioning in a manner comprehensible to the patient, ensuring the patient's active engagement in the decision-making process.

This aligns with Robles' communicational theory, emphasizing that communication in healthcare must transcend a one-sided transfer of information, becoming a dynamic and interactive dialogue. By fostering mutual understanding and shared decision-making, this approach reinforces the ethical foundations of transparency, autonomy, and trust in the patient-physician relationship.

It is also important to observe that the redefinition of physicians' duties concerning AI is intrinsically linked to the *precautionary principle*, which has emerged as a contemporary legal standard in twenty-first-century medical practice. This principle advocates a proactive and preventive approach, requiring healthcare professionals to implement measures that minimise risks and uncertainties associated with technological applications.

In the medical field, the *principle of precaution* as a guiding criterion for professional practice is enshrined among the fundamental principles of the Brazilian Code of Medical Ethics (Resolution CFM No. 2.217/2018, Chap. I). For example: (i) article XII: the physician shall strive to ensure that work is better adapted to the individual and shall work toward the elimination and control of health risks inherent in professional activities"; and (ii) article XIII: "the physician shall report to the competent authorities any form of ecosystem deterioration harmful to health and life". Similarly, contracts for medical services, governed by the Brazilian Consumer Code, underscore the basic rights to protection and prevention. Article 6 includes provisions such as: (i) clause VI: "the effective prevention and redress of patrimonial and moral damages, whether individual, collective, or diffuse"; (ii) clause VII: "the provision of adequate and clear information about the risks posed by products and services".

Nowadays, by transcending the legal framework of addressing harm after its occurrence, the *precautionary principle* prioritises continuous vigilance, the adoption of safe practices, and the clear communication of risks. This approach underscores the centrality of patient safety, dignity, and autonomy, compelling physicians to actively monitor the performance of technologies in clinical practice. Such vigilance aligns closely with the ethical AI principle of *fostering responsibility and accountability* (data-informed duties).

Moreover, when adjudicating cases involving AI in healthcare, judges are confronted with intricate dilemmas, such as determining liability and ensuring accountability in instances of adverse events—whether it falls on the physician, the healthcare institution, or the technology developer—and balancing the imperative of technological innovation with the protection of patients' fundamental rights. Robles emphasises that judicial decisions in this domain must transcend the mere formal application of legal norms, instead actively communicating ethical values and fostering public trust in emerging technologies.

Within the framework of AI in medicine, values such as autonomy, safety, and ethics acquire heightened significance. Autonomy mandates comprehensive disclosure to patients regarding the use and functioning of technologies; safety requires ongoing vigilance to mitigate risks; and ethics demands transparency and equity in the development and application of AI. These values, as recognised in the WHO's guidelines on the ethical principles of AI in medicine, redefine traditional physician's duties of conduct, fostering practices rooted in good faith and the preservation of human dignity.

In summary, in these demands involving medical law and AI, judges will inevitably face challenges involving medical ethics, professional accountability, and the utilisation of emerging technologies. Justice in these cases requires a contextual interpretation that considers: (i) the protection of patients and their fundamental rights; (ii) the promotion of technological innovation without obstructing advancements that benefit society; and (iii) the redefinition of physicians' duties of conduct based on ethical principles inherent to AI.

It is important to note that excessively rigid decisions, which penalise well-intentioned physicians acting in good faith, could deter the adoption of innovative technologies that serve the interests of patients. This underscores the necessity of consistently treating medical liability as subjective, even when professionals rely on novel technologies—a theme to be explored in the subsequent chapter of this book. Conversely, the integration of AI into clinical practice imposes heightened duties of diligence and vigilance upon physicians, alongside an expanded burden of continuous supervision of the technologies employed. This responsibility reinforces the imperative of redefining medical duties in light of AI's ethical principles, aligning them with contemporary societal demands for safety and transparency.

As Robles eloquently asserts, the interpretation and application of law in such cases must extend beyond normative formalism, effectively communicating ethical values and striking a just balance between technological innovation and the safeguarding of patients' fundamental rights. Finally, Robles's *Communicational Theory of Law* highlights the pivotal role of judges as communicators of essential values. At the intersection of medicine and AI, judges are called upon to redefine duties and responsibilities, preserving the legitimacy of the legal system, protecting patients, and promoting the responsible adoption of technology. This approach, harmonised with the *precautionary principle*, illustrates how law, as a communicative act, not only resolves disputes but also strengthens a society committed to balancing innovation and justice.

To facilitate an understanding of the intersections between AI's ethical principles and the duties of medical conduct (stemming from the principle of objective good faith), the comparative Table 4.2 is proposed. It is important to note that this is not a rigid classification; in many instances, one or more ethical principles of AI may correlate with one or more duties of medical conduct, and vice versa.

Table 4.2 Comparative table created by the author of this book, examining the physician's duties of contractual conduct redefined in light of the ethical principles proposed by the World Health Organization

Ethical principles of AI in medicine	Physician's duties of conduct	
(1) *Protecting human autonomy*	Duty of information	(I) Duty of information, disclosure and explanation
(2) *Ensuring transparency, explainability and intelligibility*		(II) Duty of documentation and confidentiality/secrecy
(3) *Promoting AI that is responsive and sustainable*	Duty of loyalty	(III) Duty of cooperation and loyalty *stricto sensu*
(4) *Ensuring inclusiveness and equity*		(IV) Duty to refrain from abuse or misuse of power
(5) *Promoting human well-being and safety and the public interest*	Duty of protection	(V) Duty of up-to-date knowledge
(6) *Fostering responsibility and accountability [data informed duties]*		(VI) Duty of care and vigilance

(1) Protecting Human Autonomy

It is imperative that humans maintain control over healthcare systems and medical decision-making processes, ensuring that ultimate decision-making power is never transferred to a superintelligent machine. AI should be designed to augment and complement human cognitive, social, and cultural capabilities, with human oversight and control over the technology consistently guaranteed.

In this regard, Pasquale (2020) emphasises the necessity of fostering a future in which AI primarily assists, rather than replaces, physicians. He underscores that there will always be a role for specialists to verify the accuracy of algorithmic recommendations and assess their real-world applicability. Moreover, he asserts that professional judgment and final clinical diagnoses cannot be automated, as there will inevitably be instances where sound scientific reasoning compels the physician to deviate from algorithmic suggestions. Consequently, human-validated AI could become the standard for diligent care in medicine, a standard that every patient deserves when seeking medical treatment.

The American Medical Association (AMA) and the World Medical Association (WMA) have deliberately chosen to use the term *augmented intelligence* instead of artificial intelligence to emphasise AI's role as a supportive tool in the field of medicine. This distinction reflects a conceptual shift, aiming to underline that AI is designed to complement and enhance, rather than replace, the intelligence and capabilities of healthcare professionals. Crigger et al. (2022) explain that the term *augmented intelligence* captures the synergy between human decision-making and algorithmic insights, where technology acts as an extension of the clinician's analytical abilities. By highlighting this collaborative dynamic, the terminology underscores the principle that healthcare decisions remain fundamentally human-centric, enriched by computational precision and efficiency.

The AMA argues that *augmented intelligence* more accurately conveys how computational systems can empower clinicians to make better-informed decisions, improving the quality of patient care. Unlike artificial intelligence, which is often perceived as autonomous systems producing outputs independently, *augmented intelligence* integrates human judgment with machine-generated data. This collaborative model ensures that the clinician remains at the forefront of decision-making, using AI-derived outputs as tools to enhance diagnostic accuracy, treatment planning, and overall clinical outcomes (AMA 2024). In this context, it is essential for manufacturers to provide AI users with the necessary information to ensure the safe and effective use of these technologies, as well as a comprehensive understanding of the roles individual algorithms can play in healthcare.

This discussion connects directly to the physicians' duties of conduct, grounded in the principle of contractual good faith, particularly in relation to the ethical AI principle of respecting human autonomy. There is a duty to inform, explain, and advise patients about autonomous systems. The WHO guidelines unequivocally stipulate that AI must not be employed for experimentation or to manipulate individuals within a healthcare system without valid informed consent.

Sá and Naves (2021) caution that technological advancements can't displace the doctor-patient relationship, with sophisticated equipment reducing personal interaction and distancing the warmth of human care. Topol (2019) advocates for *prioritising patient values and preferences* in human-machine collaborations, ensuring that the adoption of AI in clinical practice does not reinforce medical paternalism but instead creates time for more meaningful doctor-patient engagement. This vision is achievable only if the practice of medicine transcends technical procedures and adheres to a framework that embraces the principles of *person-centred medicine*.

The concept of informed consent must be adapted and reinforced within the context of the emerging technological framework, as it brings profound changes to healthcare delivery models. The use of algorithms in diagnosis, prognosis, and treatment planning should form an integral part of the process of obtaining valid informed consent. Transparency is also required to inform individuals that they are interacting with an AI system, giving them the option to choose or decline human-machine interaction, as Ferreira and Pereira (2021) argue.

Furthermore, the ethical principle of autonomy is closely tied to the medical duty of confidentiality in protecting personal health data, especially sensitive data. Health data, which serve as the *fuel* for algorithms, go beyond merely reflecting a person's health status; they are integral to the individual's personality rights. As Rodotà (2006) notes, in the post-modern society, the *constitutionalisation of the person* encompasses not only the protection of the *physical body* (the right to personal integrity) but also the *electronic body* (the right to data protection), representing a constellation of rights that define citizenship in the new millennium. This concept of the electronic body, as explained by Rosenvald and Faleiros Júnior (2022), portrays a natural person as possessing not only physical substance but also a digital projection.

The manner in which data are shared—both the purpose of their use and the entities granted access—is a significant issue in the development of the technological framework within the healthcare sector. Moreover, automated decision-making systems must ensure privacy and data protection throughout their lifecycle, covering both the initial data provided by users and those generated during interactions with the AI system. In this context, *privacy by design* represents a fundamental approach to embedding privacy and data protection into the design of AI systems from their inception.

Rather than treating privacy as a secondary concern, this strategy makes it a core element in developing technological solutions. Companies are required to adopt measures such as data anonymisation, minimisation of data collection, and implementation of robust access controls to prevent unauthorised access. By proactively integrating safeguards, this approach aims to protect sensitive patient data and significantly reduce the risk of data breaches. Coupled with compliance measures aligned with regulations like the General Data Protection Laws—GDPR in the EU and LGPD (Lei Geral de Proteção de Dados—LGPD) in Brazil, organisations must implement rigorous internal policies, including regular audits, continuous staff training, and appointing data protection officers. Technical measures such as end-to-end encryption, multi-factor authentication, and real-time monitoring systems are equally vital, ensuring that patient data remain secure throughout their lifecycle while fostering innovation without compromising privacy.

According to a 2024 report by the European—*Healthcare as a Use Case for Standardisation in the Field of Artificial Intelligence*—authored by Nick Guldemond, an independent expert under the EU-funded *International Outreach for a Human-Centric Approach to AI* (InTouchAI.eu), manufacturers of medical devices and AI systems are required to prioritise privacy and data security by the GDPR and other EU data protection regulations (ePrivacy Directive, Clinical Trials Regulation, and Medical Device Regulation—MDR). The Document highlights that these regulations require responsible handling of personal data, including minimising data collection to what is strictly necessary for the functionality of the system or device. Moreover, manufacturers must adopt a *privacy by design* approach, integrating privacy and security features such as encryption and access controls to mitigate both known and unforeseen security risks during the manufacturing stage. Furthermore, technical and organisational measures are essential to protect personal data from unauthorised access, disclosure, or destruction.

The report also underscores the importance of patient rights in the context of data processing by medical devices and AI systems. Patients must receive clear and transparent information regarding how their data is collected, used, and shared. Explicit and informed consent is required before any data processing occurs, with patients retaining the right to withdraw consent at any time. Additionally, patients must be able to access, correct, or delete their personal data, and manufacturers are obligated to facilitate these rights. Transparency, combined with robust security measures, is deemed essential to ensuring compliance with regulations and maintaining patient trust.

(2) Ensuring Transparency, Explainability and Intelligibility

AI systems must be intelligible to developers, healthcare professionals, patients, general users, regulatory bodies, and other relevant stakeholders. To achieve intelligibility, transparency must be ensured at three levels: traceability/auditability, explainability, and communication.

Traceability refers to the process of examining and evaluating the technology by documenting the dataset, identifying the algorithm employed, and recording the processes that produce the decisions of the automated system. Explainability, on the other hand, pertains to the requirement that decisions made by AI systems must, to the greatest extent possible, be comprehensible to humans. Healthcare institutions and regulatory bodies are expected to publish information about how the decision to adopt a specific AI system was reached, the methods used to evaluate the technology periodically, its applications, known limitations, and the role it plays in decision-making. This approach facilitates external auditing and oversight of AI systems.

However, as discussed in the preceding chapter of this book, the *black box problem* persists. Algorithms may execute certain actions to produce outcomes without humans being able to explain the AI's decision-making process. This justifies the need for transparent communication among all stakeholders, including users and those affected by AI systems, regarding the technology's capabilities and limitations (Dignum 2019).

The requisite degree of explainability depends on the context in which AI is applied and the severity of potential consequences arising from inaccurate or erroneous outcomes. Particular attention must be given to contexts involving vulnerable groups (Boddington 2017). Teffé and Medon (2020) emphasise the importance of understanding the limitations of automated decision-making systems and the factors they consider when making decisions. Such understanding helps to critically assess the outputs of AI systems and avoid simplistic or reductionist views, which might otherwise render individuals unduly dependent on decisions made within the black box of algorithms.

Thorough documentation is imperative to maximise traceability and, by extension, transparency in AI systems. This becomes especially important when investigating why an erroneous decision was made. For instance, as discussed in the previous subchapter, in the case of the algorithm error involving photographs of huskies and wolves, it was only through documenting the AI's dataset and the patterns of photos used in the algorithmic programming that the error could be identified and rectified.

These principles underscore the ethical importance of explainability in the doctor-patient relationship, highlighting the evolving nature of the informed consent process discussed earlier in this book. Beyond merely informing the patient that, for example, an AI algorithm was employed to support the assessment of a clinical condition, the physician must also explain the technology's functioning in accordance with the patient's level of understanding. Failure to do so may result in what was described in the previous subchapter as *explanatory opacity* (Nogaroli and Faleiros Júnior 2023).

With advancements in healthcare technology, it is crucial to recognise that providing information is just one component of informed consent. A patient's right to adequate information—which corresponds to the physician's duty to inform—encompasses *specific consent for each technology used*. This *qualified consent* requires providing the patient with knowledge about the technology's functioning, objectives, benefits, costs, risks, and alternatives (Dantas and Nogaroli 2020, 2021). Such a *process* involves a dialogue to obtain free and informed consent, which, although more demanding, offers significantly greater legal security for the physician in potential litigation.

In the current era of Person-Centred Medicine and the Contractual Model of the patient-physician relationship, it is imperative to reinterpret the concept of duty to inform and the principle of patient self-determination, especially within the context of artificial intelligence. This shift moves away from the mere right to information towards a broader informational framework, encompassing a *right to explanation and justification*.

(3) Promoting AI that Is Responsive and Sustainable

AI systems must be designed to address social and public health needs in an adaptive and sustainable manner. This entails that AI should be sensitive to the realities of its users and the contexts in which it is applied, working to reduce inequalities while delivering precise and relevant outcomes. Moreover, AI must be environmentally efficient, economically viable, and accessible, ensuring ongoing benefits to public health without compromising future resources. This principle seeks to ensure that AI, guided by ethical values, generates long-term positive impacts, promoting equity and global sustainability.

All stakeholders involved in the development and implementation of AI systems in the healthcare sector bear the responsibility of ensuring that appropriate conditions are established for their use by adequately trained individuals. This entails the continual evaluation and monitoring of AI technologies after their deployment. Regular and systematic checks are required to verify whether AI systems respond appropriately and align with the legitimate expectations and requirements communicated to users. This responsibility is shared to varying degrees by the algorithm's developers and manufacturers, as well as by healthcare institutions and medical professionals implementing the technology.

From the perspective of AI developers and manufacturers, special attention must be given during the design, development, and implementation stages to the potential impacts of the technology, including those that may emerge in the more distant future. This reflects the broader obligation to ensure that AI benefits society as a whole, rather than serving only a specific subgroup. At the governmental level, appropriate mechanisms must be established to regulate and oversee AI technologies, prevent harm, and provide satisfactory remedies for any harm caused by automated decision-making. Furthermore, governments and organisations must ensure that AI technologies align with broader goals of sustainability within healthcare systems, workplaces, and the environment, while also providing training opportunities to help healthcare professionals adapt to the use of automated decision-making systems.

To ensure the development of *responsible AI*, Dignum (2019) highlights the importance of studying various aspects of the technology: (a) an analysis of the distributive nature of AI applications, given their integration into socio-technical systems involving complex human-machine interactions; (b) a reflection on the societal implications of AI and its global effects; (c) an examination of AI's positive and negative influences, particularly on human rights, democracy, and education; (d) an understanding of AI governance and normative issues—not only in terms of competencies and responsibilities but also regarding health, safety, risk, predictability, and transparency; and (e) an investigation of the consequences of AI integration, informed by an awareness of the societal, legal, and economic models underpinning socio-technical systems (human-AI interactions).

When this debate is brought into the context of physicians' duties derived from the principle of contractual good faith, the relevance of the duty of cooperation and loyalty *stricto sensu* becomes evident. This duty requires healthcare professionals to act in accordance with standards of honesty and transparency, respecting the legitimate expectations of patients. Physicians must maintain active communication, share information, and engage in dialogue with their patients to avoid fostering false expectations about the success of AI systems in delivering healthcare.

Healthcare institutions, in turn, have a duty to establish bioethics committees to conduct detailed assessments of which AI technologies should be implemented.

These committees are tasked with examining the scientific integrity, effectiveness, and feasibility of proposed technologies, as well as ensuring the appropriate training of professionals within the institution. Continuous monitoring of AI use must prioritise patient benefit. Physicians should consult these bioethics committees when facing moral or ethical dilemmas arising from the use of AI-driven medical assistance, particularly when algorithmic outcomes present challenges to clinical decision-making (Nunes et al. 2022).

In summary, the ethical principle of *promoting responsive and sustainable AI*, as outlined by the WHO, is closely tied to the *physician's duty of cooperation and loyalty stricto sensu*, because it is required from the healthcare professionals to act collaboratively and with dedication, prioritising patient well-being and the integrity of treatment. AI's responsiveness complements this duty by enabling personalised care, enhancing access to precise diagnoses and efficient treatments. Meanwhile, the sustainability of AI ensures that its use aligns with the long-term values of medical care, promoting practices that respect available resources and address future needs. By integrating responsive and sustainable AI systems, physicians not only meet the ethical standards of cooperation and loyalty but also strengthen the trust inherent in the patient-physician relationship by demonstrating a commitment to technologies that uphold patients' rights and interests.

(4) Ensuring Inclusiveness and Equity

There must be a firm commitment to ensuring the equitable and fair distribution of the benefits derived from AI systems, as well as the elimination of unfair biases, discrimination, and stigmatisation against individuals and groups. This entails the promotion of equal opportunities concerning the accessibility of AI technologies.

According to the European Commission's *2019 Ethics Guidelines for Trustworthy AI*, substantial fairness requires that professionals using AI adhere to the principle of proportionality between means and ends, balancing the interests and objectives at stake. Procedural fairness, on the other hand, demands the provision of mechanisms for individuals to challenge and seek effective remedies against decisions made by AI systems and the human operators employing them.

Furthermore, the 2021 *Ethics and Governance of Artificial Intelligence for Health* (WHO) stress the importance of promoting diversity—across gender, cultural, and ethnic backgrounds—not only within the datasets used for algorithmic programming but also among the teams responsible for developing the technology. Such teams should include scientists from various disciplines, including the exact sciences, humanities, and social sciences, to ensure a holistic approach to AI development. To understand the ethical, social, legal, and economic impacts of automated systems and assess how development decisions influence these outcomes, professionals must have a basic understanding of fields such as philosophy, social sciences, law, and economics. Technologies in the healthcare sector must not perpetuate biases against specific groups.

In this context, the *American Medical Association* (AMA) highlighted in a recent study on the challenges of AI in healthcare the importance of applying the principle of equity to medical algorithms. The AMA noted that inequities and discrimination arise when datasets used to train algorithms exclude or underrepresent historically marginalised and minority patient populations, failing to account for significant differences in experiences or outcomes associated with patient identity (Crigger et al. 2022).

The *2022 European Framework on Ethical Aspects of Artificial Intelligence, Robotics and Related Technologies* also underscores the necessity of identifying and addressing discriminatory biases in datasets used to train and execute AI systems. Such biases must be detected, reported, and mitigated as early as possible to prevent harm and ensure fairness in AI outcomes. Building upon this, automated decision-making systems must be continuously monitored and evaluated to identify and address any disproportionate impacts on specific demographic groups.

Moreover, their development must prioritise inclusivity and accessibility, ensuring universal access, particularly for vulnerable populations such as the elderly and persons with disabilities. This involves designing user-friendly interfaces, providing clear guidance for use, and accommodating the needs of diverse populations to avoid creating technological barriers. Equally important is the integration of diverse perspectives during the design phase, involving stakeholders from marginalised and underrepresented communities to ensure that the technology serves broader societal needs rather than perpetuating existing inequalities.

The ethical principle of inclusiveness and equity in AI is closely linked to the physician's duty to *abstain from abuse or misuse their professional discretion*, a duty grounded in the principle of contractual good faith. Physicians are expected to exercise professional judgement free from impulsivity, imprudence, or arbitrariness. This includes critically assessing whether the AI algorithms they employ have been trained on small or homogenous datasets with limited population diversity, which may reflect discriminatory programming and risk harming patients.

It is, therefore, crucial that professionals using AI uphold the principle of equity, ensuring proportionality between the means employed and the ends sought, while balancing competing interests and objectives. This commitment fosters trust in AI applications and safeguards the integrity of patient care.

(5) Promoting Human Well-Being and Safety and the Public Interest

Artificial intelligence (AI) solutions must be consistently directed towards areas of global interest, sustainability, and ecological responsibility. Technology should benefit all human beings, including future generations, necessitating a thorough assessment of its social impact and its effects on institutions and democracy itself.

Regarding the principle of safety, as highlighted by the WHO in the *Ethics and Governance of Artificial Intelligence for Health*, developers of automated decision-making systems must comply with regulatory requirements for safety, accuracy, and efficacy. These systems should be carefully designed for specific use cases to avoid harm to human beings. This includes a duty of *harm prevention*, ensuring that AI does not result in avoidable psychological or physical harm that could have been mitigated by adopting alternative practices or approaches during its development. Post-market quality control and efficacy measures are also imperative to ensure the continued reliability and safety of such technologies.

Technical robustness and safety demand that automated systems perform according to their intended accuracy and purpose, while minimising unintentional or unforeseen harm. Additionally, AI systems must incorporate safeguards against vulnerabilities, such as contingency plans for damage control in the event of hacking or other technological issues.

For example, consider an automated system designed to assist visually impaired individuals in safely crossing streets by identifying pedestrian crossings. If the system is hacked, it should automatically activate an emergency protocol that temporarily disables crossing identification and issues an alert to the user, thereby preventing accidents or harm to this vulnerable group. Manufacturers must continuously evaluate the impact and safety of their AI products even after market introduction, including conducting simulated hacker attacks on automated decision systems to minimise potential negative impacts.

From the perspective of the doctor-patient relationship, *patient safety* can be promoted through the *physician's duty of up-to-date knowledge*. While technical and scientific advancements are essential, as emphasised by Nordlinger et al. (2020), the doctor of the future must be both *intelligent* in terms of embracing technological innovations and AI systems in clinical practice, and *better educated and informed* to prevent, analyse, decide, and treat diseases with empathy and a human touch.

Although physicians retain professional autonomy in choosing diagnostic methods and therapeutic approaches, they are also accountable for the consequences of their choices. This highlights the importance of *continuous medical education*, beginning in medical school, concerning the benefits and risks associated with health technologies. Without such education, AI may lead to suboptimal patient outcomes due to a lack of medical understanding of which tools add value or how to appropriately integrate AI into clinical workflows. Notably, there is a growing tendency among universities worldwide to *integrate AI systems into formal medical education curricula* (Paranjape et al. 2019).

The integration of AI into medical practice underscores the growing need for comprehensive medical education that begins during university training and contin ues throughout a physician's career. A robust curriculum should incorporate theoretical and practical knowledge about AI, emphasising its benefits, risks, and limitations in clinical contexts. For example, medical students could engage with AI-driven diagnostic tools, while residency programmes might include simulations that incorporate AI to solve complex clinical problems. Such education must also address ethical considerations, ensuring that future physicians understand not only how to use AI but also when it may be inappropriate or insufficient for patient care.

A central question shaping the future of AI in medicine is how effectively medical education can prepare healthcare professionals to navigate this evolving landscape. For clinical decisions based on algorithms to fulfil their potential, it is crucial to raise awareness among developers, healthcare providers, and policymakers about the challenges and limitations of AI technologies. Specialised and continuous education, tailored to address the demands of the AI era in medicine, will be key to ensuring that these innovations enhance healthcare outcomes without compromising ethical and safety standards.

As AI becomes more prevalent in the healthcare sector, medical students, residents, and practising physicians must acquire and maintain a deeper understanding of emerging technologies. Structuring this education within formal curricula and ensuring its adaptability to advancements in AI will remain a critical area of focus in the coming years.

(6) Fostering Responsibility and Accountability [Data Informed Duties]
The development of appropriate regulatory oversight mechanisms is essential to ensuring that the healthcare sector remains accountable and responsive to those who benefit from AI in medicine. Such mechanisms must guarantee transparency in decision-making processes and operational activities within the sector. Furthermore, in the event of adverse outcomes involving AI technology, it is important to establish robust systems that enable individuals negatively affected by algorithmic decisions to challenge these decisions and seek compensation for damages.

In this context, the *principle of accountability* emerges as a cornerstone, reinforced by healthcare compliance frameworks, incorporating preventive regulatory parameters into the use of AI in clinical practice, whether on an *ex-ante* or *ex-post* basis.

As explored throughout this book, the concept of civil liability has evolved in recent years worldwide to extend beyond its traditional reparatory function. It now incorporates additional roles, such as prevention, precaution, and the promotion of desirable behaviour—developments necessitated by the novel challenges posed by AI in medicine.

This scenario aligns with Hans Jonas's proposition of an ethics of responsibility, which provides ethical guidance for technical activities (Jonas 1979). Such an ethic shifts its focus from merely assessing the outcomes of actions to anticipating and preventing undesirable consequences. It requires a prognostic and prophylactic approach aimed at mitigating risks before they materialise. Nowadays, in the face of the demands of complex, pluralistic, and highly technological societies—characterised by uncertainty and emergent risks—it becomes evident that the monofunctional nature of civil liability must be transcended. Civil liability must extend far beyond compensating for harm already inflicted. It should function not only as a damage-control mechanism but also as a *behaviour-modifying tool.*

The contours of an ethics of responsibility, as argued by Ehrhardt Júnior (2014), necessarily involve defining a commitment to the future, focused on *prevention* and *precaution*. This forward-looking perspective underscores the importance of embedding responsibility into the design, implementation, and oversight of AI technologies in medicine, ensuring both ethical alignment and societal benefit.

When examining the duties of conduct expected of physicians in the twenty-first century, it becomes evident that civil liability holds a particularly prominent place within global legal systems, especially when understood through a *polyfunctional lens*. Brazilian scholars such as Nelson Rosenvald and José Faleiros Júnior argue that civil liability is undergoing a significant transformation, increasingly oriented towards protection through the principles of prevention and precaution. This shift reflects a global trend towards protective justice, expanding the role of civil liability beyond mere compensation.

Rosenvald and Faleiros Júnior (2021) advocate for the polysemy of civil liability within the framework of *Brazillian General Data Protection Law* (*Lei Geral de Proteção de Dados*—LGPD). Their theory is rooted in comparative law, analysing the terms used in common law systems—liability, responsibility, accountability, and answerability. They highlight the need to broaden the concept of civil liability within civil law systems, particularly in the context of Brazilian jurisprudence. This polysemic approach challenges the traditional civil law view that liability is limited to its compensatory function, characterised by monetary remedies aimed at restoring the injured party to their pre-damage condition. According to the authors, *liability* is not the central feature of tort law but merely its surface. For instance, they argue that *responsibility* encompasses a moral dimension, integrating ethical considerations and the necessity of specialised education in the application of technologies.

This perspective aligns with Hans Jonas' *principle of responsibility* (1979), which advocates for an ethical approach to technology that anticipates and mitigates potential risks. In the context of medicine, where the implementation of new technologies is increasingly pervasive, civil liability must evolve into a framework that not only addresses harm but also proactively curbs harmful behaviour.

This rationale resonates with the 2023 proposal by the Senate's Commission of Jurists to reform Brazil's 2002 Civil Code, currently under review in the Federal Senate (Bill No. 4/2025). The proposal introduces provisions that redefine civil liability to encompass not only compensatory functions but also preventive and punitive measures (proposed Article 926-A). This marks a significant departure from traditional views, broadening the legal framework to include mechanisms for pre-emptive action and behavioural deterrence as integral components of civil liability.

Furthermore, the proposal includes a new Article 926-B, which establishes: "every person has a duty to adopt, in good faith and in accordance with the circumstances, measures within their reach to avoid the occurrence of foreseeable harm". This provision reinforces the principle of good faith, emphasising a proactive obligation to prevent harm and reflecting the growing recognition of civil liability as a tool for fostering precautionary and ethical conduct in contemporary society.

This framework illustrates the progressive evolution of civil liability, particularly within the context of medical ethics and consumer protection. It underscores the prioritisation of prevention in contemporary legal and ethical thought. In an era marked by the emergence of novel risks capable of causing irreparable harm, civil liability must transcend its traditional reactive function. It is no longer sufficient to address harm post-facto; instead, the focus must shift towards foresight and precaution. Rosenvald (2019) captures this transformation succinctly:

> We live in pluralistic and complex societies where unjust harm multiplies quantitatively and becomes qualitatively refined due to the daily emergence of new risks affecting the patrimonial and existential spheres of every individual. (...) The traditional remedies of private law are characterised as post-facto, focusing on addressing harm after it has occurred. However, this approach ceases to suffice if we consider the duty to act diligently as the fundamental concept of civil liability, rather than the harm itself. The duty to act prudently in view of potential harm to others logically precedes the responsibility to compensate them.

This evolving perspective redefines civil liability as a forward-looking mechanism that prioritises the prevention of harm and the cultivation of ethical and precautionary behaviours. Such an approach aligns with the demands of modern risk management and reflects the complexities of contemporary society, positioning civil liability as an essential tool for ensuring justice and safeguarding the future.

The *principle of accountability* in new health technologies has been a prominent subject of discussion in Brazil, particularly in the context of technological innovation. The recent enactment of Law No. 14.510/2022 (the Telehealth Law) has reinforced the importance of *health data governance*. In the domain of telematics applied to health—encompassing telehealth and telemedicine—the law assigns the need to implement practices and strategies designed to ensure the safe and effective use of telematic resources.

The *principle of digital accountability*, identified as a guiding principle of telehealth in Article 2 of Law No. 14.510/2022 (Article 26-A, IX, of Law No. 8.080/1990), aligns with what Schaefer (2023) describes an essential aspect of data governance, incorporating preventive compliance measures to expand the scope of civil liability. Such measures aim to include regulatory parameters that function in both ex-ante and ex-post capacities, fostering a governance framework oriented towards the responsible and ethical handling of health data.

Baptista dos Santos (2023) echoes this interpretation, asserting that *digital accountability* in the Telehealth Law involves adherence to standards issued by the governing body of the Unified Health System and ethical norms established by the Federal Council of Medicine. It also encompasses compliance with personal data protection regulations to prevent harm. In instances where harm occurs and there is non-compliance with such standards, this may establish a causal nexus for liability, thereby grounding the obligation to provide compensation.

In its *ex-ante* application, the principle of accountability serves as a guide for AI programmers, manufacturers, and users, ensuring the integration of governance rules and best practices. This includes establishing procedures, technical standards, and security norms—a process enabled by implementing compliance programmes in the healthcare sector.

Compliance programmes in clinics and hospitals are not merely intended to align institutional activities with existing legislation. More importantly, they aim to proactively identify risks, establish protocols, and provide continuous training. Such programmes prevent adverse events and medical errors, aligning with ethical standards, organisational codes of conduct, and stakeholder expectations. As Felipe (2022) emphasises, compliance represents a cultural shift within corporate environments, prioritising integrity and accountability.

Effective compliance implementation requires robust risk management at the initial stages of failure mitigation. This involves identifying internal and external risk factors, enabling the creation of specific strategies that align with the programme's goals. These strategies typically include training, communication, monitoring, disciplinary incentives, and whistleblowing channels as part of the damage mitigation plan.

Automated decision-making in clinical practice expands the existing healthcare ecosystem to include algorithm developers, software engineers, and data scientists. While AI offers undeniable benefits—such as rapidly identifying health data patterns that would be imperceptible to humans—it also introduces new risks requiring heightened compliance and adherence to ethical and legal standards. The integration of AI into healthcare systems introduces unique challenges in managing four primary risks: (i) system malfunction; (ii) privacy violations (e.g., breaches of data protection); (iii) non-compliance with informed patient consent requirements; (iv) insufficient professional training or expertise.

A particularly pressing concern is the potential harm to patients arising from AI's fallibility, algorithmic bias, or discrepancies between training data and real-world applications. Cases where implemented algorithms fail to achieve the accuracy claimed by their manufacturers, especially when derived from limited or demographically skewed datasets, have highlighted this issue. Misdiagnoses, improper treatments, and inappropriate medical interventions can result in severe consequences for patients, thereby exposing healthcare providers to liability. In this context, it becomes crucial to clarify who bears responsibility for AI-related harm and to implement appropriate mitigation measures at every stage of the supply chain. Failing to address these issues effectively exposes healthcare organisations, professionals, and technology providers to significant legal and ethical risks.

In summary, from an *ex-ante* perspective, accountability involves embedding best practices, technical standards, and security protocols into healthcare technologies. From an *ex-post* standpoint, it requires continuous assessment of the effectiveness of governance programmes and best practices after the technology's deployment.

Frank Pasquale's concept of *data-informed duties* further emphasises the importance of compliance frameworks and data curation. Pasquale advocates for ongoing quality assessments of AI data and algorithms, alongside post-market evaluations by suppliers, healthcare institutions, physicians, and patients. This approach complements his *Fourth Law of Robotics*, which stipulates that robots must disclose their creators, owners, and levels of autonomy through identifiable information, such as serial numbers or public registries (Pasquale 2020).

Healthcare compliance programmes must be recognised as more than mere tools for corporate conformity and risk management. They should be elevated to the status of legal instruments capable of identifying and quantifying responsibilities across the healthcare sector. This transition is essential for reconciling the desire for innovation with the imperative of legal security, particularly as preventive and precautionary functions increasingly guide technological development in healthcare.

The ethical principle of accountability also reframes the duties of care and vigilance expected of healthcare professionals. As previously discussed, physicians are bound by a professional duty to maintain up-to-date knowledge. However, in the age of AI, this duty extends beyond personal expertise to encompass vigilance over the external tools and technologies employed in medical practice. For instance, a physician who observes frequent inaccuracies or systemic failures in an AI tool has both an ethical and legal duty to cease its use. If an AI system consistently delivers erroneous results or fails to meet the manufacturer's claimed accuracy under real-world conditions, the physician must prioritise patient safety and discontinue reliance on the technology.

The dual dimensions of accountability—*ex-ante* and *ex-post*—offer a roadmap for integrating innovation and legal security within healthcare. They demonstrate how civil liability's preventive and precautionary functions can serve as foundational principles in technological development. Moreover, the principle of accountability underscores the evolving responsibilities of healthcare professionals, compelling them to align technological innovation with ethical and legal imperatives to safeguard patient welfare.

Based on the discussions presented throughout this subsection of the book, it can be concluded that, in the context of the six ethical principles of artificial intelligence (AI) in medicine and the redefinition of physician's duties of conduct derived from the principle of objective good faith, various scenarios can be identified where medical civil liability may arise. This is particularly relevant in the current era of the *Post-Constitutionalisation of Civil Law* and within the framework of *Person-Centred Medicine*, which adopts an expanded perspective on the obligations of healthcare providers.

The *Post-Constitutionalisation of Civil Law*, as explained in Chapter 2, refers to the process whereby constitutional values and principles, such as human dignity, equality, and solidarity, directly influence private law relations. This development has broadened the scope of civil obligations, particularly in fields like medicine, where the consequences of professional actions have profound and immediate impacts on individuals' lives. Within this framework, a physician's obligations are no longer confined to the primary duty of performing a diagnosis or providing treatment. Instead, these obligations are accompanied by numerous ancillary duties arising from the principle of objective good faith. These duties include transparency, diligence, clear communication, respect for patient autonomy, and precautionary measures to mitigate potential risks.

Person-Centred Medicine, as discussed in detail in Chapter 2, redefines the doctor-patient relationship, focusing on the individuality and personal values of the patient at every stage of care. This model requires a holistic approach that goes beyond technical practice, encompassing respect for patient autonomy through the provision of clear, comprehensive, and comprehensible information about the risks, benefits, and alternatives of treatments, particularly when utilising technologies such as AI. Additionally, personalised attention is necessary, adapting practices and recommendations to each patient's unique needs and preferences. Furthermore, the principles of prevention and precaution obligate physicians to evaluate and mitigate risks associated with medical interventions, including those posed by technological tools such as algorithmic diagnostics or decision-support systems.

The redefined duties of physician's conduct are closely intertwined with the principle of precaution, which has emerged as a new legal standard for medical practice in the twenty-first century. These duties, rooted in the principle of contractual good faith, transcend traditional obligations by emphasising loyalty, disclosure, cooperation, and vigilance, among others. When viewed through the lens of precaution, these duties gain an additional dimension, aiming not only to address harm after its occurrence but to actively prevent its realisation. The principle of precaution sets a proactive and preventive framework, requiring the professionals to adopt measures that minimise risks and uncertainties. This standard represents a shift from reactive approaches—focused primarily on compensation for damages—toward a more protective and forward-looking paradigm. It integrates seamlessly with the broader goals of Person-Centred Medicine, where patient safety, dignity, and autonomy are prioritised within a framework of preventative care.

By embedding the principle of precaution into the fabric of physicians' conduct, the legal systems encourage them to exercise heightened diligence in their practices. This includes the adoption of safer techniques, the transparent communication of risks, and adherence to modern scientific developments. Thus, the principle of precaution is not only an ethical imperative but also a legal standard that reinforces the professional's duty to prevent harm and uphold the patient's right to informed, risk-aware decision-making. This alignment of redefined physician's duties with the principle of precaution reflects a broader evolution in legal and ethical standards, adapting to the complexities of modern medicine and the heightened expectations of contemporary society.

The expansion of the concept of medical liabilitty to include ancillary duties creates new situations in which civil liability may arise. For instance, a failure to adopt preventive measures could expose a physician to liability. If a doctor employs an AI system without conducting regular performance checks and notices recurring errors, they may be held liable for damages resulting from such omissions. Similarly, a failure to communicate transparently could lead to liability; for example, if a physician does not adequately inform a patient about the limitations of a technology, such as a diagnostic AI system that relies on specific data, and the patient suffers harm, this could constitute a breach of the duty to inform. Additionally, a failure to observe the duty of vigilance, such as neglecting to monitor the efficacy or risks of technologies used in clinical practice, may result in adverse outcomes that render the physician liable.

Objective good faith acts as a guiding principle that determines the scope of physicians' duties of conduct. In contemporary medical practice, this principle imposes ethical and preventive obligations that transcend mere technical proficiency. It underpins the physician's duty to act not only with technical competence but also with empathy, respect, and attentiveness to the human and technological contexts of each patient.

Consequently, medical civil liability must be understood as encompassing a wide array of responsibilities that include both technical performance and ancillary duties. These duties, reinforced by the ethical principles of AI, aim to protect patients in an increasingly complex technological and social landscape. By redefining the role of the physician, objective good faith demands practices that focus not only on achieving therapeutic outcomes but also on preventing risks, promoting autonomy, and maintaining high ethical standards in interactions with emerging technologies.

To conclude, it is essential to acknowledge the profound connection between the themes explored throughout this subchapter and Friedrich Nietzsche's concept of the *transvaluation of values*. The concept of transvaluation critiques the values inherited from tradition, advocating for their revaluation to meet the demands of the present. His philosophy invites the abandonment of outdated paradigms that no longer address societal needs and the creation of new, more relevant values that align with the current technological and ethical landscape.

Nietzsche offers a philosophical framework for understanding the necessity of redefining physician's duties of conduct in light of the unprecedented challenges introduced by artificial intelligence (AI). His philosophy encourages a departure from the rigid paradigms of the past—values that no longer address the complexities of contemporary society—and advocates for the construction of new, more relevant frameworks that align with the realities of the present era.

Traditionally, physicians' duties of conduct such as diligence, the obligation to inform, and the duty of vigilance were developed within a physician-centred model of care, where the doctor represented the sole authority in knowledge and decision-making. However, the integration of AI has fundamentally transformed this dynamic, decentralising certain aspects of decision-making and positioning the patient as an active participant in their own care. Nietzsche's notion of transvaluation provides a lens through which this relationship can be recalibrated, placing the patient at the core of healthcare practices while enabling physicians to employ AI as an extension of their clinical expertise.

In this context, it becomes imperative to ensure that technological advancements serve the purpose of human care, rather than relegating humanity to a secondary role. The failure to embrace this transvaluation risks fostering a form of *technological nihilism*, wherein technology is perceived as an end in itself, thereby dehumanising healthcare and undermining the trust essential to the doctor-patient relationship. This underscores the necessity of understanding that medical ethics and professional duties are not immutable; rather, they are dynamic constructs that must evolve to reflect the demands of an ever-changing society. The intersection of physician's duties of conduct with the ethical principles inherent to AI highlights the importance of this transvaluation, offering a pathway towards a more ethically grounded and patient-centred integration of technology in modern healthcare.

4.2.2 The AI Act and the European Framework for Civil Liability for Damages Involving AI Systems in Healthcare

The complexity of AI systems, coupled with their opacity, autonomy, and self-learning capabilities, often makes it difficult—or even impossible—to ascertain the proximate cause of harm, namely, the product defect and the causal link to the injury sustained by the individual. This unpredictability stems from the inherent sophistication of AI, where systems are designed to respond not only to predefined stimuli but also to new, unforeseen inputs, resulting in reactions that are not pre-programmed. Such self-processing capabilities render it challenging to anticipate the precise impact of AI once operational. Consequently, decisions made by AI systems may deviate from what was intended or foreseen by their developers, and this unpredictability becomes particularly problematic when it leads to harm (Wesendonck 2021). Given this context, it is imperative to acknowledge the impossibility of infallibility in machines. Errors are unavoidable, and this reality persists in the realm of AI, thereby necessitating a critical examination of the application of civil liability to address potential damages.

Given the difficulty of auditing the technological pathways undertaken by AI, the issue of causality becomes particularly challenging in cases where harm involves an autonomous system (Barbosa 2022). In this context, the law, in a symbiotic relationship with technological development, must evolve to address the new challenges posed by automated decision-making systems, striving to provide a legally satisfactory response within the framework of the existing legal order and updating it where necessary.

In Brazil, discussions on civil liability in Artificial Intelligence have been largely influenced by the European Union, which has emerged as a global leader in this field since 2017 (Medon 2022a, b). This prominence is attributed to its pioneering efforts, including extensive studies by renowned experts on the ethical and legal dimensions of artificial intelligence. The EU has proposed legislative reforms aimed at modernising existing civil law frameworks, with a particular focus on civil liability, to align them with the realities of the highly technological society of the twenty-first century.

This book aims to provide an overarching view of the ongoing discussions at the European level, with the subsequent objective of outlining potential pathways within the framework of Brazilian law. It is important to clarify that this work does not seek to conduct an exhaustive analysis of the liability of AI manufacturers. Instead, its primary focus is to explore the civil liability of medical practitioners in the context of automated decision-making systems. Accordingly, it is essential to present an overview of the current debates surrounding AI regulation, the ecosystem of potential stakeholders involved, and the inherent complexity of identifying the efficient cause of harm and determining where responsibility should be assigned.

In 2017, the European Parliament adopted the Resolution of 16 February 2017 with Recommendations to the Commission on Civil Law Rules on Robotics, identifying civil liability for damages involving autonomous robots as a critical issue to be addressed by Member States. In relation to the legal basis for liability, the resolution suggests choosing between two distinct approaches: risk management or strict liability. Additionally, it highlights the establishment of a mandatory insurance regime as a potential solution to the complexity of attributing responsibility for damages caused by increasingly autonomous AI systems.

As a complementary measure, the 2017 Resolution proposes the creation of a *guarantee fund* to compensate for damages not covered by existing insurance schemes. It further suggests that manufacturers, programmers, owners, or users of the technology could benefit from limited liability if they contribute to such a fund or jointly secure insurance coverage. One of the more controversial aspects of this Resolution is its suggestion to consider a special legal status for robots, recognising them as *electronic persons*. This notion has been the subject of significant academic discourse, with prominent contributions from scholars such as Pagallo (2013), Turner (2019), and Ferreira (2016).

Nonetheless, the prevailing view is that granting electronic personality to robots is both impractical and unnecessary at this stage of technological development. Most experts argue that existing legal mechanisms can be adapted to address the complexities introduced by autonomous systems, rendering the recognition of robots as legal persons neither viable nor beneficial in the current context. The focus, instead, remains on enhancing regulatory frameworks to address liability effectively while avoiding the complications associated with conferring legal personhood on machines.

In 2019, as previously discussed in an earlier subsection of this book, a *High-Level Expert Group*, established by the European Commission, published the *Ethics Guidelines for Trustworthy AI*. This document provides a comprehensive overview of ethics and values aimed at all individuals and entities involved in the development, use, or impact of automated decision-making systems, including businesses, institutions, organisations, and civil society. The ethical principles outlined are linked to seven (non-exhaustive) requirements for achieving trustworthy AI: human agency and oversight; technical robustness and safety; privacy and data governance; transparency; diversity, non-discrimination, and fairness; societal and environmental well-being; and accountability.

In February 2020, a report was prepared by experts addressing the various challenges artificial intelligence poses to the legal field, as outlined in the *White Paper on Artificial Intelligence: A European Approach to Excellence and Trust*. The document argues that the principal legal challenges associated with the use of AI concern the application of rules aimed at protecting fundamental rights (including personal data, privacy protection, and non-discrimination), as well as issues of safety and liability.

In recent years, the technological advancements observed have underscored the challenge of regulating AI in a manner that promotes progress and innovation while simultaneously ensuring robust protection for fundamental rights and freedoms within a democratic environment. This challenge is explicitly articulated in the white paper published by the European Commission, wherein the entity delineates its aim to establish a regulatory framework that achieves a balance between enabling the development of AI tools and safeguarding fundamental rights and freedoms. As will be examined further in this subsection of the book, the AI Act (2024) serves as the tangible realisation of this objective, with the risk-based regulatory model being the legal instrument selected to accomplish this purpose.

The *White Paper* highlights that automated decision-making systems can introduce new safety risks for users when integrated into products and services. Examples provided include: (i) an autonomous vehicle erroneously identifying an object on the road, causing an accident resulting in injuries and property damage; or (ii) harm caused by design flaws in AI technology, such as issues with the availability and quality of data or other problems arising from machine learning processes. These examples illustrate the potential for AI systems to generate risks that extend beyond traditional safety concerns, requiring careful legal scrutiny.

The document also underscores concerns that, in the context of AI-based systems, it may be challenging to establish both the existence of a defect in the product and the causation between the defect and the resulting harm. This difficulty arises from the complex and often opaque nature of AI systems, which involve multiple layers of decision-making and data processing that can obscure the root cause of an error. Moreover, the self-learning capabilities of AI may lead to unforeseen behaviours not directly attributable to the original design or programming.

In light of these issues, the *White Paper* stresses the importance of evaluating the adequacy of the existing legal framework, particularly the rules set forth in *Directive 85/374/EEC* (repealed by Directive 2024/2853), which holds manufacturers strictly liable for damages caused by defective products. The document suggests that this Directive may require updates to address the unique challenges posed by AI systems. Proposed adaptations include revising definitions of *defect* and *product*, as well as clarifying the allocation of liability among various stakeholders in the AI ecosystem, such as developers, manufacturers, and operators. These considerations are critical to ensuring effective consumer protection while fostering innovation and maintaining public trust in AI technologies.

In September 2020, two significant studies were published: *European Framework on Ethical Aspects of Artificial Intelligence, Robotics and Related Technologies* and *Civil Liability Regime for Artificial Intelligence: European Added Value Assessment*. The latter document outlines the general context of how legal issues raised by AI could be addressed by the civil liability systems of EU Member States, thereby strengthening the call for the development of a Directive by the European Parliament to effectively regulate civil liability issues associated with AI systems.

In October of the same year, the European Parliament issued a Resolution titled *Civil Liability Regime for Artificial Intelligence* (2020). This Resolution recognises that technology poses significant challenges to the existing legal framework on liability. It highlights that combining robust ethical standards for AI with sound and fair compensation mechanisms could address these legal challenges while also mitigating the risk of user hesitancy in adopting emerging technologies.

The *2020 Resolution* posits that it is unnecessary to overhaul the existing liability regimes of EU Member States entirely. Instead, it underscores the need for specific adjustments that can adequately accommodate the complexities of AI systems, including their connectivity, opacity, vulnerability, potential for modification through updates and self-learning capabilities, autonomy, and the multiplicity of stakeholders involved. In this regard, the Resolution reaffirms the importance of updating the existing rules under Directive 85/374/EEC (1985) on liability for defective products.

A notable recommendation within the *2020 Resolution* concerns the application of rules on the reversal of the burden of proof in specific instances involving harm caused by automated decision-making systems. It is also worth noting that since

2017, Germany has mandated the provision of a black box in autonomous vehicles. Following amendments to the *Road Traffic Act* (Straßenverkehrsgesetz—StVG), victims of road traffic accidents are granted the right to access the black box data of vehicles equipped with autonomous driving functions (Section 63a(3) StVG). This measure aims to facilitate the determination of the cause of an accident, specifically whether it was attributable to the automated system or the human driver. Similarly, French law, through the *Decree of 28 March 2018*, explicitly requires autonomous vehicles to be equipped with recording devices that preserve trip data for the 5 min preceding an accident (Soares 2019).

Additionally, the *2020 Resolution* underscores the critical importance of ensuring that liability mechanisms facilitate an appropriate, efficient, and fair allocation of responsibilities. Key principles such as explainability, interpretability, and traceability of AI systems are identified as essential. The role of civil liability insurance in automated decision-making systems is also emphasised, being identified as a determinant of the successful deployment of new technologies. The Resolution mandates *compulsory liability coverage* for all operators of technologies classified as *high-risk AI systems* and emphasises the necessity of establishing differentiated liability rules calibrated to reflect varying degrees of risk.

In summary, given the legal challenges posed by AI systems to existing liability frameworks, the *2020 Resolution* advocates for: (i) establishing a common strict liability regime for autonomous high-risk AI systems; and (ii) adopting a risk-based approach that incorporates multiple levels of risk, supported by clear criteria and an appropriate definition of high risk to ensure legal certainty. An AI system is considered *high-risk* if its autonomous operation poses a significant and random risk of harm to one or more persons, exceeding what can reasonably be expected. This classification should consider the sector in which substantial risks are likely to arise and the nature of the activities undertaken. The assessment of risk significance should take into account the relationship between the severity of potential harm, the likelihood of the risk materialising, and the specific manner in which the AI system is deployed.

The wide-ranging risks associated with autonomous systems render it particularly challenging to devise a single, universally applicable legal solution for all AI-related damages across diverse sectors. Accordingly, the 2020 Resolution advocates for a risk-based approach to AI regulation that accounts for varying levels of risk to consumers across different applications and sectors. It proposes the use of pilot projects, regulatory sandboxes, and data-driven experimental environments to identify proportionate solutions tailored to specific circumstances and industries.

The proportion of liability should be determined by the degree of control exercised by operators over the risk arising from the operation and functioning of the AI system. In this context, the *Annex to the 2020 Resolution* provides detailed recommendations for drafting a European Parliament regulation on the liability arising from the operation of AI systems. Key concepts such as *operator* and *control* of AI are defined, alongside discussions about provisions for strict or fault-based liability for high-risk AI systems. Furthermore, the Resolution addresses the allocation of joint liability where multiple operators are involved and proportional liability where several actors contribute to the harmful event.

In general terms, the *2020 Resolution* departs significantly from the earlier proposal to create an electronic personality for AI systems, as suggested in the 2017 Resolution. Instead, it adopts a *risk-based approach*, tailoring the content of regulations to the degree of risk posed by AI systems. The Resolution thus emphasises that a full-scale reform of existing civil liability frameworks is unnecessary, with only specific adjustments to the current rules needed to effectively address emerging challenges. Finally, it calls upon the European Commission to issue guidelines to prevent fragmented regulatory approaches at the national level, taking into account Directive 85/374/EEC and existing national liability regimes.

In evaluating the principal contributions of the 2020 Resolution, Medon (2020, 2022a, b) highlights that: (i) while a full revision of existing civil liability norms is unwarranted, the complexity, opacity, self-learning capacity, and programmability of AI, coupled with the involvement of multiple actors, present significant challenges to the effectiveness of existing norms; and (ii) since damages caused by AI are often linked, at least partially, to human involvement, granting legal personhood to AI systems is unnecessary and should therefore be avoided.

It is evident that Europe's approach emphasises the indispensable role of human oversight in AI development, risk management, and the integration of existing norms with mandatory securitisation mechanisms. These structures would vary depending on the degree of risk posed by each entity involved in the market introduction of AI systems or robots.

Following the publication of the 2020 Resolution and the studies and reports referenced above, the *Artificial Intelligence Act* (AI Act—AIA) was finally proposed in 2021. This legislation adopts a *risk-based regulatory approach*, categorising AI systems into levels of risk: unacceptable risk, high risk, limited risk, and minimal risk.

The AI Act represents a global milestone with the potential to serve as a model for other nations seeking to develop national regulations for emerging technologies. The European Parliament adopted the AI Act in March 2024, followed by the Council's approval in May 2024. The legislation will become fully enforceable 24 months after its entry into force, though specific provisions will apply earlier. AI systems deemed to pose unacceptable risks will be prohibited 6 months after the Act's commencement. Codes of practice will be implemented within 9 months, and general-purpose AI systems subject to transparency requirements will need to comply within 12 months. High-risk AI systems will have an extended compliance period, with their obligations becoming enforceable 36 months after the Act takes effect.

On 28 September 2022, the European Commission introduced two proposed Directives of the European Parliament and Council. The first aims to update the rules of Directive 85/374/EEC on civil liability for defective products (the *Product Liability Directive*—PLD). The second seeks to adapt non-contractual civil liability rules to address damages arising from the use of AI systems (the *AI Liability Directive*—AILD).

As of December 2024, the updated Product Liability Directive (*Directive (EU) 2024/2853*) has been adopted by the European Parliament and the Council, published in the Official Journal of the European Union on 18 November 2024, and entered into force on 8 December 2024. EU Member States are required to transpose the directive into their national laws by 9 December 2026. The *AI Liability Directive*, by contrast, remained under discussion within the legislative process for an extended period until its eventual withdrawal in February 2025, as will be explained in due course. This proposed directive sought to harmonise non-contractual civil liability rules applicable to AI systems across Member States.

There are 5 key significant updates introduced by the new Product Liability Directive (Directive (EU) 2024/2853) as follows: (i) the definition of *product* is expanded to include intangible items, such as software and AI systems; (ii) the concept of *defect* now considers the potential effects of a product's ability to continue learning (machine learning), even after being placed on the market; (iii) victims are granted the right to request, through judicial proceedings, that manufacturers provide evidence regarding an AI system suspected of causing harm, a process known as disclosure of evidence, which carries a presumption of non-compliance with a duty of care if the manufacturer fails to comply; (iv) if a claimant faces undue difficulty in proving a defect and/or causation due to the technical or scientific complexity of the product, the defect and/or causation may be presumed, provided there is sufficiently relevant evidence; (v) manufacturers are not exempt from liability (where the AI system remains under their control) if a product defect arises from the failure to provide necessary software updates required to maintain safety.

It is worth emphasising that the *AI Act* focuses on safety and the prevention of harm that may be caused by AI systems, whereas the *Product Liability Directive (Directive (EU) 2024/2853)* and the *AI Liability Directive* primarily address redress in contractual and non-contractual relationships, respectively, following the occurrence of harm involving such technology. These three regulatory proposals are designed to operate as a *Tripartite Framework*, complementing one another to create a cohesive and comprehensive approach to regulating AI systems.

The *AI Act* establishes preventative measures by setting safety standards and compliance requirements to minimise risks before they materialise. In contrast, the new Product Liability Directive ensures accountability for defective products, including AI-enabled ones, by providing clear pathways for victims to claim compensation. Meanwhile, the *AI Liability Directive* addresses specific gaps in non-contractual liability regimes by introducing provisions tailored to the unique characteristics of AI systems, such as their complexity, autonomy, and opacity.

Together, these measures reflect a dual emphasis on pre-emptive safety and effective post-harm remedies, illustrating that safety and liability are two interconnected elements of the same regulatory goal. Through future national laws derived from these instruments, EU Member States aim to adapt existing liability frameworks to the Digital Age, addressing the unprecedented challenges posed by automated decision-making systems while fostering trust and accountability in AI technologies.

It is important to note that the primary objective of the AI Act is to establish a governance infrastructure designed to prevent and mitigate the harmful outcomes of automated systems. This is achieved through preventative measures and security mechanisms, including a *security-by-design* approach at every stage—before, during, and after the deployment of AI systems in consumer markets. For certain high-risk products, more stringent accountability measures are required, including rigorous audit controls.

As previously noted, the AI Act adopts a *risk-based approach*, categorising AI systems into low or minimal risk and high risk. It also outlines scenarios in which the use of AI is strictly prohibited, such as technologies designed for credit scoring in the style of China's social credit systems, AI systems that exploit specific vulnerabilities of individuals or groups (e.g., children or persons with disabilities) to cause harm, and systems used to subliminally manipulate behaviour or opinions in a manner detrimental to individuals.

A recent study by van Leeuwen et al. (2021) examined 100 artificial intelligence systems from 54 different providers available for clinical radiology. The findings revealed that 64 of these systems lacked evaluations regarding their diagnostic effectiveness. Furthermore, only 18 systems demonstrated evidence of achieving level 3 or higher diagnostic accuracy, a critical standard required of human physicians in the field. The researchers highlighted concerns about the heterogeneity of tools and the lack of transparency regarding their functionality and outcomes, emphasising that failures in such systems could jeopardise patients' lives and physical integrity.

In response to these challenges, the AI Act was designed to ensure the safety of products and services incorporating AI systems, either as components or final products. Safety in this context entails implementing measures throughout the system's lifecycle, from the selection of data and model training to testing and accuracy evaluation. This process continues with market introduction, accompanied by assessments of the system's practical use and societal impact, and concludes with post-market calibration and compensatory measures to address outcomes deemed undesirable by society.

The risk-based approach adopted in the AI Act goes beyond a purely technical focus on system malfunctions stemming from their characteristics; it also includes an assessment of how the results generated by such systems may infringe on individuals' fundamental rights. As Mahler (2022) explains, this broadens the concept of risk within the AI Act, incorporating a legal dimension that considers not only the probability of system failure but also the likelihood of outcomes that negatively impact fundamental rights in Europe. This shift reflects a recognition of the multifaceted nature of risks posed by artificial intelligence.

The European legislator's choice of a *risk-based regulatory model* stems from the understanding that traditional regulatory approaches, such as command-and-control, are ill-suited to address the complexities of emerging technologies, particularly AI. The risk-based approach aims to ensure regulatory longevity and cost-effectiveness by focusing on auditing governance structures and documentation rather than direct supervision. Rooted in proportionality, this framework seeks to balance fostering innovation within the European Digital Single Market while safeguarding fundamental rights. It aligns with broader EU strategies, including the *Digital Single Market Strategy* (2020), and reflects principles of *accountability*, as seen in existing frameworks like the General Data Protection Regulation (GDPR) and the Digital Services Act (DSA). The AI Act operationalises this strategy with a structured risk classification system, defining specific legal consequences for each risk level, such as prohibitions, governance requirements, or transparency obligations.

As mentioned, the General Data Protection Regulation (GDPR) and the AI Act both rely on a risk-based approach to regulation, however they implement this principle in different methods. While the GDPR adopts a *bottom-up approach*, granting data controllers the flexibility to identify and mitigate risks within their specific operational contexts, the AI Act employs a *top-down framework*, defining risk categories and prescribing specific governance measures for high-risk systems. These contrasting methodologies reflect the differing regulatory challenges posed by personal data protection and artificial intelligence systems.

Under the GDPR, the responsibility for identifying high-risk data processing activities lies with data controllers. They must assess the risks associated with their processing operations and adopt appropriate measures to mitigate those risks. This process is formalised through the Data Protection Impact Assessment (DPIA), which documents the evaluation and mitigation efforts undertaken by the controller. In summary, the GDPR does not provide an exhaustive list of high-risk activities; instead, it encourages controllers to evaluate risks in the context of their specific operations, making the regulation adaptable to diverse industries and use cases.

In contrast, the AI Act employs a predefined risk classification system, which identifies specific types of AI systems as high-risk based on their potential to impact health, safety, and fundamental rights. Article 6 of the Act outlines the conditions under which an AI system is deemed high-risk. Paragraph 1 specifies two primary criteria: i) the AI system is used as a safety component of a product or the product itself and is covered by harmonised EU legislation listed in Annex I; and ii) the product, either as a whole or as a component, requires a third-party conformity assessment—typically conducted by a public authority—before being placed on the market or put into service.

A practical example involves AI-powered medical devices, such as automated insulin pumps equipped with glucose sensors. These devices are classified as high-risk in multiple jurisdictions, including Brazil, where the ANVISA RDC No. 751/2022 designates them as high risks. Similarly, in the EU, these devices are evaluated using parameters established by sectoral legislation referenced in Annex I of the AI Act. This alignment ensures that existing risk classifications are consistently applied under the AI Act framework.

Paragraph 2 of Article 6 introduces an additional mechanism for identifying high-risk activities, referring to the specific applications outlined in Annex III. The AI Act provides an illustrative list of eight predefined high-risk areas: (i) biometrics: includes remote biometric identification, sensitive categorisation systems, and emotion recognition technologies, excluding systems solely confirming an individual's identity; (ii) critical infrastructure: AI systems used as safety components in managing digital infrastructure, road traffic, or essential utilities such as water, gas, heating, and electricity; (iii) education and vocational training: systems determining access to educational opportunities, assessing learning outcomes, or monitoring prohibited behaviours during examinations; (iv) employment and workforce management: AI tools for recruitment, performance monitoring, task allocation, promotions, or contract terminations; (v) access to essential services and benefits: AI used for evaluating eligibility for public benefits, credit scoring, insurance risk assessment, or emergency call classification; (vi) law enforcement: systems for criminal risk assessment, evidence verification, behaviour analysis, and profiling in investigations; (vii) migration, asylum, and border control: AI applications for security risk assessments, processing asylum claims, and border management; (viii) judicial and democratic processes: tools for legal research, applying laws, or influencing electoral outcomes.

Although Annex III provides a structured overview of high-risk applications, it remains an exemplificative list, allowing for the inclusion of unlisted activities if they meet the high-risk criteria. This flexibility enables the regulation to adapt to emerging technologies while maintaining a consistent framework for enforcement.

Furthermore, the AI Act imposes mandatory governance obligations for high-risk AI systems. These include continuous risk management processes (Article 9), documentation of datasets used for training and validation (Article 10), technical compliance documentation (Article 11), and automated logging for traceability (Article 12). High-risk systems must also provide clear and comprehensible user instructions (Article 13), enable human oversight (Article 14), and incorporate cybersecurity measures (Article 15).

As observed, automated decision-making systems classified as *high-risk* are subject to a *special compliance regime* both before and after being introduced to the market. This includes obligations related to data quality, transparency, governance, and measures to mitigate discrimination. Non-compliance exposes manufacturers to sanctions. The *AI Act* mandates stringent controls over transparency and accountability, requiring manufacturers to implement continuous risk management systems throughout the AI's lifecycle. Failure to comply with the provisions of the AI Act may result in severe penalties, as stipulated in Article 99. Fines can reach up to €35 million or 7% of the company's annual global turnover, whichever is higher, as outlined in Article 99(3).

In summary, the text of the EU *AI Act* underscores the *principle of risk management*, accompanied by obligations related to the *accountability* of AI systems. These obligations require the preparation of technical documentation detailing general characteristics, capabilities, and limitations of AI systems, as well as the implementation of transparency measures and the adoption of internal routines and procedures to ensure robust data governance (Negri 2021). The core objective is harm prevention, which highlights the necessity of a *precautionary* and *promotive* role for civil liability. A risk-based approach must therefore be complemented by solid transparency measures aimed at evaluating the safety, robustness, accuracy, and performance of automated systems.

It is worth noting that the previously mentioned *2020 Civil Liability Regime for Artificial Intelligence* also emphasised the importance of establishing clear parameters for determining civil liability in automated systems. Similarly, the *European Framework on Ethical Aspects of Artificial Intelligence, Robotics, and Related Technologies*, published in the same year, highlighted the necessity of an accountability framework to ensure the effective protection of fundamental values within the EU.

As discussed earlier in this book, the global legal community has, in recent years, emphasised the importance of *accountability* in transitioning from traditional strict liability models to a framework that prioritises both preventive and precautionary functions (Vedder and Naudts 2017). According to Comandé (2019a, b), the concept of *multilayered (accountable) liability* for artificial intelligence must be taken into account. This notion suggests that accountability operates across multiple layers, incorporating distinct legal, ethical, and social dimensions. For example, accountability mechanisms should identify obligations at different stages of AI development and use, ensuring that liability is distributed fairly among the parties involved, such as developers, deployers, and operators of AI systems. Additionally, the party best positioned to assume data-informed duties bears the responsibility of justifying their decisions to those affected by them.

In this sense, as Faleiros Júnior (2021) argues, accountability represents more than a duty—it embodies a culture. It extends beyond merely providing justification for decisions made; rather, it aspires to ensure that the responsible party is held accountable, within appropriate spheres (whether political, civil, criminal, administrative, ethical, or social), for potential shortcomings or deficiencies in their choices.

It is important to highlight a significant debate surrounding the EU's *AI Act*. During a plenary session of the European Parliament on 13 April 2023, several criticisms of the initial draft were raised, focusing particularly on prohibited AI practices classified as *unacceptable risk* and the criteria used to categorise *high-risk technologies*. The original AI Act proposal introduced a strict regime for high-risk systems, enumerated in specific areas and use cases as outlined in Annex III.

One of the primary concerns raised during the session was how to ensure that foundational generative AI models, such as OpenAI's ChatGPT, cannot evade risk-based regulation by arguing the absence of a defined purpose. The initial draft of the *AI Act* included an intermediate category for technologies like chatbots and deepfakes, which were not subject to all compliance requirements applicable to high-risk AI systems. The European Commission had deliberately avoided addressing generative AI in the original text, given the limited understanding at the time of its potential risks and implications.

This omission highlights the inherent challenge of regulating emerging technologies, which can quickly evolve and outpace legislative processes, potentially rendering regulatory frameworks outdated even before they are enacted. In the latest version of the text, incorporating amendments proposed by the European Parliament on 14 June 2023, provisions concerning *general-purpose AI* (GPAI) were introduced, specifically addressing foundational models.

These provisions include requirements related to transparency, privacy, intellectual property rights, and other additional compliance obligations. GPAI is now subject to specific transparency requirements, including: (i) disclosing that content has been generated by AI; (ii) designing the model to prevent the generation of illegal content; (iii) publishing summaries of copyrighted data used during training. Rather than focusing solely on specific high-risk AI applications, these new provisions apply to technologies with varying levels of risk and broad potential uses across multiple sectors. This adjustment reflects the EU's commitment to a more comprehensive and adaptive approach to AI regulation, ensuring that foundational and generative AI models meet stringent standards while addressing their multifaceted impact on society.

Considering the broader debate proposed in this subchapter on the regulation of emerging technologies, several key considerations emerge in the specific context of medical devices. AI systems used for diagnostics and treatment recommendations fall under the regulatory category of *Software as a Medical Device* (SaMD). SaMD refers to software intended for medical purposes that functions independently of physical medical devices. These systems leverage advanced algorithms, including machine learning, to analyse medical data, support clinical decisions, and improve patient outcomes.

In the European Union, SaMD must comply with the stringent requirements of the *Medical Devices Regulation* (MDR—Regulation (EU) 2017/745) and, the *In Vitro Diagnostic Medical Devices Regulation* (IVDR—Regulation (EU) 2017/746). These regulations provide comprehensive frameworks to ensure safety, efficacy, and performance. Compliance is demonstrated through the *CE marking*, certifying that the device meets EU standards. MDR regulates medical devices used for diagnosing, preventing, monitoring, treating, or alleviating diseases or medical conditions in humans. This includes devices like pacemakers, surgical instruments, implants, software as a medical device (SaMD) for general diagnosis, and diagnostic or treatment systems. On the other hand, IVDR regulates in vitro diagnostic (IVD) devices, which are used to examine biological samples (e.g., blood, tissue) taken from the human body to provide information about a person's health, such as diagnosis, prediction, or monitoring of diseases. Examples include blood glucose meters, pregnancy tests, laboratory reagents, and genetic testing software.

The MDR, adopted on 5 April 2017, replaced Directives 90/385/EEC and 93/42/EEC, establishing a new regulatory framework for medical devices. Although it entered into force on 25 May 2017, its full application was initially scheduled for 26 May 2020. However, due to the COVID-19 pandemic, the application date was postponed to 26 May 2021. Since then, the MDR has been the applicable regulation for medical devices in the EU. The In Vitro Diagnostic Medical Devices Regulation (IVDR—Regulation (EU) 2017/746) was adopted on 5 April 2017 and entered into force on 25 May 2017. Its full application began on 26 May 2022. The IVDR replaces Directive 98/79/EC, establishing a new regulatory framework for in vitro diagnostic medical devices within the European Union.

An example of SaMD is the Paige Prostate Detect system, mentioned in a previous subchapter of this book, which was developed to assist pathologists in identifying prostate cancer. Another noteworthy SaMD already mentioned is LuminetícsCore, an AI-based tool approved for diagnosing diabetic retinopathy. Similarly, the Viz.ai LVO system represents a significant advancement in stroke management, analysing CT angiograms to detect large vessel occlusions (LVOs) in stroke patients and immediately alerting healthcare teams.

For the approval processes for these three notable examples—Paige Prostate Detect, LuminetícsCore, and Viz.ai LVO—there was rigorous standards required for SaMD certification within the EU. Each of these systems has achieved the CE marking, signifying compliance with the Medical Devices Regulation (MDR) or In Vitro Diagnostic Medical Devices Regulation (IVDR), depending on their classification.

The evaluation includes thorough assessments of clinical safety, accuracy, and reliability, alongside evidence of their ability to improve clinical workflows and patient outcomes. These approvals underscore the EU's commitment to fostering innovation in healthcare technology while maintaining robust safeguards to ensure that such tools meet the highest standards of medical efficacy and patient safety. Beyond compliance and certification, another significant discussion relates to the traceability of medical devices. The EU mandates the Unique Device Identifier (UDI) system, ensuring that devices and their manufacturers can be tracked throughout the supply chain. This system allows for swift corrective actions if issues arise with an AI-powered device. With over 500,000 types of medical devices currently available in the EU market—including software, contact lenses, X-ray machines, ventilators, and pacemakers—the importance of robust traceability mechanisms cannot be overstated (European Commission 2021).

The MDR and IVDR have become benchmarks for regulating medical technologies, covering risk classification, liability, and safety requirements. These frameworks are complemented by the General Data Protection Regulation (GDPR), the Market Surveillance Regulation (Regulation (EU) 2019/1020), the AI Act, and the Product Liability Directive (PLD).

As mentioned previously, the AI Act (2024) incorporates a *risk-based regulatory framework* for AI systems, categorising them into prohibited, high-risk, limited-risk, and minimal/no-risk categories. While some AI-enabled medical devices are indeed classified as high-risk, *not all medical devices with AI are automatically deemed high-risk.* The classification depends on several factors, including the system's intended purpose, its application in clinical settings, and its potential impact on health and safety. For example, devices directly influencing critical medical decisions, such as diagnostic tools for life-threatening conditions, are typically classified as high-risk. However, less critical applications, such as tools for administrative purposes or non-critical data analysis, may fall into lower risk categories. This distinction reflects the flexibility of the AI Act, which shapes regulatory demands to the specific risks posed by each device.

Although many recent academic articles claim that the AI Act considers all medical devices incorporating artificial intelligence to be classified as high risk, this interpretation does not fully align with the regulation's nuances. The AI Act establishes a structured risk-based framework, and while it does classify many AI-enabled medical devices as high risk due to their potential impact on health, safety, and fundamental rights, it does not automatically place all such devices into this category. It is true that a significant majority of medical devices on the market may end up being considered high risk, but some key considerations must be made.

AI systems are classified as high risk under two main conditions. The first occurs when an AI system is designed to function as a safety component of a product or is itself a product regulated under EU harmonisation legislation listed in Annex I, such as the Medical Devices Regulation (MDR) or the In Vitro Diagnostic Medical Devices Regulation (IVDR). These systems are subject to a third-party conformity assessment under the relevant EU legislation (Article 6(1)). Importantly, compliance with the AI Act does not exempt the system from adhering to all other applicable harmonisation regulations required for market placement.

For instance, under the MDR, only Class I medical devices are exempt from third-party conformity assessments. By contrast, all medical devices using AI that fall into Class IIa or higher must comply with the requirements of the AI Act for high-risk systems, such as those applied to AI-assisted tools for medical imaging analysis (Busch et al. 2024).

The second condition for an AI system to be classified as high risk applies to technologies that are explicitly listed in Annex III as involving high-risk applications and which pose a substantial threat to the health, safety, or fundamental rights of individuals (Articles 6(2) and 6(3)). Examples of such high-risk use cases in healthcare include systems for emotion recognition or those used in emergency triage to prioritize patients. However, AI systems performing narrowly defined tasks may be exempt from the high-risk classification under certain conditions. For example, if the AI system is intended to carry out a specific procedural task, assist in improving the outcome of a human-performed activity, identify decision-making patterns, or highlight deviations without replacing prior human assessment, it may not fall under the high-risk category. Additionally, systems designed solely for preparatory tasks related to Annex III use cases may also be exempt (Article 6(3)).

Consequently, common administrative applications of AI in healthcare, such as medical text classification (e.g., ICD-10 coding) or structured radiology reporting, are generally not considered high risk unless they meet the first condition outlined above. To provide further guidance, the European Commission is expected to publish a more detailed list of high-risk and non-high-risk AI use cases within 18 months of the regulation's entry into force (Article 6(5)). This clarification will aid stakeholders in understanding the specific obligations for different AI systems and ensure consistent application of the AI Act.

Examples of high-risk AI-enabled medical devices include automated insulin pumps with glucose sensors, which ensure patient safety through real-time monitoring and delivery of medication, and AI systems for diagnostic imaging, such as those used to analyse CT scans for cancer detection. These devices are categorized as high risk because they not only influence essential healthcare decisions but also demand high reliability and rigorous conformity assessments to mitigate potential risks.

Beyond these specific examples, other applications of AI in the medical field also fall under high-risk classification. According to Busch et al. (2024), devices such as AI-assisted X-ray diagnostic tools, which help healthcare professionals detect abnormalities in imaging, and systems used in emergency triage, where AI assists in prioritizing patients based on urgency, exemplify the extensiveness of applications under this category. Similarly, AI applications in medical training assessments and asylum health risk screenings are also classified as high risk due to their significant implications for health, safety, and fundamental rights.

The inclusion of these devices in the high-risk category under the AI Act highlights the stringent regulatory oversight necessary for technologies that interact with vulnerable populations or perform critical healthcare functions. This classification ensures that such systems adhere to robust safety, accuracy, and performance standards, reinforcing trust in their deployment in sensitive contexts like healthcare, workforce management, and public services.

On the other hand, it is important to observe that certain AI-enabled medical devices can be classified by AI Act as medium or low risk. Examples include health monitoring applications, such as fitness trackers that provide general wellness information but do not make critical clinical decisions or perform medical diagnoses, and symptom checker tools that suggest users seek medical assistance based on self-reported symptoms but do not make autonomous clinical decisions. These devices pose fewer risks to patient safety and are subject to less stringent regulatory requirements under the AI Act.

This distinction is critical for understanding the regulatory landscape and avoiding overly broad generalizations about the classification of AI-enabled medical devices under the AI Act. While the AI Act classifies many medical devices with AI as high risk, this does not mean all such devices fall into this category automatically. The classification depends on factors such as the device's function, its potential impact on health and safety, and whether a third-party conformity assessment is required. The assertion that all medical devices are high risk oversimplifies the regulatory approach, failing to account for the nuances introduced by the AI Act. To accurately determine the classification of a specific device, both the MDR/IVDR and the AI Act must be consulted.

As observed by Porsdam Mann et al. (2024), a significant number of AI-based medical systems are expected to be classified as high risk under the AI Act. Supporting this view, Busch et al. (2024) report that approximately 75% of all commercial AI-enabled medical devices currently available on the market are associated with radiology, a field where such technologies are particularly prominent. Of these devices, nearly all are classified as Class IIa or higher under the Medical Devices Regulation (MDR), with only one exception. This classification places the vast majority of radiology-related AI systems firmly within the high-risk category as defined by the AI Act. The stringent requirements imposed on these devices reflect their critical role in healthcare delivery and the potential impact they have on patient safety and outcomes.

Consequently, these medical devices will be required to adhere to the stringent requirements for high-risk AI systems within 36 months of the AI Act coming into force on 1 August 2024, as mandated by Article 113(b). This compliance timeline underscores the urgent need for manufacturers to assess their products and ensure conformity with the AI Act's provisions, including rigorous risk management, transparency, and cybersecurity measures, to maintain market access and regulatory compliance.

For high-risk AI systems used in medical devices, the AI Act imposes stringent requirements throughout the system's lifecycle. These include ensuring high-quality data for training and validation, transparency of algorithms, explainability of decisions, and robust post-market monitoring. In this scenario, the AI Act seeks to maintain consistency across regulatory frameworks and existing sectoral legislation, such as the MDR and IVDR. Conformity assessment procedures for high-risk AI systems will incorporate these additional AI-specific requirements, ensuring comprehensive oversight without duplicating regulatory burdens. This harmonisation ensures that high-risk classifications are applied proportionately, avoiding unnecessary restrictions on devices that pose lower risks to health and safety.

The AI Act's risk-based approach is pivotal for fostering a regulatory environment that balances innovation and safety. By differentiating risk levels among medical devices, the regulation avoids treating all AI-powered tools the same, recognising that their impact and importance vary widely. This proportionate framework aligns with broader EU objectives to encourage the development of transformative medical technologies while safeguarding patients and public trust. It also ensures that only those devices posing substantial risks to health or fundamental rights are subject to the most stringent controls, allowing lower-risk tools to navigate less burdensome pathways to market approval.

The AI Act's Recitals indicate its provisions concerning high-risk AI systems will be aligned with existing sectoral legislation to promote consistency, prevent overlap, and minimise additional regulatory burdens. Specifically, for high-risk AI systems associated with products covered under the new legislative framework, such as machinery, medical devices, and toys, the AI requirements set out in the proposal will subsequently be verified as part of the conformity assessment procedures under existing specific legislation.

In summary, the integration of AI into medical devices presents both transformative potential and significant regulatory challenges. Harmonisation between the AI Act, MDR/IVDR, and PLD is essential to minimise duplication, streamline approval processes, and foster an environment conducive to innovation while ensuring safety, efficacy, and public trust in these groundbreaking technologies.

Bringing the discussion to the realm of a physician's liability when utilizing AI-based diagnostic technology, the impact of the EU's regulatory framework, particularly the AI Act, is significant. The regulation establishes clear obligations for developers, providers, and users of AI systems, including medical practitioners. While physicians are not directly involved in the design or implementation of these systems, their role in supervising, validating, and applying AI-generated results is pivotal and carries specific responsibilities under the AI Act.

The AI Act, especially through Article 14, mandates that high-risk AI systems, such as diagnostic tools, must be designed to allow for human oversight. This requirement specifically emphasizes that the performance of the AI system must be effectively supervised by human operators, such as physicians, to ensure that the system functions reliably and safely. For diagnostic tools, this means that physicians must actively monitor the system's outputs, validate its recommendations, and intervene when necessary, particularly when critical patient outcomes are at stake. Failure to supervise effectively may result in claims of negligence, even if the error originates from the AI system itself. This underscores the necessity for healthcare professionals to acquire sufficient technical understanding of AI functionalities to critically evaluate and challenge its outputs when required.

In addition, the regulation's requirements for transparency and explainability significantly affect medical practice. Articles 13 and 14 of the AI Act oblige developers to ensure that their systems provide interpretable and comprehensible outputs. However, if these transparency requirements are inadequately implemented, physicians may face challenges in justifying decisions made based on AI recommendations. This could lead to scenarios where liability is shared between the physician and the developer, particularly if the physician relies excessively on opaque or unclear AI-generated conclusions.

Finally, there is one final discussion proposed in this book regarding the regulation of AI within the European Union. The AI Act stands as a pivotal piece of legislation with significant global implications, particularly due to its broad scope, as outlined in Article 2. The Act applies not only within the EU but also extends to organisations and individuals outside its borders, including those in countries such as the United States and Brazil. Its provisions cover entities that develop and make AI systems available in the EU (providers), use AI systems or produce AI-generated outputs within the EU (deployers), import AI systems into the EU (importers), or distribute AI systems in the EU market (distributors).

This extraterritorial reach underscores the AI Act's importance as a cornerstone of governance, shaping the development, deployment, and regulation of AI technologies across borders. In this context, it is worth highlighting the example provided in the article *The EU AI Act: Implications for U.S. Health Care* by Porsdam Mann et al. (2024). The authors describe how the AI Act applies to deployers, such as a U.S. hospital collaborating with an EU research institution. If the hospital uses an AI-based diagnostic tool to analyse medical images of EU patients, it would be subject to the AI Act's deployer obligations. These include ensuring the system is used in accordance with the provider's instructions, maintaining human oversight, monitoring the system's operation, and promptly reporting any risks associated with the AI system. This example illustrates the extraterritorial reach of the AI Act and its practical implications for international organisations engaging with the EU market.

The authors mentioned above highlight that AI Act sets rigorous standards for AI systems, particularly in healthcare, to ensure transparency, accuracy, robustness, and cybersecurity. Transparency requires that users are informed when interacting with AI, with synthetic content clearly labelled. Moreover, accuracy standards demand that devices meet declared performance metrics throughout their lifecycle, while robustness ensures resilience to errors or environmental inconsistencies.

Finally, cybersecurity measures protect against unauthorised access or manipulation of the system.

For instance, an AI-based diagnostic system that fails to disclose its accuracy metrics in its documentation would violate the AI Act's accuracy requirements (Porsdam Mann et al. 2024). Furthermore, the Act mandates ongoing post-market monitoring to identify and address issues arising during real-world use and to ensure compliance with EU laws, such as copyright regulations for training data.

The AI Act's scope and regulatory requirements underscore its impact beyond Europe, imposing obligations on international stakeholders that engage with the EU market. It highlights the necessity for organisations in countries like the U.S. and Brazil to align their practices with the European legislation to ensure compliance, market access, and the safe and ethical deployment of AI technologies. As already mentioned, this demonstrates the AI Act's significance as a global benchmark for AI governance, shaping the development and use of AI systems worldwide.

In light of the general overview of the European landscape, it becomes clear that a single, universally applicable legal solution to address all damages arising from the use of AI across various fields is unachievable. An approach tailored to specific situations and sectors is necessary. In summary, 7 significant European legislative trends can be identified as follows:

1. *Expansion of the definition of product*: the definition of *product* has been broadened to include intangible items, such as software and AI systems. This ensures that emerging technologies are fully integrated into the scope of product liability laws.
2. *Broadening the concept of defect*: the concept of *defect* now encompasses the effects of machine learning, acknowledging that products can undergo changes and adaptations after being placed on the market. This shift accounts for the evolving nature of AI-driven technologies and raises new considerations for defences, such as development risks, particularly in scenarios where products autonomously alter their performance or features.
3. *Use of presumptions of fault and causation*: presumptions of fault and causation have been introduced to address the difficulties in proving defects or causal links in cases involving complex AI systems. This mechanism shifts the evidentiary burden in favour of victims, facilitating legal redress.
4. *Facilitation of evidence-gathering for victims*: victims are now granted the right to access critical data, such as the black box of automated decision-making systems. This reversal of the burden of proof ensures transparency and supports victims in substantiating their claims.
5. *Imposition of heightened transparency and accountability obligations*: manufacturers of high-risk AI systems must adhere to stricter post-market surveillance and transparency requirements. These obligations are designed to ensure ongoing compliance and reduce the risks associated with advanced AI technologies.
6. *Establishment of risk-based liability criteria*: liability rules are now tailored to the degree of autonomy and associated risks of the AI system. The framework

allows for strict or fault-based liability, depending on the classification and potential dangers of the technology.

7. *Implementation of mandatory civil liability insurance*: civil liability insurance is now compulsory for automated decision-making systems, particularly those classified as high risk. This measure provides an additional layer of protection for victims and ensures that operators can fulfil their liability obligations.

These legislative EU trends reflect a comprehensive effort to modernise liability frameworks, aligning them with the unique challenges posed by AI technologies while ensuring fair and effective remedies for those impacted. They also serve as a model for other legal systems worldwide, offering valuable guidance on how to address the complexities of regulating emerging technologies in a manner that balances innovation with accountability and the protection of fundamental rights.

An uncritical adoption of solutions developed for the European Union's legal framework into Brazilian law should be avoided (Medon 2022a, b). Nonetheless, the debates in the European context provide an excellent reference for fostering reflections and developing proposals aimed at delivering satisfactory legal responses to damages involving artificial intelligence in Brazil. It is also important to note that, despite certain similarities between the Brazilian Consumer Protection Code and Directive 85/374/EEC (repealed by Directive 2024/2853), there are clear distinctions between the two frameworks.

For instance, the European directive allows for the *development risk defence* (Article 7 of Directive 85/374/EEC; Article 11 of Directive 2024/2853), whereas the Brazilian Consumer Protection Code do not have such provision. Directive 2024/2853 enables Member States to allow manufacturers to invoke the development risk defence, also known as the *state-of-the-art defence*. This defence exempts manufacturers from liability for defects that could not have been discovered based on the state of scientific and technical knowledge at the time the product was placed on the market. However, the new directive preserve the possibility for Member States to maintain their previous decisions not to apply this defence within their legal systems, as expressly provided in its text.

A significant innovation introduced by Directive 2024/2853 concerns the treatment of products incorporating Artificial Intelligence (AI) components. Specifically, Article 11 establishes that the development risk defence cannot be invoked in relation to products that include AI components. This represents a clear shift from the previous framework under Directive 85/374/EEC, where the applicability of this defence was entirely at the discretion of Member States, regardless of the nature of the product. The rationale behind this restriction lies in the inherent characteristics of AI systems, particularly their complexity, opacity (the so-called "black-box" problem), capacity for autonomous learning, and the difficulty of predicting how such systems may behave over time. In this context, the legislator considered that consumers should not bear the risks associated with technological unpredictability or insufficient knowledge about AI-related defects at the time the product is placed on the market. Consequently, manufacturers of products with AI components are subject to strict liability for defects, even if those defects could not have been detected based on the scientific and technical knowledge available at the relevant time.

On the other hand, under the Brazilian Consumer Protection Code, as explained in subchapter 3.2.2 of this book, manufacturers are strictly liable for damages, even when risks were unforeseeable at the time of production. Liability is grounded in the failure of the product to meet legitimate safety expectations, irrespective of whether the risk was knowable. This underscores the Code's commitment to prioritising consumer safety and well-being over the unforeseeability of certain risks.

Furthermore, a substantial difference in these legal frameworks lies in the absence of a general clause of strict liability for product or enterprise risks in most European legal systems, in contrast to Article 927, sole paragraph, of the Brazilian Civil Code. This article imposes strict liability for damages arising from the inherent risks of a business or activity, regardless of fault, thereby embodying a broader principle of risk allocation within Brazilian law.

The Brazilian legal framework places significant emphasis on the precautionary and protective functions of liability, requiring businesses engaged in high-risk activities to bear the financial consequences of their operations, even when no fault can be established. Conversely, the European approach generally necessitates proof of a product defect and often permits defences such as the development risk defence, which exempts manufacturers from liability for unforeseeable risks at the time of market entry. This divergence underscores the distinct underlying philosophies: while the Brazilian Civil Code prioritises consumer and societal protection through a broad application of strict liability, European legal systems seek to balance liability with innovation and economic incentives, providing manufacturers with certain exemptions aligned with technological progress and the unpredictability of emerging risks.

To a large extent, this tension prompted the recent debate and reform of the directive on liability for defective products, aiming to accommodate technological evolution and the novel risks associated with emerging technologies.

In conclusion, the EU's regulatory efforts in the field of artificial intelligence, exemplified by the AI Act and the accompanying frameworks, reflect a comprehensive approach to balancing innovation with the protection of fundamental rights. By integrating principles of risk management, transparency, and accountability, these instruments aim to address the unique challenges posed by automated systems. The emphasis on clear liability parameters and ethical accountability underscores the EU's commitment to fostering trust and safety in AI technologies while ensuring they align with the Union's core values. This multifaceted strategy provides a robust foundation for the responsible development and deployment of AI, serving as a model for global regulatory standards in the Digital Age.

Finally, it is worth noting that, more recently, in 2025, a repositioning movement has been observed within the European Union regarding AI regulation. This shift became particularly evident during the AI Summit 2025, held on February in Paris, which brought together representatives from over 100 countries, including heads of state, international organisations, civil society, the private sector, and academia. Unlike previous regulatory discussions that shaped the AI Act (2024), the Paris

Summit's final declaration did not endorse restrictive measures on AI development and deployment. Instead, European leaders signalled a shift towards a more business-friendly regulatory approach, acknowledging the need to simplify rules, foster innovation, and align Europe's regulatory landscape with global trends. This repositioning reflects growing concerns that excessive regulation could stifle AI-driven economic growth and weaken Europe's technological competitiveness.

The United States' influence on this shift was particularly evident in US Vice President JD Vance's speech, in which he strongly criticised AI overregulation, warning that "excessive regulation of the AI sector could kill a transformative industry just as it's taking off". His remarks reinforced the Trump administration's pro-growth AI policies, which contrast sharply with the EU's traditionally cautious regulatory approach. This external pressure, combined with internal political and economic factors, appears to have shaped the European Commission's 2025 work programme.

Released in February 2025, under the title "Moving forward together: a bolder, simpler, faster union", the EU's programme marked a distinct shift from previous regulatory approaches. Among its most notable decisions was the withdrawal of 37 legislative proposals, including the AI Liability Directive (AILD), which was intended to address legal gaps in civil liability related to autonomous systems and facilitate claims for compensation in cases of AI-related harm. Initially designed to shift the burden of proof onto AI providers and facilitate access to technical documentation in legal disputes, the directive was seen as a major step in strengthening user protections. The regulation responded to concerns that current national liability laws, based on fault, were not suited for AI due to its complexity, autonomy, and opacity (black box effect), making it difficult for victims to prove responsibility. The proposal aimed to reduce legal uncertainty, prevent fragmentation of national laws, and support AI adoption in the EU by harmonizing liability rules.

Nevertheless, its withdrawal highlights the EU's changing priorities, now favouring economic growth over stringent legal constraints on AI. Beyond external influences, domestic political and economic factors have also contributed to this regulatory shift. French President Emmanuel Macron, under pressure from national AI companies—particularly the generative AI startup Mistral, seen as Europe's response to OpenAI—has actively lobbied for a more flexible regulatory framework. His opposition to including Foundation Models (FMs) within the scope of the AI Act was already evident in December 2023, when he led a joint initiative with Germany and Italy advocating for self-regulation of these models.

This push for a lighter regulatory approach reflects broader efforts to position Europe as a leader in AI innovation, ensuring that European firms can compete globally without excessive constraints. As mentioned before, The 2025 Paris Summit reinforced this shift, with European policymakers increasingly prioritising a regulatory approach that balances oversight with competitiveness. The withdrawal of the AI Liability Directive was widely interpreted as a signal of openness to investment and innovation, particularly in light of the EU and France's announcement of AI investment commitments worth hundreds of billions of euros.

This scenario also appears to be a gesture of "goodwill" towards the US, given the Biden-Trump administration's strong opposition to restrictive AI policies. From both a technical and political perspective, it is alleged that the directive had been losing momentum, especially after the adoption of the AI Act, which already regulates AI systems based on risk levels. A separate liability framework was increasingly seen as redundant and burdensome, particularly since the AI Act already addresses fundamental legal risks associated with AI deployment. The European Commission justified its decision by citing the lack of political consensus on the AI Liability Directive and announced that it would consider alternative approaches in the future.

Despite concerns that this shift signals deregulation, EU officials insist that the objective is to enhance competitiveness, not succumb to US tech industry pressure. Henna Virkkunen, the European Commission's executive vice-president for digital policy, stated that the EU seeks to support businesses rather than burden them with additional reporting obligations. The Commission also confirmed that the AI Act remains central to AI governance in Europe, classifying AI systems based on three risk levels and imposing transparency and compliance obligations on high-risk models such as GPT-4 and Google Gemini.

While the AI Act remains intact, the withdrawal of the AILD reflects a clear regulatory recalibration, suggesting that Europe is moving towards a more flexible and industry-friendly approach to AI governance. It remains to be seen what impact this regulatory shift will have on patients who suffer harm from these technologies in future litigations, particularly in the absence of a specific and uniform legal framework for civil liability in cases involving AI systems.

4.3 Frameworks and Perspectives for Regulation of Artificial Intelligence in Brazil

The regulation of artificial intelligence (AI) in Brazil is a pressing issue in the country's legislative agenda, exemplified by Bill No. 2338/23. This proposed framework aims to establish comprehensive rules governing the development, implementation, and use of AI systems across all sectors. Recently approved by the Federal Senate in December 2024, the bill now moves to the House of Representatives for further evaluation and voting. Its final text and effective date remain pending, as additional scrutiny and potential amendments may alter the current provisions before receiving presidential approval.

The primary distinction between the EU AI Act and Brazil's Proposed AI Regulation (Bill No. 2338/2023) lies in the inclusion of a dedicated chapter, specifically Chap. II (Articles 5–11), which establishes a comprehensive framework of rights related to artificial intelligence, alongside various aspects of AI governance. Article 5 provides that individuals affected by artificial intelligence systems are entitled to: (i) prior information regarding their interactions with such systems; (ii) explanations of decisions, recommendations, or predictions made by these systems; (iii) the ability to challenge decisions or predictions that produce legal effects or significantly impact their interests; (iv) the right to human determination and participation in AI-driven decisions, taking into account the context and state of the art in technological development; (v) protection against discrimination and the rectification of discriminatory biases, whether direct, indirect, unlawful, or abusive; and (vi) the right to privacy and the protection of personal data in accordance with relevant legislation. Furthermore, the law mandates that artificial intelligence operators provide, in a clear and easily accessible manner, the necessary procedures for individuals to exercise these rights.

Complementing this, Article 6 of the proposed regulation ensures that the defence of the interests and rights established under the legislation may be pursued both before competent administrative bodies and in court, whether individually or collectively, in accordance with the provisions of relevant legislation governing individual, collective, and diffuse remedies. This legal framework emphasises that obligations associated with artificial intelligence extend beyond regulatory authorities, encompassing accountability towards citizens and users who may be affected by these technologies. Consequently, the judiciary may assume an active role in enforcing AI legislation, providing individuals with a direct mechanism for seeking remedies through legal channels.

However, this approach has sparked considerable debate among legal scholars. Critics, including Maranhão (2024), contend that judicial enforcement of AI-related rights could engender legal uncertainty and inconsistency. The complexity and novelty of AI governance may result in courts issuing divergent interpretations and rulings on analogous issues, which not only complicates compliance for stakeholders but may also undermine trust in the legal framework governing artificial intelligence. Moreover, the integration of judicial oversight raises additional concerns regarding the judiciary's capacity to address the technical and multifaceted nature of AI systems effectively. Questions have been posed as to whether courts possess the requisite expertise to evaluate algorithmic decisions and their societal implications comprehensively. While judicial involvement adds a crucial layer of accountability, it simultaneously risks creating a fragmented body of precedent, potentially jeopardising the uniform application of AI regulations, as noted by Maranhão (2024).

It is important to observe that, while Brazil currently lacks a dedicated AI regulatory framework, several existing laws indirectly affect the development and use of AI systems. These laws provide a foundational legal environment and offer essential safeguards: (i) *General Data Protection Law* (Law No. 13,709/2018): governs the processing of personal data, requiring AI systems to comply with principles of transparency, purpose limitation, and security; (ii) *Consumer Protection Code* (Law No. 8078/1990): protects consumers from unfair practices, ensuring that products (AI technologies) used in consumer-facing sectors uphold their rights and interests; (iii) *Civil Code* (Law No. 10,406/2002): establishes general rules concerning civil liability, contractual obligations, and extracontractual liability. While these laws provide a preliminary regulatory foundation, they do not comprehensively address AI-specific risks, such as algorithmic bias, automated decision-making accountability, or ethical concerns in AI deployment. Consequently, discussions on establishing a dedicated AI regulatory framework in Brazil continue to evolve, drawing insights from international regulations such as the EU Artificial Intelligence Act and the UK's AI governance strategies.

Brazilian legal scholarship has increasingly aligned with the approach advocated within the European Union scenario, suggesting that rather than proposing the creation of an entirely new legislative framework—or a comprehensive legal regime—on liability involving artificial intelligence (AI), the existing legislative system should be adapted on a *case-by-case basis* (Tepedino and Guia da Silva 2019).

A noteworthy contribution in this regard is the proposal by Filipe Medon (2022), which draws upon European experience while also considering the peculiarities of the Brazilian legal system. He suggests a *dual system of civil liability for AI*, delineating between the internal or personal liability of agents (of a subjective nature) and external liability (towards consumers and individuals affected by automated decisions—of an objective nature).

Concerning the civil liability of manufacturers in AI, as previously discussed in an earlier chapter of this book, Brazilian law provides for liability arising from defective products or services under the Consumer Code (CDC). The objective liability of manufacturers is considered the most appropriate mechanism to protect victims from damages involving automated systems, given the unique challenges that will be further elaborated upon below. Article 12, paragraph 1 of the CDC, stipulates that a product is considered defective when it "fails to provide the safety that one may legitimately expect," taking into account: "I - its presentation; II - the use and risks that may reasonably be expected of it; III - the time it was placed on the market". Conversely, paragraph 2 clarifies that a product is not deemed defective "merely because another of superior quality has been introduced into the market".

A contentious issue within Brazilian legal doctrine, as already explored in this book, is the potential applicability of an exclusionary cause of liability when damage arises from an event beyond the manufacturer's foreseeability—referred to as the *development or unknowable risk*. In the context of AI systems, there is the potential for autonomous decision-making, independent of the manufacturer's or algorithm developer's intent, combined with self-learning and experience accumulation. This capacity could lead to unpredictable outcomes.

At first glance, it might be argued that a manufacturer of an automated decision-making system, when facing legal claims, could rely on the defence that the product, at the time of its market introduction, was equipped with the highest accuracy and technology in line with the scientific knowledge of that period. This argument could ostensibly justify the exclusion of liability for unforeseeable behaviour resulting from machine learning.

However, as Rosenvald (2020) and Barbosa (2021) have persuasively argued, the advent of new AI technologies necessitates an updated interpretation of the concept of *defect* in legal frameworks worldwide. This concept should evolve to encompass a *breach of a general duty of safety*, meaning the standard of safety required in the realm of AI and similar technologies (Soares 2019). The unpredictable effects of machine learning, in this sense, represent a disparity between the legitimately expected standard of quality of AI and what is actually delivered by the manufacturer, particularly concerning its safety (Nalin and Nogaroli 2020).

In this context, the notion of *defect* is identified as an unlawful circumstance, representing a deviation between an expected standard of quality of a product or activity and the insecurity to which the psychophysical integrity of the consumer is actually exposed (Rosenvald 2022). This evolving understanding underscores the need for a proactive approach to AI-related liability, ensuring that legal protections keep pace with technological advancements and the inherent risks they entail.

The degree of care required of a supplier to ensure safety, as articulated by Soares (2019), depends on the specific circumstances of each case. She contends that this duty of care increases proportionately with the level of risk associated with the provision of products or services, as well as the characteristics of their intended recipients. Moreover, the implementation of algorithmic activities and the unpredictable events inherent to machine learning encompass the concept of an *inherent risk* associated with the activity itself. This aligns with the provisions of Articles 927, sole paragraph, and 931 of the Brazilian Civil Code. It is worth noting that this provision introduces a general clause regarding the risk inherent to certain activities under Brazilian law. This clause underscores the recognition that certain activities inherently carry risks, thereby establishing a framework of strict liability, where those engaging in such activities are liable for damages caused by their inherent risks, irrespective of negligence or fault.

Thus, the manufacturer cannot invoke the self-learning capability of the technology as an unforeseeable defect at the time the product was introduced into circulation, as this feature is intrinsic to the technology itself (machine learning). Furthermore, it constitutes a breach of a general duty of safety (Godinho and Rosenvald 2019).

In addition to the aforementioned update to the concept of defect, it is essential to recognise that any damage caused by AI will necessarily stem from human error, under the principle of *res ipsa loquitur*—such as an error in design, manufacturing, assembly, or the provision of information regarding the product's safety and appropriate use. In such cases, the manufacturer bears the burden of proving an exclusionary cause of liability (such as the exclusive fault of the victim or a third party, or a fortuitous event or force majeure).

The principle of *res ipsa loquitur*, Latin for *the thing speaks for itself*, is a doctrine that infers liability from the very nature of the damage or outcome, even in the absence of direct evidence of the defendant's conduct in relation to the harmful event. For liability to arise in these cases, the following elements must be established: a duty, a breach of that duty, causation, and damage. When a harmful outcome is observed, it is accepted as circumstantial evidence that the event would not have occurred without the defendant's conductaction. The elements of duty of care and breach can be inferred from the nature of the harmful event itself, even without direct evidence of the defendant's actions.

As Pires and Peteffi da Silva (2017) explain, this approach makes no distinction between cases involving defects in the design or production of AI and cases where damage caused by the independent acts of AI occurs while the product is functioning perfectly but presents significant risks due to the state of the art. In practice, whether the damage results from an algorithm programming error or an effect arising from machine learning, it will inevitably be classified as a product defect.

With respect to the Brazilian Consumer Code (CDC), and building upon the previously discussed arguments regarding the concept of product defect (as applied to AI systems), as well as drawing inspiration from Article 6 of the new Product Liability Directive (Directive (EU) 2024/2853) in the European Union, it is proposed—*de lege ferenda* proposed—that the concept of *defect* within the CDC be expanded. This expansion would encompass the effects of products arising from machine learning, thereby introducing a new understanding of exclusionary liability clauses and the development risk doctrine.

To achieve this, it is suggested that a new subsection IV be added to paragraph 1 of Article 12 of the CDC, as follows: Article 12, § 1°: "A product is deemed defective when it fails to provide the safety that one may legitimately expect, taking into account relevant circumstances, including: I - its presentation; II - the use and risks reasonably expected of it; III - the time it was placed on the mark et; *IV - the inherent effects of the product arising from its capacity for self-learning after being placed on the market*".

This proposed amendment aims to modernise the Brazilian Consumer Code by addressing the complexities introduced by AI systems and their capacity for autonomous learning, thereby providing a clearer legal framework for assessing product defects and determining liability in cases involving advanced technological products.

It is also worth highlighting that, regarding the manufacturer of an AI system, the strict liability established under Article 14, caput, of the CDC will apply whenever the defect in the product or service is the proximate cause of harm to the consumer. However, the substantial complexity in such cases will inevitably concern the evidentiary challenge of establishing the causal nexus.

In the European context, the new directive (Directive (EU) 2024/2853, Article 10) on product liability establishes the possibility of presuming either the defective quality of a product, the causal link between the defect in an AI system and the damage, or both, under certain conditions. These conditions include: (1) excessive difficulty in proving the case due to technical and/or scientific complexity; (2) the claimant providing sufficiently relevant evidence demonstrating that the product contributed to the damage; and (3) the likelihood that the product is defective and that the harm suffered is of a type typically associated with such a defect, making the defective quality a probable cause of the harm. The directive also allows the defendant to rebut any of these presumptions.

In this regard, Barbosa (2022) illustrates the concept of presumed causation with a practical example. She explains that the presumption of fault, combined with the presumption of causation, as proposed in the European regulatory framework, provides greater clarity in resolving such disputes. For instance, in situations where it is uncertain whether the damage resulted from the system's initial programming, subsequent security updates, or the data collected by the system, liability would rest with the party responsible for the system, as defined in the directive. This responsibility could, however, be excluded if one of the potentially liable parties can prove that the harm did not result from the realisation of the relevant risk or from a failure to fulfil any specific duties.

This approach shifts the burden arising from the system's technological opacity onto the party in control of the AI system, thereby reducing the scope of corporate opacity and ensuring accountability for the harm caused. In essence, the party responsible for the system must bear the consequences of its inherent complexity unless they can clearly establish that the damage was not attributable to their conduct or product.

In the Brazilian legal context, it would be feasible to consider the application of the aforementioned solution, which allows for the presumption of either the defective quality of a product or the causal link between the defect and the resulting harm. This approach finds support among Brazilian legal scholars, notably Hironaka (2005) and Mulholland (2010), who advocate the view that the concept of causation within the Brazilian legal system is undergoing a process of flexibilization. They further emphasise the necessity of a presumption of causality as a legal tool in certain contexts.

According to Mulholland (2010), establishing such a presumption of causation and liability requires three steps: (i) the harmful event must be accurately described, identifying both the damage and the conduct or activity that is purportedly linked to it; (ii) the causal chain must be correctly decomposed, pinpointing the sine qua non cause(s) of the damage; and (iii) statistical techniques must be employed through expert analysis to scientifically calculate the probability that a specific activity or conduct caused the damage.

However, in scenarios where only a single incident has been recorded and no similar events exist, it becomes impossible to predict statistically whether the outcome was due to a calculable probability. In such cases, Mulholland (2010) refers to the *Theory of Logical Probability*, which does not rely on numerical or percentage criteria to establish causation. Instead, it uses logical and inductive reasoning to infer the causal relationship.

This perspective is particularly relevant to the challenge of determining the defect in an AI system or the causal link to the harm caused. Such challenges can be addressed by recognising the degree of plausibility of the causal connection. This approach is akin to the concept of loss of chance, as advocated by Frada (2010), who highlights the challenges posed by new risks in contemporary society worldwide. In many cases, it is either impossible or extremely difficult to establish a clear and unequivocal link between a specific event and the resulting harm, as harmful causal processes are often neither singular nor transparent.

To mitigate the evidentiary difficulties in proving causation in adverse events involving AI systems, the establishment of presumptions of causation is recommended. This mechanism assigns certain harms to specific risk domains, reinforcing the preventive function of civil liability. Such liability is imposed on the agent who increased the likelihood of harm by failing to meet their duty of safety or care.

This presumption of causation—where any doubt about the causal link is interpreted in favour of the victim—is justified by the *social function of contracts*, as explained by Rosenvald (2007). This function serves a critical role in the provision of healthcare services involving AI, ensuring that individuals are not rendered victims of their own vulnerabilities in contractual relationships. Even under the principle of contractual freedom, such relationships must not instrumentalise individuals, reducing them to mere means for achieving external objectives, rather than treating them as ends in themselves.

In this context, the standards of proof become highly pertinent. Maranhão (2006) notes that, in judicial decision-making, the most common *standards of proof* include *preponderance of evidence*, *clear and convincing evidence*, and the *inference to the best explanation*. In consumer relations, Article 6, item VIII, of the CDC stipulates the consumer's basic right to have their defence facilitated, including the reversal of the burden of proof in civil proceedings. This reversal is contingent upon the judge's determination of the plausibility of the consumer's allegations and their technical vulnerability, based on ordinary experience.

The recognition of consumer vulnerability is a fundamental principle of Brazil's National Consumer Relations Policy (Article 4, item I, CDC). This principle significantly distinguishes Brazilian legislation in the field of comparative law, serving as a premise to justify and guide consumer protection, including in judicial contexts (Article 6, item VIII, CDC). As Miragem (2002) notes, these protections derive from constitutional foundations and public policy norms aimed at serving the consumer's social interests.

Maranhão (2006) also observes that the reversal of the burden of proof in Brazilian law constitutes a *reduction in the standard of proof*, effectively serving as an example of a less stringent evidentiary requirement to facilitate consumer rights.

Following the CDC's goal of providing effective legal protection by facilitating consumers' defence in court, the author of this book proposes that, in certain situations, consumers should be granted the right to request access to the black box of an AI system during legal proceedings. To address concerns about trade secrets, judges should adopt specific measures to ensure confidentiality, such as mandating that inspections of algorithms and databases be conducted under seal or within a framework that protects sensitive proprietary information. This balanced approach seeks to uphold consumer rights while respecting the legitimate interests of manufacturers and developers.

In the European Union, the new Product Liability Directive explicitly recognises the possibility of a right to request disclosure of evidence related to an AI system suspected of causing harm (Article 9(4)). It also establishes a presumption of non-compliance if the manufacturer fails to provide such evidence (Article 10(2)(a)).

Adopting a similar approach within Brazilian law, the author of this book proposes a *de lege ferenda amendment* to Article 6 of the CDC to include a new subsection IV, addressing consumers' basic rights. The suggested wording is as follows: "Article 6. Consumers' basic rights include: (…) *IV – In cases where the burden of proof is reversed in favour of the consumer in civil proceedings, the disclosure of the black box of an autonomous system must be required at the judge's discretion, with due respect for trade secrets. Failure to comply shall result in a presumption of the product's defectiveness against the manufacturer*".

In conclusion, even when harm caused by AI falls outside the manufacturer's or programmer's expectations, and establishing a causal nexus is exceedingly difficult or impossible, these parties may still be held liable. This is predicated on the occurrence of a harmful event during the interaction between humans and the AI system, provided the criteria for presumed causation are met. Such liability exists regardless of whether the consumer was adequately warned about potential risks.

Finally, it is important to emphasise that while the CDC already provides mechanisms for reversing the burden of proof against manufacturers of allegedly defective AI systems (Article 6, item VIII, CDC), the proposed right to request access to the AI system's black box is a *de lege ferenda suggestion* put forward by the author of this book. This proposal seeks to address the heightened vulnerability of consumers and the need for stronger protections in cases involving autonomous systems. It should be noted, however, that the Brazilian legal community continues to engage in ongoing discussions on this matter, reflecting diverse perspectives on how best to balance consumer protection with the promotion of technological innovation.

In light of the foregoing, two key points must be considered when analysing liability involving AI in the healthcare sector. Firstly, the absence of presumptions of causation to address the evidentiary challenges posed by AI, particularly its lack of transparency in the machine learning process, would reduce manufacturers' incentives to invest in preventive measures and resources to mitigate potential harm. Such presumptions not only promote accountability but also reinforce the manufacturer's duty to ensure safety in the deployment of AI systems.

Secondly, it is essential to balance this need for accountability with the recognition of the significant technological advancements brought about by AI in healthcare. These innovations have the potential to revolutionise patient care and improve health outcomes. To avoid disincentivising manufacturers from developing new technologies, the adoption of mandatory civil liability insurance for medical devices equipped with AI is proposed. This approach would serve as a protective mechanism, ensuring compensation for potential harm while fostering a regulatory environment that supports innovation.

By mandating liability insurance, manufacturers would remain accountable for their products without bearing prohibitive risks that might stifle technological progress. At the same time, this system would provide greater security for consumers and patients, ensuring that they are adequately protected in the event of harm arising from the use of AI-enabled medical devices. This dual approach strikes a balance between fostering innovation and safeguarding public trust in emerging technologies.

Regarding the nature of medical civil liability, when a harmful event arises in the context of an AI medical device, significant considerations emerge under the framework of Bill No. 2338/2023. This legislative approach aligns with risk-based regulation, akin to the provisions established by the EU AI Act.

Under this framework, the liability of AI actors is deemed strict for high-risk AI systems, as stipulated in Article 27, §1: "In cases involving high-risk or excessively risky AI systems, the supplier or operator shall be held strictly liable for any damage caused, proportional to their degree of involvement in the harm". This category explicitly includes AI systems deployed for "healthcare purposes, including those designed to assist in medical diagnoses and procedures" (Article 17, IX).

Article 17 provides an extensive list of high-risk AI applications, including systems used in critical infrastructure management, education and professional training, recruitment and employment, eligibility for public and private services, credit assessment, emergency response prioritisation, justice administration, autonomous vehicles, healthcare diagnostics, biometric identification, criminal investigation, and migration management. These applications are deemed high-risk due to their significant societal impact and the potential for harm if misused.

Article 18 empowers the relevant authority to update the list of high-risk AI systems by considering various criteria, such as the scale of implementation, potential negative impacts on rights and freedoms, discriminatory or irreversible harmful effects, and the system's level of transparency and auditability. This process must include regulatory consultations, public hearings, and an impact assessment, ensuring that the framework remains adaptive and reflective of evolving technological advancements.

It is worth noting a distinction between Bill No. 2338/2023 and the EU AI Act. Under the proposed Brazilian legislation, all medical devices are categorised as high-risk by default (Article 17, IX). In contrast, the EU AI Act allows for a nuanced discussion regarding the classification of certain medical devices (Article 6), as elaborated in the preceding subchapter of this book. Furthermore, even where the AI system is not classified as high-risk, it can be presumed the culpability of the party responsible for the harm. In such cases, the burden of proof is shifted in favour of the victim, pursuant to Article 27, §2: "The fault of the party causing the damage shall be presumed, with the burden of proof being reversed in favour of the victim".

Finally, it is important to note that Article 29 of the proposed legislation states that "in cases of civil liability arising from damages caused by artificial intelligence systems within consumer relations, the provisions of Law No. 8,078, of 11 September 1990, shall apply". Accordingly, in the context of the doctor-patient relationship, which is governed by the Brazilian Consumer Code (CDC), the personal liability of the physician, as a liberal professional, continues to be assessed based on fault, pursuant to §4 of Article 14. This demonstrates the legislator's intent to preserve the existing legal framework for professional liability, ensuring consistency in the evaluation of fault even in cases involving AI systems.

References

Abràmoff MD et al (2018) Pivotal trial of an autonomous AI-based diagnostic system for detection of diabetic retinopathy in primary care offices. NPJ Digital Medicine 1(1):39

Ali R (2023) Performance of ChatGPT and GPT-4 on neurosurgery written board examinations. Available via Medrxiv. https://www.medrxiv.org/content/10.1101/2023.03.25.23287743v1.full.pdf

Alper BS et al (2004) How much effort is needed to keep up with the literature relevant for primary care? J Med Libr Assoc 92(4):429–437

American Medical Association (2023) Augmented intelligence research. Physician sentiments around the use of AI in health care: motivations, opportunities, risks, and use cases. https://www.ama-assn.org/system/files/physician-ai-sentiment-report.pdf

American Medical Association (2024) Augmented intelligence in medicine. https://www.ama--assn.org/practice-management/digital/augmented-intelligence-medicine

Ariyaratne S et al (2023) A comparison of ChatGPT-generated articles with human-written articles. Skeletal Radiol 52(9):1755–1758

Baptista dos Santos R (2023) A responsabilidade digital na lei da telessaúde. O que é isso?. Available via Migalhas de Responsabilidade Civil. https://www.migalhas.com.br/coluna/migalhas-de-responsabilidade-civil/381128/a-responsabilidade-digital-na-lei-da-telessaude-o-que-e-isso. Acesso em: 14 fev. 2023

Barbosa MM (2021) Responsabilidade civil pelos danos causados por entes dotados de inteligência artificial Mafalda Miranda Barbosa. In: Barbosa MM, Braga Netto FP, César Silva M, Faleiros Júnior JLM (eds) Direito digital e inteligência artificial: diálogos entre Brasil e Europa. Foco, Indaiatuba

Barbosa MM (2022) Sistemas autónomos e responsabilidade autoria e causalidade. Revista de Direito da Responsabilidade 4:1122–1173

Barrie R (2024) Ultromics's EchoGo misses primary endpoint in heart disease trial. While the trial's endpoint did not show statistical significance, the AI-augmentation tool showed promise for less-experienced clinicians. Available via Clinical Trials Arena. https://www.clinicaltrialsarena.com/news/ultromicss-echogo-misses-primary-endpoint-in-heart-disease-trial/

Boddington P (2017) Towards a code of ethics for artificial intelligence. Springer, Cham

Brady AP et al (2024) Developing, purchasing, implementing and monitoring AI tools in radiology: practical considerations. A multi-society statement from the ACR, CAR, ESR, RANZCR & RSNA. Can Assoc Radiol J 75(2):226–244

Brag J (2020) Artificial intelligence in medical imaging. In: Nordlinger B, Villani C, Rus D (eds) Healthcare and artificial intelligence. Springer, Cham

Buijs E et al (2024) Clinical impact of AI in radiology department management: a systematic review. Radiol Med 129(11):1656–1666

Busch F et al (2024) Navigating the European Union artificial intelligence act for healthcare. NPJ Digit Med 7(1):210

Cerka P, Grigien J, Sirbikyt G (2015) Liability for damages caused by artificial intelligence. Computer Law & Security Review 31(3):376–389

Chinese Academy of Sciences (2022) LAIP – Linking Artificial Intelligence Principles. International Research Center for AI Ethics and Governance, Institute of Automation. Available at: https://www.linking-ai-principles.org/

Comandé G (2019a) Intelligenza artificiale e responsabilità tra liability e accountability. il carattere trasformativo dell'IA e il problema della responsabilità in Analisi Giuridica dell'Economia. In: Nuzzo A, Olivieri G (eds) Analisi giuridica dell'economia: studi e discussioni sul diritto dell'impresa. Il Mulino, Bologna

Comandé G (2019b) Multilayered (accountable) liability for artificial intelligence. In: Lohsse S, Schulze R, Staudenmayer D (eds) Liability for artificial intelligence and the internet of things. Nomos, Baden-Baden

Crigger E et al (2022) Trustworthy augmented intelligence in health care. J Med Syst 46(2):12

Dantas E, Nogaroli R (2020) Consentimento informado do paciente frente às novas tecnologias da saúde (telemedicina, cirurgia robótica e inteligência artificial). Lex Medicinae—Revista Portuguesa de Direito da Saúde 13:25–63

Dantas E, Nogaroli R (2021) The rise of robotics and artificial intelligence in healthcare: new challenges for the doctrine of informed consent. Med Law 4:15–62

Dignum V (2019) Responsible artificial intelligence. How to develop and use AI in a responsible way. Springer, Cham

Ehrhardt Júnior M (2014) Responsabilidade civil pelo inadimplemento da boa-fé. Fórum, Belo Horizonte

European Commission (2021) Public health: stronger rules on medical devices. https://ec.europa.eu/commission/presscorner/detail/en/ip_21_2617
Faleiros Júnior JLM (2021) Discriminação por algoritmos de Inteligência Artificial: a responsabilidade civil, os vieses e o exemplo das tecnologias baseadas em luminância. In: Barbosa MM, Braga Netto FP, César Silva M, Faleiros Júnior JLM (eds) Direito digital e inteligência artificial: diálogos entre Brasil e Europa. Foco, Indaiatuba
Felipe MG (2022) A aplicação do compliance em hospitais privados para prevenção de erro médico e mitigação de danos. Lawinter Editions, New York
Ferreira AE (2016) Responsabilidade civil extracontratual por danos causados por robôs autônomos. Revista Portuguesa do Dano Corporal 27:39–63
Ferreira AE, Pereira AGD (2021) Uma ética para a medicina pós-humana: propostas ético-jurídicas para a mediação das relações entre humanos e robôs na saúde. In: Rosenvald N, Menezes JB, Dadalto L (eds) Responsabilidade civil e medicina, 2nd edn. Foco, Indaiatuba
Fjeld J et al (2020) Principled Artificial Intelligence: mapping consensus in ethical and rights-based approaches to principles for AI. Berkman Klein Center for Internet & Society. Available at: https://dash.harvard.edu/handle/1/42160420
Floridi L (2023) Artificial intelligence: principles, challenges, and opportunities. Oxford University Press, Oxford
Ford RA, Price WN (2016) Privacy and accountability in black-box medicine. Mich Telecommun Technol Law Rev 23:1–43
Frada MAC (2010) Direito civil, responsabilidade civil: o método do caso. Almedina, Coimbra
Future of Life Institute (2023) Pause giant AI experiments: an open letter. Available at: https://futureoflife.org/open-letter/pause-giant-ai-experiments/
Godinho AM, Rosenvald N (2019) Inteligência artificial e a responsabilidade civil dos robôs e de seus fabricantes. In: Rosenvald N, Dresch RFV, Wesendonck T (eds) Responsabilidade civil: novos riscos. Foco, Indaiatuba
Hironaka GMFN (2005) Responsabilidade pressuposta. Del Rey, Belo Horizonte
Jie Z, Zhiying Z, Li L (2021) A meta-analysis of Watson for oncology in clinical application. Sci Rep 11(1):5792
Jonas H (1979) Das Prinzip Verantwortung: Versuch einer Ethik für die technologische Zivilisation. Suhrkamp Verlag, Frankfurt. Portuguese edition: Jonas H (2007) O princípio da responsabilidade. Ensaio de uma ética para a civilização tecnológica (trans: Lisboa M, Montez LB). Contraponto, Rio de Janeiro
Kung TH et al (2023) Performance of ChatGPT on USMLE: potential for AI-assisted medical education using large language models. PLoS Digit Health 2(2):e0000198
Ledford H (2019) Millions of black people affected by racial bias in health-care algorithms. Nature 574(7780):608–609
Ledley RS, Lusted LB (1959) Reasoning foundations of medical diagnosis. Science 130(3366):9–21
Lee P, Goldberg C, Kohane I (2023) The AI revolution in medicine: GPT-4 and beyond. Pearson, London
Lottenberg C, Ellen da Silva P, Klajner S (2019) A revolução digital na saúde: como a inteligência artificial e a internet das coisas tornam o cuidado mais humano, eficiente e sustentável. Editora dos Editores, São Paulo
Mahler T (2022) Between risk management and proportionality: the risk-based approach in EU's Artificial Intelligence Act Proposal. In: Colonna L, Greenstein S (eds) Nordic yearbook of law and informatics 2020–2021: law in the era of artificial intelligence. The Swedish Law and Informatics Research Institute, Oslo
Maranhão CA (2006) Standards de prova no processo civil brasileiro. Revista Judiciária do Paraná 1(1):221–258
Maranhão J (2024) AI and Law in Brazil with Juliano Maranhão. Online lecture delivered at Podcast "Monday Bagel Bytes: Legal Tech & AI Insights", on September 16, 2024. https://www.youtube.com/watch?v=p4mGveKOW2k

Maranhão J, Santos TTC, Wassermann R (2024) Artificial Intelligence in Brazilian Law Courts: risks and governance standards. In: Anais da Conferência latino-americana de ética em inteligência artificial. https://doi.org/10.5753/laai-ethics.2024.32456

Medeiros da Silva L et al (2021) Independent real-world application of a clinical-grade automated prostate cancer detection system. J Pathol 254(2):147–158

Medon F (2022a) Inteligência artificial e responsabilidade civil: autonomia, riscos e solidariedade, 2nd edn. JusPodivm, São Paulo

Medon F (2022b) Tendências para a responsabilidade civil da Inteligência Artificial na Europa: a participação humana ressaltada. Available via Migalhas de Responsabilidade Civil. https://www.migalhas.com.br/coluna/migalhas-de-responsabilidade-civil/335801/tendencias-para-a-responsabilidade-civil-da-inteligencia-artificial-na-europa%2D%2Da-participacao-humana-ressaltada

Miotto R et al (2016) Deep patient: an unsupervised representation to predict the future of patients from the electronic health records. Sci Rep 6(1):1–10

Miragem B (2002) O direito do consumidor como direito fundamental: consequências jurídicas de um conceito. Revista de Direito do Consumidor 43:111–132

Mittelstadt BD, Floridi L (2016) The ethics of biomedical big data. Cham: Springer

Mittelstadt BD (2021) The impact of artificial intelligence on the doctor-patient relationship. Available via Council of Europe. https://rm.coe.int/inf-2022-5-report-impact-of-ai-on-doctor-patient-relations-e/1680a68859

Mulholland CS (2010) A responsabilidade civil por presunção de causalidade. GZ Editora, Rio de Janeiro

Nalin P, Nogaroli R (2020) Perspectivas sobre ética e responsabilidade civil no contexto dos robôs inteligentes de assistência à saúde. In: Campos AF, Berlini LF (eds) Temas contemporâneos de responsabilidade civil: teoria e prática. D'Plácido, Belo Horizonte

Negri SMCA (2021) Sergio Marcos Carvalho de Ávila. Personalidade, responsabilidade e classificação dos riscos na Inteligência Artificial e na robótica. Available via Migalhas de Responsabilidade civil. https://www.migalhas.com.br/coluna/migalhas-de-responsabilidade-civil/347862/personalidade-responsabilidade-e-classificacao-dos-riscos-na-ia

Nogaroli R, Faleiros Júnior JLM (2023) Ethical challenges of artificial intelligence in medicine and the triple semantic dimensions of algorithmic opacity with its repercussions to patient consent and medical liability. In: Antunes HS et al (eds) Multidisciplinary perspectives on artificial intelligence and the law. Springer, Cham

Nordlinger B, Villani C, Rus D (eds) (2020) Healthcare and artificial intelligence. Springer, Cham

Nunes HC, Guimarães RMC, Dadalto L (2022) Desafios bioéticos do uso da inteligência artificial em hospitais. Revista de Bioética 30(1):82–93

Obermeyer Z et al (2019) Dissecting racial bias in an algorithm used to manage the health of populations. Science 366(6464):447–453

Oliveira L et al (2022) PathoSpotter: computational intelligence applied to nephropathology. In: Bezerra da Silva Junior G, Nangaku M (eds) Innovations in nephrology. Springer, Cham

Pagallo U (2013) The laws of robots: crimes, contracts, and torts. Springer, London

Paranjape K et al (2019) Introducing artificial intelligence training in medical education. JMIR Med Educ 5(2):e16048

Pasquale F (2015) The black box society: the secret algorithms that control money and information. Harvard University Press, Cambridge

Pasquale F (2020) New laws of robotics: defending human expertise in the age of AI. The Belknap Press of Harvard University Press, Cambridge

Pires TCF, Peteffi da Silva R (2017) A responsabilidade civil pelos atos autônomos da inteligência artificial: notas iniciais sobre a resolução do Parlamento Europeu. Revista Brasileira de Políticas Públicas 7(3):238–254

Poplin R et al (2018) Prediction of cardiovascular risk factors from retinal fundus photographs via deep learning. Nature Biomedical Engineering 2(3):158–164

Porsdam Mann S, Cohen IG, Minssen T (2024) The EU AI Act: implications for US health care. NEJM AI 1(11):AIp2400449

Riotto E et al (2024) Accuracy of autonomous artificial intelligence-based diabetic retinopathy screening in real-life clinical practice. J Clin Med 13(16):4776

Robbins R (2020) An experiment in end-of-life care: tapping AI's cold calculus to nudge the most human of conversations. Available via Stat News. https://www.statnews.com/2020/07/01/end-of-life-artificial-intelligence

Robbins R, Brodwin E (2020) An invisible hand: patients aren't being told about the AI systems advising their care. Available via Stat News. https://www.statnews.com/2020/07/15/artificial-intelligence-patient-consent-hospitals

Robles G (2009) La justicia en los juegos: Dos ensayos de teoría comunicacional del derecho. Trotta; Madrid

Rodotà S (2006) La vita nella società della sorveglianza: la privacy oggi. Laterza, Roma-Bari. Portuguese edition: Rodotà S (2008) A vida na sociedade da vigilância: a privacidade hoje (trans: Doneda D, Doneda LC). Renovar, Rio de Janeiro

Rosenvald N (2007) A função social do contrato. Revista MPMG Jurídico 9

Rosenvald N (2019) A responsabilidade civil pelo ilícito lucrativo: o disgorgement e a indenização restitutória. JusPodivum, Salvador

Rosenvald N (2020) Foundations of civil liability in the face of the challenges of new technologies. Online lecture delivered at the meeting of the research group in Philosophy of Private Law, Federal University of Rio Grande do Sul (Brazil), on May 28, 2020. https://www.facebook.com/filosofiadpufrg

Rosenvald N (2022) A falácia da responsabilidade subjetiva na regulação da IA. Available via Migalhas de Proteção de Dados. https://www.migalhas.com.br/coluna/migalhas-de-protecao-de-dados/365913/a-falacia-da-responsabilidade-subjetiva-na-regulacao-da-ia

Rosenvald N, Faleiros Júnior JLM (2021) Accountability e mitigação da responsabilidade civil na Lei Geral de Proteção de Dados. In: Frazão A, Cueva RVB (eds) Compliance e políticas de proteção de dados. Thomson Reuters, São Paulo

Rosenvald N, Faleiros Júnior JLM (2022) A despersonalização da personalidade: reflexos sobre o corpo eletrônico e o artigo 17 da Lei Geral de Proteção de Dados Pessoais. In: Colombo C, Engelmann W, Faleiros Júnior JLM (eds) Tutela jurídica do corpo eletrônico: novos desafios ao direito digital. Foco, Indaiatuba

Ross C (2021a) As the FDA clears a flood of AI tools, missing data raise troubling questions on safety and fairness. Available via Stat News. https://www.statnews.com/2021/02/03/fda-clearances-artificial-intelligence-data

Ross C (2021b) Machine learning is booming in medicine. It's also facing a credibility crisis. Available via Stat News. https://www.statnews.com/2021/06/02/machine-learning-ai-methodology-research-flaws

Rudnicka AR et al (2022) Artificial intelligence-enabled retinal vasculometry for prediction of circulatory mortality, myocardial infarction and stroke. Br J Ophthalmol 106(12):1722–1729

Sá MFF, Naves BTO (2021) Bioética e biodireito, 5th edn. Foco, Indaiatuba

Salim SV et al (2020) Heart disease and stroke statistics-2020 update: a report from the American Heart Association. Am Heart Assoc Circ 141(9):e139–e596

Schaefer F (2023) Telessaúde e responsabilidade digital na lei 14.510/22. Available via Migalhas de Responsabilidade Civil. https://www.migalhas.com.br/coluna/migalhas-de-responsabilidade-civil/381503/telessaude-e-responsabilidade-digital-na-lei-14-510-22

Schwab K (2017) The fourth industrial revolution. Crown Currency, New York

Shaban-Nejad A, Michalowski M (2020) From precision medicine to precision health: a full angle from diagnosis to treatment and prevention. In: Shaban-Nejad, Arash; Michalowski, Martin (Org.). Precision health and medicine. A digital revolution in healthcare, Studies in Computational Intelligence. Cham: Springer, 2020, v. 843. Cham: Springer, 2020, p. 1–7

Soares FR (2019) Veículos autônomos e responsabilidade por acidentes: trajetos possíveis e desejáveis no direito civil brasileiro. In: Rosenvald N, Dresch RFV, Wesendonck T (eds) Responsabilidade civil: novos riscos. Foco, Indaiatuba

Teffé CS, Medon F (2020) Responsabilidade civil e regulação de novas tecnologias: questões acerca da utilização de inteligência artificial na tomada de decisões empresariais. Revista Estudos Institucionais 6(1):301–333

Tepedino G, Guia da Silva R (2019) Inteligência artificial e elementos de responsabilidade civil. In: Frazão A, Mulholland C (eds) Inteligência artificial e direito: ética, regulação e responsabilidade. Thomson Reuters, São Paulo

Topol E (2013) The creative destruction of medicine: how the digital revolution will create better health care. Basic Books, New York

Topol E (2015) The patient will see you now: the future of medicine is in your hands. Basic Books, New York

Topol E (2019) Deep medicine: how artificial intelligence can make healthcare human again. Basic Books, New York

Topol E et al (2022) Multimodal biomedical AI. Nat Med 28(2):1773–1784

Turner J (2019) Robot rules: regulating artificial intelligence. Palgrave Macmillan, Cham

UCI Beall Applied Innovation (2017) Husky or wolf? Using a Black Box learning model to avoid adoption errors. http://innovation.uci.edu/2017/08/husky-or-wolf-using-a-black-box-learning-model-to-avoid-adoption-errors

van Leeuwen KG et al (2021) Artificial intelligence in radiology: 100 commercially available products and their scientific evidence. Imag Inform Artif Intell 31:3797–3804

van Noordt C, Medaglia R, Tangi L (2023) Policy initiatives for artificial intelligence-enabled government: an analysis of national strategies in Europe. Public Policy Admin 0(0):09520767231198411

Vedder A, Naudts L (2017) Accountability for the use of algorithms in a big data environment. Int Rev Law Comput Technol 31(2):206–224

Wesendonck T (2021) Inteligência Artificial e responsabilidade civil pelos riscos do desenvolvimento: um estudo comparado entre as propostas de regulamentação da matéria na União Europeia e o ordenamento vigente brasileiro. In: Barbosa MM, Braga Netto FP, César Silva M, Faleiros Júnior JLM (eds) Direito digital e inteligência artificial: diálogos entre Brasil e Europa. Foco, Indaiatuba

World Health Organization (2021) Ethics and governance of artificial intelligence for health. https://www.who.int/publications/i/item/9789240029200

Yahav-Dovrat A et al (2021) Evaluation of artificial intelligence-powered identification of large-vessel occlusions in a comprehensive stroke center. Am J Neuroradiol 42(2):247–254

Zeng Y, Lu E, Huangfu C (2019) Linking artificial intelligence principles. In: Proceedings of the 2019 AAAI workshop on artificial intelligence safety. Available via Cornell University. https://arxiv.org/pdf/1812.04814

Chapter 5
Artificial Intelligence and Medical Liability in Hypothetical Cases

5.1 Medical Malpractice in Errors Related to Diagnosis, Prognosis, and Treatment Through AI Systems

It was observed in the preceding chapter of this work that artificial intelligence (AI) holds significant potential to support physicians in achieving more accurate and efficient diagnoses and clinical decision-making. However, the risks associated with this technology were equally noted, revealing potential scenarios in which harm may be caused to patients. Furthermore, ethical principles of AI in medicine and their impact on professional's duties of conduct were highlighted. Building upon the preceding analysis of the legal framework and regulatory approaches of the European Union and Brazil regarding AI, this chapter offers practical reflections on the rules governing the attribution of civil liability to medical practitioners for harm suffered in cases involving automated decision-making systems.

It is worth emphasising that this book adopts a multijurisdictional perspective, exploring medical liability and physician's duties of conduct in the context of AI systems across Brazil and European jurisdictions. By focusing on universal principles of medical law and AI ethics, it underscores the adaptability of its insights across various legal systems. The legal framework outlined in the initial chapters serves as a foundation for addressing hypothetical disputes and legal claims, enhancing the book's relevance in international markets.

In November 2022, the Ada Lovelace Institute and The Alan Turing Institute conducted a survey titled *How do People Feel About AI? A Nationally Representative Survey of Public Attitudes to Artificial Intelligence in Britain*, which gathered insights from over 4000 adults to explore public attitudes towards AI. Their findings reveal a complex and nuanced perception of AI's role in public and personal life. While many respondents in UK viewed AI positively, especially in areas like health, science, and security, concerns persisted regarding specific applications.

R. Nogaroli, *Medical Liability and Artificial Intelligence*,
https://doi.org/10.1007/978-3-031-94306-5_5

For instance, while nine out of ten people appreciated AI's potential in detecting cancer, over half worried about over-reliance on technology over professional judgment, and nearly half expressed concerns about accountability for mistakes. A significant majority (78%) feared that the adoption of AI in healthcare could lead to a loss of human interaction, aligning with previous findings from the *2019 Public Attitudes to Science* survey. These insights suggest that while the British public supports AI as a complementary tool to enhance human capabilities, there is resistance to its use as a replacement for human care, particularly in sensitive areas like healthcare.

The survey underscores the public's cautious optimism about AI. While its potential to revolutionise fields like healthcare is widely recognised, there is a strong desire to balance technological innovation with the preservation of human interaction and accountability. For AI to gain broader public acceptance, its role must be framed as a supportive tool that complements rather than replaces human expertise and empathy, mostly in critical sectors like medicine.

Watson for Oncology (WFO), a machine learning platform developed by IBM, as explained in Chap. 4, is designed to assist oncologists in recommending cancer treatments by analysing vast amounts of structured and unstructured medical data. Despite its promise, studies reveal inconsistent concordance rates between WFO's recommendations and oncologists' decisions, ranging from 30% in Denmark to 90% in India. These discrepancies are attributed to the platform's reliance on US-based treatment guidelines and a lack of transparency in its scoring criteria for clinical studies. Concerns about bias, inadequate adaptation to local practices, and varying availability of treatments globally highlight the challenges of adopting WFO in diverse healthcare settings (Tupasela and Di Nucci 2020). Furthermore, the AI system has been criticised for its black box nature, where the algorithm's value judgements and ranking criteria for clinical evidence remain opaque. This raises critical questions about its reliability and applicability, particularly in settings where local expertise and guidelines differ significantly from those embedded in the platform. While WFO holds potential in resource-limited regions, it also underscores the need for transparency, inclusivity, and long-term validation of outcomes to ensure that its recommendations align with global best practices and local healthcare needs.

The case of Watson for Oncology presents a broader ethical and legal challenge: how should medical liability be addressed when artificial intelligence (AI) platforms influence treatment decisions? If harm occurs due to a physician's reliance on or deviation from AI-generated recommendations, should the professional bear responsibility, or should the accountability extend to the developers of the AI? Moreover, in instances where an algorithmic error leads to an adverse outcome, such as the patient's death, how should the physician's decision to trust or override the AI be assessed? These critical questions demand careful examination of the interplay between AI tools and professional judgement, emphasising *the need for robust ethical and legal frameworks in the era of AI-driven medicine*.

As observed throughout this book, the task of assessing individual professional fault becomes exceedingly complex, particularly with the advent of advanced technological tools. Given the intricate nature of such technology—including its coding language and the algorithms underpinning its functionality—one might anticipate that courts would deem it *unjust* to hold a healthcare professional liable for adhering to the outcomes provided by an autonomous system, especially when the *errors* committed by the technology lie beyond the physician's control or capacity for correction. In cases of adverse events involving automated decision-making systems in clinical practice, civil liability should fundamentally be determined on a case-by-case basis, requiring an investigation into the physician's involvement in the decision-making process, including their choice to employ the AI system for a particular clinical scenario.

Where an evident technological defect is identified, the liability would, in principle, fall upon the product manufacturer. However, if elements of human error are also present, liability may need to be apportioned proportionally. In this regard, a critical distinction must be made between *joint liability* and *proportional liability*, as delineated in this work in Chap. 3.

Joint liability arises when two or more parties are collectively responsible for fulfilling an obligation. For instance, where a physician acts negligently, thereby breaching their duty of care, the hospital employing the professional may bear joint liability due to their vicarious responsibility. *Proportional liability*, on the other hand, pertains to situations where a breach of obligation or harm results from the conduct of multiple parties, each of whom bears responsibility commensurate with their contribution to the damage or contractual breach. For example, consider a scenario where a patient suffers harm caused both by a physician's lack of proficiency with an AI system and by a defect in the system itself. In such a case, liability may be distributed proportionally between the professional and the product manufacturer based on their respective roles in causing the harm.

Demonstrating the defect in an AI system and establishing its causal link to the damage can be an exceedingly complex task. As discussed in the previous chapter, presumptions regarding the defectiveness of the product and its causal connection to the harm may be considered. Furthermore, akin to legislative approaches in some European states concerning the provision of black box data for autonomous vehicles, patients should have a recognised right to request the black box data of an AI system in court. Failing this, a presumption of defect against the manufacturer may arise, as explained earlier in this book.

To avoid liability for medical negligence, healthcare professionals must demonstrate diligence, providing care at the reasonable standard expected of a competent physician within their speciality, given the available resources. When evaluating negligence, a key question arises: *would a prudent physician, under the same external conditions, have acted in the same manner as the individual accused of causing harm?* However, defining what constitutes a *prudent physician* can be particularly challenging in the context of AI-assisted clinical decisions. The assessment of medical negligence becomes even more intricate when algorithmic recommendations are involved in diagnosis, prognosis, or treatment planning. Demonstrating causation in cases of patient harm is already a nuanced and probabilistic endeavour, where outcomes often lack determinism. Introducing autonomous systems into healthcare adds further complexity, particularly in litigation, making the demonstration of causality even more challenging.

This context raises other critical questions: (1) to what extent should the physician question algorithmic recommendations, especially given the black box nature of AI systems?; (2) even if the professional cannot fully discern the reasoning behind an algorithmic output, should he or she assess the indicators of its quality and reliability, as well as the methodology used in its development and validation?; (3) can the minimum standard of professional diligence be evaluated on whether such questioning and investigation occur?; and (4) as AI becomes another tool in the display of clinical practice instruments, how should it be used to ensure that professional conduct meets the standard of diligence?

Inevitably, these examinations are going to come before courts worldwide soon. This is why the comprehensive proposal in this book to redefine the duties of medical conduct, derived from principles of objective good faith and ethical AI guidelines, is especially relevant to the practical analysis of medical liability.

At present, there is no reported case law addressing medical liability involving AI systems. However, a rise in such disputes appears likely, given the increasing adoption of automated systems in clinical decision-making in recent years. This underscores the urgent need to explore how contemporary legal frameworks can address these scenarios through a reinterpretation of general principles in civil law, contractual law, and the doctrine of civil liability itself.

Regarding the legal nature of medical civil liability—particularly with respect to its objective or subjective dimension—it is essential to highlight the global debate concerning the rejection of all approaches advocating for the strict liability of operators of AI systems classified as high-risk in the context of *physicians identified as front-end operators* of AI systems. Buchner (2022) argues that extending the scope of physician's liability towards product liability fails to account for the legal distinction between *product safety liability*, on the one hand, and *treatment-related medical liability*, on the other. Consequently, applying strict liability to physicians is deemed inappropriate.

It is worth emphasising, as previously mentioned in Sect. 4.2.2, that the European Commission advocates that AI regulation should seek proportionate and evidence-based solutions tailored to specific situations and sectors, with liability attribution and proportionality determined by the respective level of control operators have over the risk related to the operation and functioning of the AI system. In this regard, Buchner (2022), a German professor at the University of Bremen, explains that physicians do not inherently create risks but instead fulfil their medical treatment obligations in accordance with the *lege artis* of the profession and the rules of medical care.

It is unacceptable to alter the subjective liability regime applicable to medical professionals by imposing strict liability on the basis that their activity is inherently risky. The risk faced by the patient does not arise from the medical intervention itself but rather from the patient's underlying illness, their intrinsic reaction to the treatment, or risks associated with the manufacturer's product. As Nilo (2020) aptly notes, *the application of risk theory to medical practice is unsupported*, as neither the *created risk* nor the *profit risk* theories align with the nature of medical activity.

A physician is not liable for harm caused by a defective or unsuitable medical product or technology when such issues are impossible to detect, either by the professional or other members of the healthcare team (Aguiar Dias 2006). As Kfouri Neto (2024) highlights:

> when prostheses are implanted, for example, harm may result from manufacturing or design defects, for which the manufacturer is liable. In such cases, there can be no suggestion that the physician promised a specific outcome.

However, consider a scenario in which a physician performs a breast augmentation surgery, and the implanted prosthesis later ruptures. A second procedure is performed to explant the defective product, but the prosthesis is discarded, precluding future technical examination to determine the cause of the rupture. In addition to potential manufacturer liability for a defective product, one might argue that the physician has breached their duty of vigilance, rooted in the principle of good faith, by failing to report the adverse event to the manufacturer and regulatory body. Such a report would include the suspected association with the prosthesis, even if not yet confirmed. Similarly, a physician breaches this duty if they observe over time that a medical device repeatedly malfunctions, causing harm to patients, as exemplified in the Cobalt-60 case in Sect. 3.2.1 of this book. Nevertheless, a physician cannot reasonably be expected to bear the burden of immediate knowledge of so-called unknown or unknowable risks.

Given this context, it is concluded that in medical service contracts involving AI, when the harm suffered by the patient is related to an *essentially medical service*, the personal liability of the physician needs to be assessed based on *fault*, as provided in Article 14, §4 of the Brazilian Consumer Protection Code (*Código de Defesa do* Consumidor—CDC). In European countries, Buchner (2022) explains that the same reasoning should apply in cases involving AI-based algorithms functioning as medical devices.

It is important to note that, in such scenarios, primary responsibility is attributed to the manufacturer and the hospital. However, this does not absolve physicians, as operators of the technology, from all liability in cases involving defective AI systems. When the recommendations provided by such algorithms contradict the clinical expertise of the attending physicians, these professionals have a duty—derived from their treatment obligations—to exercise independent judgment and refrain from relying on the algorithm if reasonable doubts about its reliability exist.

This duty, nevertheless, does not stem from any form of operator liability for a defective product (Buchner 2022). Instead, it is rooted in the traditional framework of fault liability, applicable when physicians breach their duty of care and vigilance. Such breaches occur, for instance, when a professional, based on their medical expertise, could reasonably recognise that the medical decision in question did not adhere to the required *lege artis* standards.

In the Brazilian context, it is essential to highlight the discussions advanced by the preeminent Brazilian scholar on medical law, Miguel Kfouri Neto, in his seminal work *Civil Liability of the Physician* (2024). In this classic text, the author underscores the impossibility of assessing a physician's liability in any scenario without establishing the element of fault, as illustrated in the excerpt below:

> The liability of the medical professional (...) can never be separated from the traditional concept of fault when qualifying the physician's conduct as harmful and capable of generating an obligation to indemnify. The objectification of liability, so favoured by a considerable segment of contemporary legal scholarship, cannot be applied here. (...) Such an approach would equate the diligent, attentive, and well-read physician with the careless professional who has not opened a medical book since graduating. Moreover, an insurmountable difficulty arises in applying the theory of no-fault liability to the medical profession: how can one determine whether death or disability resulted from medical error or the natural course of human life? Equally absurd would be the imposition of liability on the collective body of medical professionals for any and all harm, as these are precisely the individuals who collectively alleviate human suffering. Finally, human beings are subject to disease and suffering, and any attempt to eliminate the element of fault would transform the duties owed by physicians into obligations of result, which is entirely unacceptable.
>
> Pain, illness, death, and health impairments are not, in principle, risks inherent to medical activity but are intrinsic to human existence. Each physician, and the collective medical profession worldwide, seeks to alleviate this suffering, remedy illness, and restore health. The patient, by their very nature, carries a risk derived from their pathology—and it is not the physician who creates it. Adopting strict liability in this context would amount to opposing the very essence of human nature. To cover all risks of illness or death in medical activity would equate to obliging physicians to grant health to the ill, to prolong life indefinitely, thereby exceeding the human capabilities of the physician and transforming them into a deity.

In the same sense, Brazilian scholars such as Facchini Neto and Costa (2023) underscore similar concerns, both in Europe and Brazil, regarding the potential adoption of strict liability for physicians employing AI systems in their professional practice. They emphasise the paradoxical consequence that a physician employing AI systems to provide optimal patient care would be subjected to a stricter liability regime than a colleague who refrains from such use and would therefore remain liable only for fault. This could inadvertently promote a defensive, omission-based approach to medicine, as professionals might opt to avoid utilising technologies that, while useful or even indispensable, expose them to a disproportionately greater burden of civil liability. Consequently, the rigorous liability regime could deter physicians from adopting advanced AI technologies, undermining their potential to enhance healthcare outcomes and leaving practitioners vulnerable in potential litigation.

Thus, the debate on the appropriate liability framework for medical professionals in the context of AI underscores the need for balanced legislation that safeguards patients' rights while promoting the responsible adoption of innovative technologies. By *distinguishing product liability from professional liability*, legislators can ensure that medical practitioners are held accountable for breaches of professional duty without deterring them from leveraging AI systems to improve healthcare. This balance is crucial to fostering trust, innovation, and fairness in the evolving intersection of technology and medicine.

Finally, it is worth reflecting on the fact that medical civil liability, while subjective in nature and necessitating a thorough analysis of fault, is intrinsically tied to the fulfilment of professional duties that, in the context of artificial intelligence (AI), are redefined and interconnected with the ethical principles governing this technology. The integration of AI into medical practice imposes on professionals an obligation to uphold elevated standards of diligence and care, as discussed throughout this book and further explored in practical terms in the present chapter.

When a physician chooses to follow or disregard the recommendations provided by an AI system, and such a decision results in harm to the patient due to improper treatment, the judge may invoke rules of presumption, assuming *prima facie* that the professional acted negligently. It is important to underline that this does not establish strict liability; rather, the burden shifts to the physician to justify their conduct and demonstrate that all reasonable measures were taken to ensure their actions were both diligent and necessary to prevent harm. This presumption serves to reinforce the expectation of professional conduct that is not only prudent but also ethically aligned with the principles underpinning the responsible use of AI in medical care. It is worth noting that this reflection regarding presumptions was discussed in Sect. 4.2.2.

Building on these preliminary considerations about medical liability in AI systems, this book proposes a practical analytical approach of key parameters of professional conduct and potential legal consequences, which outlines general principles for assessing diligence in medical conduct across various scenarios.

The goal is to assist in the resolution of concrete cases that may come before the courts. Table 5.1 presents *eight (8) scenarios* (first column) illustrating potential interactions between physicians and AI—when an automated decision-making system recommends a specific medication and its dosage for a cancer patient. Originally developed by Professors Nicholson Price II, Sara Gerke, and I. Glen Cohen (2020), the table has been reinterpreted and adapted for this work, with the addition of a final column to evaluate breaches of auxiliary duties of conduct.

This book proposes the analysis of general principles to assess diligence in medical conduct across diverse scenarios, providing guidance for resolving concrete cases that may arise in litigation. The table presents *eight possible scenarios* for physician-AI interaction (first column)—for instance, where an automated decision-making system recommends a specific dosage of a chemotherapeutic drug, such as 15 mg/kg every 3 weeks (standard dosage), or a significantly higher dosage, such as 75 mg/kg every 3 weeks (non-standard recommendation).

In the *first scenario*, a physician follows the AI's correct recommendation and prescribes 15 mg/kg for cancer treatment, leading to the successful eradication of the tumour and the patient's cure. However, despite this favourable outcome, the patient experiences adverse side effects, such as complications in diabetes management, which could potentially have been avoided if the alternative treatment—CAR-T cell therapy—had been pursued. This innovative genetic therapy could reprogram the patient's own immune cells to target and destroy cancer cells, offering a less aggressive and potentially more beneficial approach compared to traditional chemotherapy when widely recognised by the medical community.

Table 5.1 Table adapted by the author of this book from the table originally proposed by Nicholson Price II, Sara Gerke, and I. Glen Cohen in the article Potential Liability for Physicians Using Artificial Intelligence (2019)

Potential legal outcomes related to AI use in clinical practice						
Scenario	AI recommendation	AI accuracy	Physician action	Patient outcome	Legal outcome (probable)	Breach of auxiliary duties of conduct
1	Standard of care [15 mg/kg]	Correct	Follows	Good	No injury and no liability	**Liability when fault is not established**
2			Rejects	Bad	**Injury and liability**	Increase in the awarded damages
3		Incorrect (standard of care is incorrect)	Follows	Bad	Injury but no liability	**Liability when fault is not established**
4			Rejects	Good	No injury and no liability	**Liability when fault is not established**
5	Nonstandard care [75 mg/kg]	Correct (standard of care is incorrect)	Follows	Good	No injury and no liability	**Liability when fault is not established**
6			Rejects	Bad	Injury but no liability	**Liability when fault is not established**
7		Incorrect	Follows	Bad	**Injury and liability**	Increase in the awarded damages
8			Rejects	Good	No injury and no liability	**Liability when fault is not established**

The patient's recovery and successful treatment clearly demonstrate that there was no medical error per se—a fact that underscores the physician's competence in delivering effective care. However, there is a breach of the physician's duty of information. While the patient received appropriate care and achieved a successful outcome, the failure to disclose the full range of therapeutic options—particularly those recommended by the AI, such as potentially less invasive or more effective treatments—constitutes a violation of this critical duty.

In this case, there is a failure to provide the patient with comprehensive knowledge for informed decision-making, especially regarding viable alternatives recognised by the medical community. The duty of information, increasingly redefined in light of ethical principles governing AI, requires *transparency, explainability, and intelligibility* in all aspects of clinical decision-making (as further discussed in Sect. 5.2). Patients have the right to be fully informed of all reasonable treatment options, particularly when an alternative may significantly reduce risks, such as secondary health complications or adverse effects. This reinforces the ethical and legal imperative for transparency when utilising AI technologies to assist in formulating diagnostic, prognostic, or therapeutic recommendations. By failing to fulfil this obligation, the physician compromises the patient's autonomy and their ability to participate meaningfully in their own healthcare decisions.

Moving on to further reflections on the scenarios outlined in the table above, it is important to consider that the AI's recommendation (second column) can either be correct or incorrect (third column). While 15 mg/kg is generally the *standard of care*, there could be circumstances in which a higher dosage is appropriate for a particular patient, reflecting the broader goals of the Digital Era of Medicine and AI algorithms to personalise medical care (precision medicine). The physician may choose to accept or reject the AI recommendation (fourth column), and the outcome may be favourable or harmful to the patient (fifth column). These variations lead to potential legal outcomes, considering the physician's liability for the damage suffered (sixth column) or, alternatively, the physician's liability for breaching ancillary duties (seventh column). It is worth emphasising again that, the seventh column, which addresses ancillary duties—and liability even when fault is not established—was introduced by the author of this book to build upon the framework initially proposed by Nicholson Price II, Sara Gerke, and I. Glen Cohen, thereby broadening the analysis of the physician's responsibilities in scenarios involving AI-assisted decision-making

The professional may be held liable in cases where they follow or reject an AI system's recommendation, and the patient suffers harm (*scenarios 2 and 7*). In *scenario 2*, the AI provides an accurate recommendation consistent with the standard of care for the clinical situation (e.g., administering 15 mg/kg every 3 weeks of a chemotherapeutic drug). However, the physician disregards this recommendation, prescribes a different medication or dosage, leading to harm. Here, the physician must justify their decision to deviate from the algorithmic recommendation with reference to medical science and literature. Failure to demonstrate diligence in deviating from the standard care could result in liability for medical negligence.

Additionally, in *scenario 2*, a breach of the physician's duty of conduct, such as failing to adequately inform the patient about the AI's recommendation and the reasons for deviating from it, may further exacerbate the physician's liability. This is the position advocated by the author of this book, emphasising that in any potential litigation, two distinct issues must be considered: the physician's liability for medical negligence in the treatment itself and the separate issue of informational negligence, represented by a breach of the duty of information. The latter pertains to the physician's failure to provide the patient with sufficient and accurate information to enable an informed decision. This lack of transparency, which undermines the patient's autonomy, constitutes an independent violation and could serve as an aggravating factor in the calculation of damages when medical negligence is also considered. Such an approach highlights the multifaceted nature of medical liability, ensuring that both the quality of medical care and the integrity of the informed consent process are appropriately addressed.

On the other hand, in *scenario 7*, the AI recommends a non-standard dosage, which ultimately proves to be incorrect, and the physician follows it, resulting in harm to the patient. In such cases, physicians who rely thoughtlessly on AI recommendations without critically evaluating them against the standard of care established in the broader specialised medical literature, and without conducting proper anamnesis, physical examinations, and complementary tests, may be deemed negligent. This failure to exercise due diligence highlights the physician's responsibility to integrate AI recommendations into their clinical decision-making process thoughtfully and cautiously. Negligence arises not from the use of AI itself but from the physician's overreliance on it without appropriate scrutiny, which contravenes their duty to ensure that the proposed treatment aligns with established medical standards and the specific needs of the patient.

In situations where no harm occurs to the patient, medical liability is generally not established (*scenarios 1, 4, 5, and 8*). The treatment chosen by the physician results in a good outcome for the patient, whether the physician follows a correct AI recommendation (*scenarios 1 and 5*) or rejects an incorrect AI recommendation (*scenarios 4 and 8*). However, even in these cases, the physician could still be held accountable for breaching contractual obligations, such as failing to adequately inform the patient or violating other ancillary duties, including duties of vigilance (data-informed duties). These issues will be discussed later in this chapter (Sects. 5.2–5.4).

There are also situations where the physician, in principle, would not be held liable for patient harm, even if an alternative course of action might have been better in a specific case (*scenarios 3 and 6*). In *scenario 3*, the AI recommends the standard dosage of 15 mg/kg for the drug, consistent with medical literature and commonly applied in similar cases. However, the AI's prediction proves incorrect, and the physician, having acted diligently, follows the recommendation. If it is later discovered that the patient had an extremely rare and difficult-to-diagnose condition, the physician would not be liable, as their actions reflected the diligence and prudence expected of a competent professional under similar circumstances.

Scenario 6 warrants special consideration. Here, the AI provides a non-standard recommendation that proves correct, but the physician disregards it, adhering instead to the standard dosage of 15 mg/kg. If the patient suffers harm as a result, the physician may not initially be held liable, as they acted in line with the standard treatment for the patient's clinical condition. However, as scientific studies evolve, it could become evident that an alternative treatment—precisely the one suggested by the AI—would have been more appropriate.

It is important to recall that AI algorithms are trained on vast datasets comprising millions of clinical studies, scientific research, and medical literature. AI systems may propose innovative treatment approaches, such as higher medication dosages or entirely different drugs, which may be shown to be more effective for specific patient profiles. In such situations, physicians must demonstrate diligence by critically evaluating whether the AI's recommendation necessitates reconsidering their initial treatment plan. Physicians could, therefore, incur liability for rejecting correct but non-standard AI recommendations without proper reflection, as a lack of due diligence in disregarding these recommendations could constitute grounds for liability.

Based on the structure of the proposed table and the general principles discussed earlier to guide the assessment of diligence in medical conduct across various scenarios, considering possible legal consequences in the context of physician-AI interaction, this section investigates the legal repercussions of several hypothetical cases. These situations were developed based on reports (Rohaidi 2016; Fikes 2022) detailing physicians' practical experiences with AI in clinical decision-making.

In 2015, an intriguing case involving AI-supported medical diagnosis was reported in Japan. A cancer patient was hospitalised at a facility affiliated with the University of Tokyo's Institute of Medical Science (Rohaidi 2016). She was initially diagnosed with acute myeloid leukaemia—a type of blood cancer—and underwent what appeared to be a successful round of chemotherapy. However, her unusually slow recovery during post-remission therapy prompted the physicians to reconsider the diagnosis, suspecting a different type of leukaemia.

Faced with this diagnostic challenge, the hospital's medical team turned to IBM's Watson for Oncology. This AI-powered tool cross-references and analyses information from thousands of clinical cases, extensive specialised literature, and millions of oncology studies conducted by research institutions worldwide. Remarkably, the AI system identified the patient's condition within just 10 min—a task that would typically take human specialists around 2 weeks to accomplish. Watson's diagnosis revealed that the patient was suffering from a rare secondary leukaemia caused by myelodysplastic syndromes, a group of disorders in which the bone marrow fails to produce adequate healthy blood cells (Rohaidi 2016). Acting on Watson's recommendation, the physicians implemented a treatment plan specifically tailored to this type of leukaemia (the legal implications of this case were thoroughly examined in an academic study by Nogaroli and da Guia Silva 2022).

In another instance, at a hospital affiliated with the University of California, San Diego, a positive outcome was reported with the so called *I-PREDICT system*, an AI and genetic engineering platform (Fikes 2022). This system allows physicians to analyse the DNA profile of cancerous cells to provide more precise diagnoses and treatment proposals.

I-PREDICT uses AI algorithms to analyse genetic variants in the patient's DNA, cross-referencing them with a database of thousands of research studies, hundreds of medications, and millions of drug combinations. Its goal is to identify the optimal treatment for the individual patient's tumour, based on its unique characteristics rather than its location in the body or the cancer type affecting a broader population group. This is an example of *Precision Medicine*, which enhances the development of new drugs and offers better disease understanding by considering a patient's clinical and genetic profile, the interaction between genomics, drug responses, and potential treatment options.

The case of a patient called Teresa McKeown serves as a compelling example within this context (Fikes 2022). Initially diagnosed with breast cancer, she underwent a double mastectomy and chemotherapy, successfully achieving remission. However, the cancer eventually recurred, progressing to an advanced metastatic stage that was deemed lethal. Standard chemotherapy and other conventional treatments failed, as the cancer had spread extensively throughout her body, rendering surgical intervention unfeasible. Teresa was subsequently enrolled in the clinical trial *I-PREDICT—Study of Molecular Profile-Related Evidence to Determine Individualised Therapy for Advanced or Poor Prognosis Cancers*. This trial utilised a genetically tailored drug specifically designed to target the mutations within her tumour. Remarkably, the personalised treatment proved successful, leading to the complete disappearance of her tumours.

The positive outcomes in both cases described above do not eliminate a critical question: how should physicians' conduct be assessed if they choose to disregard a correct recommendation provided by AI and instead follow their own judgment, resulting in a patient's death due to an incorrect diagnosis or inappropriate treatment? The answer depends on the specific circumstances of each case. To address this issue effectively regarding medical liability for diagnostic or treatment errors, the reflections here will focus on legal scenarios 2 and 6 outlined earlier in this section.

In *scenario 2*, consider an oncological patient whose clinical data is provided to *Watson for Oncology* (WFO) by their physician. The AI system suggests a treatment aligned with established medical literature and standard practices. However, the physician chooses to disregard this recommendation and instead prescribes an alternative drug or dosage, ultimately causing harm to the patient due to inappropriate treatment. In such a case, it would be challenging to absolve the professional of liability, particularly since WFO's recommendation reflects what a prudent and diligent physician, in similar circumstances, would have prescribed. Neglecting to provide a well-supported justification for deviating from the AI's recommendation and opting for a treatment outside the standard of care would likely constitute medical negligence.

Conversely, in *scenario 6*, consider a situation where a physician inputs a patient's data into WFO, which recommends a treatment involving a non-standard but correct chemotherapy drug, differing from the standard approach the physician has relied upon for years. The physician disregards the AI's recommendation, maintaining their belief that the patient's case is best addressed with the standard treatment. However, this decision results in harm to the patient due to an inappropriate course of treatment.

In principle, the physician may not be held liable if they acted diligently by conducting a thorough anamnesis, requesting the necessary diagnostic tests, and reasonably determining that the standard treatment was appropriate for the patient's clinical condition. Nevertheless, as scientific research progresses, it may become evident that the previously accepted standard treatment is no longer optimal and that the AI-recommended drug would have been significantly more beneficial.

When confronted with an unconventional AI recommendation, physicians have a duty to exercise heightened diligence in determining whether their preferred treatment is truly the best option for the patient. This diligence involves conducting supplementary tests or thoroughly reassessing the patient's clinical condition, and critically evaluating the algorithmic recommendation within the context of the broader medical literature and established practices. Failure to undertake these steps may expose the physician to liability, particularly where harm arises from an inappropriate diagnosis or treatment decision that could have been prevented through a more diligent assessment of the AI recommendation.

The author of this book strongly advocates for the importance of *specialised legal guidance* for physicians, particularly concerning the proper documentation of their decision-making process. In cases where the physician either follows or disregards an AI recommendation, it is essential to record the rationale behind their choice in the patient's medical record. This documentation could include attaching a document or image of the AI system's output, which serves as evidence of the technology employed and the recommendation provided during clinical practice.

Such meticulous record-keeping is not merely a bureaucratic formality; it serves as a critical means of proving the physician's professional diligence in the event of any future legal or ethical scrutiny. By ensuring that decisions are transparently justified and properly documented, physicians can better demonstrate adherence to the standard of care and protect themselves from allegations of negligence.

This preventive legal approach—referred to as *Medical Preventive Law*—emphasises the need for physicians to proactively safeguard their professional practice by integrating both legal and medical diligence. In doing so, they not only enhance the quality of patient care but also mitigate potential litigation arising from the integration of AI in clinical decision-making. Balancing technological innovation with robust professional accountability ensures that physicians responsibly leverage AI to improve patient outcomes without compromising ethical and legal standards.

It is worth noting that, in 2018, reports highlighted a significant issue with WFO, which was frequently recommending unsafe and blatantly incorrect treatments for oncology patients (Ross 2018). On one occasion, the AI system suggested the use of a chemotherapy drug called bevacizumab (commercially known as Avastin) for a lung cancer patient undergoing chemotherapy with a history of severe bleeding.

The issue arises from the known side effect of this drug, namely its potential to cause bleeding—a risk widely acknowledged within the medical community. Consequently, bevacizumab is prescribed only for specific cases of lung cancer. In a situation where a patient dies as a result of such inappropriate treatment, establishing medical negligence becomes relatively straightforward. Following an evidently flawed and non-standard recommendation from the AI would unequivocally amount to gross negligence, as highlighted in *scenario 7* of the table outlined at the beginning of this section.

As Price et al. (2023) argue, it is the physician's responsibility to assess whether to use AI in any specific situation and, if so, whether to follow or disregard an algorithmic recommendation. Physicians may be held accountable for their choices, including the decision to rely on the technology in the first place.

A practical reflection on the diligence required when using automated decision-making systems like WFO is necessary. When a physician inputs a cancer patient's data into the AI system, there is a predictive analysis on an extensive database curated by Memorial Sloan Kettering (USA), which includes medical journals, textbooks, clinical cases, and scientific literature. The system then classifies potential cancer treatments into three categories—recommended, for consideration, and not recommended. The physician views this ranked list alongside published articles and statistics supporting each treatment option. While Watson cannot fully explain why it selects a particular treatment, it provides *clues* or scientific evidence to aid physicians in their decision-making. Thus, a physician cannot simply adopt the AI-recommended treatment without further scrutiny. They must exercise due diligence by reviewing the scientific studies supporting the recommendation to confirm whether it is appropriate for their patient.

If the physician, based on their expertise, determines that the information provided by the AI is incorrect for the specific case, they must disregard it, as Molnár-Gábor (2020) asserts. This minimum standard of diligence requires a critical evaluation of the AI system's outputs. The more severe the potential consequences of an error in the AI's recommendations, the greater the physician's duty to question the basis of the algorithm's decision-making. This underscores the importance of maintaining a balance between leveraging AI as a tool for improving medical care and ensuring that physicians remain the ultimate arbiters of clinical decisions.

It is worth making a distinction when bringing the debate into the field of medical fault in diagnosis errors compared to treatment errors. In practice, it is significantly more challenging to establish a physician's liability because the assessment of fault in diagnostic errors is characterised by notable complexities, as explained in Chap. 3, and only gross negligence can justify liability (Pereira 2015; Kfouri Neto 2024), as discussed in Sect. 3.1.1.

If a similar situation were to be reviewed by a court today, where AI suggests a diagnosis (X) that significantly deviates from the standard diagnosis (Y) initially determined by the physician, and the patient suffers harm because the physician chose not to follow the AI's recommendation (X), medical liability would not, in principle, be established. This is because the process of diagnosis inherently involves uncertainties and probabilistic outcomes. If the professional conducts a thorough examination of the patient, gathering comprehensive information through anamnesis, tests, and all scientific tools available, and determines a diagnosis (Y) that diverges from the AI's result (X), they would not be held liable, even if the AI's diagnosis (X) is ultimately proven correct.

However, a different conclusion might be reached if the physician ignores the AI's result about the diagnosis (X) and fails to investigate evident symptoms or test results that clearly warrant further examination. In such cases, the refusal to conduct complementary examinations or to re-evaluate the clinical scenario could be considered *gross negligence*. This would indicate unacceptable ignorance or carelessness, leading to fault-based liability and the obligation to compensate the damages. This evolving standard reflects the growing integration of AI into medical care and the heightened responsibility on physicians to engage critically with its outputs.

Looking ahead, as automated decision-making systems become an integral part of clinical practice, the expectation for physicians to leverage the full spectrum of available technological tools will inevitably rise. By applying the *Theory of Changed Circumstances* to the medical field, the standard of diligence required to assess professional liability is undergoing a significant evolution. As mentioned earlier, if AI provides a diagnostic or treatment recommendation that deviates from established standards, a physician's failure to investigate or critically assess the AI's suggestion could be seen as a lack of due diligence.

Furthermore, medical negligence and *the minimum diligence required of a physician will soon be evaluated based on whether they utilised an AI system* that is widely recognised by the medical community and implemented within the hospital where they practice. This reflects a growing consensus that adopting proven AI systems is not merely optional but may become a professional obligation for physicians operating in technologically advanced healthcare settings.

The *Theory of Changed Circumstances*, traditionally applied in contract law to account for evolving conditions, has become increasingly relevant in medicine, especially in light of rapid technological advancements. It suggests that as circumstances shift—with the implementation of numerous AI systems becoming part of the daily routine in clinical practice—the duties and responsibilities of physicians must evolve accordingly. Practices that were once considered diligent may now be deemed insufficient in light of tools and specific conditions of medical activity that significantly enhance diagnostic accuracy or optimise treatment outcomes.

An example of this theory's application comes from an interdisciplinary study conducted by Brazilian, Portuguese, and Spanish legal scholars—Rosenvald et al. (2021). They demonstrate how the Theory of Changed Circumstances was invoked globally during the COVID-19 pandemic to adapt judicial analyses of professional standards to the extraordinary context of a public health emergency. This adaptation recognised that the pandemic imposed unique challenges on healthcare systems and professionals, requiring a temporary recalibration of conduct standards to reflect the altered reality.

Drawing on this pattern, it is important to consider the theory's application in technologically advanced medical practice, where AI systems are increasingly being integrated into clinical workflows. For instance, if a widely recognised AI system capable of delivering highly accurate diagnoses or treatment recommendations is available, a physician's decision not to use it—absent a valid justification—might be viewed as a negligent conduct.

However, it is crucial to emphasise that this logic represents a standard that may be expected to apply in the near future. At present, it is not yet possible to uniformly impose such an expectation because we are still in a phase of initial technological development worldwide. Many hospitals and clinics do not yet have access to AI systems, and their integration into everyday clinical practice remains inconsistent.

This expectation, as argued by the author of this book, reflects the evolving standards of diligence in medicine, drawing parallels to historical shifts in what constitutes essential medical tools. For example, the stethoscope, now indispensable for auscultation, was not always part of standard medical practice. Its adoption marked an evolution in the standard of care, establishing new benchmarks for diligence. Similarly, as AI systems gain widespread acceptance and validation within the medical community, failing to utilise them when they are available and appropriate could breach the expected standard of care. Ignoring such tools would be akin to neglecting the use of a stethoscope for auscultation today—a clear departure from the diligence required of a diligent medical professional.

Hospitals and healthcare systems play a pivotal role in this transition. They must actively educate physicians about the capabilities and limitations of AI technologies, fostering their seamless integration into clinical workflows. By mandating the use of well-validated AI systems, healthcare institutions—and professional regulatory bodies—can establish clear benchmarks for diligence, ensuring that physicians stay up to date with advancements in their respective fields. Furthermore, incorporating formal medical education on emerging technologies, with dedicated courses for medical students to understand and utilise these tools, will be essential for preparing future professionals.

It is worth highlighting that throughout the debate proposed in this section, a foundational principle remains constant in the legal analysis of adverse events arising from medical acts: the inherent uncertainty of medical practice (therapeutic risk) makes it impossible to impose on physicians an obligation of infallibility or absolute accuracy in diagnosis. Medicine is not an exact science, and the inherent unpredictability of clinical care must be recognised and factored into the assessment of medical responsibility.

In conclusion, a physician presented with an AI-generated diagnostic or prognostic result occupies a challenging position and must justify: (1) why they followed the diagnosis or treatment suggested by the AI; or (2) why—and based on which factors—they deviated from the algorithmic recommendation. While physicians retain authority over their clinical decisions, they are equally accountable for their choices. They must balance their professional autonomy with the duty to critically evaluate AI-generated insights, ensuring that every decision aligns with the patient's best interests and is grounded in sound clinical reasoning.

All the situations discussed above underscore the growing complexity of evaluating medical liability in the context of AI-assisted decision-making. While AI systems like *Watson for Oncology* and *I-PREDICT* can significantly enhance diagnostic accuracy and treatment precision, their recommendations do not absolve physicians of their duty to exercise independent, informed judgment. Physicians must critically evaluate AI outputs within the broader clinical context, incorporating their expertise, patient-specific factors, and the latest scientific evidence.

As observed, the legal repercussions of ignoring or improperly relying on AI recommendations depend on the circumstances of each case, but they invariably hinge on the physician's diligence and adherence to professional standards. As medical technologies evolve, so too must the interpretation of the legal frameworks governing their use. The incorporation of AI necessitates a nuanced approach that balances the benefits of technological innovation with the ethical and professional responsibilities of healthcare providers.

Ultimately, the responsibility rests with the physician. Regardless of the sophistication of the AI system, the physician is the final decision-maker and remains accountable for the choices made in a patient's care. This accountability arises from the foundational principle that medical professionals, by virtue of their specialised knowledge and ethical obligations, are entrusted with safeguarding the health and well-being of their patients. AI can provide valuable insights and recommendations, but it is the physician's role to interpret these outputs critically and make decisions that align with the best interests of the patient. Thus, while AI offers significant support, it does not—and cannot—displace the physician's ultimate responsibility for ensuring appropriate and ethical medical care.

This foundational understanding of the professional's accountability seamlessly connects with recent advancements in AI, particularly in its application to sensitive areas such as palliative care, where decision-making requires both technological support and profound ethical considerations. Recently, AI systems have been developed to predict survival probabilities for hospitalised patients, triage individuals in need of palliative care, and even estimate the time to death for terminally ill or incurable patients. These technologies, referred to by Topol (2019) as *AI Dying Algorithms*, aim to support physicians in efficiently identifying cases where palliative care is appropriate, thus promoting timely and dignified end-of-life medical care.

While these tools hold significant promise as decision-support systems, challenges related to their accuracy have been reported. For instance, the *Jvion CORE algorithm* has a 40% accuracy rate in predicting high-risk patients who will pass away within the following month, leaving a concerning 60% error margin (Robbins 2020). This level of algorithmic fallibility underscores the critical need for caution and supplemental judgment in their use.

As Topol (2019) notes, AI can aid patients and physicians in making informed decisions about medical treatment, whether palliative or curative. Additionally, these systems could positively influence resource allocation in healthcare settings, such as ICU beds, resuscitation equipment, or ventilators. However, until more precise models are developed, uncertainty remains about the role AI should play in palliative care decisions.

Physicians must approach these tools with wisdom, carefully evaluating which technologies add value to their practice and how to integrate them appropriately into clinical workflows. Failure to do so risks exacerbating epistemic opacity, where the rationale behind AI-driven decisions becomes unclear. To avoid this, the ethical *principle of promoting human well-being, safety, and public interest* must guide the adoption of AI in medicine, aligning with the professional duty of continuous medical education and technological literacy.

Ravi Parikh, an oncologist leading an AI and palliative care project at the University of Pennsylvania (USA), advises caution: "If the algorithm is the only reason you are having this conversation with the patient and recommending palliative care, that is not a good (or sufficient) reason". He highlights that AI systems only estimate higher risk of mortality or clinical decline, not definitive outcomes—often within uncertain timeframes, such as 3–6 months.

Molnár-Gábor (2020) aptly emphasises that "the physician is free to choose their diagnostic and therapeutic means but is also responsible for their choices". Thus, the decision to initiate end-of-life discussions or recommend palliative care must rest on a broad spectrum of factors, not solely the results of an AI Dying Algorithm. This reinforces the indispensable role of human judgment, ethics, and expertise in ensuring that AI complements, rather than replaces, the nuanced decision-making processes essential to high-quality medical care.

Finally, as the closing discussion of this section, it is essential to observe that, while this book primarily focuses on physician liability in the context of AI, civil liability issues are far more complex in practice. Medical negligence constitutes merely one facet of a broader ecosystem of accountability, involving diverse stakeholders and considerations that transcend the physician-patient relationship. Hospitals and clinics that purchase and implement automated decision-making systems, as well as the manufacturers of such products, may also bear liability for adverse events involving patients.

Therefore, it is crucial to emphasise that the analysis of civil liability in this context must be based on a thorough investigation of the efficient cause of the harm. This requires determining whether the harm suffered by the patient arises from conduct exclusively attributable to the physician, a defect in the product, or a failure by the hospital to properly maintain and update the AI system, as examined in Sect. 3.2 and further discussed in the subsequent section.

5.2 Data-Informed Duties (Duty of Vigilance) and the Multifunctionality of Medical Liability in the Twenty-First Century

Hospitals may be held accountable in certain situations for errors committed by their employee or agent. For instance, in Brazil, legal doctrine supports the concept of *vicarious hospital liability*, which is contingent upon first establishing the fault of the physician or another healthcare professional. In such cases, liability may arise from *culpa in eligendo* (fault in selection) or *culpa in vigilando* (fault in supervision), in accordance with Articles 932 (III), 942, and 933 of the Brazilian Civil Code. This aligns with the previously discussed (Sect. 3.1.1) *Theory of Mitigated Objective Liability* (Barbosa and Mascarenhas 2021), according to which the hospital's strict liability is established only after the professional's fault has been recognised.

Additionally, hospitals assume direct and strict liability for ensuring the proper maintenance of medical devices and equipment installed on their premises, particularly in the context of AI system implementation. Price (2018) aptly highlights that, although hospitals are not directly accountable for inherent defects in the medical devices they use, they are obligated to diligently and continuously monitor the quality and performance of these technologies. This duty extends to ensuring that maintenance is performed in accordance with the manufacturer's guidelines and that any necessary updates are promptly implemented to maintain the device's functionality and safety.

The hospital's responsibility also includes assessing the scientific integrity of algorithms both before deciding to integrate them into the institution and after their implementation, to periodically verify their accuracy and performance as claimed by the manufacturer. Additionally, they have an obligation to maintain consistent training and qualification programs for their medical staff. Failure to meet these obligations may result in strict liability, reflecting the hospital's non-delegable duty to safeguard patient safety through the proper management of medical technologies.

On the concept of prevention as a general legal duty and a cornerstone of contemporary civil liability, Zampier (2022) argues that as technological societies uncover more risks, the greater the need for a legal system that fosters virtuous behaviour among agents who might potentially infringe upon the rights of others. This underscores the importance of regulating sectors exposed to direct or indirect risks through specific legislation designed to play a preventive role *ex ante*. Such an approach aligns with the evolving role of civil liability, which seeks not only to compensate for harm but also to mitigate risks by proactively influencing conduct. In high-risk fields like medicine, particularly with the integration of AI technologies, this preventive framework is essential to ensure accountability and protect fundamental rights, thereby promoting a more responsible and ethical approach to innovation.

An illustrative example can be found in the Brazilian resolution regulating robotic surgeries (Resolution No. 2,311/2022 of the Federal Council of Medicine). This regulation demonstrates the importance of ensuring that hospitals and clinics implementing new technologies possess the necessary technical conditions, equipment, physical facilities (Art. 2), as well as support services for all potential complications and adequate human resources for specialised care (Annex 1 of the Resolution). Moreover, the resolution imposes a duty on the hospital's technical director to verify documentation confirming the medical team's training and competence with the technology (Art. 5). It also sets out requirements for the training and qualification of physicians using the technology (Arts. 3 and 4, and Annex 2).

Ensuring appropriate conditions for the use of AI by adequately trained professionals, coupled with ongoing evaluation and monitoring, should be achieved through a compliance program aligned with the hospital's bioethics committee. This obligation stems from two AI ethical principles: (1) *promoting AI that is responsive and sustainable*, and (2) *fostering responsibility and accountability*. These principles should be incorporated into future regulations governing AI technology in Brazil, both legislatively—through the anticipated publication of a legal framework for AI—and ethically, applying norms issued by the Federal Council of Medicine. However, it is hoped that Brazil's regulatory body will not delay nearly 15 years to issue ethical standards for AI, as occurred with robotic surgeries, which were implemented in 2008 but only regulated in 2022 by the Federal Council of Medicine.

A compliance program must align with the hospital's bioethics committee and, in evaluating AI systems, should fulfil at least five obligations:

1. Assess which AI system is most appropriate for each purpose, considering the scientific integrity of the system. It is essential to evaluate the AI system's design, methodology, and evidence base to ensure its suitability for the intended clinical application. This assessment should also examine whether the AI system incorporates local population biomedical data and adheres to the clinical guidelines and healthcare standards of the region where the technology will be implemented. Such considerations are crucial to ensure the system's recommendations are relevant, applicable, and tailored to the specific needs of the local patient population.
2. Account for specific use cases, identify relevant regulatory requirements, and monitor compliance post-implementation in the clinical environment. Each AI system must be assessed for its applicability to particular medical scenarios, considering factors such as patient demographics and local healthcare practices. Once implemented, continuous oversight should ensure the system adheres to all legal and regulatory obligations, including updates to applicable standards or guidelines.
3. Develop a comprehensive AI governance and risk management strategy, ensuring the necessary technical conditions, physical infrastructure, and clearly defined roles and responsibilities among the involved professionals. Governance frameworks should establish robust protocols for risk assessment, incident reporting, and corrective measures. Hospitals must also allocate sufficient resources, including specialised facilities and advanced equipment, to support AI operations while defining the responsibilities of every stakeholder involved in its usage.
4. Allocate accountability and governance not only internally but also with partner organisations, ensuring the teams managing and developing the AI project have the requisite skills and resources, including ongoing training and capacity building. Collaboration with external developers and vendors must include clear contractual agreements on accountability and compliance with regulatory standards. Internally, teams using the AI system must undergo regular training to ensure they remain competent and up-to-date on technological advances and operational protocols.
5. Provide continuous monitoring post-implementation, with adequate support services for potential complications and resources for specialised care, ensuring the AI system performs as expected and engaging the hospital's bioethics committee to address moral or ethical dilemmas. Post-implementation monitoring should involve periodic performance reviews to verify the AI's accuracy and efficacy against its stated objectives. Additionally, hospitals must prepare to address any ethical concerns or dilemmas that arise, ensuring timely intervention by the bioethics committee to uphold patient rights and medical integrity.

Finally, it is worth noting that physicians also bear certain responsibilities—duties of conduct—regarding the technological tools they employ in their clinical practice.

Among these duties is the obligation to monitor the technological framework they utilise (duty of vigilance), ensuring that its functioning complies with clinical standards and safeguards patient safety, within the scope of their practical capabilities. This duty, redefined under the ethical principle of *fostering responsibility and accountability*, highlights the need for data-informed oversight, requiring physicians to remain attentive to the reliability and effectiveness of the tools integrated into their practice.

Consider a hypothetical scenario involving Richard, a patient who consults an ophthalmologist (Physician 1) using an AI-based diagnostic software to assess his ophthalmological condition. This technology is presumed to enhance diagnostic precision by supporting clinical decision-making. However, over time, Richard notices a significant worsening of his vision despite adhering to the diagnosis and treatment plan prescribed by Physician 1. Dissatisfied with the lack of improvement, he decides to seek a second opinion.

Richard then consults another ophthalmologist (Physician 2), who employs a more advanced automated decision-making system, akin to an *AI Model 2.0*. During the consultation, Physician 2 observes that the *AI Model 1.0* used by Physician 1 is outdated and known for its high rate of inaccuracies, with numerous reports of erroneous results in clinical practice. Physician 2 further remarks that he has not used that older model for a considerable time, opting instead for the updated *AI Model 2.0* due to its superior reliability and precision. Supported by this more advanced AI system, Physician 2 provides Richard with an accurate diagnosis and prescribes a new treatment plan. As a result, Richard experiences significant improvement in his vision. However, he is left with permanent partial vision loss, likely attributable to the delayed initiation of appropriate treatment caused by the erroneous diagnosis provided by Physician 1.

In such a scenario, several critical issues emerge regarding liability. Firstly, could Physician 1 be held accountable for the diagnostic error and for continuing to use an outdated AI system? Secondly, if it is later discovered that the older AI system contained a programming flaw, who should bear responsibility for the harm caused—the physician, the manufacturer, or both? These questions necessitate a detailed analysis of the physician's obligations and the broader implications of integrating AI technologies into clinical practice.

Physicians are bound by two fundamental duties: the duty of updating their knowledge and skills to keep pace with advancements in medical technology, and the duty of vigilance regarding the tools and equipment they use in their practice. While these duties are integral to professional medical conduct, the standards to which a physician is held vary according to the specific circumstances of each case. For instance, it is unreasonable to expect a physician practising in a rural clinic to have access to the same advanced technologies available to practitioners in cutting-edge urban hospitals. Nevertheless, a minimum standard of diligence is always required, regardless of the setting.

If a physician relies on an outdated AI system known to produce frequent inaccuracies and this reliance results in a gross diagnostic error, they may be held liable for medical negligence. Such liability could be further aggravated if the physician failed to monitor or update the AI system, thereby breaching their duty of vigilance. This principle is consistent with precedents such as the Cobalt-60 radiotherapy incidents in Panama, as explained in Chap. 3, where inadequate maintenance of medical equipment led to significant patient harm. These examples underscore the importance of vigilance not only in monitoring patients but also in assessing the reliability of the tools and technologies employed in clinical practice.

Even if it is determined that Physician 1 did not directly cause the final harm—Richard's permanent partial vision loss—their gross diagnostic error may have reduced Richard's likelihood of achieving a full recovery. In this context, the *Loss of a Chance Doctrine* becomes relevant (see Sect. 3.1.1). This doctrine considers the lost opportunity for a better outcome as an independent harm, even when a direct causal link between the physician's negligence and the ultimate harm cannot be conclusively established. Richard's case exemplifies how this legal principle can provide recourse for patients in complex scenarios involving delayed or inadequate medical intervention.

When the diagnostic error arises from a defect in the AI system itself, the focus shifts to the manufacturer's liability. As Buchner (2022) argues, manufacturers hold primary responsibility for defective algorithms because they design and program the decision-making processes underlying these technologies. If a physician diligently uses a certified AI system approved by regulatory authorities and an error results from a programming flaw, the manufacturer, rather than the physician, should be held accountable under product liability laws. However, scenarios of concurrent causation may arise, where both the physician's actions and the defective AI system contribute to the harm. In such cases, the physician may still face liability if they continued to use the AI system despite being aware of its evident flaws, constituting a breach of their professional and ethical duties, especially the duty of vigilance.

The physician's duty of vigilance must be redefined to reflect the realities of technological integration in healthcare. This duty should extend beyond monitoring the patient's clinical condition to include, within the concrete possibilities of the situation, the continuous assessment of the tools and technologies employed in clinical practice. Such an expanded understanding is particularly relevant in an era where AI systems are increasingly central to medical decision-making. By adopting this broader perspective, the duty of vigilance evolves into a framework that ensures physicians remain proactive in safeguarding the reliability of their instruments while maintaining their commitment to patient care.

Ultimately, the physician-patient relationship is founded on trust and an ethical obligation to prioritise the patient's well-being. This existential nature of the contractual relationship between physician and patient demands that the physician exercise prudence and dignity in their professional conduct, ensuring that both the patient and the technologies employed in their care receive the necessary attention. In an era of rapid technological advancement, these duties acquire new dimensions, underscoring the need for continuous professional education and the careful integration of AI systems into clinical workflows.

In this context, it is pertinent to highlight a recent study provided by the *American Medical Association*, establishing three critical questions that physicians should consider when deciding whether to implement (or continue using) an algorithm in their clinical practice (Crigger et al. 2022):

1. *Does the AI work?* (Is the technology safe and effective, supported by scientific evidence, and consistent with ethical principles?)
2. *Does the AI work for my patients?* (Was the algorithm validated in a population and healthcare setting that reflects my clinical practice? Does my workplace have the resources, infrastructure, and training to implement the technology ethically? Am I, alongside the healthcare institution, conducting continuous monitoring of the AI's performance to communicate any observed performance issues to the developer or manufacturer?)
3. *Does the AI improve clinical outcomes?* (Has the AI improved patient care and enhanced my relationship with patients? Does the technology demonstrate a positive impact on health outcomes, minimising harm to my patients? Are diagnoses, prognoses, and treatment proposals more efficient with AI support?)

A physician who regularly evaluates these three questions fulfils their duties of care and vigilance underpinned by the principle of good faith. These guidelines reinforce the notion that physicians must diligently monitor the performance of AI systems, ensuring that an algorithm advertised as highly accurate by the manufacturer also performs at the same level when exposed to the real-world variables of diverse patient populations and clinical environments.

It is important to emphasise that the standard of diligence required in a physician's conduct is modulated over time, as previously discussed in this book, through the application of the *Theory of Changed Circumstances* in the medical context. The landscape of medical practice has been profoundly transformed by the integration of automated decision-making systems, necessitating periodic redefinition of professional duties—such as duty of vigilance—imposed by the principle of good faith. These duties must evolve to reflect the realities introduced by the new technological framework.

Acting in good faith, a physician who identifies that an AI system adds no value to their practice or consistently produces erroneous results has both an ethical and legal duty to cease using the technology. Failure to comply with such preventive duties may give rise to civil liability on the part of the physician. For example, in the case of Richard, if Physician 1 had observed over time that the AI system frequently generated inaccurate results or failed to enhance clinical decision-making, they would have an ethical-legal obligation to discontinue its use in their practice.

While the manufacturer of a defective algorithm may bear liability for its flaws, the broader debate centres on the physician's adherence to the ethical AI principle of fostering responsibility and accountability (data-informed duties). This principle is closely tied to the physician's duty of care and vigilance, which derives from the broader concept of good faith in contractual obligations. In this context, physicians must balance technological adoption with professional discretion, ensuring that any tools they use serve the best interests of their patients while maintaining accountability and oversight.

It is important to emphasise that, given the potential for inaccurate or inadequate data contaminating machine learning processes, Frank Pasquale's proposal for the *parametrisation of data-informed duties* in the use of AI has been previously highlighted. Within this framework, specific obligations are imposed on algorithmic operators—including physicians as front-end operators of autonomous systems.

As Miragem (2007) asserts, it is an inescapable requirement that medical professionals remain up-to-date in their field of practice. Continuous education and training are integral to the professional duty of technical knowledge, ensuring that physicians align themselves with the current scientific advancements and the evolving standards of medical science. Moreover, as argued by Faleiros Júnior (2020), this encompasses an adapted range of duties of care, including: (1) the selection of appropriate technology; (2) proper monitoring of its performance; and (3) verification of maintenance, addressing general issues of safety and necessary repairs. Failure to fulfil these obligations may lead to liability, underscoring the need for vigilance and adherence to professional standards in the use of AI technologies in medical practice.

Furthermore, as argued previously in this section, compliance programs in healthcare institutions must be afforded appropriate legal recognition, elevating them to a critical tool for identifying and quantifying responsibilities rather than merely a corporate mechanism for compliance and risk management. The ethical principle of accountability—applied both *ex ante* and *ex post*—offers pathways to reconcile the desired innovation with necessary legal certainty. Regarding civil liability, the preventive and precautionary functions serve as guiding principles for technological development in the healthcare sector, reflecting a redefinition of the duty of care and vigilance for hospitals and healthcare professionals.

In Italy, Comandé (2019a, b) advocates for the concept of a multilayered *accountability framework for artificial intelligence*, a concept that merits thorough examination. This perspective highlights that responsibility functions on multiple tiers, integrating legal, ethical, and social elements. For example, accountability mechanisms should delineate obligations across various phases of AI development, deployment, and operation, ensuring that liability is equitably shared among developers, deployers, and operators of AI systems. Furthermore, such mechanisms must identify the party best positioned to undertake data-driven responsibilities, requiring them to provide transparent justification for their decisions, particularly when these affect individuals or groups. This approach not only ensures fairness but also promotes trust in AI systems by aligning accountability with the capacity to manage risks and mitigate harm effectively. The integration of these principles into regulatory and organisational frameworks strengthens the legitimacy and reliability of AI-based technologies in sensitive domains such as healthcare and public services.

As previously discussed in this work, the advent of artificial intelligence in medicine has prompted the evolution of civil liability to operate *ex ante facto*, advancing toward the recognition of a precautionary function. This shift is crucial for harmonising technological development with the protection of fundamental rights, aiming to minimise algorithmic biases or defects while fostering a culture of accountability.

In the context of complex, plural, and highly technological societies characterised by uncertainty and emerging risks, the necessity of transcending the monofunctional nature of civil liability becomes evident. Baptista dos Santos (2018) stands out as a prominent voice in Brazilian legal doctrine, emphasising the need to realign the theory of civil liability with contemporary ethics—advocating for a forward-looking approach centred on precautionary duties.

In today's landscape of increasingly integrated medical technologies, the objective of civil liability, as argued by Rosenvald and Clemente (2022), extends far beyond merely compensating for damages already incurred. They contend that civil liability should function not merely as a mechanism for damage containment but also as a tool for the regulation of behaviour, thereby fostering responsibility and accountability within the technological and medical domains.

On the significance of the preventive and precautionary function in the context of AI in medicine, German professor Buchner (2022) provides a critical perspective. He argues that the preventive role of civil liability rules is essential to ensuring that AI does not prematurely enter everyday clinical practice under the often-invoked banner of necessary medical and technological progress. The author points out that there are numerous examples of seemingly innovative advancements in medicine—whether new treatment methods, pharmaceuticals, or medical devices—where the anticipated benefits ultimately fell short of the associated risks.

A preventive liability regime, with clearly defined responsibilities, serves a crucial deterrent function in this regard. This is particularly vital in the realm of AI-based medicine, where such a framework can act as a safeguard to ensure that an ostensibly AI algorithm does not later prove to be poorly designed or unwisely programmed. As Buchner (2022) aptly warns, the potential for harm underscores the need for robust regulatory oversight and accountability to balance the promise of innovation with patient safety and ethical medical practice. This preventive approach highlights the broader importance of incorporating precautionary principles into legal frameworks governing AI in healthcare, reinforcing the need for rigorous evaluation before integrating new technologies into clinical practice.

Furthermore, within Brazilian legal doctrine, some scholars have advocated for a promotional function of civil liability (Braga Netto and Nogaroli 2023). Following this perspective, in cases where an adverse event involving AI occurs, but it is established, for instance, that the physician and/or hospital invested in compliance and adhered to best practice standards—upholding ethical principles and duties of conduct stemming from good faith, while maintaining constant monitoring of the technology—it may be possible to consider an equitable reduction of damages. This concept draws from Article 944, sole paragraph, of the Brazilian Civil Code, *in verbis*: "If there is excessive disproportion between the severity of the fault and the damage, the judge may equitably reduce the compensation".

This approach introduces an element of promotional civil liability, aiming to encourage meritorious behaviour. By recognising and rewarding efforts to implement robust compliance frameworks, adhere to ethical practices, and maintain diligent oversight of technological tools, this model seeks not only to address harm but also to incentivise proactive measures that align with the principles of responsibility and accountability in healthcare.

The Brazilian legal scholars Rosenvald and Faleiros Júnior (2021) highlight that the *ex post* dimension of accountability serves as a guide for judges in identifying and quantifying responsibilities. It allows for the establishment of proportional and appropriate remedies tailored to the circumstances of each technology and specific situation, rooted in a comprehensive understanding of civil liability. In this context, emphasis is placed on the potential to consider effective compliance investments as a mitigating factor for damages, as provided for in the sole paragraph of Article 944 of the Brazilian Civil Code, which permits judges to equitably reduce compensation when there is a disproportion between the severity of fault and the harm caused.

The core idea is that recognising compliance efforts as a form of *reward-based sanction* enables the legal system to incentivise economic agents and organisations to adopt additional safety and diligence measures. This approach diverges from traditional civil liability models, which often disregard preventive efforts, particularly in cases of strict liability. By rewarding commendable practices, such as robust compliance programs, the accountability model acquires a multifunctional role that transcends mere compensation or damage neutralisation. This perspective fosters risk prevention and promotes more responsible and diligent behaviour among economic actors, a principle that is increasingly vital in the context of technological advancements, such as the integration of AI, which heighten the complexities of civil liability frameworks.

Beyond doctrinal discussions regarding the interpretation of Brazilian legislation, the ideas presented above align with the systematic approach outlined in the recent proposal to reform the Brazilian Civil Code. In August 2023, a commission of legal experts was established to review the Civil Code, chaired by Minister Luis Felipe Salomão of the Superior Court of Justice. In April 2024, the proposed revisions were submitted to the Senate as a bill for debate and voting (Draft Bill No. 4/2025).

As previously discussed, the concept of civil liability has evolved in recent years to encompass an *ex ante* function, incorporating roles beyond mere reparation, such as prevention, precaution, and the promotion of responsible behaviour. These additions are particularly significant given the new challenges posed by emerging medical technologies.

Within this context, the proposal to include §1° in Article 927-A introduces a duty for individuals and organisations to take measures to prevent foreseeable harm, *in verbis*:

> Anyone who creates a risk situation or is responsible for containing the resulting harm is obliged to take measures to prevent it. §1° Every person has a duty, acting in good faith and in accordance with the circumstances, to adopt measures within their reach to prevent the occurrence of foreseeable harm that could be attributed to them, mitigate its extent, and avoid aggravating the harm if it has already occurred.

Additionally, the Report of the Subcommittee on Civil Liability, represented by Nelson Rosenvald and other jurists, created as part of the Civil Code reform process, emphasised the need to explicitly assess whether the individual acted in good faith. The report also proposed extending the possibility of equitable reduction of damages to include cases of strict liability—an interpretation already supported by some legal scholars. In this regard, the proposed Article 944, §1° states:

> If there is an excessive disproportion between the act committed by the individual and the extent of the resulting harm, according to the principles of good faith, or if the compensation provided for in this article deprives the offender or their dependents of necessities, the judge may equitably reduce the compensation, including in cases of strict liability.

The proposed amendments to the Brazilian Civil Code reflect a modernised approach to civil liability, incorporating preventive and precautionary principles that are essential in addressing the complexities introduced by technological advancements, particularly in fields such as medicine. By requiring individuals and organisations to act in good faith and take proactive measures to mitigate harm, these provisions aim to promote greater accountability and foster a culture of responsibility. Moreover, the explicit recognition of equitable reduction in strict liability cases ensures that compensation mechanisms remain fair and balanced, further advancing the multi-faceted role of civil liability in contemporary legal systems.

In summary, the interplay between human expertise and algorithmic intelligence demands a redefinition of diligence and accountability in clinical practice. Legal systems and scholars worldwide must adapt to these challenges, fostering an environment where AI serves as a tool to complement—not replace—the critical thinking and ethical obligations of medical professionals. By ensuring that physicians remain vigilant and proactive in their interaction with AI systems, it is possible to maximise the potential of these technologies while safeguarding patient welfare and maintaining the integrity of medical decision-making.

5.3 Breach of Patient Trust as a Basis for Medical Liability in AI

In recent years, there has been a proliferation of sensationalist advertisements on social media platforms portraying medical technologies as revolutionary solutions with guaranteed success rates. These campaigns contribute to heightened patient expectations, potentially leading to misconceptions about the capabilities and limitations of such systems. Physicians who echo these claims, explicitly or implicitly, risk undermining the trust-based nature of the physician-patient relationship and exposing themselves to liability if outcomes fail to meet the inflated expectations.

This raises critical questions: how would such assurances impact the assessment of medical liability for adverse events? Does the physician's obligation remain one of means, wherein they are expected to act diligently and within professional standards, or *does it shift to an obligation of result*, implying a guarantee of success? Such scenarios demand nuanced legal and ethical analysis, particularly in the context of emerging AI technologies, where transparency, explainability, and professional diligence are paramount in maintaining patient trust and safeguarding against liability.

To address these issues, it is helpful to examine the discussions within the American medical and legal communities regarding surgical assistance robots. In the landmark case *Zarick v. Intuitive Surgical* (2016) and other litigations involving patients in the United States, during the early 2000s, it was discussed that the Da Vinci robotic systems were heavily marketed as the best—and sometimes the only—treatment option for the patient. The technology was described as exceptionally precise, almost guaranteeing success with no adverse events. However, several patients suffered serious injuries from defective robotic components that were later recalled.

This issue was prominently highlighted in the Netflix documentary *The Bleeding Edge*, which reveals how regulatory gaps have allowed insufficiently tested and potentially harmful technologies to enter the healthcare market. These cases also underscore the crucial duty of physicians to inform patients about both the benefits and risks of new technologies. While robotic-assisted surgery offers numerous advantages, its use must be restricted to conditions where efficacy and safety are well-established. Traditional open or laparoscopic surgery often remains the preferred option in specific clinical scenarios. In 2021, the Food and Drug Administration (FDA) issued a communication emphasising the lack of robust evidence supporting the safety and efficacy of Da Vinci robots in mastectomy procedures for breast cancer prevention or treatment.

This context highlights the need for continuous and adequate medical education, enabling physicians to critically evaluate which technologies enhance their clinical practice and benefit individual patients. Similar concerns extend to the use of automated decision-making systems in diagnosis, prognosis, and treatment recommendations. A lack of education regarding these technologies, coupled with overreliance on algorithmic predictions, risks misleading patients into believing that such tools are infallible and guarantee specific outcomes.

Moreover, physicians have a duty to respect patients' legitimate expectations through transparent communication and dialogue. This *responsibility includes avoiding explicit or implicit promises of guaranteed success when employing AI in healthcare*. In this regard, adherence to the ethical *principle of promoting responsive and sustainable AI* aligns with the contractual *duty of cooperation and loyalty* arising from the principle of good faith.

The violation of the duty of cooperation and loyalty differs fundamentally from the duty of information, particularly in the context of AI in healthcare. While the second focuses on ensuring that patients receive accurate, comprehensive, and transparent information, the first addresses a distinct issue.

The *duty of loyalty* is breached when there is an active conduct by the physician in conveying imprecise, inaccurate, or outright incorrect information to the patient. For instance, this might involve overestimating the accuracy or capabilities of an AI system, or falsely assuring the patient of a guaranteed positive outcome simply because the AI was utilised. Such conduct fosters unrealistic expectations and undermines the patient's ability to make an informed and autonomous decision.

In the case of AI, a breach of the patient trust occurs when the physician rely excessively on algorithmic predictions and present them as infallible, failing to acknowledge the inherent limitations and fallibility of the autonomous system. By actively providing misleading information, the professional not only compromises the patient's legitimate expectations but also violates the ethical *principle of promoting AI that is responsive and sustainable*.

This distinction is critical because the duty of cooperation and loyalty pertains to the active creation of undue reliance on the AI system, whereas the duty of information focuses on ensuring that the patient is sufficiently informed to consent to or reject a proposed course of action. Both duties are integral to respecting the patient's autonomy and maintaining the integrity of the physician-patient relationship.

The *principle of trust* is paramount in physician-patient relationships, ensuring the fulfilment of legitimate expectations and forming a cornerstone of contemporary contractual good faith. As César Silva (2018) notes in his analysis of contractual law, existential contracts—those involving the human body as their subject—demand relationships founded on fidelity, transparency, and trust. Any breach of these elements may constitute a violation of good faith, resulting in a breach of contract.

However, as demonstrated in Sect. 4.1.2 by the risks of *epistemic opacity*, a physician's lack of understanding of an AI system's functionality and limitations can lead to its *misuse as an end in itself* rather than a tool. If a physician fails to understand the system's limitations and guarantees absolute success to a patient due to reliance on the technology, two legal pathways may emerge.

First, as already mentioned, such conduct could breach the *duty of loyalty* and its corresponding ethical *principle of promoting responsive AI*. Misrepresenting AI's capabilities violates the patient's legitimate expectations and constitutes a breach of contract based on good faith. Second, if a physician presents the technology as infallible, this might shift their obligation from one of means to one of result, given the promise of guaranteed success. This misrepresentation undermines trust and may redefine the juridic nature of physician's liability under contract law.

In other words, *the legal repercussions of qualifying the physician's obligation as one of result, rather than means*, merit careful consideration. When physicians explicitly or implicitly guarantee a specific outcome based on the use of AI, they risk elevating their contractual responsibility, moving beyond the expectation of diligence to one of assured success. Such a transition would not only reshape the dynamics of the physician-patient relationship but also redefine the legal framework governing medical liability. Physicians must tread carefully, balancing the promise of technological advancements with the inherent uncertainties of medical practice. Overpromising the capabilities of AI systems undermines patient trust and potentially creates a pattern for liability that extends beyond their traditional professional standards.

As discussed in Sect. 2.2.2, some Brazilian scholars argue that breaching these duties may transform the physician's obligation from one of means to one of result, as it creates a legitimate expectation of a specific outcome. This principle is particularly relevant in medical advertising, which is regulated by Resolution CFM No. 2.336/2023 and the Brazilian Consumer Protection Code (CDC). Articles 6(IV), 30, 31, 35, 36, and 38 of the CDC prohibit misleading and abusive advertising, with non-compliance attracting sanctions under Articles 56, 60, 67, 68, and 69. Physicians must navigate the balance between innovation and ethical responsibilities, preserving patient trust and adhering to legal standards.

The issue of binding promises in medical advertising is also addressed in Spanish law, as highlighted by Cortés (2024). Jurisprudence from the Spanish Supreme Court, including rulings from 14 June 1976 and 27 January 1977, based on Article 1258 of the Spanish Civil Code, establishes that advertising forms part of the contract under the principle of good faith. For example, the 27 January 1977 decision asserts that promises made in promotional materials become binding when they create legitimate expectations in consumers, even if such details are not explicitly stated in the contract. Additionally, Article 61.1 of the General Law for the Protection of Consumers reinforces that advertising terms can be enforced by consumers, obligating the provider to honour what was promoted. Applied to medical advertising, this means that physicians who promise specific outcomes through social media promotions create legitimate expectations in patients and may face legal consequences (liability) for failing to meet these promises. This underscores the importance of ethical advertising practices in medicine, grounded in good faith and professional integrity.

As observed, respecting patients' legitimate expectations is essential to the practice of medicine worldwide. They rely on healthcare professionals to provide accurate, transparent information and to manage their care responsibly. The inherent uncertainties of medicine, coupled with the risks of therapeutic outcomes, mean that no technology can offer absolute infallibility. Physicians must therefore approach AI as a decision-support tool rather than a guarantee of success, ensuring patients are informed of both its potential and its limitations.

Continuous medical education is vital to staying abreast of technological advancements and adopting best practices. By critically assessing AI outputs and integrating them responsibly into clinical workflows, physicians can make informed decisions that benefit their patients. As Zampier (2022) highlights,

> understanding the functioning of algorithms, particularly regarding the production of their results, is essential for detecting and resolving contradictions. Such diligence preserves the legitimate exercise of legal rights and compliance with the duties of good faith.

Therefore, education plays a central role in responsibly integrating AI into medical practice, bridging ethical and technical implications. At the same time, respecting patient expectations is crucial to maintaining trust and fostering collaboration. Through continuous professional development, physicians can ethically employ AI, deliver high-quality care, and uphold their obligations, meeting the needs and expectations of their patients.

As the integration of AI in healthcare advances, it becomes crucial to establish clear legal and ethical boundaries that uphold the physician's role as a diligent and transparent practitioner, rather than an infallible guarantor of outcomes. This approach ensures that the adoption of AI enhances medical care while preserving the trust, autonomy, and rights of patients.

5.4 Medical Liability and Patient Consent in AI-Assisted Clinical Decisions

Numerous criticisms have arisen regarding the fact that patients are frequently not informed or asked to consent to the use of AI systems in their healthcare (Robbins and Brodwin 2020). This underscores the critical importance of debating the contours of the doctrine of informed consent and determining the circumstances under which a physician might be held liable.

Many physicians still adhere to a markedly paternalistic approach, claiming mastery of the leges artis of their profession and therefore believing they are not obligated to inform patients about all the tools employed—such as AI systems—in the clinical decision-making process. In a recent interview, Jessica Hamzelou archive (2023), a professor of technology and regulation at the University of Oxford (USA), expressed concern about the rise of what is known as *AI Paternalism* as these technologies become embedded in healthcare environments. AI Paternalism refers to the tendency to rely heavily on AI systems in decision-making while withholding information about the technology's involvement from patients. This practice shifts power and control to AI-driven processes, often undermining patient autonomy and transparency by prioritising efficiency or professional authority over full disclosure.

In 2020, it was reported that thousands of patients hospitalised at one of the largest healthcare entities in Minnesota, USA, had their discharge planning decisions supported by an AI system. However, none of these patients was informed about the technology's involvement in the medical decision-making process (Robbins and Brodwin 2020). One physician at the facility remarked: "Just as I wouldn't tell a patient that an X-ray 'decided' they are ready to go home, in practice, we generally don't mention the use of AI either." She further argued that disclosing the autonomous system to patients made little sense, stating that doing so "could result in lengthy discussions with curious individuals about the technology and how the algorithm was created," which "might divert valuable time away from more critical medical and logistical details".

The lack of disclosure about the technology employed in healthcare means that patients may never know if an AI model made an incorrect recommendation, contributing to improper treatment or unnecessary, costly, or even harmful interventions. Physicians often argue that revealing the use of AI to patients has the potential to create unnecessary distractions and negatively impact the trust patients place in their medical care. However, the author of this book disagrees with this justification, as previously outlined in Chap. 4. The forthcoming lines will argue that full transparency regarding AI systems is essential not only to uphold the physician's duty to inform but also to reinforce patient trust through ethical and open communication.

Automated systems should represent a gain in time, enabling physicians to spend more of it engaging in meaningful dialogue with patients during the process of obtaining free and informed consent. Rather than being viewed as an obstacle, AI disclosure can serve as a foundation for building trust and ensuring that the integration of such technologies aligns with the ethical tenets of patient-centred care.

As discussed throughout this book, patient consent is a fundamental prerequisite for medical practice. It represents a permissive decision that authorises the physician's actions, arising from an informative and decisional process that varies in length and detail according to the specific circumstances of each case. A physician may, depending on the situation, be held liable for harm resulting from the instruments, devices, or equipment used in their care. On this subject, Aguiar Dias (2006) warns:

> If the application of an instrument entails risks, it is the physician's duty to inform the patient, bearing responsibility for any harmful consequences if they fail to do so; acceptance of risks cannot be presumed.

When analysing the peculiarities of patient consent in the context of artificial intelligence, based on the table presented in the preceding section regarding the standard of medical diligence required when utilising such technology, it becomes evident that even when the physician is not at fault (scenarios 1, 3, 4, 5, and 8), they may still be held directly liable for breaching a duty of conduct stemming from the principle of good faith. Conversely, when fault is established—such as in scenarios 2 and 7—and is compounded by a breach of the duty to inform the patient, this breach may serve as a factor to increase the quantum of damages awarded as compensation (Maranhão and Nogaroli 2022). This aligns with the interpretation outlined in Sect. 2.2.3, where such violations are considered aggravating factors in the quantification of damages.

The breach of a physician's duty to inform gives rise to an obligation to compensate. For civil liability to be established due to a failure to obtain proper consent, a clear causal relationship must be demonstrated between the lack of (or incorrect) information provided and the ultimate harm suffered. The harm arises from a risk about which the patient should have been informed, thereby enabling them to deliberate and decide whether to accept a particular treatment, for instance. The reinterpretation of the doctrine of patient consent, as advocated in this book, requires that the concept of *consenting* be understood as a process rather than an isolated act.

Furthermore, the content of the information that must form part of this informative-decisional process remains the subject of ongoing doctrinal debate, particularly in the context of artificial intelligence. For this reason, several critical issues must be carefully considered. In general, both in Brazil and European countries such as Portugal, legal doctrine and case law have endorsed the *Theory of Significant Risks* (see Sec. 2.2.1), which requires physicians to disclose significant risks—those that a medical professional knows or ought to know are important and relevant to the average person placed in similar circumstances as the patient. In this context, careful consideration of the frequency and severity of the risk is essential to determine the scope of information that must be conveyed to and comprehended by the patient.

Moreover, an essential factor in analysing the minimum content of informed consent, as Pereira (2004) argues, is the *novelty of the treatment*. The newer a therapeutic or diagnostic procedure, the greater the rigor required in the information provided to the patient. Similarly, the introduction of novel technologies, especially those involving AI or other advanced systems, necessitates heightened transparency and detailed explanations of potential risks, limitations, and uncertainties.

As highlighted in the preceding section of this book, a table was presented outlining possible legal scenarios in physician-AI interaction. In the first scenario, a physician adheres to the AI's accurate recommendation by prescribing 15 mg/kg for cancer treatment, successfully curing the patient and eradicating the cancer. Nevertheless, despite this positive outcome, the patient develops adverse side effects, such as difficulties in managing diabetes, which might have been avoided had an alternative treatment—CAR-T cell therapy—been selected.

CAR-T cell therapy, an innovative form of genetic treatment, offers a less aggressive and potentially more beneficial option compared to traditional chemotherapy, particularly as it gains broader recognition within the medical community. The physician's failure to inform the patient about this alternative, even when it is available and recommended by the AI, represents a violation of the duty of information. Conversely, if the physician does disclose the possibility of using such technology, the process of obtaining informed consent must still be carefully examined, particularly considering the criterion of treatment novelty.

In this context, it is essential to address findings such as those revealed in January 2024 by a study conducted at Massachusetts General Hospital in the United States, which investigated the communication profile between oncologists and patients (and their families) regarding CAR-T Cell therapy. The research found that physicians often focus on the innovative and effective aspects of this therapy but rarely discuss specific risks, the possibility (even if small) of treatment failure, or the planning of advanced care. While emphasising the positive outcomes of the technology is appropriate and important (Dhawale et al. 2024), it leaves a significant gap in patient understanding of potential negative results, risks, treatment failures, toxicities, and other side effects.

As with any medical intervention, CAR-T Cell therapy involves inherent risks and therapeutic uncertainties, with each patient potentially responding differently to the same treatment. A comprehensive explanation of CAR-T Cell therapy should encompass how it works, why it is innovative, and the types of cancer for which it is currently approved—specifically tailored to the patient's case. This foundational understanding allows patients to weigh the associated benefits and risks effectively.

Healthcare professionals should also commit to continuous communication, enabling patients to ask questions, express concerns, and revisit decisions as treatment evolves or new circumstances arise. For example, during a consultation observed in Brazil by the author of this book, an oncologist explained:

> Mr. Peter, one treatment option we are considering at this point is CAR-T Cell therapy. This is a form of treatment that uses your own immune system to fight cancer. It involves genetically modifying some of your immune cells so that they can better recognise and attack cancer cells.

Such a simplified yet precise introduction helps patients grasp the fundamental mechanism of the therapy.

An integral part of the informed consent process involves discussing risks and side effects—at least the most common and specific to the proposed treatment. For CAR-T Cell therapy, this includes potential complications like Cytokine Release Syndrome (CRS), neurotoxicity, infections, cytopenias, and toxicity to non-target organs.

Managing patient expectations is equally crucial, particularly with medical innovations. While CAR-T Cell therapy holds significant promise for treating specific haematological cancers, particularly those unresponsive to previous treatments, public perception often exceeds realistic outcomes. Media coverage frequently highlights success stories of cures or complete remissions, which, while genuine, do not represent every patient's experience.

Cancer patients, especially those in advanced stages or who have exhausted other options, may cling to the hope of a "miraculous cure." Although fostering optimism is essential, physicians must carefully manage these expectations to prevent disappointment and avoid potential civil liability for breaches of the duty of information. Given the complexity of CAR-T Cell therapy and the heightened vulnerability of oncology patients, each case requires a personalised approach. Consent should address the patient's individual history, hopes, fears, and expectations, fostering open dialogue about the potential benefits, risks, side effects, and possible outcomes of success or failure.

In this context, *qualified consent* is particularly critical when introducing innovative technologies. This approach ensures that patients receive thorough, accurate, and comprehensible information, empowering them to make informed decisions. For groundbreaking therapies like CAR-T Cell, qualified consent not only enhances patient autonomy but also protects healthcare providers by demonstrating adherence to ethical and legal standards in obtaining informed consent. By bridging the gap between medical innovation and patient understanding, qualified consent strengthens trust and supports ethically sound clinical practices.

Moreover, the integration of AI systems in clinical practice raises additional considerations for informed consent. Patients should be made aware of the AI's role in their diagnosis or treatment, including the system's capabilities, limitations, and the extent of its involvement in clinical decisions. This obligation becomes even more pronounced when the technology introduces complexities that may impact the predictability or reliability of outcomes.

In conclusion, as medical practice evolves with the introduction of emerging technologies, the doctrine of informed consent must likewise adapt to ensure that patients are fully aware of and actively participate in decisions about their care. A failure to uphold these standards not only undermines patient autonomy but also exposes healthcare providers to potential liability for inadequate disclosure or negligent use of technological tools.

The discussion on patient consent in the context of AI intersects with two of the previously mentioned semantic dimensions of AI in Medicine: *opacity due to non-disclosure* and *explanatory opacity* (a thesis originally developed by Nogaroli and

Faleiros Júnior 2023). In this regard, there is a dual risk: the physician may fail to disclose that an automated decision-making system was used to support the clinical decision, and/or they may neglect to explain the functioning and role of the technology in a manner aligned with the patient's level of understanding.

In 2020, Glenn Cohen published the article *Informed Consent and Medical Artificial Intelligence: What to Tell the Patient?*, which is widely regarded as the first comprehensive academic work to deeply examine how AI systems interact with the doctrine of patient informed consent. The article includes an illustrative example, which we adapt below for further analysis.

Imagine a scenario where you are a patient diagnosed with prostate cancer. There are two primary treatment approaches available:

1. Expectant management/active surveillance: this approach involves less intensive management, relying on regular medical monitoring and periodic tests. Based on changes in symptoms or clinical status, the physician determines whether intervention via radiation therapy or surgery is necessary. Prostate cancer often grows slowly, and for some patients—particularly older men or those with other significant health issues—immediate treatment may not be required. In such cases, physicians may recommend expectant management, also referred to as watchful waiting, or active surveillance, to delay or avoid unnecessary treatment.
2. Radical prostatectomy (surgical removal of the prostate): this option involves surgically removing the prostate gland to eliminate the tumour. If robotic-assisted surgery is employed, it offers distinct benefits compared to traditional techniques, such as smaller incisions, reduced trauma, enhanced precision through high-definition imaging, and improved preservation of critical structures like nerves controlling erectile function and urinary continence. These advancements contribute to quicker recovery times, shorter hospital stays, and a lower risk of side effects, optimising outcomes while aiming to maintain the patient's quality of life.

Despite the advantages of each treatment approach, it is crucial for physicians to discuss both the benefits and potential risks, ensuring patients make informed decisions that align with their individual preferences and medical circumstances.

However, imagine a scenario where your physician does not disclose that their recommendation for prostatectomy (instead of active surveillance) was based on a decision made with the aid of an artificial intelligence (AI) system. The AI recommended the treatment plan after analysing factors such as your age, tumour size, other health data, and personal characteristics found in your electronic medical record, combined with its database. This raises a critical question: has the physician ensured informed consent—interpreted as free and fully informed consent—from both an ethical and legal perspective?

Conversely, suppose the physician chooses to disregard the AI's recommendation and instead advises you to opt for active surveillance rather than undergoing prostatectomy. If this decision is contrary to the AI's algorithmic output and the physician does not disclose this deviation, could it be argued that they violated a legal or ethical obligation related to informed consent?

Additionally, the following considerations become pertinent: If you later discovered that an autonomous system was used to make recommendations about your care without your knowledge, how would you feel? Upon reflection, do you know if an AI algorithm was involved the last time you consulted with a physician?

In the scenario described above—an adaptation of the example created by Cohen (2019)—the author concludes that, generally, physicians are not held civilly liable for failing to inform patients about the use of AI in formulating diagnoses, prognoses, and/or treatment proposals. However, the author of this book disagrees with this position. This disagreement is based on the *sui generis* nature of medical practice, the hyper-vulnerability of patients in the context of AI, and the premise that the physician-patient relationship, as an *existential contract*, must be functionalised in light of the *Post-Constitutionalisation of Civil Law* globally and the emerging model of *Person-Centred Medicine*, as outlined in Sect. 2.1.

Globally, the doctrine of informed consent has been evolving, as highlighted throughout this book, particularly in Sects. 2.2.1 and 4.2.1. Guided by the constitutional reinterpretation of the principle of self-determination, priority is given to the effective fulfilment of the duty to inform. This means that the information and explanations provided must be tailored to the specific patient (Soares 2021). Consequently, generic consent is deemed invalid and, therefore, subject to annulment.

As previously explained, the medical duties of informing, clarifying, and advising—rooted in the principle of contractual good faith—are closely aligned with two ethical principles specific to AI: (1) protecting human autonomy, and (2) ensuring transparency, explainability, and intelligibility.

It is essential to emphasise that informational transparency must include informing the patient that they are interacting with an AI system, thereby allowing them the choice to accept or reject the human-machine interaction (in line with the ethical principle of human autonomy). On this topic, as previously discussed in this book, reference must be made to the work of Ferreira and Pereira (2021), who reflect on patient autonomy and consent to being treated by a medical assistance robot. The authors argue that respecting a patient's refusal to engage with AI in healthcare is "a fundamental claim of the technological transition in health."

Moreover, the physician has a duty not only to disclose that an AI algorithm was used to support their clinical evaluation but also to explain how the technology works, tailoring the explanation to the patient's level of understanding (aligned with the ethical principles of transparency, explainability, and intelligibility). Failing to do so risks creating what is known as *explanatory opacity*.

Consider the example of the physician treating the Japanese patient who used Watson for Oncology to support the diagnosis and treatment proposal for cancer. The physician might explain:

> Joana, based on your clinical condition, it initially appears that you have a type of cancer X. However, we attempted a specific chemotherapy treatment without success. Therefore, we will input your data into Watson, which will cross-reference it with an extensive database and may reveal a different diagnostic picture, possibly presenting new treatment proposals ranked by confidence levels. But please note, Joana, while Watson offers various benefits, such as R and S, it has a fallibility rate of X% and involves other risks, such as Y and Z.

This example highlights the importance of respecting the informational and decisional process. The simple act of a patient reading and signing a consent form is insufficient to discharge the physician's duty to inform, even though such a document is valuable evidence of diligent medical conduct.

Professional diligence must permeate the entire process of obtaining free and informed consent, which should be understood not as a single act but as "a process that results in the emergence of shared responsibilities" (Dantas and Nogaroli 2020, 2021).

Shared decision-making, as described earlier in this book, is integral to the framework of *Person-Centred Medicine*, aiming to promote the patient's personal autonomy and active participation as an effective agent in their health decisions. This approach ensures that the patient is not only informed but also empowered to engage meaningfully in their treatment journey.

To address the complexities of patient autonomy in the era of AI, it is essential to adopt innovative tools such as *legal design* and *visual law* (Faleiros Júnior and Calaza 2021). These approaches aim to overcome the inherent challenges of informational asymmetry, especially in scenarios involving advanced technologies like AI systems. By fostering a *fair by design framework*, these tools ensure that patients are not only informed but also empowered to make well-considered decisions about their healthcare.

E-consent, a fully electronic consent mechanism, exemplifies this paradigm. Grounded in *design thinking principles*, e-consent transforms the traditional consent process into an interactive, patient-centric experience. Through visual aids, simplified explanations, and dynamic interfaces, it enhances patient understanding of medical procedures, risks, benefits, and, critically, the role of AI systems in clinical decision-making. However, it is fundamental to emphasise that e-consent is designed to complement, rather than replace, the personal explanation provided by the physician. This synergy ensures that the patient benefits from both advanced technological tools and the irreplaceable human element of clinical communication.

For instance, graphical representations of an AI's decision-making process or video tutorials about its capabilities and limitations can make abstract concepts more accessible. The system allows patients to review the provided information at their own pace, ask questions in real-time, and revisit sections to ensure comprehension. Simultaneously, the physician remains actively engaged in the process, personally addressing the patient's specific concerns, clarifying any ambiguities, and contextualising the AI's role within the overall treatment strategy.

This concept is further reinforced by the informed consent model developed by Carvalho and Tatagiba (2021), which highlights the importance of creating an inclusive and efficient informational framework. While e-consent platforms provide essential foundational knowledge, the physician's direct involvement ensures that the information is tailored to the patient's unique clinical circumstances and cognitive understanding. This dual approach safeguards the ethical principles of patient-centred care, bridging technological efficiency with human compassion.

In scenarios where AI supports medical decisions, this partnership between e-consent tools and physician explanations addresses a critical need: ensuring that the AI's role and functionality are understood in a manner aligned with the patient's level of comprehension. By clarifying how the AI was used, the rationale behind its recommendations, and the physician's interpretation of these suggestions, the combined approach reinforces the *ethical principles of transparency, explainability, and intelligibility* inherent in AI.

The benefits of this integrated process extend beyond the patient experience. By *streamlining the informational-decisional process, e-consent can reduce the time physicians need to spend explaining technical details, allowing them to focus more on patient-specific care*. Additionally, the detailed record generated by e-consent platforms can serve as evidence of professional diligence in legal disputes, further aligning with preventive legal principles. Ultimately, the *collaboration between e-consent tools and personal physician explanations* represents a critical advancement in healthcare. It harmonises the benefits of AI with the ethical and legal imperatives of patient-centred care, ensuring that technology and human engagement work together to uphold autonomy, trust, and truly informed decision-making.

This evolving understanding reframes the very notion of consent—not merely as a procedural formality, but as a substantive ethical and legal process grounded in transparency, autonomy, and mutual trust. It is important to note that the redefinition of the patient's right to information, as outlined here, represents a form of *gold standard in treatment*. Thus, the unique circumstances of each case must be carefully considered when evaluating the feasibility of requiring specific conduct from a physician. Factors such as precarious working conditions or the structural limitations of the healthcare facility where the treatment occurred may impact the physician's ability to meet this standard. Balancing these considerations is essential to ensuring that the implementation of advanced tools and frameworks does not inadvertently impose unreasonable burdens on medical professionals while still upholding the patient's right to autonomy and informed decision-making.

References

Aguiar Dias J (2006) Da responsabilidade civil, 11th edn. Renovar, Rio de Janeiro

Baptista dos Santos R (2018) Responsabilidade civil por dano enorme. Juruá, Porto

Barbosa ABN, Mascarenhas IL (2021) Responsabilidade hospitalar por erro médico: a necessidade da comprovação da culpa em razão da aplicação da Teoria da Responsabilidade Objetiva Mitigada. In: Rosenvald N, Menezes JB, Dadalto L (eds) Responsabilidade civil e medicina, 2nd edn. Foco, Indaiatuba

Braga Netto FP, Nogaroli R (2023) Tecnologias digitais emergentes e o direito civil e médico no prelúdio de um admirável mundo novo. Available via Migalhas de Direito Médica e Bioética. Disponível em: https://www.migalhas.com.br/coluna/migalhas-de-direito-medico-e-bioetica/383226/tecnologias-digitais-emergentes-e-o-direito-civil-e-medico

Buchner B (2022) Artificial intelligence as a challenge for the law: the example of "Doctor Algorithm". Int Cybersecur Law Rev 3(1):181–190

Carvalho C, Tatagiba L (2021) A utilidade das ferramentas de legal design para o consentimento efetivamente esclarecido. In: Faleiros Júnior JLM, Calaza T (eds) Legal design: teoria e prática. Foco, Indaiatuba

César Silva M (2018) Convergências e assimetrias do princípio da boa-fé objetiva no direito contratual contemporâneo. In: Braga Netto FP, César Silva M (eds) Direito privado e contemporaneidade: desafios e perspectivas do direito privado no século XXI. Lumen Juris, Rio de Janeiro

Cohen IG (2020) Informed consent and medical artificial intelligence: what to tell the patient? Georgetown Law J 108:1425–1469

Comandé G (2019a) Intelligenza artificiale e responsabilità tra liability e accountability. il carattere trasformativo dell'IA e il problema della responsabilità in Analisi Giuridica dell'Economia. In: Nuzzo A, Olivieri G (eds) Analisi giuridica dell'economia: studi e discussioni sul diritto dell'impresa. Il Mulino, Bologna

Comandé G (2019b) Multilayered (accountable) liability for artificial intelligence. In: Lohsse S, Schulze R, Staudenmayer D (eds) Liability for artificial intelligence and the internet of things. Nomos, Baden-Baden

Cortés JCG (2024) Responsabilidad Civil Médica, 9th edn. Civitas, Navarra

Crigger E et al (2022) Trustworthy augmented intelligence in health care. J Med Sys 46(2):12

Dantas E, Nogaroli R (2020) Consentimento informado do paciente frente às novas tecnologias da saúde (telemedicina, cirurgia robótica e inteligência artificial). Lex Medicinae – Revista Portuguesa de Direito da Saúde 13:25–63

Dantas E, Nogaroli R (2021) The rise of robotics and artificial intelligence in healthcare: new challenges for the doctrine of informed consent. Med Law 4:15–62

Dhawale T et al (2024) Communication about chimeric antigen receptor T-Cell (Car-T) Therapy. Transplant Cell Ther 30(4):402–4e1

Facchini Neto E, Costa AP (2023) Responsabilidade civil do médico e do desenvolvedor no diagnóstico algorítmico. In: Pinho A (ed) Manual de direito na era digital - médico. Foco, Indaiatuba

Faleiros Júnior JLM (2020) Discriminação por algoritmos de inteligência artificial: a responsabilidade civil, os vieses e o exemplo das tecnologias baseadas em luminância. Revista de Direito da Responsabilidade 2:1007–1043

Faleiros Júnior JLM, Calaza T (eds) (2021) Legal design: teoria e prática. Foco, Indaiatuba

Ferreira AE, Pereira AGD (2021) Uma ética para a medicina pós-humana: propostas ético-jurídicas para a mediação das relações entre humanos e robôs na saúde. In: Rosenvald N, Menezes JB, Dadalto L (eds) Responsabilidade civil e medicina, 2nd edn. Foco, Indaiatuba

Fikes BJ (2022) Woman's lethal cancer disappears after gene-matched therapy, leaving her in full remission. Available via The San Diego Union Tribune: https://www.sandiegouniontribune.com/business/biotech/story/2019-04-22/lethal-cancer-disappears

Hamzelou J (2023) Artificial intelligence is infiltrating health care. We shouldn't let it make all the decisions. Available via MIT Technology Review: https://www.technologyreview.com/2023/04/21/1071921/ai-is-infiltrating-health-care-we-shouldnt-let-it-make-decisions

Kfouri Neto M (2024) Responsabilidade civil do médico, 12th edn. Thomson Reuters Brazil, São Paulo

Maranhão C, Nogaroli R (2022) O método bifásico como critério de quantificação dos danos morais e estéticos decorrentes da atividade médica na jurisprudência do TJ/PR. Available via Migalhas de Responsabilidade Civil: https://www.migalhas.com.br/coluna/migalhas-de-responsabilidade-civil/372731/metodo-bifasico-como-criterio-de-quantificacao-dos-danos-morais

Miragem B (2007) Responsabilidade civil médica no direito brasileiro. Revista de Direito do Consumidor 16(63):52–91

Molnár-Gábor F (2020) Artificial intelligence in healthcare: doctors, patients and liabilities. In: Wischmeyer T, Rademacher T (eds) Regulating artificial intelligence. Springer, Cham

Nilo AT (2020) Direito médico: o contrato de tratamento no direito brasileiro. Juruá, Curitiba

Nogaroli R, da Guia Silva R (2022) Inteligência artificial na análise diagnóstica: benefícios, riscos e responsabilidade do médico. In: Kfouri Neto M, Nogaroli R (eds) Debates Contemporâneos em direito médico e da saúde, 2nd edn. Thomson Reuters Brazil, São Paulo

Nogaroli R, Faleiros Júnior JLM (2023) Ethical challenges of artificial intelligence in medicine and the triple semantic dimensions of algorithmic opacity with its repercussions to patient consent and medical liability. In: Antunes HS et al (eds) Multidisciplinary perspectives on artificial intelligence and the law. Springer, Cham

Pereira AGD (2004) O consentimento informado na relação médico-paciente. Estudo de direito civil. Coimbra Publisher, Coimbra

Pereira AGD (2015) Direito dos pacientes e responsabilidade médica. Coimbra Publisher, Coimbra

Price WN (2018) Medical malpractice and black-box medicine. In: Cohen IG et al (eds) Big data, health law, and bioethics. Cambridge University Press, Cambridge

Price WN, Gerke S, Cohen IG (2019) Potential liability for physicians using artificial intelligence. J Am Med Assoc (JAMA) 322(18):1765–1766

Price WN, Gerke S, Cohen IG (2023) Liability for use of artificial intelligence in medicine. In: Cohen IG, Solaiman B (eds) Research handbook on health, AI and the law. Edward Elgar, Cheltenham

Robbins R (2020) An experiment in end-of-life care: Tapping AI's cold calculus to nudge the most human of conversations. Available via Stat News: https://www.statnews.com/2020/07/01/end-of-life-artificial-intelligence

Robbins R, Brodwin E (2020) An invisible hand: patients aren't being told about the AI systems advising their care. Available via Stat News: https://www.statnews.com/2020/07/15/artificial-intelligence-patient-consent-hospitals

Rohaidi N (2016) IBM's Watson detected rare leukemia in just 10 minutes. Available via Asian Scientist: https://www.asianscientist.com/2016/08/topnews/ibm-watson-rare-leukemia-university-tokyo-artificial-intelligence/

Rosenvald N, Clemente GT (2022) A multifuncionalidade da responsabilidade civil no contexto das novas tecnologias genéticas. Available via Migalhas de Direito Médica e Bioética: https://www.migalhas.com.br/coluna/migalhas-de-direito-medico-e-bioetica/360773/a--multifuncionalidade-da-responsabilidade-civil

Rosenvald N, Faleiros Júnior JLM (2021) Accountability e mitigação da responsabilidade civil na Lei Geral de Proteção de Dados. In: Frazão A, Cueva RVB (eds) Compliance e políticas de proteção de dados. Thomson Reuters Brazil, São Paulo

Rosenvald N, Pereira AGD, Doménech JB (2021) Proteção jurídica dos profissionais de saúde envolvidos no atendimento em contexto da pandemia da COVID-19. Cadernos Ibero-Americanos de Direito Sanitário 10(2):151–182

Ross C (2018) IBM's Watson supercomputer recommended 'unsafe and incorrect' cancer treatments; internal documents show. Available via Stat News: https://www.statnews.com/2018/07/25/ibm-watson-recommended-unsafe-incorrect-treatments

Soares FR (2021) Consentimento do paciente no direito médico: validade, interpretação e responsabilidade. Foco, Indaiatuba

Topol E (2019) Deep medicine: how artificial intelligence can make healthcare human again. Basic Books, New York

Tupasela A, Di Nucci E (2020) Concordance as evidence in the Watson for Oncology decision-support system. AI Soc 35:811–818

Zampier B (2022) Estatuto jurídico da inteligência artificial. Entre categorias e conceitos, a busca por marcos regulatórios. Foco, Indaiatuba

Chapter 6
A New Chapter for Medical Liability: Fifteen Legal and Ethical Lessons in the Age of AI

Humanity stands at the dawn of a new chapter in medical history. Artificial intelligence (AI) in healthcare represents the advent of a transformative era, offering the potential to automate routine tasks and allocate valuable time to medical professionals. By streamlining processes such as analysing vast datasets, monitoring medical histories, and conducting initial diagnostics, AI enables physicians to concentrate on more complex and critical challenges. Its ability to identify patterns, correlations, and trends within clinical data facilitates groundbreaking insights, particularly in early disease detection, personalised treatments, and the prediction of health outcomes.

Nevertheless, the adoption of AI also introduces considerable risks and challenges, including algorithmic biases, technological fallibility, and the potential erosion of patient trust due to epistemic opacity. These complexities necessitate a *revaluation* of traditional legal and ethical frameworks and require the redefinition of key concepts such as physician's duties of conduct, medical liability, and patient rights.

By alleviating administrative burdens, AI empowers healthcare professionals to devote more attention to their patients, fostering stronger connections and promoting a more humanised approach to care. Such interactions underscore that while AI enhances efficiency, it cannot replace the essential *human touch*. Healthcare professionals remain indispensable in providing compassionate care, emotional support, and shared decision-making.

The implementation of AI in healthcare has necessitated a shift in the understanding of the physicians' obligations, framing them as part of a continuous process shaped by the so-called *Post-Constitutionalisation of Civil Law* and the globally recognised paradigm of *Person-Centred Medicine*. The evolving dynamics of this relationship underline the urgency of developing clear interpretations and adaptive legal responses to the ethical and operational complexities presented by AI technologies.

R. Nogaroli, *Medical Liability and Artificial Intelligence*,
https://doi.org/10.1007/978-3-031-94306-5_6

The incorporation of AI into medical practice presents a landscape characterised by contemporary ethical and legal challenges, demanding a comprehensive understanding of how AI-specific ethical principles intersect with the contractual duties of healthcare professionals. While establishing rigid boundaries for medical liability in AI-related contexts remains impractical due to the diversity of scenarios, the analyses provided herein have aimed to elucidate standards of care, duties of conduct, and the diligence expected of physicians across varied circumstances.

At this pivotal juncture in the history of medicine, a new chapter emerges where the traditional principles of medicine intersect with the transformative capabilities of artificial intelligence. This moment calls for a thoughtful balance between innovation and the timeless values that underpin the physician-patient relationship.

The discussions within this book reflect on the intricate legal, ethical, and practical challenges AI introduces into the realm of medical liability. As these reflections are drawn to a close, it is essential to emphasise that progress must not come at the expense of humanity, and precision must not compromise empathy.

The author hopes that the reflections presented throughout this work have contributed to a deeper understanding of the delicate balance required—a balance where innovation lights the path forward, while the revaluation of concepts and legal frameworks ensures that patients' rights and medical accountability are upheld with clarity and integrity.

Considering the discussions presented throughout this book, *fifteen principal conclusions* can be summarised in the following key points outlined below.

1. It is essential to analyse the contractual relationship within medical agreements in its entirety, perceiving it as a comprehensive sequence of interconnected phases aimed at achieving a common purpose. While the central obligation remains the *duty to deliver care*, due attention must also be given to the *ancillary duties* embedded in this contract. The *physician's duties of conduct (standards)*, as debated throughout this work, represent a kind of *gold standard in treatment*. However, the peculiarities of each case must be carefully considered to determine whether it is both reasonable and feasible to demand a particular conduct from the physician, especially in the face of precarious working conditions or systemic issues related to the infrastructure of the medical facility where the care was provided. This perspective underscores the *importance of balancing the expectations placed on healthcare professionals with the realities of their working environments*, ensuring that assessments of professional responsibility are fair, context-sensitive, and aligned with the broader principles of justice and equity in medical practice.
2. To assess the right to information and any breach of patient consent, it is imperative to consider the contemporary model of *Person-Centred Medicine*, which reflects the current evolution of the physician-patient relationship. This model shifts from an authoritarian and hierarchical structure to a more *democratic and horizontal approach*, emphasising enhanced *clinical communication skills* and recognising the unique characteristics and values of each patient. In this context, the reinterpretation of the doctrine of patient consent increasingly requires

that consent be viewed as a dynamic process rather than an isolated act. This process must involve a genuine, prior, and continuous engagement in the requisite informative and decision-making procedures. By prioritising ongoing dialogue and mutual understanding, this approach fosters greater respect for patient autonomy, enabling informed and *collaborative clinical decision-making* that aligns with ethical and legal standards in modern medical practice.

3. In the context of increasingly complex, pluralistic, and technologically advanced societies characterised by uncertainty and emerging risks, the importance of an *ethics of responsibility* becomes undeniable, providing a critical foundation for the ethical governance of technical and professional activities. Modern developments in civil liability indicate a paradigm shift, grounded in the *principles of prevention and precaution*, with a heightened focus on mitigating harm and safeguarding rights. This evolution aligns with the framework of protective justice articulated by *Hans Jonas* in the *principle of responsibility* and is further exemplified in the convergence of physicians' duties of conduct, derived from the principle of contractual good faith, with the ethical imperatives associated with artificial intelligence. These duties are being redefined and expanded through the ethical principles of AI, such as transparency and accountability, which now play a crucial role in shaping the standards of professional diligence. Such an approach underscores the necessity of *reconciling technological innovation with rigorous ethical standards*, thereby preserving the integrity of patient care and addressing the inherent risks of contemporary medical practice.
4. The integration of physicians and artificial intelligence holds the potential to streamline workflows, enhance individual physician performance, and reduce the risk of human error. However, while algorithmic technologies can enable a larger number of patients to be treated more efficiently, their use may simultaneously erode the non-mechanical dimensions of care. For this reason, healthcare professionals must apply the transformative potential of technology responsibly, adhering to specific duties of conduct revaluated by the AI ethical principles. Such an approach ensures that healthcare becomes *more efficient without compromising the humanistic essence of medicine*. Humanisation in medicine is vital to fostering trust, empathy, and personalised care, elements that are essential for effective healing and patient satisfaction. To achieve this, AI should be strategically utilised for logistical and data-intensive tasks, *allowing physicians to dedicate more time to building meaningful relationships with their patients*. By doing so, the *balance between technological innovation and compassionate care* can be preserved, ensuring the well-being of patients remains at the forefront of medical practice.
5. The standard of diligence in professional conduct is subject to modulation through the *Theory of Changed Circumstances* in the healthcare context. The evolving landscape of medical practice, marked by the integration of AI systems, necessitates a *periodic revaluation and reinterpretation of physicians' duties of conduct*. These duties, traditionally grounded in principles of good faith and professional ethics, must now adapt to a reality increasingly shaped by technological advancements. The incorporation of AI in clinical workflows

introduces new tools and possibilities but also imposes heightened expectations regarding the physician's decision-making process, technical competence, and vigilance. This *resignification (revaluation) of contractual duties is not merely theoretical but practical*, as it requires healthcare professionals to respect the AI ethical principles, remaining continuously updated on emerging technologies and to exercise critical judgement in their application. Furthermore, healthcare institutions must provide the necessary infrastructure, training, and support to ensure that such tools are used effectively and ethically. Ultimately, this dynamic standard aims to harmonise technological innovation with the enduring principles of patient-centred care, ensuring that advancements enhance, rather than diminish, the quality and humanistic essence of medical practice.

6. This book has embraced a multijurisdictional perspective, reflecting on the intersection of artificial intelligence and medical liability in a manner that transcends the boundaries of specific legal systems. By analysing principles of good faith, contractual duties, and ethical obligations alongside the evolving standards of care, it provides a *framework applicable to diverse jurisdictions*. The discussions within emphasise the universal need for harmonising technological innovation with legal safeguards, balancing the transformative potential of AI with the foundational values of patient-centred care and trust. Regardless of the jurisdiction, the guiding principles of transparency, diligence, and accountability resonate as cornerstones of ethical and legal approaches to AI in medicine. Furthermore, the minimum standard of medical diligence required to establish potential liability when an AI system is involved is *evaluated consistently across legal systems*. This standard focuses on whether the physician acted in accordance with the best practices available, critically assessed AI-generated recommendations, and exercised professional judgment to ensure patient safety. This perspective reinforces the *need for a proactive, forward-thinking legal response* that accommodates the unique challenges posed by emerging technologies, while ensuring that the integrity of medical practice and the protection of patient rights remain paramount.
7. The AI ethical principle of artificial intelligence to ensure *transparency, explainability, and intelligibility* profoundly impacts the evolving *process of informed consent* in medical practice worldwide, revaluating the physician's duty of information. This ethical principle demands a reinterpretation of patient autonomy and self-determination, moving beyond a mere right to information toward a more comprehensive *right to explanation and justification*. This expanded obligation requires not only disclosing the use of AI systems but also providing a clear and accessible explanation of their role and functioning, tailored to the patient's level of understanding. Patients must be empowered with an understanding of how AI contributes to their diagnosis, prognosis, or treatment recommendations. It is not sufficient for a physician to simply inform that AI was employed; the explanation must include its purpose, the data it processed, the logic behind its outputs, and the degree of reliability and uncertainty associated with the system. Such transparency allows patients to grasp how AI assists in medical decision-making while also understanding its inherent limitations and

potential risks. This nuanced approach to informed consent ensures that patients can meaningfully participate in their care, fostering trust and enhancing shared decision-making. Tailoring these explanations to each patient's cognitive and emotional capacity underscores the ethical imperative to respect individual values and circumstances. By embracing this expanded duty, healthcare providers not only meet legal and ethical obligations but also reinforce the humanity and dignity central to the doctor-patient relationship.

8. In the pursuit of mitigating the effects of informational asymmetry in emerging technologies, the adoption of *legal design* and *visual law* tools becomes crucial. These innovative frameworks aim to create a *fair by design* environment, facilitating genuinely informed consent that empowers patients through clarity and accessibility. The concept of *e-consent* embodies this approach, leveraging digital platforms to enhance the process of obtaining informed consent. E-consent integrates interactive, user-friendly technologies with principles of *design thinking* to improve patient engagement, comprehension, and decision-making. By employing visual aids, simplified language, and customisable content tailored to individual needs, e-consent seeks to bridge communication gaps that often arise in traditional consent processes. For instance, graphical representations, videos, or infographics can help patients better understand complex medical procedures, risks, and benefits, especially when AI-based decision-making systems are involved. Moreover, *e-consent platforms* allow for real-time interaction, enabling patients to ask questions, revisit specific sections, and even access additional explanatory materials. This dynamic process not only enhances transparency but also respects the ethical *principles of explainability and intelligibility* inherent in AI technologies. Importantly, e-consent tools are designed to be inclusive, accommodating diverse literacy levels, languages, and cognitive capacities, thereby ensuring equitable access to information. By integrating e-consent into healthcare practices, physicians can foster greater patient autonomy, strengthen trust, and align with contemporary standards of diligence. Such advancements also serve to protect healthcare providers by documenting the depth and scope of the informed consent process, reducing legal disputes and potential liabilities. In this way, e-consent represents a transformative step toward harmonising technological innovation with the ethical and legal imperatives of patient-centred care. It is important to note that *e-consent is designed to supplement, not replace, the personal interaction between physician and patient*, ensuring the indispensable human aspect of clinical care remains integral. This *combined approach* clarifies the role and functionality of AI in medical decisions, aligning explanations with the patient's understanding while upholding the principles of transparency, explainability, and intelligibility. Finally, this book underscores a crucial issue: the unique circumstances of each case must be carefully evaluated to determine the practicality of imposing specific expectations on the physician, even as the redefinition of the patient's right to information establishes a benchmark for excellence in medical treatment.
9. The intersection between the ethical *principle of promoting AI that is responsive and sustainable* and the physicians' *duty of conduct of cooperation and*

loyalty arising from the objective good faith highlights the importance of acting with integrity and honesty. Such medical conduct must respect the patient's legitimate expectations and avoid creating false assurances regarding the success of autonomous systems, failing which civil liability may arise. Moreover, when a physician fails to recognise *AI as a decision-support tool* (AI-as-a-tool) and instead presents the technology—explicitly or implicitly, configurating the so-called *epistemic opacity*—as a guarantee of success in medical practice, this undermines the trust and legitimate expectations of the patient. This *misrepresentation could potentially alter the legal characterisation of the physician's obligation from one of means to one of results.* The principle of trust emerges as a safeguard for fulfilling the legitimate expectations established in contractual relationships between physician and patient. It plays a pivotal role in evaluating the substantive content of the principle of objective good faith.

10. The physician bears not only an *intrinsic duty to stay on up to date with medical knowledge* but also an *extrinsic duty related to the tools* utilised to support clinical decision-making. Acting in good faith imposes a *duty of vigilance* concerning the patient's clinical condition and, within the physician's concrete possibilities, the *technological framework employed* in healthcare. This duty of vigilance, rooted in the principle of objective good faith, aligns with the ethical *principle of AI to promote responsibility and accountability*. The healthcare professional must diligently monitor the performance of the technology, ensuring, as far as practically possible, that the algorithm functions with the same level of accuracy claimed by the manufacturer when exposed to real-world variables, including diverse patient populations across various locations. Given the potential for inaccurate or inadequate data to contaminate machine learning processes, Frank Pasquale's concept of *data-informed duties* offers a valuable framework for addressing the use of AI. As a front-end operator of autonomous systems, the physician must fulfil the following duties of conduct, failure of which may lead to liability: (1) the appropriate selection of technology; (2) continuous monitoring of its performance; and (3) conducting maintenance checks, including matters related to system updates. Furthermore, acting in good faith, if the physician determines that AI does not add value to clinical practice or frequently yields erroneous results, *there arises an ethical—and legal—duty to terminate its use*. Failure to do so may constitute a medical negligence. This position aligns with the stances adopted by certain medical associations globally, exemplified in this book through the guidelines of the American Medical Association. The principle of *accountability*, by offering pathways to reconcile the desirable pursuit of innovation with the essential requirement of legal certainty, demonstrates how the *preventive and precautionary functions of civil liability* shape the technological advancements in healthcare during the first quarter of the twenty-first century.
11. *Healthcare institutions* employing AI technologies on their premises have also to respect the *ethical principle of accountability* which is reinforced by healthcare compliance frameworks. These frameworks, with their prospective function, incorporate preventive regulatory parameters for the use of AI in clinical

practice, whether in an *ex ante* or *ex post* context. On the *ex ante* level of accountability, *hospital compliance programmes* play a crucial role by integrating best practice rules, establishing procedures, implementing continuous medical education programmes focused on technologies, and defining technical standards and safety protocols. In contrast, on the *ex post* level of accountability, the compliance programme must *align with* the efforts of the *hospital bioethics committee*. Together, these bodies should conduct continuous assessments of the *effectiveness of governance* and best practice programmes already implemented. Furthermore, they are pivotal in resolving disputes arising from adverse events involving AI systems in clinical settings. In summary, the ethical principle of accountability—addressed in both *ex ante* and *ex post* dimensions—offers potential pathways for reconciling the desirable pursuit of innovation with the indispensable requirement for legal certainty. Regarding civil liability, the *preventive and precautionary functions* once again emerge as guiding principles for technological development in the healthcare sector.

12. *Healthcare compliance programmes* must be afforded *appropriate legal recognition*, elevating them to the status of a vital instrument for *identifying and quantifying liabilities*, rather than being regarded merely as corporate tools for ensuring compliance and managing risks. In this regard, it has been argued in this book that when physicians and/or healthcare institutions invest in robust compliance frameworks and adopt best practice standards — demonstrating adherence to ethical principles and professional duties of conduct—there is a legal and doctrinal basis to consider an *equitable reduction in the amount of compensation* owed in the event of an adverse event. This exemplifies the *promotional function of civil liability*, aimed at *fostering meritorious behaviours* and encouraging adherence to exemplary standards of care.
13. In this book, the author defends that it is impossible to adopt strict liability—without the analysis of medical fault—even when assessing a breach of a physician's duty of conduct in the provision of services involving AI. The contract between physician and patient constitutes a *juridical transaction of an existential nature*, imbuing certain duties with distinctive meanings. This unique character necessitates a *form of legal protection distinct* from the traditional framework of contractual civil liability. In this context, the obligations inherent in the physician-patient relationship extend beyond the mere fulfilment of agreed services; they encompass duties deeply rooted in trust, care, and respect for the patient's dignity. These obligations, shaped by the particularities of the *existential contract*, require an evaluative approach that considers the transformative role of technologies such as AI in medical practice. The breach of a medical contract, assessed through a subjective lens, is justified by the fact that duties of conduct within the physician-patient relationship take on a *qualified nature*, functioning almost as principal obligations. In this existential contract, *fault serves as the legal foundation* for the professional's liability. Similarly, the failure to fulfil any of the physician's duties of conduct—information, disclosure and explanation; documentation and confidentiality/secrecy; cooperation and loyalty *stricto sensu*; refrain from abuse or misuse of power; up-to-date

knowledge; care and vigilance—must be evaluated subjectively. To understand this differently would risk undermining the viability of the medical profession and depersonalising the physician-patient relationship, which is inherently founded on trust and tailored, personalised care. As Miguel Kfouri Neto states, "strict liability is not compatible with medical activity, given the singularity of the service provided: healing the sick and saving lives". In summary, the redefined duties of conduct, as presented in this book, call for a nuanced framework of liability—one that acknowledges the unique ethical and legal complexities of modern medical practice while accommodating the integration of advanced technologies. However, this adaptation must remain anchored in the fundamental principle that medical liability must be predicated on an analysis of fault, preserving the core notion of culpability as the basis for determining medical responsibility.

14. In addition to the preceding conclusion, it is essential to offer further reflections. Regarding the debate concerning the legal nature of civil liability for physicians involved in the use of AI systems in healthcare, all approaches advocating for the imposition of strict liability on the operator of high-risk AI systems must be categorically rejected when applied to medical professionals in their role as front-end operators of AI. Extending the physician's liability towards a product-based framework disregards the *legal distinction between product safety liability*, which pertains to the technology itself, and medical liability, which is tied to the treatment provided. Consequently, *imposing strict liability on medical professionals is not appropriate*. Moreover, *adopting a risk-scaling approach to determine the nature of civil liability for physicians leads to a paradoxical situation in which* those who employ autonomous systems to improve patient care would be subjected to a stricter liability regime than their counterparts who refrain from using such technologies, whose liability continues to be asseded under a fault-based system. This paradox undermines the incentives for innovation and technological adoption in medical practice, penalising those who seek to integrate advanced tools for enhance safety, accuracy, and treatment outcomes. As advocated by the European Commission in its deliberations on AI regulation, it is evident that *designing legal solutions are required to regulate technology within specific sectors*. In the healthcare context, these solutions must *respect the nuanced division between product liability and professional liability*, ensuring that the regulatory framework does not unduly burden medical practitioners. Such an approach balances the dual imperatives of fostering innovation and maintaining legal certainty, safeguarding both patient welfare and the integrity of the medical profession.
15. The civil liability ecosystem in healthcare must be carefully examined when an adverse event involving an AI system affects a patient. The assessment of liability in such cases should be based on identifying the efficient cause of the harm. Hospitals may be held strictly liable for adverse events linked to AI systems implemented on their premises if there is a failure in the proper maintenance of the technology or in fulfilling their duty to diligently and continuously assess the quality and performance of the automated decision-making system. On the

other hand, it is equally critical to emphasise that the manufacturer bears liability for defects in the AI system itself. As explained through this book, the *AI manufacturer is not entitled*, in legal proceedings, to *invoke the development risk defence* as a ground for excluding liability by arguing that the effects of machine learning represent an unforeseeable defect given the state of technical knowledge at the time the product was introduced to the market. This is because such *self-learning capabilities are an intrinsic characteristic of the technology itself* (machine learning) and constitute a *breach of the general duty of safety*. This allocation of responsibility reinforces the distinction between product liability—attributable to the manufacturer for problems with the technology—and professional or institutional liability for its use. This framework ensures that *accountability is distributed appropriately* across all stakeholders in the healthcare ecosystem, fostering both patient safety and technological innovation.

In light of the reflections presented throughout this work and the fifteen lessons outlined above, a vision emerges of a future in which Medicine, transformed by the presence of artificial intelligence, not only redefines the contours of professional responsibilities but also reinterprets the essence of human relationships in healthcare. AI systems, imbued with promises and challenges, compels medical professionals to transcend the boundaries of technical knowledge, combining scientific expertise, robust ethics, and human sensitivity. In this context, as *Eric Topol* asserts, *all doctors will eventually adopt AI algorithms as their frequent work partners*. This new panorama of available scientific knowledge will inevitably lead to a new type of challenge: identifying and continuously training professionals endowed with the highest levels of wisdom, intelligence, and diligence in the utilisation of these new technologies.

This discussion warrants a parenthesis to demonstrate that the rationale for redefining physicians' duties of conduct in the implementation of AI systems can be derived from *Gregorio Robles's Communicational Theory of Law*, as presented through his book. Based on this theory, it is possible to understand the need for a dynamic interaction between ethical and juridical imperatives and the evolving technological landscape, emphasising the *resignification of legal norms and juridical concepts* in contemporary medical practice.

Robles argues that law should be understood as a social phenomenon shaped by processes of communication and interpretation. His theory portrays *law as a communicative process* among judges, lawyers, legislators, and citizens, *requiring norms to be both comprehensible and perceived as legitimate*. In the context of Medical Law, this perspective holds particular significance, especially in addressing the ethical and legal dilemmas of AI in healthcare. For example, the duty to inform, *traditionally a one-sided obligation* to convey information, now necessitates an *interactive dialogue* in which *physicians must explain and justify* the use of AI in terms comprehensible to patients, *as well as listen* to the patient, ensuring their *active engagement in shared decision-making*.

Such an approach represents the new model of what is currently considered valid patient consent. It aligns with Robles's view that *justice is a dynamic ideal*, contextualised by social, cultural, and moral influences, and *communicated effectively to preserve the legitimacy of law* and the integrity of professional relationships.

The (near) future of medicine expects new physicians operating in a universe of possibilities, integrating various automated decision-making systems to combine technology, science, and interpersonal skills, thereby delivering healthcare that is more personalised, effective, and accessible. As the society worldwide advance toward this horizon filled with possibilities, it is imperative to reflect upon the limits and responsibilities that lie before each agent. Technology, as a tool, must not eclipse the timeless values that underpin the doctor-patient relationship.

Friedrich Nietzsche's philosophy, as discussed in this book, also provides a foundation for reinterpreting medical duties in light of the transformative impact of AI, which offers a new background for this resignification. His concept of transvaluation emphasizes the need to move beyond outdated paradigms, encouraging the establishment of new approaches rooted in the ethical principles of AI. It is worth stressing that the rupture Nietzsche proposes is that we must not continue perpetuating values that are already in place; instead, we need to reconstruct new values, understanding that the revaluation of concepts is built upon contextual and experiential backgrounds, rather than being simply given.

In this process, medical duties—such as diligence, the obligation to inform, and vigilance—are revaluated and understood in a new way through the reconstructed meaning of these concepts. By aligning these revaluated medical duties with AI ethical guidelines, technology becomes a tool to support and enhance clinical practice without undermining the essential human aspects of healthcare, paving the way for a more ethically aligned and patient-centred medical framework.

Whether the implementation of AI will dehumanise or depersonalise the doctor-patient relationship will depend on *how the technology is utilised and the meaning attributed to it* within the diverse contexts of medical practice. New paradigms for medical service contracts involving AI are emerging, making it essential to understand and adapt to them. This underscores the need to foster critical thinking and the *continuous process of gradual refinement and/or resignification of existing legal frameworks and institutions*, a trend likely to become increasingly prominent in the next years.

The challenge lies in balancing *progress with values*, *efficiency with empathy*, and *innovation with compassion*. May this balance, comparable to a fair and just scale, stand as the legacy of this generation of professionals and scholars, laying the foundation for healthcare systems that resonate not only in their technical excellence but also in human essence, embodying the aspirations of our global society.

The manufacturer's authorised representative in the EU is Springer Nature Customer Service Centre GmbH, Europaplatz 3, 69115 Heidelberg, Germany. If you have any concerns regarding our products, please contact ProductSafety@springernature.com

Printed and bound by CPI Group (UK) Ltd, Croydon, CR0 4YY
30/09/2026
02225570-0005